TEXT/POLITICS IN ISLAND SOUTHEAST ASIA

CONTRIBUTORS

Keith Foulcher is senior lecturer in the Discipline of Asian Studies in the Flinders University of South Australia. He has an international reputation in Indonesian literature, in which he is one of Australia's leading specialists.

Jose Mario C. Francisco, S.J. was trained at the Graduate Theological Union, University of California at Berkeley. He is an assocate professor and dean, Loyola School of Theology, Ateneo de Manila University, of which he is a graduate. Religious narrative in general and Tagalog studies in particular are his chief areas of research.

David T. Hill was formerly with the Department of Indonesian and Malay at Monash and is currently lecturer in Southeast Asian Studies, Murdoch University, Western Australia. He is the author of articles in English and Indonesian.

H. M. J. Maier holds the Chair of Malay and Indonesian Language and Literature in the Royal University of Leiden, the Netherlands.

Vicente Leuterio Rafael is associate professor in the Department of Communication at the University of California at San Diego. He is a graduate of the Ateneo and Cornell and formerly taught at the University of Hawaii. He is known for his studies of Tagalog literature.

D. M. Roskies has taught at the Universities of London and Singapore and was Visiting Fellow at the Southeast Asia Program, Cornell University, during 1986-88. He holds the University Professorship of Language and Literature in the University of Papua New Guinea. Indonesian and Philippine literatures are his main areas of interest.

Paul Tickell was formerly with the Department of Chinese and Indonesian Studies at Monash University and is now lecturer in the Discipline of Asian Studies at Flinders. He is the author of monographs and articles on Indonesian fiction and journalism past and present.

C. W. Watson is senior lecturer in Sociology at the University of Kent at Canterbury (UK) and former chairman of the University's Centre of South-East Asian Studies. He has published studies of modern Indonesian literature, and of the Kerinci district of Sumatra.

TEXT/POLITICS IN ISLAND SOUTHEAST ASIA

Essays in Interpretation

edited by
D. M. Roskies

Ohio University Center for International Studies
Monographs in International Studies

Southeast Asia Series Number 91
Athens, Ohio 1993

Library of Congress Cataloging-in-Publication Data

Text/Politics in Island Southeast Asia : essays in
    interpretation / edited by D. M. Roskies.
        p. cm. – Monographs in international studies.
Southeast Asia series ; no. 91
    Includes bibliographical references.
    ISBN : 0-89680-175-6
    1. Politics and literature–Southeast Asia. 2. Politics in
literature–Southeast Asia. 3. Southeast Asian literature–
20th century–Political aspects. 4. Southeast Asian litera-
ture– 19th century–Political aspects. 5. Indonesian litera-
ture– 20th century–Political aspects. 6. Indonesian litera-
ture– 19th century–Political aspects. 7. Philippine litera-
ture– 20th century–History and Criticism. 8. Philippine lit-
erature–19th century–History and Criticism.
    I. Roskies, D. M. II. Series.
PL3508.05T49 1993
809'.8959–dc20   92-37869
                                                            CIP

99 98 97 96 95 94 93   5 4 3 2 1

CONTENTS

ILLUSTRATIONS

1. Ferdinand Marcos as *Malakas* (Strong).

2. Imelda Marcos (painted by Claudio Bravo).

3. Imelda Marcos (painted by Federic Aguilar Alcuaz).

4. Imelda Marcos "A-Go-Go" (painted by Antonio Garcia Llamas).

after page 68

ACKNOWLEDGMENTS

A volume such as this—to paraphrase Samuel Johnson—borrows rays from diverse origins and brings them to a focus. The debts therefore are many and none can be repaid in full. The warmest is owed to the Southeast Asian Program and Modern Indonesia Project at Cornell University, with which I had the privilege of being associated during the years 1986 to 1988.

At the University of Papua New Guinea I received help from Miss Fiona Pirie and Mr. Jackson Rannells, both of the Michael Somare Library. I am grateful to Dr. Daniel Bryant and his colleagues in the Department of Pacific and Asian Studies at the University of Victoria, British Columbia, and to the staff at its McPherson Library, for making my short visit to the university a useful and productive one. It was there, in my green and pleasant native land, that the labor for this project was carried to within striking distance.

James L. Cobban, editor of the Monographs in International Studies at Ohio University, showed extraordinary patience with my numerous submissions in the process of producing the manuscript in its final form.

All the essays contained herein were either commissioned or solicited specially for this volume by the editor. In the interim, however, circumstances compelled publication of one elsewhere. Permission to reprint it here in revised form has been secured from the Syndics of the Cambridge University Press and Editors of *Comparative Studies in Society and History*, to whom kind thanks are offered.

1

PERMISSION, VOICE, AND SILENCE: INSCRIPTIONS OF AUTHORITY

D. M. Roskies

"Beginnings," Edward Said remarks, "have to be made for each project in such a way as to *enable* what follows from them."[1] Our enabling beginning lies with the attested realities of conquest, resistance, penetration, and dominion in the two great archipelagic nations of Southeast Asia. The principal concern is with imaginative production from Indonesia and the Philippines since, roughly, 1890 to the present day. More particularly is it with literature which speaks from within or is brought forth from great conjunctural crisis: in Indonesia, the fight for *kemerdekaan* (independence) from 1945 to 1949 and the abortive coup of 30 September 1965 and its bloody dégringolade; in the Philippines, the "Revolution" of February 1986 associated with the ouster of Ferdinand Marcos and his succession by Corazon Aquino. The idea for a volume devoted to these matters—an effort felt to have been long overdue—grows from an interest in the making and remaking of identities in an island Malay world whose historical experience has been at once so discontinuous and contiguous.[2] It is a relationship understood here as having been formed through discourse, defined by Michel Foucault as "the power to be seized" and posing the question which is the heart of the matter: "How does the struggle for the taking over of the discourse take place between classes, nations, linguistic, cultural, or ethnic collectivities?"[3]

At the heart of our enquiries lies a recognition of the equal insistence with which this question has borne upon Tropical Holland, postrevolutionary Indonesia, and the Philippines from the time of its absorption into the American domain and up to the recent, ambiguous

1

overthrow of constitutional dictatorship. Overall, however, the case for vision of this quarter of Southeast Asia through bifocals is well established. It was the geographer Charles Robequain who observed more than thirty years ago that archipelagic Southeast Asia—in commercial, demographic, physical, and climatic terms—is such that the Philippines in several important respects may be seen as "part of the East Indies."[4] Students of politics, too, have advanced the view that both archipelagoes "are similar enough to be discussed together, yet different enough to make comparison interesting."[5] A speculative foundation for a perspective in double focus has been laid in the work of contemporary historians.[6] The most important precedent is Theodore Friend's comprehensive study in comparative tropical history, which elucidates the psychologies which after 1945 led to reoccupation and upheaval under Sukarno and Hatta and to "liberation" and restoration in a setting presided over by McArthur and Benigno Aquino.[7] Its importance lies in its attempt to bring into resolution an image of that part of Southeast Asia which has undergone the most harrowing experience of formal conquest, popular uprising (and its suppression), and informal dominion.

Comparative literature, however, not comparative tropical history, is our field. It is one similarly sited in an island region considered as a universe, a "discursive entity." I take this useful term from Peter Hulme, who brings it to bear on "the extended Caribbean," an entity assumed to owe less to subsequent political boundaries and more to "features— environmental, ideological—that lay beyond national difference."[8] I take a similar view of Indonesia and the Philippines, a view supported by existing scholarship. The treatment of their literatures in this volume lies impenitently between the disciplines of literature and history. The contributors have taken as given a need to juxtapose the examination of the particularities of literary and cultural texts with analysis of the engendering moment in which those texts have their being. In varying degrees all are curious about the "afterlives" of such texts, reading them for the way "authority is carried . . . circumstantially from the State down into a society [and into] institutions and establishments."[9]

Behind this volume's conception lies an excitement over ways of talking about literature in general, and about Southeast Asian literature in particular, which—influenced to an extent by Geertzian anthropology—are open to the variety and complexity of interpretative practices.[10] The excitement extends to the prospect of subversion in

2

the midst of orthodoxy and, equally, to exceptions to the ideological containment of genre. It has yielded an enterprise which extends onto hitherto unexplored terrain a view of texts as being inseparable from the conditions of their production and reception in history. That view is not propounded dogmatically; certainly it is in debate here with more orthodox standpoints. But it is a shared view inasmuch as it sees literature as involved in the making of cultural meanings, which, in the last analysis, are political meanings. Political, in that what are figured forth are social and economic relations of power. Power must be a matter of rights to speech as well as of institutional arrangements. Rights to speech are instantiated, and ultimately validated—or not—by authority and by resistance of the subject to authority.

The terms *text* and *ideology* being recurrent, some account of their referents is necessary.[11] Anybody familiar with even a fraction of contemporary literary criticism will recognize that its ways and means have come under sustained, comprehensive, and some might say irreversible attack.[12] A younger generation has been fretful when faced with the continued traditional study of an accepted canon of works in a clearly defined national language. It is a canon some see as cordoned off with disconcerting neatness into periods and rendered internally seamless.[13] Of course, the canon was never perhaps *quite* as seamless as it is sometimes made out to be. It is correct to say, however, that until not very long ago the activity of literary criticism in the West was defined above all by the determination of *a* canon. Is the Argentinian Miguel Angel Asturias a greater Latin American novelist than his Brazilian counterpart Sarmiento? Is Chinua Achebe the most important novelist of postcolonial Anglophone Africa? The questions have been, Which writers are worthy of detailed study? and more important, perhaps, Who is moving from contemporaneity into canonicity? These debates were accompanied by an immense technical effort to establish reliable texts. They presupposed notions of cultural and moral excellence, of tradition, and of an educated audience, notions which have come to be seen as having been compromised by valorizing assumptions, latent or patent. The received view has not lacked for defenders.[14] But these have been unable satisfactorily to parry the complaint lodged against it by those who see it as a redoubt of essentialism and of mechanistic thinking.

The complaint has come to be associated with the New Historicism, which has set its face against a privileging of literature and/or history.[15] It has jibbed at terms set in dyadic or hierarchical opposi-

3

tion, as these so often are. Instead, it prefers to see the kinds of knowledge which are literature and history as being conditioned, made available, by present determinations as well as past—both disciplines furnishing a frame in which "the past" is set, within which it has its meaning, value, and utility in the present. It sees signification, the manufacture of meaning, as being imbricated with the set of discourses instrumental in the maintenance of forms of social and historical life. Those forms themselves are seen as varying greatly, from institutional protocols (including the institution of literature, its forms and conventions), to categories constitutive of an entire rationality (e.g., "colonialism," "imperialism," "revolution"), to more direct forms of partisanship and intervention.

This is an approach which stresses the sociomaterial instance rather than the timeless essence of the artifact, and which, insofar as it aims to deconstruct, is nothing like the free-play-of-meaning or anything-goes notion of criticism that the later phase of the Saussurean movement is sometimes taken to be. Its interest here is in the circumstantial network of options seized and refused, which enables a text to come into being in the first instance. The interest encompasses the key business of self-legitimation, whereby a cultural product strives to persuade those who consume it that it, and it alone, speaks the language of truth. The meaning of the "social text," as it has been called, is juridical.[16] Far from inhering in verbal structures, it is a function of the ends envisaged for it by persons and organizations, though it is precisely through scrutiny of verbal structures that meaning, often contradictory, typically bound up with conflict, can be ascertained. This species of historicist criticism is attuned to the Babel within the text, which in turn is perceived as mired in the materialities of production, reproduction, and consumption. Vicente Rafael, in his analysis of the potency of spectacle under Marcos, acknowledges this criticism as a source of inspiration. He shows how the special attention required to be given to the literary, the linguistic, the pictorial, makes possible an understanding of the experience distilled in word, narrative, and image while pointing to a comprehension of that which lies beyond these particular manifestations of a system of signs generally.[17]

There arise here questions of means and ends which are of relevance alike to students of history and literature. Are we to read literature as a form of historical knowledge giving immediately onto the past? In which case, would we not be privileging history, literature merely assisting in the understanding of past societies? There are

4

difficulties here: exactly what kind of access does literature give to what has happened which is not on offer from other sources? How do we justify the study of minor or forgotten artifacts; will not any work evoke its own past, and why then should we not want that past?[18] This, in turn, begs the possibility of a complete recovery of times gone by, whose "presentness," it has been said, "can be recuperated only as writing, not as event."[19] We need not be detained here by the need to answer these questions, except to say that whatever the answer may be, it will insist on making the point that the pursuit of knowledge is qualified in advance by the interests of those who undertake it. It must address not only the record of the past but also the hidden forces shaping the imaginative complexes in and through which the past is perceived.

So if the contributors to this book share any bias, it is one which favors a view of past political conflict as existing not somewhere beyond the work but as a struggle, within the particulars of composition, amongst competing ways of representing power. Interpretation here is seen as having to do not just with investigation of features or phenomena. Its business is with the kinds of effects which discourses produce, and with how these are brought about.[20] Whence the view, undergirding this book, that textual and historical/political action are consubstantial. On this understanding, the matters perennially at issue are consciousness, process, and above all, hegemony.

This last is a controlling concept in the thinking of Antonio Gramsci and offers a positive alternative to reductionism by rethinking the role of class and economy in literary production. It is distinguished from domination associated with the agencies of government and—from "political society"—tends towards equilibrium, not coercion. Gramsci's concept refers to the pervasive though not irresistible force by which a class or a people is persuaded of the naturalness of its condition—persuaded, that is, to tacit agreement as to what shall count as indisputably real, what counts as real being that which, in the realm of values and practices, is held to be so by a ruling class. There is implied a selection of one version of the real from among several such, the outcome of competition between rival experiences and clashing perspectives. And the best way of endorsing such an outcome is by articulating it, embodying it in the comparatively permanent form of the written word.

Hegemony, in other words, in Gramsci's view is to be identified and countered; hence the importance he lays on the "organic intellectuals" with a cause, a movement, and a collective program—men and women equipped, by dint of a "sentimental connection with the people-nation" and through work with words, to unmask coercive force. Suspension of hegemony is possible when a governing elite or administrative caste appears poised to fail in an undertaking requiring a measure of popular consent, for it is then that there are likely to be "put forward formal demands, which taken together . . . add up to revolution."[21]

A helpful supplement to analyses of hegemony and its remission is available in two key formulations developed by Said. He speaks of the "strategic location" of intellectuals, understood as "the author's position in a text with regard to the . . . material he writes about," and of "strategic formation," understood as "a way of analysing the relationship between textual genres, acquiring mass, density and referential power among themselves and thereafter the culture at large."[22] From this viewpoint, "culture" is to be thought of as a contest among discourses, literary and otherwise, to render the individual subject in both (contrary) senses of the word. Forms of order and regulative practices—laws, institutions, sociological concepts, historiographical as well as imaginative categories—place the author at the receiving or at the executive end of unofficial controls. Hence the suggestiveness of Foucault's idea of an interpretative enterprise bent on discovering "how it is," in a given setting, that "subjects are progressively . . . constituted," and his ideas of "discourse-as-the-power-to-be-seized."[23] Hence his view of textual analysis as persuasive in the degree that it registers such things without reduction.

Behind the conception of this book is a suspicion that such revisionary thinking about state, class, and social control may have as much to say to students of Southeast Asian literatures in particular as it has had to students of literature generally. Our domain embraces writing which, though inevitably uneven in quality, is remarkably variegated. As well as fiction, poetry, and drama, it comprehends personal and official memoirs, accounts of travel and exile, and autobiography. Generalizations about so varied a domain would be rash, but one may be attempted by way of prolegomenon. Whether conceived in standard or variant Malay, in Tagalog, Pilipino, Cebuano, or in the principal contact languages of English, Spanish, and Dutch, this material can be said to be absorbed more complexly in the contentions of its time, place, and moment than is apparent at first blush. This is so, one might add, whether it exemplifies the domesticated category of the literary or whether it evinces more combustible alignments—formations antagonistic or peripheral to a state (colonial or postcolonial) operating by the principle of what may be called Devise and Rule.

Caution is necessary here. To speak, for example, of a "dominant culture" in the colonial Philippines even by way of shorthand is unsatisfactory, inasmuch as it elides local intractabilities which are not susceptible of handy definition. Father de la Costa is right to forewarn "against the shock of finding somewhere in this vast area an Asian nation of Malay stock, socially structured on a basically Indonesian pattern, containing a large infusion of Chinese blood and attitudes but with a cultural heritage in part Spanish, in part Anglo-Saxon."[24] Attempted control of such multiform communities from above and from within is, nonetheless, an aboriginal theme, one with variations. Political control through an evangelical *mission civilisatrice* to the Tagalogs was, clearly, far from being a traffic in one direction. It was negotiated intricately, not passively received; European ideas of hierarchy and indebtedness were parried, adulterated through contact and propinquity.[25] From the perspective of a history from below, Tagalog accommodation to hispanidad was an irregular, shifting, segmented affair, an act of fealty certainly, but also an exercise in counter-demarcation. Counterconsciousness, as Renato Constantino has called it, was an intricate, above all a contradictory, unity, mixed in prove-nance, not always audible, sometimes invisible, often carried in one narrative which served as a screen for another.[26] The point has been taken up by Reynaldo Ileto, who has demonstrated how Tagalog jacquerie movements from Apollinario de la Cruz in the nineteenth century and beyond, to Macario Sakay and Felipe Salvador in the twentieth, drew upon a species of folk enthusiasm which recontext-ualized ecclesiastical dogma and reversed its totalizing charge.[27] As Ileto has insisted in his researches, the capacity of such subterranean popular-religious phenomena to give a voice to the voiceless, during Malolos and well after, is difficult to overestimate.[28]

But voice depends upon permission, approved or circumvented. And in the last three decades of Spanish rule the making of texts, where text is taken to mean the visually experienced medium of print implicated in monetized systems of exchange, in large part has been the preserve of those entitled to make their voice heard above all others. An *ilustrado* prerogative, it reaches its apogee in the decade previous to the proclamation of the Republic at Malolos in 1899 and is coextensive with shifts in orientation within a colonial intelligentsia whose fiscal and

7

political estate had latterly been augmented.[29] Changes in the institution of literature in the Philippines in the period 1865-1901 articulate with a shift in general mode of production, as Spanish imperialism, declining in the measure that it is geared to entrepôt trading, cedes to American, whose proficiency in extraction, of surplus wealth is the greater. Feudal, tributary arrangements come to be overlaid by sophisticated mechanisms of accumulation (merchant house, sugar exchange, stock exchange, sugar hacienda), whose nodal points are in the regional capitals (Cebu, Iloilo) as well as in the metropolis. Monoculture specialization in a few primary commodities gives way to markets for manufactured goods calibrated to global and continental flux in supply and demand. In short, it is permissible to speak of a political economy coming by the 1870s to be ordered to laissez-faire in the classical acceptation of the phrase.

Insofar as it can be described without simplification, the impact of these changes upon habits of literary reception and expression of the ilustrado-mestizo elite was differential.[30] Internationalization of the political economy of the archipelago was accompanied by the growth, in the cities, of a constituency of readers with disposable income, readers attuned to developments overseas (including liberal political thought in the nation-states of late nineteenth-century Europe). Within this elite formation there was fostered an appetite for books in the sense recognizable by a European bourgeoisie. It was an appetite, a variety of literacy, being stimulated in its turn by a proliferating apparatus of book publishing, book circulation, and book consumption. Reading became privileged, institutionalized within and mainly for an indigenous elite becoming affluent and horizontally integrated, an elite whose sons had as often as not been educated abroad and whose patresfamilias were joining commercial activity in the towns to management of latifundia in the countryside. As regards the *Katipunan*, moreover, equivocal feelings among this elite characterize its stand towards the prospect of jacobinical mobilizations from below. The radicalism that was to produce a Bonifacio, an Aguinaldo, and a Mabini, provincial leaders of the 1896 revolution of artisanal extraction both appealed to and repelled a mestizo stratum with as much to lose as it stood to gain from drastic change, in the same way that, a century later, its descendants were to find themselves in two minds about the kind and degree of assent commanded by suspension of constitutional democracy.[31]

What was the imprint on imaginative writing by ilustrado authors of this revised sociology of literature, together with the effect of such a

8

"legitimation crisis"? It is to be expected that such writing may vivify, while commenting upon, a historical and cultural problematic external to it. Yet at the same time that writing invites scrutiny in relation to two other things: first, a model of discontinuous internal history—the work's, as well as that of the conjunctural period whose disturbance it communicates; second, a literary-critical renegotiation of that history in which individual agency, alike of author and of hero, disperses into a decentered subjectivity, in turn determining the text's "affiliation" (to adopt a term of Edward Said) with "other texts, classes, and institutions."[32]

Rizal's *Noli Me Tangere* (1987) is clearly the signal instance. Written in the language of the conqueror, this most famous of all Philippines fictions registers in its subtitle an identity as a "Tagalog novel." The contradiction bespeaks a nexus of desire and blockage within a parochial vernacular which has yet to attain the condition of a "national" language. Oriented on the fatherland, the geography of its authorship is dissipated amongst the foreign metropolises of Madrid, Paris, and Berlin, where its constitutent chapters were assembled. Published in Europe, it was proscribed within the Philippines yet infiltrated there in small numbers. It is a mutinous act, betokening an urge, in Rizal's prefatory words, to "bear witness to what I have always preached."[33] Yet it is an act constrained, internally distorted, by the way in which that urge is at variance with itself. For the *Noli* is an assertion of a bourgeois nationalism allied to a classical and quasi-aristocratic culture, its standard bearers the Catholic church (incarnated in Father Salvo and the egregious Father Damaso) and those avatars of creole and Chinese mestizo elite, Capitan Tiago, Doña Victoriana, and Capitan Basilio. These are the terms of the novel's humanist critique of key colonial institutions—church and state—and of the assumptions about obligation, loyalty, and obedience which these institutions exist to enforce. Yet it is also an assertive appropriation, at several removes, of these classical modes for historically progressive ends, by an author affiliated to the reformist Propaganda Movement nucleated around the newspaper *La Solidaridad*, an author educated by the Jesuits and scion of a wealthy principalia (landed and politically influential) family in Laguna.[34]

It is in terms of choreography of character and expedients of plot that these cloven allegiances are registered. Registered, that is, not only as a reflection of conditions within which the *Noli* is grounded, but as a torsion, a differential adjustment, at the very heart of the fiction.

9

Chrisostomo Ibarra's radicalism is shown (in the vivificatory critical idiom, derived from Lukàcs, of "showing" as distinct from "telling") to consist of a reformist trust in education, the proximate setting of the action being, we recall, the relatively tolerant administration of that very military man, Carlos Maria de la Torre (1869-71).[35] Thanks to a plot kitted out with all the statutory properties of the nineteenth-century European fiction on which Rizal was nurtured—complicated subdivision, elaborate digression, gratuitious interlude, ingenious elaboration—Ibarra is carried into a positivist suspicion of political change incited, but also curtailed, by the enigmatic Elias. The latter's eventual injunction and his disengagement, prior to the hero's "tragic" death, highlight the novel's implied refutation of the knowledge enforced by its itinerary.

In other words, the novel's official project is at variance with what it discloses; its meanings are disjunct, its texture fissiparous. What it wishes to assert through one of the chronicles at its center—Ibarra's readiness for political activism, the scales having dropped from his eyes—can be reconciled only imperfectly with what it shows through another narrative strand. That strand follows Elias's penultimate quietism, his metaphysical detachment from the cynicism he has been encouraging in his protégé. The formal structure of the novel is in this way promiscuous, distended by contrary programs. It poses a problem, the solution to which is to be observed in an activity of dislodgement and of etherealization at the core of the *Noli*. Ibarra is, so to speak, rusticated to the novel's periphery, through a transparently engineered "sensational" conclusion, as if in retribution for lack of adamantine will and comprehensive vision; while Elias, his doppelgänger, loitering hesitantly in the margins, is given a charismatic presence at the fore of the dramatic action, a presence which compensates for the deadlock into which he has led Ibarra's liberalism.

Rizal's origins, in "the new elite elements, substantially drawn from the old but critical of the status quo in the Philippines," may serve as a point of access to an understanding of the uneasy alignments and partial disjunctions of his fiction, a fiction at odds with a dominant ideology yet simultaneously isomorphous with it.[36] Such a way of seeing depends in its turn on a complexified view of how world and work are related. Certainly the two are in homology here, but the homology is highly mediated. For one thing, Rizal's mode of disinheritance from his contemporary moment is dictated by the nature of that moment itself. This, thanks to Rizal's martyrdom, gave a local habitation and a name to the prophetic rebel diffidently marginal to a

Europeanized ruling caste and fated to be destroyed for sake of its perpetuation. Then there is the very character of the literary product. Its realism is customary, derivative, liberal. It involves a tactful unravelling of interlaced processes, an equable distribution of authorial sympathies.[37] It rests upon an attempt to hold competing points of view in precarious equipoise. It involves, that is, the creation of a municipal rhetoric and the enlistment in its name of a naturalism consistent with that of a Balzac, a Eugene Sue, or a Dumas. The rationale is likewise "*je ne propose rien, je n'impose; j'expose.*" An improving reformism is the ideological correlative as well as the pretext of this essentially civil, and civic, mode of narrative. It is a narrative intended for indigenes but actually postulating a European or at least European-oriented audience, one, moreover, which has interiorized the thought-processes of a visual, manuscript literacy.

This is to emphasize that the literary product that is Rizal's *Noli* also wears a material aspect. It is that reified article, a bound volume in chapters meant as an article of exchange. It enshrines writing which, through the relatively sophisticated means of typographic preservation and reproduction, ensures the fixity of the "work," copies of which can be disseminated and multiplied. It exemplifies the idea of "literature" as spatially-fixed print, designed for aural ingestion, conceived neither as epiphany nor as participatory dialogue, but seeking an entrée in the first instance to an educated universe of soirées, salons, bookshops, and weeklies.[38] It seeks (and, like all nineteenth-century novels, creates) its putative reader, who is imagined in the act of reading as inhabiting an atoll of privacy, light, and stillness. Rizal's reader, in these ways, is constructed in and by the fiction. He or she is assumed to be in possession of those goods, just as he or she is assumed to be on easy terms with that well-tempered, linear meditation from an omniscient, superior position imported lock, stock, and barrel from afar and advertising itself as The Novel.

To say that the *Noli* is at bottom compliant with the conditions within which it is generated is scarcely to patronize. No one would wish to demote Rizal's masterwork or to permit the sophistication of current critical theories to negate the attractive urgency which it has had and continues to have for Filipino readers. Its "revolutionary use value," as Benjamin calls it, will always derive from its raising of a sceptical mirror to authority, in its time and beyond.[39] Yet, in its resort to an englobing, overviewing, classical naturalism, the *Noli*, and the particular kind of classical writing it represents, leaves fundamentally

11

unchallenged the discursive vocabularies which shore up that authority. We might go so far as to say that in speaking of "Rizal" as author we are speaking, inter alia, of an aesthetic formation which, in the way it selects and constitutes its human subject, accords with a prevailing ideological formation. That formation sustains, and is sustained by, tacitly held values, by certain representations: psychological inwardness; the insistently seriocomic dissection of manners; conventions of linear, progressive plot; character portrayed both discretely and in the round. The whole is embedded in a technology of commerce and competition. An instance of a familiar realism, standing in a relationship of consanguinity to a range of nineteenth-century European forerunners, this novel is submissive to the arbitrament of different interpretative contracts; encoded in its artifice are the print-futures it makes possible for itself. The finished product, received into those futures, is capable of becoming, simultaneously or in succession, artistic practice (available for imitation), social medium (of patriotic sentiment), national-cultural symbol, and instrumental hagiography (witness the status and institution of "Rizal" in Philippines secondary education and culture at large).[40] But finished product it is, before and beyond such uses and whatever else it may be. As such, it will be seen to be generically distinct from other literary artifacts.

The immediate point of the foregoing excursus is to illustrate what is meant by a politics *of* as well as *in* a text: a hard and sometimes brittle forging of coherences and cohesions out of materials set on flight and dispersal. In Althusserian parlance, the text is overdetermined: participating in more than one history while being, qua anticolonialist statement, inwardly distressed, rendered unstable, its surface corrugated by the tensions of its time. Notoriously in Rizal's case (others are adduced elsewhere in this volume) the posture of the State and its instruments exposes the crassest of these tensions. Censorship (pressure at the point of production, distribution, and consumption) is the darkness in which Rizal's hectically illuminated Spanish text subsists.[41] It is a perpetuation of illiteracy (itself a form of regulation), its concomitant—political impotence—being perpetuated amongst those with destinies socially more obscure than Ibarra's, Donna Consolacion's, Elias's. Indeed, the illiteracy foisted into the Southern Tagalog speech communities until the 1860s is the silence surrounding the choric, Ibero-colonial voices of the text, arguably the ground "on which it traces a figure and which constitutes its real support."[42] To read Rizal in this way is not only to meditate (and to enjoy) a "classic"; at the same time, it is to

12

think of the conditions under which a canon is constructed and of its contingency. The canon is formed here, and at the same time rendered contingent, within a nexus of class and by prevailing relations of commodity production. These include literary commodity production of the sort in force in the Philippines on the eve of the American era and during the subsequent two decades.[43]

The contrast is with a contemporaneous species of literature which speaks from beyond the pale and is more directly committed to work on the world. Its texts delimit what *rezeptionsaesthetik* calls a different "horizon of expectation."[44] Their production and consumption are at several removes from a culture of desk, light, study, and script. The remoteness is also from that intricate and sustained interest in character and in personal motive which feels most at home amid such material surroundings. In their set, in their disposition, such texts are more accurately described as being common, not personal, property, not the product of lonely authorial intention but illustrating what has been called a "socialized concept of authorship."[45] Their survival is ensured as much by dint of word of mouth and collaborative memory as by mechanical replication. They operate conventions of "impersonality" inimical to the confessional forms of a privatized Author. Yet, like the novel as received and practiced by Rizal, they encode within themselves their own ideology of how, by whom, and for whom they are written. Like the *Noli* and *El Filibusterismo*, they secrete in their forms and materials the fashion and friction of their making.

This is the orally based, communitarian, "folk" tradition brought to light by Ileto in his magisterial study. In this Little Tradition, as distinct from elite initiatives for autonomy, there can be discerned a renegotiation of relations of center and periphery in the prelude to and in the early years of Pax Americana in the Philippines.[46] Periphery becomes home to uncovenanted social formations, eccentric to the educated, propertied, urban elite's recension of nationalism, independence, and revolution. What has been termed the "subplot of provincial protest," as David Sturtevant has it, is carried on a base of peasant dissent in the Luzon countryside and is scripted to fragmented (though not, for this reason, incoherent) Tagalog hopes and expectations which had come to acquire a chiliastic aspect.[47] The expressive form it takes, at once more radical than, and categorically different from, that establishing Rizalian narrative. It may be seen as a species of subjunctive imagining, harnessing libidinal energies to a historical realization of utopia. Issuing from subaltern society, it defines a "structure of feeling" of an emergent formation.[48] Its conjunctural moment is marked by transition, never uniform, frequently interrupted, from an agrarian to an industrial capitalism. While its traditionalism might be misinterpreted as a product of a merely conservative impulse, backward-looking and anachronistic, that very same traditionalism is also a principal site of resistance, "creatively evolv[ing] its own brand of folk Christianity from which was drawn much of the language of anti-colonialism in the late nineteenth century."[49] *Pasyon* literature is a volatile mode, aimed at and consumed by readers for whom power, far from being a traditional prerogative, is lost and gained in sequences of defeat and resurgence.

Defeat and resurgence: therein lies the difficulty. Renato Constantino has envisioned an intermittent *levée en masse*, seeing "the people" as threatening, at key moments, to erupt onto the stage of patronage and power with proclamation and ritual as well as with musketry and bolo.[50] His implied caveat is that "the people" at such moments also are caught insecurely within delicate strands of paternalism, defense, and terror. To make these points is to reflect on the nature of any "folk" culture. Inasmuch as it is coterminous with the ways of the dominated and excluded, such a culture is, in its interior formations and differentiations neither, in a pure sense the national-popular tradition of refusing such containment, nor is it the forms, aesthetic or legislative, which containment takes. Rather it is the background on which these transformations have been worked. "Tradition"—that weasel word—has little to do, really, with mere persistence in time of old forms. Really it refers to the way components have been linked together, conjugated, to take on a new meaning or relevance, or to the way these intersect with different, opposing components to receive new resonances and accents. Popular tradition is not paradigmatically fixed forever in a universal position in relation to a subaltern class, nor, finally, in relation to class-against-class. In the Philippines at the turn of the century, as in other times and places, we need to speak of an alliance of classes, strata, and forces (the Manila artisanate as represented by Bonifacio, the ilustrado elite in league with plebeian impulses at work in and through the Katipunan) intersecting and overlapping in the same field. This is the field where hegemony arises and is secured, and where there is contestation, albeit irregular, of colonial Spain to begin with, then of the United States in its expansionist phase, intervening in what has aptly been termed "the first modern war of national liberation," latterly of the Marcos regime.[51]

14

Recalcitrance, of the kind implied by pasyon and enunciated through a popular tradition, arises, that is, at points of historical intersection. As James C. Scott has reminded us, it may assume a plurality of forms: negotiation, distortion, part-incorporation, refusal, singly or in combination.[52] But the sign of literary expression under revolutionary duress is always labile. It delineates a range of meanings but carries within itself no guarantee of a stable, single meaning. The Christ story carried in pasyon, Mario Francisco establishes, is a case in point. The "master narrative" within lowland Philippine society during the Spanish colonial period, it functions as a means of making sense alike of story and history (the Tagalog word *akasaysayan* embraeing both senses) and indeed continues indirectly to do so, as the turmoil of February 1986 sensationally illustrated. Yet the Christian Passion, premised on passive death and resurrection, was itself a contested metaphor, in dispute among individuals and collectivities with varying practical ends in view. Its foundation text, the *Mahal na Pasyon*, is, nevertheless, the subversive memory of a demotic literary tradition; its sublime plot carries suggestions of previous processings and intimates at a syllabus for renewal. The low-profiled anonymity of its narrative runs athwart a range of literary production, embracing pious accounts of lives of saints and exemplary stories of holy men popular during the latter part of Spanish colonization. During the first two decades of American occupation it is the "political unconscious" by which a politer literature is creased and haunted. To demonstrate this, as Mario Francisco demonstrates, is to show how the social and political content is restive beneath the becalmed surface of a fiction's formal structure.

It is difficult to think of any area of expressive activity in the Philippines (or on Luzon, at any rate) which was other than restive in this way, in the period under consideration here. Within the domain of *belles lettres* too, and of university-centered critical discourse, parallel contestments are discernible, beginning with the epochal moment framed by the withdrawal of Spain and the subsequent American drive to pacify the islands. A traditionalist outlook, exemplified in such poet-critics as Inigo Ed. Regalado and Juan Cruz Balmaseda, is well to the fore in the three decades after 1901 and particularly under the Commonwealth (1935-46). It is a rearguard activity, generally conservative of Tagalog values, crystallized in *tugma* and *sukat* and taking *Florante et Laura* (1838) as the epitome of such conventional usage. Balagtas's epic came to be monumentalized, the "anxiety of influence" generated by it going largely unassuaged until the eve of Japanese conquest.[53] It was only much later that the riposte to *Balagtasismo* was mounted, and then within a new axiomatic of Modernist poetry appearing in the late 1960s and early 1970s. The stimulus was an emerging liberal consensus amongst an urban intelligentsia, equivocally placed in relation to the radical agenda: suspended between an openly adversarial stance and a desire to improve, whilst preserving, things as they were under Martial Law. That the former stance was to prevail is, in a retrospective view, no matter for surprise, taking into account conditions of overall breakdown.[54] As well as rural insurgency, these conditions encompassed the inroads made by *cacique* oligarchy into industry and manufacturing, as distinct from land and property, together with a narrowing class representation, both in Senate and in economy, exclusive of large sectors of population whose lot was growing immiserated as never before.

The politics of interpretation, within this disturbed setting, are a displacement of more central conflicts, and turn on defense or repudiation of an accepted paradigm. A positive revaluation of *engagement* was the literary-critical accompaniment to student-driven militancy in the thoroughfares of the capital. The social matrix is a partial estrangement of a *bien-pensant* middle stratum from a corporatist regime advertising itself as fundamentally disinterested, when—as was plain for all who had eyes to see—its authority was in practice imposed through a *caudillist* despotism. This is arguably one manifestation of Gramscian general crisis in the Philippines under Marcos. Other manifestations are the implosions and dissolutions occurring within clan and family, and (as the political fiction of Linda Ty-Casper proposes) the cleavages hollowed out within the Makati bourgeoisie. In passing it will be noted that discussion of her writings about Manila under the dictator is by no means the only essay here to be brought up short by aspects of post-structuralist thinking about texts. This thinking has urged a grasp of literary works as being, in the last analysis, neither self-sufficient nor organically complete wholes but internally dissonant entities, self-divided in ways essential to their nature. In this it has performed a service. Whether it has had the final word, however, is far from clear. For it is one thing to set store by arguments for denying a work's putative integrity through an insistence on its partiality and limitation, but quite another to gainsay any notion of a realist critique; there is little in art that is more radical than a hunger for the real, as satisfied in the imitation of a human action. In the color transparency of Ty-Casper's novels—written, significantly, not in Tagalog but in American English—the imitation is of an actual historical society in emergency.

16

Novels, however, even novels which succeed in some measure in delivering the goods, are not the only things worthy of note about textual production in the Philippines in the period from the second term of office of Ferdinand Marcos to the assassination of Benigno Aquino, Jr., and since. Just as remarkable is the upsurge from a fissured base of a theatre of metaphor and protest. This theatre harks back to beginnings in oral projection. Its cardinal feature, it has been suggested, is a submerged rhetoric of insubordination.[55] Programmatically and after long inertia, theatre in the Philippines in the half-decade before the events on EDSA in 1986 had reinserted itself into traditions of ethnic ritual, game, and dance-drama adapted from such Hispanicized forms as *sinakulo, panunuluyan*, and *komedya*.[56] These were localized traditions, evolved principally (though not exclusively) in the Ilocos regions and in the Tagalog areas of Laguna and Bulacan. But they carried a larger import. The "seditious" theatre (as it came to be termed by the American insular administration) into which these local forms were repermuted flourished from the early 1900s until the late 1920s.[57] It received its quietus upon the convening of the first National Assembly: dormant since, it was revived under Martial Law, and mutated into a form whose raison d'être was the repression accompanying constitutional authoritarianism. Of this dramaturgy it is no exaggeration to remark that it contains scarcely a lyric impulse, nor any capacity for sustained eloquence, which does not spring from a deepening awareness of, and in some cases a shocked exposure to, urban poverty and political degradation.

Plays such as Chris Millado's *Buwan at Baril* [Moon and Gun] (1984), mounted by the Philippines Educational Theatre Association (PETA), are characteristic for their strategies both of identification and of abstention. Performed in the penumbra of detention and foreclosure, they resort to indirection to lodge their protest, yielding a new, uncovenanted dramaturgy in which literature returns to a parliamentary past, becoming in formal terms a regress from print to script to speech, but in ideological terms a progress, pooling knowledge, rehearsing memory, and cementing allegiances. On this reading, "low" culture in the Philippines, far from being an amorphous or an inferior residue (or a unified one, the contrary claim being, typically, the self-legitimation of an elite), is a rich plurality of separate discourses and textual practices in sophisticated competition with each other for audiences. Its theatrical expression aims at eliciting a startling alienation effect and an instantiation of carnival. Bakhtin's term, of course, has to do not with world-turned-upside-down but with a concept of the unstable underside of a culture, a sussurus of popular discontent ever-present within its "high" version and rising unpredictably to the surface when established authority is absent in mind, its overseeing gaze distracted. Drawing from stock, this carnivalesque theatre mixes entertainment, edification, and collusion with its audience by way of corrective rejoinder to a fraudulent official patriotism and the presumptive histories manufactured to match it.

So short a reconnaissance cannot hope to do more than identify one problematic at work in vernacular literature in the Philippines since 1896. The problematic is that of a variety of writing formed on real foundations of entailment from without and division from within. That is to say, writing and reading in Tagalog share the conditions of many another indigenous tongue in active use in the basement of a subordinate or colonized entity. They are inhabited by structures of consciousness as real as those of finance or of military intervention, and as manifoldly responsive to the direction of lives and fates. Of the manifold responses, two intrigue many of the contributors to this book. One, mentioned earlier, is the process through which the argot of a successful group, together with its outlook, carry all before them, or fail to do so. The other, correspondingly, is the means by which a subjugated entity—a state, a region, a class, a community of speech, an individual—preserves and perpetuates, thinks or unthinks, its historical identity.

In modern Indonesia, as in the Philippines since its failed revolution of 1896-98, of the structures of consciousness just alluded to the most momentous is, of course, nationalism, its discursive idiom characteristically subsuming difference and marginality, the whole and its parts, the legitimate and the delinquent, in a binary relation. Indonesia was never, of course, a colony in quite the same sense as was the Philippines. Nonetheless, its movement for independence emerges similarly in a phase when state monopoly gives way to private capital investment. More important, in both countries emergent nationalism asks to be understood as the product of the essential, and essentially anomalous, colonial condition. Colonialism implies dependence; dependence enjoins at once conformity and defiance: conformity, in some degree to be established experimentally as necessary for survival; defiance, in some degree to be established experimentally as necessary for self-regard. There is no better expression of this involuted dilemma

18

than the anguished introspection of the narrator in Pramoedya Ananta Toer's great novel *Rumah Kaca* [House of Glass] (1988):

> Perjalanan hidupku tidak berliku-liku, lurus seperti kawat yang lempang. Hanya setelah tuga pembasmian sisa Gerombolan Pitung, kawat itu tak pernah lagi lurus, bukan sekadar bengkok, tapi sudah jadi ruwet. Dan aku sendiri tak dapat melihat begaimana meluruskan kekusutan itu. Kekuatan dari luar, uang bernama jabatan, semakin hari semakin melilit leher. Aku harus merobohkan orang-orang seperti Bonifacio dan Rizal di Filipina. . . . Cuma nurani ini mengapa terus saja mengusik? Aku telah menjadi penumpas bayaran. . . . Kenaikanku sebagai Pribumi dari Inspektur jadi Ajung Komisaris, kemudian Komisaris, bukan hanya tak menyenagkan rekan-rekan uang tertinggal, juga mencurigakan mereka . . . aku merasa disisihkan. . . . Aku menjadi seekor merak di tengah-tengah ayam hutan. Ke mana pun dan di mana pun rasa-rasanya mereka selalu memperhatikan dan mencari-cari kesalahan . . . aku dipaksa hidup sewaspada dan seteliti mungkin. . . . Demikianlah maka kepolisian menjadi sumber penghidupan dan sekaligus tawanan polisi. Seakan sudah kelilangan kemauan "sendiri."

Aku menyadari, aku jijik terhadap pekerjaanku setelah meningkat jadi Ajung Komisaris, semua kemuliaan uang ada dalam diriku tertindas demi menghidupi keluargaku. Untuk keselamatan diri hanya ada satu jalan yang bisa ditempuh: bermuka dua dan berhati banyak dengan sadar. . . . Namun aku selalu saja merindukan manusia Pangemanann yang dulu, yang tulus, yang sederhana, yang percaya pada kebajikan manusia. Dan kalian, anak-anakku, jangan sampai mencontoh ayahmu, budak penghidupan yang kehilangan prinsip. Jangan contoh aku. Anggaplah ayahmu sebagai pribadi yang punah, pribadi yang kalah budak . . . Ampuni ayahmu ini, karena dia tidak mampu memberikan contoh sebaik-baiknya sebagaimana ia sendiri kehendaki. Anggaplah aku sebagai wakil generasi Pribumi yang kalah, dikalahkan oleh kekuatan dan kekuasaan. . . .

Bukankah sudah jelas? . . . Pitung-Pitung modern yang meng-usik-usik kenyamanan Gubermen—semua telah dan akan kutempat-patkan dalam sebuah rumah kaca yang kuletakkan dimeja kerjaku. Segalanya menjadi jelas terlihat. Hindia tidak boleh——harus dilestarikan. Maka bila aku berhasil dapat menyelamatkan tulisan ini, dan sampai pada tangan kalian, hendaknya kepada catatan-catatanku ini kalian beri judul Rumah Kaca. . . .[58]

(My life's journey was not entangled but was straight as a wire pulled taut. Only after being assigned the task of wiping out the remnants of the Pitung gang, it was never to be straight again, not merely bent but all tied up in knots. And I'm unable myself to see how to sort out the tangle. An external force, calling itself my Official Duty, is winding itself round my neck with each passing day. I'm to bring about the downfall of people very like Bonifacio and Rizal in the Philippines. . . . Why then does my heart keep disturbing me? . . . I've become a paid exterminator. . . . My promotion as a *pribumi* from Inspector to Deputy Inspector, then to Commissioner, not only displeased my remaining colleagues, it made them suspicious as well. . . . I felt rejected. . . . I've become a peacock in the midst of jungle fowl. Everywhere and anywhere it seems they're forever taking note, forever looking to catch me out. . . . I'm forced to live as warily and as meticulously as possible. . . . So it is that the Police have become at once a way of life and a cage. I'm an officer of the Police, but at the same time its detainee. It's as if my own will's vanished. . . . I was conscious of being filled with disgust towards my work after having been promoted to Deputy Commissioner, sensing all the grandeur within me crushed for the sake of keeping my family alive. . . . From this day on I'm to become a scribe, . . . working not for knowledge and its improvement but for the power of Government. . . .

For my own survival there is but one road to take: to be two-faced, consciously to have more than one purpose. Nevertheless I always pine for the human being Pangemanann formerly was, sincere, simple, a believer in service to mankind . . . and you, children, Don't take after me. . . . Think of your Father as a destroyed self, a lost self, a slave. You've got to become men who are pure of heart, principled, individuals . . . forgive your father here, who is unable to set you as good an example as he might have wished himself . . . look upon me as a representative of the generation of *pribumis* who failed, defeated by the might and main of colonialism . . .

It's crystal clear the latter-day Robin Hoods who disturb Government's security—all these I shall place in a glass house, to be set on my worktable.[59] This is my work. . . . Everything becomes clearly visible. The Indies cannot change, must be preserved as is. And so, should I succeed in safeguarding this piece of writing, and if it falls into your hands, it is my wish that you give to these notes of mine the rubric House of Glass. . . .)

This is an extraordinary interior monologue. The testimony it delivers is immolating in its veracity. It is sage, rigorous, unforgiving. We are bystanders at the spectacle of a dissection of *un moi haïssable*, a dissection both merciless and comprehensive. The speaking "I" is Jacques Pangemanann, a minor character first encountered in *Jejak Langkah* [Footsteps], the third volume of Pramoedya's tetralogy. A former commissioner of police in the Netherlands East Indies, he is a ruthless and dedicated servant of the colonial government. The year is 1912, moment of catalysis in early modern Indonesian politics when, as has been observed, "Dutch control [over the archipelago] was extended . . . new agencies of government were created . . . [and] the need for a Western-educated Indonesian bureaucracy became ever greater." The period is also one in which Indies society was becoming internally partitioned, fissiparous as never before.[60] Pangemanann's mission, accepted with resolve, even glee, is, as he says, *"menyingirkan inisiator atau Sang Pemula dari suatu Kebangkitan Nasional"* (to remove the initiator or originator from a National Awakening).[61] The resolve comes from the knowledge that behind him lies the iconic force and executive might of the *Beamtenstaat*, whose *"kekuatan . . . adalah hasil seni pedang, mesin dan modal"* (power . . . is the product of the art of sword, machine and capital).[62] The glee comes from the knowledge of being (he fancies) in complete control of events as they unfold and able with ease to overcome resistance to his direction of them. He exults in his ability *"mendiskreditkan pimpinan Syarikat yang tersangkut sebagai perusuh dan kepala huru hara . . . mengikuti betapa benggol-benggol Syarikat masuk perangkap seperti tikus"* (to discredit the leader of Syarikat [Islam] who is involved as a disturber of the peace and as the leader of rioters . . . to watch how the ringleaders of the *Syarikat* enter the trap like mice).[63] Yet he is at the same time excruciated by the awareness that the service rendered unto his masters, the loyalty he bears them, is an act of profoundest treachery because he acknowledges them as his own people.

It is also an exquisitely futile gesture against the drift of events. Hence the guilty self-recrimination working its way through Pangemanann's miserable meditations. These flow from the plenitude of his understanding (he is far too intelligent not to face the truth when it confronts him) of *"betapa menjijikan tugas peradaban Eropa—nasionalisme yang sangat muda"* (how disgusting was this recent job of mine: fighting against the best product of European civilization—a fledgling nationalist movement).[64] It is this quandary which elicits interest in the character Pramoedya has created, a quandary whose tragic resolution supplies the motive for the writing of the novel and for its narration in forsaken *propria persona*. And it is this which ceaselessly torments and ultimately destroys him.

Pangemanann's emplotment in the tetralogy is revealing, both in its own right and as an index of putative authorial guile. Earlier, he had been proffered as one of the arch enemies of Minke, the name Pramoedya gives to the central character representing Raden Mas Tirto Adisoeryo (b. circa 1890), founder of Sarekat Dagang Islam (Association of Islamic Traders) and first native journalist, whose life story, unfolding between 1900 and 1919 (the year of the foundation of the Volksraad), forms the cynosure of the four novels.[65] As well, this story serves as the *point d'appui* for a political history of the Indonesian nationalist awakening, a history as comprehensive in scope here as it is minutely detailed. Hitherto it is Minke, the *pribumi* intellectual, who is made to stand at the center of his own heroic narrative. Now, in a surprising reversal, he is expelled to its margins, his position occupied by none other than his tormentor and pursuer, whose ordeal of consciousness the book explores with a mixture of compassion and dispassion. It is the ordeal of the outsider alienated from the values of colonial society yet, in a paralyzing contradiction, retaining its essential perspective. Not for nothing does he refer to himself bitterly as *"seorang birokrat yang hendak menyenangkan dan memenangkan diri pribadi dengan kekuasan yang ada padanya"* (a bureaucrat who seeks to gratify and vanquish himself with the power rendered unto him).[66]

Pangemanann, like Minke himself an "Inlander" by birth, is ethnically a Menadonese but has been adopted by a French chemist, at whose expense he had been sent to the homeland to be educated.

Retired, he has been appointed to the Algemeene Secretariat under the direct control of Governor-General Idenburg and charged with monitoring the exponential growth of political activity and publication in the Indies. His brief is to know about everything and everyone: the rise of Sarekat Islam and the government's use of agents to engineer its demise by fomenting ill will between Chinese and Indonesian members; the foundation of the Indische Partij, earliest political party in the Indies and its triumvirate leadership by Douwes Dekker, Suwardi Surjadiningrat, and Tjipto Mangunkusomo; the fortunes of Boedi Oetomo and of activists such as Sitti Soendari, first woman political activist in the colony. To want to know, or to want to be able to *claim* to know everything, is partly cause and partly effect of the veridical narrative. Pramoedya is writing in keeping with the nineteenth-century European genealogy of the novel, and with its betokening conventions of panoramic compass, its stress on fidelity to fact and on solidity of specification. This is historical fiction with (literally) a vengeance.

For the representation of a devouring will-to-omniscience is a means, not just of plotting a career, but of plotting *against* the character whose life is so highly evolved and whose career is so fastidiously logged. More to the point, it is, a sort of detective mania. Pangemanann is, in every sense of the word, sentenced: psychologically disabled to the extent that he is at the mercy of a need to give tongue. His anxieties and desires for revenge, though not wholly text-bound, appear to be so, which in dramatic terms matters greatly in the world of the work. Early on in the story, he escorts Minke into exile on the island of Ambon; five years later he is instructed to meet him on arrival from exile in Surabaya and secure his signature to a document renouncing any further political activity. On each occasion Minke treats his escort with withering contempt. It is to the manuscript which comprises the novel that he, Pangemanann, confides his confusion when faced with a conflict between pleasure in the exercise of the authority vested in him and a literally unspeakable respect for Minke's personal integrity struggle.

Unspeakable, except in soliloquy, because it threatens everything Pangemanann has been brought up to believe, everything he stands for. It must for this reason be celebrated through absence of mind, in the interstices of reading, and through his setting down of expiatory commentary of Minke/Pramoedya's three novels *Bumi Manusia* (This Earth of Mankind), *Anak Semua Bangsa* (Child of All Nations), and *Jejak Langkah*, whose drafts have been included among the personal papers officially confiscated. The interest, in other words, is in the prison house of language and its matrix, in the carceral nature of a policed and surveyed society whose operational norms are subdivision and oversight—a veritable *rumah kaca*, or glass house.

So the central trope of the text—Pangemanann's Indies as a transparent labyrinth, exposed to view from all sides, nothing escaping invigilation, but an enclosure which is at the same time a cage (*krangkeng*) in which the invigilator is himself trapped and delivered to judgment—this trope communicates a predicament at once private and public. It is a plight refracted through the optic of Foucault's view of knowledge as a form of manipulation. The metaphor of *rumah kaca* brings to mind of course the compelling image of Bentham's Panopticon, epitome of perfect surveillance, whose establishment, like that of institutions of curtailment and classification generally, entails the operation of all kinds of normalizing cognitive procedures.[67] The social question we are invited to consider turns on vocabularies of management and penalty, of distinction of offense and distribution of punishment, a vocabulary sited not on law but on the norm, and where not acts but identities are named.

To come with these provoking insights to *Rumah Kaca* is to discover several things. It is to see how a twentieth-century Indonesian text is independently aware of the creation of supervisory power and oppression that Foucault (in the detailed analyses, as distinct from his grand generalizations) has charted so effectively. It is to contend with magisterial depictions of (at least metaphorically) prisonous environments—for instance, the environment contrived and controlled by the colonial *apparat* in the Dutch East Indies in the first quarter of the century. It is to see such surroundings as impinging in a sinister way on questions of language and the control of language, which of course entails ways of thinking, a whole discourse. The novel lies smack at the center of this discussion, so keenly does it register the fact that to acquire knowledge from a standpoint of enmeshment in the bureaucratic "nightwatchman state" is ineluctably to enter into the dominant discourse.[68] It is intimately to have learned, and to have learned to beware, the language of oppression.

This much is evident from Pangemanann's anxious and scrupulous analysis of his dealings with Minke, ironically adverted to as *guruku* (my teacher). Candor, confidence, and trust: these are the rule between master and pupil; here, however, disguise, self-betrayal, secrecy above all, are the keys, and not simply secrecy as involving an undeclared complicity of attitude and outlook, important though this is.

24

The relationship also pivots on the sense of intermittently observing without in turn being observed. It turns on identity as, in part at least, constituted out of having something shameful or illicit to hide, not least the writing itself, here plainly transgressive. It involves the self-perception of an oppressor in which, more accurately, the oppressor is really the victim and in which a scapegoat is needed by the persecutor to assure the latter that his powers and properties are more than hallucinatory. This ambivalent liaison is sustained by Pangemanann's sense of criminality as being fed by each act and by its consequences. It also feeds off a Nietzschean *ressentiment,* that quality Foucault has made much of in discussing the origins of the drive to power.[69] Pramoedya's narrator is, like Nietzsche's "reactive personality," a type that, characteristically fired by rancor, tries to move into a legislative position. But, in historical perspective, he is also the model of helplessness; and the more cut off the more he is aware of his position—the dominators no less than the dominated being marked off, indeed receiving their very individuality, from their location in the carceral framework.

All this can be heard in the tone and timbre of the passage just quoted. It can be felt in its carriage, which is that of a well-defended personality in which envy and hatred commingle. The self-oppressive note is sustained to the bitter end and marks the automatic, unstoppable confession, which pauses not at all in its recounting of events and in its self-accusation. The prose impersonates a consciousness that remains fixed, that of someone who seems not to have gone beyond the emotional state of fury and despair documented in the writing, so that there is nothing cathartic about the admission which, substantially, constitutes the novel. Nor is release gained, even at the end, when Pangemanann meets his death having (it is implied) assisted in bringing about Minke's. The entire novel, punctuated as it is by such tortured and tortuous inquisitions, is a brilliantly dexterous exposition of "the compelling and constricting artificiality of the colonial framework, [which] forced the intelligentsia [in Indonesia] into a psychological and political one-way street."[70]

It is a nice question whether the fiction was contrived from the outset to draw attention to the scandal enacted in the very letter of its form. Be that as it may, it is no small part of the novel's fascination, and of its centrality to this discussion, that it should evolve into an examination of its own relation to a regnant literary ideology—and this in the closest possible way. A classic realist text, satisfying an insistence on the part of critic and reader on "typicality," catering to a liberal-humanist interest in character and in the interconnectedness of lives and personalities, it comes close to suggesting that the concept of the individual is finally unhelpful; that what are important are the total manipulations of power, the range of heterogeneous languages and voices deployed by the group in Indonesia whose hands are on the levers of definition and control.[71]

The imperialism of which the likes of Pangemanann were the dedicated and vindictive servitors was, therefore, an intimately domestic phenomenon. By a peregrination of intensities it entered, among many discursive areas, that of the psyche. The force of its entry was taken most especially on ambiguously placed sensibilities of subjection. Nor, as C. W. Watson reveals in his essay, was any sensibility tenderer, or more dissociated, than that of the new *priyayi* or functional elite of administrators who advocated a course of cooperation with the Dutch.[72] The career of Achmad Djajadiningrat, scion of an old Banten (West Java) family and the first Bupati to receive a formal Western education, is exemplary here.

Achmad's *Herinneringen* (1936), as Watson shows, is in one sense an instance of autobiography as a genre defined by the attempt to reconstruct "the movement of a life, in the actual circumstances in which it was lived. Its center of interest is the self, not the outside world, though necessarily the outside world must appear so that, in give and take with it, the personality finds its peculiar shape."[73] But there is more at stake here. Concepts like "selfhood" and "personality" are always already conditioned, neither given nor natural, and narratives of their formation ask therefore to be read not only for the straightforward account of incidents but, as well, for a logic of primary selection. Achmad's memoirs, Watson demonstrates, are on the face of it submissive to the classic form of autobiography, in that they set out to establish a public self and the history of its making. Their symbolic significance, however, has, first, to do with the representativeness of events, the account of which in this case meets antiphonally the standard paradigm of Indonesian historiography, and, second, with the question- able nature of its internal address.

Watson sees Achmad's recording impulse as resolving itself out of a certain defensiveness about the correctness of the association policy, *pace* the views of nationalist sympathizers among the new *priyayi*. The address of this impulse is a *totok* (migrant Dutch) constituency, collusively engaged here in an argument whose trump is the visible

26

progress of the writer/hero "from Sundanese minor aristocrat to respected, quasi-Dutch gentleman." As in Kartini's letters to Abendanon, entry is being afforded to an accommodationist *mentalité* which, though with hindsight a lost cause, seemed at the time as if it might prevail. Hence its value. We are made privy to an unspectacular metamorphosis, which complicates a statutory view of Dutch-Indonesian social and political relations and, in complicating it, qualifies an agreed interpretation.

Foucault is again helpful, particularly if we place the *Herinneringen* alongside Pangemanann's stream of consciousness, the two figures being rough historical coevals. The similarity lies in the institutional context which gives the person a sense of uniqueness and felt a difference from others. Autobiography, an art of taciturnity as well as revelation, becomes in this instance an exercise in endorsement, a mode for self-presentation to be sure, but not a vehicle for the sensibility boldly feeling and thinking its way into an area of thought where it can question the very terms of its making. Instead, it extends an invitation for the self retrospectively to confer an order of its life—each moment now frozen in time, each scene approaching iconic stasis—strengthening the sense of inevitability with regard to final, institutionalized success.

Indeed, if the narrations of Pangemanann and of Achmad Djajadiningrat suggest anything it is that the State, the supreme institution, is not some monolithic despot sitting on high and ruling by main force (hegemony-as-coercion), but a collection of "statements" which engineer, mark, machine, making it possible only for some things to be said (hegemony-as-consent), while all that threatens the coherence of such a collection—what Foucault would designate an "archive"—is confined to silence. Ideological interpellation, as it has been called, is perhaps too kind and gentle a term for this painful tooling of individuality, of one's "place" in every sense of the term.[74] *Tuan Pangemanann; Willem van Bantem; Pangeran Ario Achmad Djajadiningrat*: these are not only designations but somatic effects, bearing upon deportment, upon conduct, upon musculature even, so that one is talking not just of ideologies or of values but of the regulated formation and nomination of subjectivities. The enormous power of the state, colonial or neocolonial, is not only external and objective, it is in equal part internal and subjective, working through the myriad ways it collectively and individually (mis-) represents and, variously, encourages, coaxes, and compels its subjects/citizens to (mis-) represent themselves. (Rafael's absorbing essay in this collection on pornography and politics (chapter

27

2) catches this point with finesse, in relation to the Philippines in the years leading up to, and immediately following, the establishment of a constitutional dictatorship.)

In both Indonesia and the Philippines the national struggle, as it moved into the phase of diversified organizational activity, became ever more ideational and sentimental in form. Increasingly the struggle, and also the imperial resistance, moved into areas of elemental feeling and antipathy. Earlier it was noted that popular tradition, including its literary outcropping, demarcates one such area. Within this area, as elsewhere in the cultural domain, the most important problem of all is arguably the presence within of a vernacular idea of the state, the multiple ways it totalizes and categorizes those "under" or "inside" it. Henk Maier elucidates the problem with reference to the genealogy of high and low Malay in the Netherlands Indies towards the end of the Liberal period. He sees these categories as taking shape within the newly imagined community of the Indies at the turn of the century, and at a time when the challenge to authority was accompanied by the breakdown of a discursive system.

Maier's Batavia is a fin-de-siècle melting pot, not unlike Carl Schorske's Vienna in 1890, its commemorative plural society about to be sundered under the shock of the modern: by the railway, by migration from Holland, by pressures of supply and demand; above all, by possibilities of mechanical duplication of works of art. Maier's analysis shows how, under these pressures, the authority of a manuscript tradition was not so much eroded as refurbished. This, at a time when newspapers, speaking from a Dutch-oriented world of business, combined with the prescriptions of colonial pedagogues as to the truest or purest Malay (the search for roots and origins being, as Said has reminded us, a characteristic reflex of the orientalist mind) to enhance Dutch colonial superintendence of an indigenous heritage.

The brief of Maier's essay (chapter 5) is "the struggle of authority that flared up once print had acquired a solid place in the textual system." To find this enacted at the margin, not the center, and in terms of the deviant and unconceptualizable, is not to be wondered at, for the reasons given earlier. Accordingly, it is in turn-of-the-century booksellers' catalogues that we are asked to search, finding there a concatenation of discourses which, though equivocal, reached a wide public and, in reaching it, attested to a new-found capacity for unification and for subversiveness on the part of Indies Malay. In poetry, on the evidence of metamorphosis of such traditional forms as *syair* and *pantun* into vehicles for stock response, easily "consumed," produced cheaply and to a formula for profit, Maier discerns a new, relatively impersonal structure of feeling taking hold of the Malay world of the Indies. No longer communal in character, it is vitally connected to the ordonnances of journalism and to the habits of reception and ways of knowing arising around it. The product of spare time (itself prerequisite for the constitution of Literature as such), it in turn occasions and panders to *iseng*, the dangerous feeling of having time on one's hands— dangerous, in the colonial setting, because unaccounted for. It compels its antidote, in the form of a variety of printed texts contrived to be read aloud rather than in the privacy of a room of one's own. Even the "readerly" text, though rapidly commodified, nonetheless showed itself capable of evolution into socioeconomic critique (for example in the short stories of Mas Marco and the novels of Semaun, Sneevliet's protégé and an early PKI stalwart).[75] It is here, in the margins, that the idea of *kesusasteraan* comes into its own, in so doing acquiring a dimension of countersuggestibility.

Enough has been said elsewhere of nationalism to warrant framing of an hypothesis about its part in the bringing to birth of literature in an extended Malay world in the early twentieth century. A "political revival in cultural terms, a cultural revival in historicist terms" in the region, nationalism is the founding moment when, within a dense constellation of social, administrative, and intellectual pressures, literary discourse emerges as a language appropriate to a now-separate, demarcated body of privileged writing.[76] It is characteristic of this body of writing, in island Southeast Asia as indeed elsewhere, that the most consequential questions capable of being addressed to it have already been set in place by such pressures, by the vicissitudes surrounding the emergence of new discursive formations. These questions are about function, purpose, origin, affiliation; they can be seen as the asymptote of all the particular, technical questions capable of being addressed to this or that memoir, novel, or poem.

Maier's essay ends by querying the role played by *sastra*, or high, literature in Indonesia in the period after 1945. Keith Foulcher's companion studies adopt an equally interrogative posture towards one of the more contentious issues in modern Indonesian literature: the emergence and consolidation since the annus mirabilis of 1945 of received views in criticism as well as in the literature itself and in particular of an aesthetic ideology with political implications.

For his point of departure he takes the mixed feelings evoked in poets and writers of fiction by the upheaval spearheaded by the *pemuda*. But, as he argues, the artistic upshot had as much to do with a strategic annexment of Modernism by Indonesian writers as with the symbiosis of fear and uncertainty, horror and compassion, called into being by the Revolusi. This annexment, he shows, had its origins in the last years of Dutch colonial rule. It received expression in the Sjahririan stream of Indonesian nationalism, whose secularism was at variance with other tendencies (Hatta's, for example) within the modernizing Indonesian intelligentsia. It was this stream which burst forth in the extraordinary conditions of Jakarta under Dutch occupation, to flow in spate through the work of Chairil Anwar, modern Indonesia's *poète maudit*.

Chairil, and the "Generation of 45" of which he is the flower, undoubtedly compose a canon. But a canonical tradition is defined, and in being defined is rendered vulnerable to skeptical examination, as much by virtue of what it fends off, excommunicates, or places under embargo, as by what it approves, ratifies, or celebrates. The *Angkatan "45"* was such a tradition, especially where it began to ossify into orthodoxy, requisitioned in the postrevolutionary period and subsequently cut down to size until it could be appropriated for mythopoeic and exclusionary purposes by those in the driver's seat in Indonesia. But the political tradition of which the Angkatan was an outcropping was ironically a failed, minority tradition, not to be mistaken for the exclusive voice of the Indonesian revolution. For that voice speaks in the accents not only of *gelora api revolusi*, of (as the jest has it) history as an interview with the victor, but of tragic suffering, and, as has been truly said, in awareness of "all the consequences of this suffering: degeneration, brutalization, fear, hatred, envy . . . born in an experience of evil made the more intolerable by the conviction that it is not inevitable, but is the result of particular actions and choices."[77]

The voice is, again, quintessentially Pramoedya's. The attention he is accorded in these pages is in need of no justification, bearing in mind Said's remarks, cited at the start, about the "strategic formation" of intellectuals. Paradoxically because he writes at several internal removes from it, Pramoedya may well be the apotheosis of the Indonesian language, the novelist in whom its persuasions and abstracts are most triumphantly effective, the best exponent of its inflections, genders, moods, word-order and latencies. He is also, as Benedict Anderson has shrewdly pointed out, a combatant in a civil war within Javanese culture.[78] And, for his subtle but unmistakable taking up of arms against it there has been reserved punishment both condign and malignant, involving the physical interdiction of writing as well as banishment to the prison camp of remote Buru island in the Moluccas, and ceaseless harrassment upon release.[79]

Pramoedya's offense can be described as consisting of having placed in parenthesis ideas of order and deference at the heart of his background, class, and Javanese upbringing.[80] The severity of the punishment reflects the insolence with which he has been felt to have held these concepts up for questioning. It is this, more than anything else, which has elicited the authorities' vengefulness towards a writer whose popularity in his own country is undisputed. Indonesia's most important author has been edited out of the national narrative, his works circulating nonetheless *di bawah tanah* (that is, in samizdat) but at personal cost to their readers, many of them young, who remain numerous. It would not be mistaken to instance Pramoedya as having paid the price for being the avatar, in a post-GESTAPU context, of Gramsci's "organic intellectual" mentioned at the start: the "artist or literary man" who comes into existence on the cusp of an emergent social class but who then confronts—and attempts to vanquish and assimilate—traditional intellectual categories surviving from previous social conditions.[81]

This, however, is not the only reason for Pramoedya's attempted silencing and for his removal from the center. For one thing, he stands foursquare in a tradition of overtly politicized writing dating back to the very beginnings of modern Indonesian literature around 1919. To be sure, he has had a place in a (fabricated) Great Tradition of Indonesian literature. It was, however, a shifting place, his connection with that tradition being, as Foulcher shows, anything but straightforward. In the contours of that connection is inscribed the story of how a canon has been contrived.

The writings of his early experimental period demarcate a "universal-humanist" position and, no less than the short stories of Idrus and poems of Chairil, admit of inner questioning and introspection. Even more disturbingly do they meditate the nature and power of rhetoric and its ability to conjure up a past. Pramoedya's relationship to the literary ideology which succeeded in gaining the upper hand is thus by turns collateral, deviant, and recidivist. But always it involves a creative reworking of his own experience together with a detached, ironized evaluation of that of the *pemuda*: an evaluation committed only spasmodically to heroic elevation.

31

Correlative with this is a style that refuses to be docketed. Early Pramoedya is a heteroglossic mélange of fastidious description, socialist-realist melodrama, philosophical rumination, and a humorous earthiness that might be called Zolaesque if that adjective did not obscure a deeper quality of Javaneseness incomprehensible finally to any but Javanese-speaking readers themselves. It is only by a process of sanitizing it, cordoning off what is disturbingly new from what is safe and predictable, only by pitting interdependent elements against one another, that the oeuvre is rendered fit for consumption, but fit only on sufferance, as Foulcher shows.[82]   Pramoedya's unclubbable versatility has thus been his greatest virtue and his chief disqualification. In combination with his avowed shift to the Left, it has accounted for his erasure from the text of Indonesian literary life today.

Though in his middle phase he was to disengage from it, Pramoedya early and late remains well within the mainstream of a figural realism. His great historical tetralogy, no less than *Keluarga Gerilya* and *Perburuan* (1950), affirms an implicit belief in the efficacy of words in recording and crystallizing truth. It is a conviction shared by other "classic" Indonesian authors, some of a very different doctrinal stripe: Armijn Pane, Sutan Takdir Alisjahbana, Achdiat Karta Mihardja.   But there is another lineage in Indonesian fiction post-*kemerdekaan,* one in which Pramoedya, in his short stories, himself occupies an impressive place. As Paul Tickell observes (chapter 10), it had evolved after the watershed year of 1965 into a carrier of oppositional feeling, filling the hiatus left by a biddable naturalism. It is a tradition which has rubbed up fricatively against the limits of a straightforward mimesis, or else has overrun these limits into satire, parody, expressionist distortion, or imaginative extravaganza.[83]   The names to conjure here are those of Danarto, Arifin Noer, Yudhistira Ardi Noegraha—all writers who have risen to prominence or notoriety under the New Order and who have shown themselves disenchanted with its values.   There is a paradoxical sense in which they inhabit the vacuum created by the destruction of the Indonesian literary Left in the period 1965-70, while taking up the cudgels of an experimentalism pioneered by the Lembaga Kebudayaan Bakyat (People's Cultural Institute, or LEKRA).[84]

The reasons for this resort to surrealist indirection and coyness after 1965 are not far to seek. If your environment allows normally for judicial opprobrium, banning, and threats of imprisonment, you are less likely to be enamored of stable, representational forms which tend, so

32

to speak, to be on the side of Caesar. Your writing, Tickell implies, will be forced into the opposite of these forms, in compensation for a harsh political actuality. If the language in which you write is the language of uncompromising authority, it is unlikely that you will avoid an intense verbal self-consciousness. Language will seem the one surviving space where one might momentarily be free, wresting a pyrrhic victory over an inexorably conditioning environment. The author, thus marginalized, pitched into permanent crisis, will not be over-impressed by the solid, well-rounded character of a classical literary realism, but will feel himself fluid, diffuse, and provisional. The same sense of provisionality will apply to his awareness of social forms and conventions, breeding an ironic awareness of their fictive, ungrounded nature.

Of contemporary Indonesian writers who, in recoil from the unscripted formalisms of New Order literary policy, have set up home within the fantastic, the Balinese writer I Gusti Ngurah Putu Wijaya is an excellent example. His career has been unusually porous to influence: Beckett and Camus alongside Javanese *ketoprak*, *ludruk*, and *wayang wong* and the sophisticated primitivism of Balinese pictorial art. It has been conducted under conditions which have made necessary an intrepid adversary dissembling. Story in Putu's hands has evolved into a difficult though impressively integrated mixture of lyricism, spectacle (running to Grand Guignol) and an unsettling general exuberance. Overall, it entails a kind of secret signalling to spectators—spectators being the operative word, for story here is nothing if not histrionic performance. An object of the exercise, albeit an undeclared one, is to evade the vigilant eye of a censorship which looks askance at writing allegedly projecting and protecting attitudes linked too closely for comfort with LEKRA, yet a censorship which blinks leniently at writing smacking of the metaphysical or which is tamely art-for-art's-sake.

Putu, in short, is a past master of camouflage. His minimalist chronicles, keyed to a deadpan oral delivery, by design or default induce in readers a kind of critical consciousness which he likes to call "mental terror." Like his celebrated novels—including *Nyali* (Guts) (1983), incisively analyzed here by Tickell—the items collected in his volumes of short stories are allegorical scenarios, containing coded criticisms of failures and encroachments on the part of patrimonial authority. The method employed has a recognizably mischievous purpose, which is to plumb currents of disturbance presumed to run well beneath the surface of the quotidian lives of their (middle-class) readers. The apparent intention is slyly to invite these readers to ponder the source of their discontents in the social mechanism.

Hence, for example, the distraction visited upon the family in the story *Mata* (Eyes) when confronted with a corpse whose organs of sight are missing, and the *cauchemar* wrangle between *seorang pemberontak* (the rebel) and *yang berwajib* (the person in charge) in *Huru-Hara* (Chaos).[85] These narratives have rightly been called subversive, but their subversiveness has nothing to do with this or that paraphasable message of disobedience. It is a function, instead, of the heroes' adventures having been conceived in such a way as to engender in readers anything but an irenic attitude towards the ordinary in Indonesian urban experience. Not only are these unmistakably fictions of and from Indonesia's seething, polyglot capital. They are tales in which the ordinary is foregrounded disconcertingly as a perfidious, opaque category and made to feel problematical by being presented as fragmentary, terrifyingly ungovernable, and wildly comic at one and the same time. This, Tickell suggests, gives his narratives, expecially *Nyali*, an atemporal quality and belies their enmeshment in the contemporary moment.

The position of Putu Wijaya, like that of playwright and enfant terrible Rendra, may be likened in some ways to that of the *punakawan* clown—retainers in *wayang*. There is a similar license employed to say what cannot be said via the polite discourse of authority, and to do so in ways calculated to outrage and to prompt reparative action however vague. The position of Mochtar Lubis, which David Hill dissects in relation to his intervention in a debate of his own making in New Order Indonesia, is rather different though again best understood in the context of the Suharto government's enhanced coercive capacity, its ritual proscription of politics, and the intensified administrative pressure it is able to bring to bear on all sections of Indonesian society. There are resonances with the failures of Indonesia since Independence: the collapse of the social revolution led by the Indonesian Communist party; the entrenchment, in the twenty-five years since the October 1965 coup, of an ethos of authoritarian "developmentalism"; and the rapidly rising inequality in Java and the Outer Islands as between wage-workers on the one hand and village society on the other.

Admirers of the author of the Indonesian novels best known overseas can be forgiven for objecting to the view of him as having been "produced" by these determinate conditions. There is, nonetheless, a sense in which the Lubis of the controversial pamphlet-lecture *Manusia*

Indonesia could only have written as he has within them. There is no need to summon his 1964 novel for which he is justly famous, *Senja di Djakarta* (Twilight in Jakarta), to argue for a shift in sympathy and in ideological stance from liberal critic of Guided Democracy to energetic opponent of the PKI. To be sure, Lubis as novelist and editor established a reputation as a scourge—he a Mandailing Batak from North Sumatra—inveighing against the corruption of Javanese *penguasa* (those with power), well understanding the price to be paid for falling foul of them. Yet, as Hill shows, we are not to take him at his own valuation as soi-disant disinterested conscience-of-the-nation. The "advocacy journalism" for which he is famed bespeaks opposition to the New Order all right, but opposition essentially loyal—far more so than he might care to concede. The key is an untranscripted belief about the nature of cultural change and a faith (belied by events) in the means to be used to bring it about. Here a contrast with the Rendra of *Perjuangan Suku Naga* (The Struggle of the Naga Tribe) suggests itself.

If, then, Mochtar belongs to his country's postrevolutionary generation of secular modernizing intellectuals, in William Liddle's term, he must also be seen in terms of his "strategic location," exemplifying the ambivalent relationship of the Indonesian national bourgeoisie, "exhibiting both confrontation and alliance with foreign international capital."[86] The text of Lubis's lecture, vocal in defense of a hypostatized concept of *Kepribadian Indonesia*, is reticent about cause, effect, and ultimate accountability for social failure within the New Order. The reticence speaks through the arrested formal itinerary of his polemical prose in a variety of unexpected ways.

It has been a twofold aim of this chapter to adumbrate some of the issues arising from the essays assembled here and to furnish a rudimentary context for their appreciation. By "context" is meant not some inert backdrop but (in the root sense of the word) something which weaves itself inextricably into literary discourse as part of its texture and is established as a condition of its textuality. Much has been heard of late of the need for criticism to step into the ancestral, the stigmatized, silences left by time and make them speak. It is a demand which assumes literature to be an agency of change as well as a repository of knowledge. It is not an easy one to satisfy, for a fully *political* criticism of literature would include literature's varying historical constructions, the force of the textual articulations of constructions, the force of the textual articulations of experience and language, and the interrelations and disjunctions of all these. A tall order, granted, and one that remains to be filled.

For it to be filled, however, attention will have had to be drawn to the hazards attending this kind of enquiry. The chief hazard is of forgetting, as much post-Saussurean theory has gone to incoherent lengths to forget, the necessary role of insight (into a reality which is revealed or disclosed, by someone in a cultural or historical situation) in the interpretative process. Literature, like political action, is part of history; and for literature, as for history, the questions asked, as with the answers returned, must finally lie not in any transhistorical general rules or in the comprehensive exposure of what the author or the thinking of his day did or did not know, but in an insight—from the point in time and space where we are now (the question and answers will change as our own situation changes)—into what is, or is not, really there.

NOTES

1. Edward Said, *Orientalism* (Harmondsworth: Penguin, 1985), 16.

2. The predecessors are A. Reid and D. Marr, eds., *Perceptions of the Past in Southeast Asia* (Singapore: Heinemann for Australian Association of Asian Studies, 1979); W. Gungwu, M. Guerrero, and D. Marr, eds., *Society and the Writer: Essays on Literature in Modern Asia* (Canberra: Research School of Pacific Studies, Australian National University Press, 1981); Pierre-Bernard Lafont and Denys Lombard, eds., *Littératures Contemporaines de L'Asie du Sud-Est* (Paris: Societé Asiatique, 1973).

3. Michel Foucault, "The Order of Things," in *Untying the Text: A Post-structuralist Reader*, ed. Robert Young (London: Routledge and Kegan Paul, 1981), 53; "The Politics of Discourse," *Ideology and Consciousness* 3 (1978): 15.

4. Charles Robequain, *Malaya, Indonesia, Borneo and the Philippines: A Geographical, Economic, and Political Description of Malaya, the East Indies and the Philippines*, 2d ed. (London: Longmans, 1958), 258.

5. R. J. Pringle, *Indonesia and the Philippines: American Interests in Island Southeast Asia* (New York: Columbia University Press, 1980),

1. The best overall comparative modern assessments are by John Bastin and Harry J. Benda, *A History of Modern Southeast Asia: Colonialism, Nationalism, and Decolonisation* (Englewood Cliffs, N.J.: Prentice-Hall, 1977); and D. J. Steinberg, ed., *In Search of Southeast Asia: A Modern History* (Honolulu: University of Hawaii Press, 1987). A useful vade mecum is Patricia Lim Pui Huen's *The Malay World of Southeast Asia: A Select Cultural Bibliography* (Singapore: Institute of Southeast Asian Studies, 1987).

6. O. W. Wolters, *History, Culture and Region in Southeast Asian Perspectives* (Singapore: Institute for Southeast Asian Studies, 1982) 99; Anthony L. Reid, *The Lands Below the Winds*, vol. 1 of *Southeast Asia in the Age of Commerce* (New Haven: Yale University Press, 1988).

7. See Theodore Friend, *The Blue-Eyed Enemy: Japan Against the West in Java and Luzon, 1942-1945* (Princeton University Press, 1988).

8. Peter Hulme, *Colonial Encounters: Europe and the Native Caribbean, 1492-1797* (London: Routledge, Chapman and Hall, 1987), 2.

9. Edward Said, quoted in Imre Saluzinsky, *Criticism and Society* (London: Methuen, 1987), 126. This collection of interviews is an excellent introduction to current thinking on its subject. Said's emphasis on the "worldliness of texts" is amplified in Edward Said, *The World, the Text, the Critic* (Cambridge, Mass.: Harvard University Press, 1985), chaps. 7, 8.

10. See Clifford Geertz, *Works and Lives: The Anthropologist as Author* (Stanford: Stanford University Press, 1988). The main argument turns on a sharply critical examination of Barthes' essay "Authors and Writers." Geertz's influence on the New Historicism discussed below is, like that of Victor Turner, crucial, and apparent for example in James Clifford and G. E. Marcus, eds., *Writing Culture: The Poetics and Politics of Ethnography* (Berkeley: University of California Press, 1988).

11. There is a useful glossary in Frank Lentricchia and Thomas McLaughlin, eds., *Critical Terms for Literary Study* (Chicago: University of Chicago Press, 1990).

12. The battle lines have been drawn since the late 1970s, with the attack led from the trenches by Tony Bennett in his *Marxism and Formalism* (London, Methuen, 1979) and by Terry Eagleton, whose writings have been influential. See Eagleton's *The Function of Criticism: From the Spectator to Post-Structuralism* (London: Verso, 1976) and *Walter Benjamin or Towards a Revolutionary Criticism* (London: Verso, 1981). For studies on the new theories in general, see J. G. Merquior, *From Prague to Paris: Structuralist and Post-structuralist Itineraries* (London: Verso, 1986). An aerial view of the battlefields is provided by Frank Lentricchia, *After the New Criticism* (Chicago: University of Chicago Press, 1981). See also Christopher Butler, *Interpretation, Deconstruction and Ideology: An Introduction to Some Current Issues in Theory* (Oxford: Clarendon Press, 1984).

13. A forceful challenge to the canon has come from Stanley Fish: see *Is There a Text in this Class?: The Authority of Interpretative Communities* (Cambridge, Mass.: Harvard University Press, 1980). But the problem as a whole has been superbly ventilated by Frank Kermode in *History and Value* (Oxford: Clarendon Press, 1989). See especially the chapters entitled "Value at a Distance" and "Canon and Period," 86-128.

14. See, for example, E. D. Hirsch, Jr., "The Politics of Theories of Interpretation," *Critical Inquiry* 9/1 (1982): 235-47; and Jerome J. McGann, "The Text, the Poem, and the Problem of Historical Method," *New Literary History* 12/24 (Winter 1981): 269-88.

15. By far the most helpful discussion of what is implied in the thinking going under this name is to be found in Jerome J. McGann, *Social Values and Poetic Acts: The Historical Judgement of a Literary Work* (Cambridge, Mass.: Harvard University Press, 1988) (see esp. chap. 5); see also his *Towards a Literature of Knowledge* (Oxford University Press, 1989).

16. See Frederic Jameson, *The Political Unconscious: Narrative as a Socially Symbolic Act* (London: Methuen, 1981).

17. See Rafael's foray into late nineteenth-century photographic portraiture, "Nationalism, Imagery and the Filipino Intelligentsia," *Critical Inquiry* 16/3 (Spring 1990): 591-611.

18. On these questions see Derek Attridge, Geoff Bennington, and Robert Young, eds., *Post-Structuralism and the Question of History* (Cambridge: Cambridge University Press, 1987); and Robert Weimann's critique of concepts of "representation" in "Text, Author-Function, and Appropriation in Modern Narrative: Toward a Sociology of Representation in Modern Narrative," in *The Aims of Representation: Subject/ Text/History*, ed. Murray Krieger (New York: Columbia University Press, 1987), 175-215. See also Dominick La Capra, *History and Criticism* (Ithaca: Cornell University Press, 1985), esp. chaps. 4, 5; and David Simpson, "Literary Criticism and the Return to History," *Critical Inquiry* 14/4 (Summer 1988): 721-47.

19. Gillian Beer, *Arguing with the Past: Essays in Narrative from Woolf to Sidney* (London: Routledge, 1990), 85.

20. For illuminating comment, see Terry Eagleton, *Literary Theory* (Oxford: Blackwell, 1984), 205-6.

21. Antonio Gramsci, "Problems of Marxism" and "State and Civil Society," in *Selected from the Prison Notebooks of Antonio Gramsci*, ed. and trans. Quintin Hoare and Geoffrey Nowell-Smith (London: Lawrence and Wishart, 1982), 418, 210. Readers will want to consult James C. Scott's chapter "Hegemony and Consciousness: Everyday Forms of Ideological Struggle" in his brilliant *Weapons of the Weak: Everyday Forms of Peasant Resistance* (New Haven: Yale University Press, 1985), 304-51, for exegesis directly related to Southeast Asia and for further bibliographical reference. See also Said, *Orientalism*, 168-71, and John Brenkmann, *Culture and Domination* (Ithaca: Cornell University Press, 1987).

22. Said, *Orientalism*, 20.

23. Michel Foucault, *Power/Knowledge: Selective Interviews and Other Writings, 1972-77*, ed. and trans. Colin Gordon (New York: Pantheon, 1980), 97.

24. Horacio de la Costa, S.J., "The Responsibility of the Winter in Contemporary Philippine Society," in *Literature and Society: A Symposium*, ed. Alberto Florentino (Manila: Florentino, 1964), 104.

25. See Vicente L. Rafael, *Contracting Colonialism: Translation and Christian Conversion in Tagalog Society Under Early Spanish Rule* (Ithaca: Cornell University Press, 1988), 121. This is the standard work in the area.

26. See Renato Constantino, *Neocolonial Identity and Counter-Consciousness: Essays on Cultural Decolonisation* (London: Merlin Press, 1978).

27. Reynaldo Clemeno Ileto, *Pasyon and Revolution: Popular Movements in the Philippines, 1840-1910* (Quezon City: Ateneo de Manila University Press, 1979). Ileto's study has occasioned sometimes tempestuous debate, summarized in his article "Critical Issues in 'Understanding Philippine Revolutionary Mentality,'" *Philippine Studies* 30 (1982): 92-119.

28. See Reynaldo Ileto, "The Past in the Present Crisis," in *The Philippines After Marcos*, ed. R. J. May and Francisco Nemenzo (London: Croom Helm, 1985), 7-16.

29. An *ilustrado* was generally of mixed Filipino, Chinese, and/or Spanish blood and a member of the social and economic elite who also had received a Western education either in the Philippines or abroad. The necessarily elliptical account in this paragraph extrapolates from Nicolas Tarling, *A Concise History of Southeast Asia* (New York: Frederick A. Praeger, 1966); Temario C. Rivera, Merlin M. Magallona, et al., *Feudalism and Capitalism in the Philippines: Trends and Implications* (Quezon City: Foundation for Nationalist Studies, 1982); and Jonathan Fast and Jim Richardson, *Roots of Dependency: Political and Economic Revolution in the 19th Century Philippines* (Quezon City: Foundation for Nationalist Studies, 1979). On exposure to, and penetration by, European and American markets, see Steinberg, *In Search of Southeast Asia*, 197-209; and Norman G. Owen, ed., *Compadre Colonialism: Studies on the Philippines Under American Rule* (Ann Arbor: University of Michigan, *Michigan Papers on South and Southeast Asia No. 3*, 1970).

30. For a masterly discussion, see Resil B. Mojares, *The Origins and Rise of the Filipino Novel: A Generic Study of the Novel Until 1940* (Quezon City: University of the Philippines Press, 1983), esp. 114-15, where attention is paid to the social origin of writers and readers of

fiction, both in Spanish and in the regional vernaculars, in the late colonial period, as well as to altering conditions in publishing and in the Manila book trade. These are discussed in relation to changes in levels of education which, Mojares notes, "were to bring to the fore . . . lawyers, clerks, merchants, native civil servants" (113). See also Eliodoro G. Robles, *The Philippines in the 19th Century* (Quezon City: Malaya Books, 1969).

31. A succinct survey can be found in Benedict R. O'G. Anderson, "Cacique Democracy in the Philippines: Origins and Dreams," *New Left Review* (May/June 1988): 1-31. See esp. pp. 5-10. On the ambiguities of *ilustrado* response, see Bonifacio S. Salamanca, *The Filipino Reaction to American Rule, 1901-1913* (Archon, Conn.: Shoe String Press, 1968), and Martin Meadows, "Colonialism, Social Structure and Nationalism: The Philippines Case," *Pacific Affairs* 4/3 (1971): 337-52.

32. Said, *Orientalism*, 174-75. On his concept of "affiliations," see his *World*.

33. Rizal in a letter to his family dated 20 June 1882; quoted in Leon Ma. Guerrero, *The First Filipino: A Bibliography of Jose Rizal* (Manila: National Historical Commission, 1974), 68.

34. On Rizal's life and writings, see Mojares, *Origins and Rise*, 137-50.

35. See Georg Lukàcs, *Writer and Critic* (London: Merlin Press, 1978), esp. the essays "Narrate or Describe" and "Art and Objective Truth."

36. Tarling, *A Concise History*, 196.

37. On this conception of the classic (European) novel Raymond Williams has much to say in *Politics and Letters: Interviews With New Left Review* (London: Verso, 1981), 201-4 and 349-50. See also J. P. Stern, *On Realism* (London: Routledge, Chapman and Hall, 1973), and W. D. Harvey, *Character and the Novel* (London: Chatto and Windus, 1965).

38. There is incisive comment on Rizal from this point of view in Benedict R. O'G. Anderson, *Imagined Communities: Reflections on the Origin and Spread of Nationalism* (London: Verso, 1983), 32-3, and by Vicente Rafael in his "Language, Identity and Gender in Rizal's Noli," *Review of Indonesian and Malayan Affairs* 18 (Winter 1984): 110-40.

39. Walter Benjamin, "The Author as Producer," in *Understanding Brecht*, A. Bostock, trans. (London: Merlin Press, 1977), 95.

40. For the reception of Rizal among the Tagalog peasantry, see Reynaldo Ileto's essay "Rizal and the Underside of History," in *Moral Order and the Question of Change: Essays on Southeast Asian Thought*, ed. D. Wyatt and A. Woodside (New Haven: Yale University Southeast Asian Studies monograph series No. 24, 1982), 274-337.

41. On censorship, in this double sense of the monitoring of what was read and by whom and of eccelesiastical oversight of a reading public, see Bienvenido L. Lumbera, "Tradition and Influences in the Development of Tagalog Poetry (1570-1898)," Ph.D. thesis, University of Indiana, 1967; and remarks passim in Domingo Abella, "Some Notes on the Historical Background of Philippine Literature" in *Brown Heritage: Essays on Philippine Cultural Tradition and Literature*, ed. Antonio Manuud (Manila: Atenio de Manila University Press, 1967), 34-48. On the absence of provision for primary education or for pedagogical training in the Philippines before 1863 and the corresponding reservation of education to the monied and to "Filipinos" (in the contemporary sense of Spaniards born in the islands) see Evergisto Bazaco, *History of Education in the Philippines* (Manila: University of Santo Tomas Press, 1953).

42. Pierre Macherey, *A Theory of Literary Production*, trans. Geoffrey Wall (London: Routledge & Kegan Paul, 1978), 85. Macherey argues that the speech of a text, novel, treatise, poem "comes from a certain silence" or is built upon "a discord in the historical reality" (238). To become alert to this incompleteness is to identify the active presence of conflict and silence at the borders of a work. The business of criticism is to reveal the limits and the conditions of this ideological incoherence.

43. On the link between the production of fiction, historical and ethnographic treatises, commercial journalism (written for pro-Spanish,

conservative newspapers), and the growth of private presses, see Mojares, 114-30.

44. See Hans-Robert Jauss, *Towards an Aesthetic of Reception* (Brighton: Harvester, 1982), who stresses a dialogue between past and present (implicit in the notion of "horizon,") and emphasizes that literary history which relates to general history both actively and passively and cannot be divided into essential and otiose elements. Robert Holub's *Reception Theory: A Critical Introduction* (London: Methuen, 1984) is a very clear account of these matters.

45. The phrase is to be found passim in Jerome A. McGann, *A Critique of Modern Textual Criticism* (Chicago: University of Chicago Press, 1983).

46. The term is Robert Redfield's, cited in Harry Benda's "Peasant Movements in Southeast Asia," in *Continuity and Change in Southeast Asia: Collected Journal Articles of Harry J. Benda* (New Haven: Yale University Southeast Asian Studies monograph series No. 18, 1972), 221-35.

47. David Sturtevant, *Popular Uprisings in the Philippines, 1840-1940* (Ithaca: Cornell University Press, 1976), 1.

48. The phrase belongs to Raymond Williams in his discussion of "The Complexity of Hegemony," in his *Problems in Materialism and Culture: Selected Essays* (London: Verso, 1980), 38-42. Williams makes a distinction between *residual* (formed in the past but still active) and *emergent* (the expression of new groups outside the dominant group), and between *oppositional* (challenging the dominant ideology) and *alternative* (coexisting with it in various degrees of unease) which may assist in defining the nature and status of *pasyon* which is at the crux here.

49. Ileto, *Pasyon and Revolution*, 15.

50. See Renato Constantino, *A History of the Philippines: From the Spanish Colonisation to the Second World War* (New York: Monthly Review Press, 1976).

51. David Joel Steinberg, "An Ambiguous Legacy: Years at War in the Philippines," *Pacific Affairs*, 45/2 (Summer 1972): 171.

52. James C. Scott, *Domination and the Arts of Resistance: Hidden Transcripts* (New Haven: Yale University Press, 1990).

53. The phrase "anxiety of influence" is, of course, Harold Bloom's, in his influential *The Anxiety of Influence: A Theory of a Poetry* (New York: Oxford University Press, 1973). This concept is put to excellent use by Dr. Soledad Reyes of the Ateneo in an unpublished paper entitled "The Balagtas Tradition: The Politics of the Modern-Traditional Debate," to which the preceding discussion is indebted, as it is to Virgilio S. Almario's *Balagtasismo versus Modernismo: Panulaang Tagalog sa-ika-20 siglo* (Quezon City: Ateneo de Manila University Press, 1984).

54. See David Wurfel, *Filipino Politics: Development and Decay* (Ithaca: Cornell University Press, 1988), esp. chaps. 4-11. This is the most comprehensive description to date of the undoing of the Philippines polity under Marcos, and of its antecedents.

55. See the important contributions of Doreen Fernandez to this field of study: "From Ritual to Realism: A Brief Historical Survey of Philippine Theatre," *Philippine Studies* 28 (4th Quarter 1980): 389-419.

56. With reference to EDSA, see "The Culture of Revolution: Tentative Notes," *Diliman Review* 35/2 (1987): 26-36. EDSA is the name of the highway around Metro Manila. On the part between Camp Crame and Camp Agunaldo a civilian and military uprising took place in 1986 which resulted in the downfall of President Marco.

57. On "seditious" theatre in Tagalog in the early American period, see Alfred W. McCoy, "Zarzuela and Welga: Vernacular Drama and the Growth of Working Class Consciousness, Iloilo City, Philippines, 1900-1932," in Gungwu, Guerrero and Marr, (eds.), *Society and the Writer*, 35-67.

58. Pramoedya Ananta Toer, *Rumah Kaca* (Jakarta: Hasta Mitra, 1988), 52-56. The translations from the Indonesian are my own.

59. The reference appears to be to a legend from the areas surrounding Batavia of *"Abang Pitung"* (Brother Pitung), an ordinary *pribumi* who in a kind of Hobsbawmian primitive rebellion took up arms against the *"tuan tanah Belanda"* (Dutch landlord), single-handedly to begin with, after the latter stole his fiancée as well as his land. With a growing

band of followers all skilled in the self-defensive martial art of *silat*, he then set out to become a sort of Robin Hood to the villagers in the neighborhood. Pramoedya's way, of course, is to have his narrator utter the soubriquet in clear reference to those in rebellion against the Dutch in the period in which the novel is set and without being quite aware—or what is more likely, all too aware—of the resonating ironies; but there is also a possible glance by the author at a popular contemporary Indonesian film entitled *"Si Pitung"* on this theme.

60. Robert Van Neil, *The Emergence of the Modern Indonesian Elite* (Dordrecht: Foris Publications, 1984), 50. On the internal compartmentalisation of Indies society, see Jacques van Doorn, "A Divided Society: Segmentation and Mediation in Late-Colonial Indonesia," in *Indonesian Politics: A Reader*, ed. Christine Doran (Townsville: Centre for Southeast Asian Politics, James Cook University of North Queensland, 1987), 5-31.

61. Pramoedya, *Rumah Kaca*, 99.

62. Pramoedya, *Rumah Kaca*, 105.

63. Pramoedya, *Rumah Kaca*, 124.

64. Pramoedya, *Rumah Kaca*, 153.

65. On the life and times of Tirto Adisoeryo, see Van Neil, *Emergence*, 88-93, 107-8.

66. Pramoedya, *Rumah Kaca*, 149.

67. See Michel Foucault, *Discipline and Punish*, trans. Alan Sheridan (Harmondsworth: Penguin, 1979).

68. The phrase is Harry J. Benda's, "Decolonization in Indonesia: The Problem of Continuity and Change," *American Historical Review* 70/4 (July 1965): 1071.

69. *Ressentiment* is translated as "rancor" and discussed in detail in the first essay of Frederich Nietzsche, *The Genealogy of Morals*, trans. Francis Golffing (New York: Garden Press, Doubleday, 1956). See esp. 170.

70. Harry J. Benda, "The Pattern of Administrative Reforms in the Closing Years of Dutch Rule in Indonesia," *Journal of Asian Studies* 25/4 (1966): 600.

71. "Typicality," of course, is not a matter of a statistical average or an aggregate of traits but of "the convergence and intersection of . . . the most important moral, social and spiritual contradictions of a time." Lukàcs, *Writer and Critic*, 78.

72. On the *priyayi* in late colonial Indonesia, see Heather Sutherland, *The Making of a Bureaucratic Elite: The Colonial Transformation of the Javanese Priyayi* (Singapore: Heinemann Educational, 1980).

73. Roy Pascal, *Design and Truth in Autobiography* (London: Chatto and Windus, 1956), 9.

74. Louis Althusser, *Essays on Ideology* (London: Verso, 1984), 45.

75. Tickell has drawn attention to the long-term consequences of deletions from the official transcript of Indonesian literary history in the introduction to his translation of *Three Early Indonesian Short Stories by Mas Marco Kartodikomo (c. 1890-1932)* (Clayton: Monash University Centre of Southeast Asian Studies, 1981), 1-6. See also Henri Chambert-Loir, "Mas Marco Kartodikromo (c. 1890-1932), ou L'education Politique," in P.-B. Lafont and D. Lombard, *Littératures Contemporaines de L'Asie du Sud-Est* (Paris: à l'Asiathèque, 1974), 203-14, for an illuminating discussion of novels *Student Hijo* (1919) and *Rasa Merdeka* (1924).

76. Donald K. Emmerson, "Issues in Southeast Asian History: Room for Interpretation," *Journal of Asian Studies* 40/1 (November 1980): 66. See also E. J. Hobsbawm, *Nations and Nationalism Since 1978: Programme, Myth, Reality* (Cambridge: Cambridge University Press, 1990). Anderson, in his *Imagined Communities*, has illuminated, contrariwise, the function of literature in the promotion of the national idea.

77. Raymond Williams, *Modern Tragedy* (London: Chatto and Windus, 1966), 77. His formulation seems to me to be profoundly germane to an understanding of such fictions as "Dendam" (Revenge), "Blora," and *Keluarga Gerilya* (A Guerilla Family) (1950).

78. See his splendid "Sembah-Sumpah (Courtesy and Curses): The Politics of Language and Javanese Culture," in Benedict R. Anderson, *Language and Power: Exploring Political Cultures in Indonesia* (Ithaca: Cornell University Press, 1990), 194-241.

79. There have been demands recently in the Indonesian press for the rearrest of Pramoedya and even for the burning of his books (see *Masa Kini*, 13 June 1988, and *Jayakarta,* 20 May 1988), concurrent with a series of arrests among students in central Java. On 3 August 1988 a ban was announced on Pramoedya's novel *Gadis Pantai*, and on 9 August the Jakarta Public Prosecutor was instructed to proceed against the firm Hasta Mitra for having published his novels and for being staffed by former *tapol* (*tahanan politik*, or political detainees).

80. See "A Note on the Author," in *A Heap of Ashes*, ed. and trans. from the Indonesian by Harry Aveling (St. Lucia: University of Queensland Press, 1975); ix-xxii, and "Pramudya Ananta Tur [*sic*]: The Writer as Outsider," in *Cultural Options and the Role of Tradition: A Collection of Essays on Modern Indonesian and Malaysian Literature*, ed. Anthony H. Johns (Canberra: Australian National University Press, 1979), 96-109.

81. See Gramsci, *Selections from the Prison Notebooks*, 15-20.

82. See also Savitri Scherer, "From Culture to Politics: The Development of Class Consciousness in Pramoedya Ananta Toer's Writings," in *Society and the Writer*, 239-61.

83. On Yudhistira's Arjuna novels, see Anderson, "Sembah-Sumpah," 227-35, and Savitri Scherer, "Introducing Yudhistira Ardi Noegraha," *Indonesia* 31 (April 1981): 31-52. Danarto's stories are discussed by Teeuw in his *Modern Indonesian Literature*, vol. 2, 3rd ed. (Dordrecht: Foris Publications, 1986), 192-6.

84. On LEKRA experimentalism, see Foulcher's authoritative study, *Social Commitment in Literature and the Arts: The Indonesian Institute of People's Culture 1950-1965* (Clayton: Monash University Centre for Southeast Asian Studies, 1986), 39-49.

85. The sources are the collections *Bom* (Jakarta: Teater Mandiri, 1978); *Es* and *Gres* (Jakarta: PNG Balai Pustaka, 1982).

47

86. Richard Robison, "Class, Capital and the State in New Order Indonesia," in *Southeast Asia: Essays in the Political Economy of Structural Change*, ed. Richard Higgott and Richard Robison (London: Routledge & Kegan Paul, 1985), 307. See Robison's *Indonesia: The Rise of Capital* (Sydney: Allen and Unwin, 1976), 315-16, for a complex discussion of class relations and inter- and intraclass conflict. Rex Mortimer, *Showcase State: The Illusion of Indonesia's Modernisation* (Sydney: Angus and Robertson, 1973), and Herbert Feith, "Political Control, Class Formation and Legitimacy in Suharto's Indonesia" in *Indonesian Politics: A Reader*, ed. Doran, 221-34, shed additional light on the topic.

2

PATRONAGE AND PORNOGRAPHY: IDEOLOGY AND SPECTATORSHIP DURING THE EARLY MARCOS YEARS

Vicente L. Rafael

In the aftermath of the February 1986 "revolution" which forced Ferdinand and Imelda Marcos out of the Philippines, the government of Corazon Aquino turned the presidential palace, Malacañang, into a museum and in doing so meant to put the Marcos's legacy of excess on display.[1] A guidebook on the presidential palace describes one instance of that excess, in which the doors leading to the Grand Staircase are said to have "depict[ed] the Philippine legend of 'Malakas' (Strong) and 'Maganda' (Beautiful), the first Filipino man and woman who emerged from a large bamboo stalk. Mrs. Marcos liked to think of President Marcos and herself in terms of these legendary First Filipinos. So thoroughly did they identify with this myth that they had portraits hung of themselves as Malakas and Maganda in the palace—seminude and emerging from a forest of bamboo stalks (fig. 1). In 1985 they went so far as to commission a group of Filipino academics to rewrite the legend which culminated in the celebration of the Marcos regime."[2]

As Malakas and Maganda, Ferdinand and Imelda imaged themselves not only as the "Father and Mother" of an extended Filipino family, they also conceived of their privileged position as allowing them to cross and redraw all boundaries, social, political, and cultural. They thought of themselves as being at the origin of all that was new in the Philippines—for example, the "New Society" (1972-81) and the "New Republic" (1981-86). To the extent that they were able to mythologize the progress of history, the First Couple could posit itself as the origin of circulation itself in the country.

In this essay I propose to trace the genesis of this authoritarian wishfulness as it first emerged during the early period of the Marcos presidency, with particular references to the ways in which the Marcoses and their supporters produced and disseminated the couple's tendentious reconstruction of history—in the sense both of what happened and what was "new" or yet to happen—in relation to prevalent ideas about the circulation and display of power in postcolonial Philippine society. Such ideas, I argue, grew out of the gap between consciousness and social experience which became particularly acute in the 1950s and 1960s, as Filipinos from different classes sought to reconstitute traditional notions of patronage within the logic of an expanding capitalist economy. At the same time, new images of female ambition and subjugation emerged in film and politics which would furnish a context for reworking the positions of leader and follower in terms of the relationship between spectators and spectacle, seer and seen. That Imelda Marcos would become as important as she did in her husband's career was an indication of the extent to which national politics had become a stage for playing out a generalized nostalgia for patron-client relationships—a nostalgia fashioned to focus upon the First Lady as a prototypical sign for the simulation of patronage within the amoral context of commodity exchange.

A Man of Destiny, A Woman of Charm

The appropriation of the legend of Malakas and Maganda was but one way in which the Marcos regime sought to set itself apart from those of its predecessors. The juxtaposition of images of primordial strength with eternal beauty was symptomatic of a dominant obsession among the Marcoses: the turning of politics into spectacle. We can begin to see this obsession at work by looking at the ways in which Ferdinand's and Imelda's private and public careers were represented prior to 1970 in the Philippine press and in their respective biographies.

In the presidential campaigns of 1965 and 1969, Ferdinand Marcos often referred to his wife as his "secret weapon." Imelda's presence was considered to be important at political rallies all over the country in attracting and holding the crowd, who waited for her to sing, something which she did after routinely appearing to be coy. Her husband would often join her in a duet, to the great pleasure of the audience.[3]

Both were adept at working their audiences. Ferdinand's rhetorical style set him apart from other politicians. The sound of his voice, rather than the content of his speeches, seemed to command attention. One account describes it as a "rich masculine boom . . . that invests him with power and authority. . . . The deep-toned voice, solemnly and slowly articulating the words, where the other [speakers] choose to be just loud and strident, is the voice of authority, no doubt." Because of the immediate distinctiveness of his voice rather than specific elements in his oratory, Ferdinand was widely regarded as "one of the best performers among present-day politicos."[4]

For her part, Imelda set a new style of political campaigning in a largely male-dominated field. She came across as a striking presence—tall and youthful in her formal gowns, generously granting requests for songs. "It did not matter whether her audience were urbanites or poor *barrio* folk: she was an actress putting on a stage appearance. She wore *ternos* even for appearances on small, rickety makeshift stages of rough wooden planks covered with nipa palms."[5] Imelda made herself accessible to an audience, but this meant that the audience in political rallies became voyeurs waiting to see and hear her. As voyeurs, they did not have to articulate their interests but only had to be alert for the appearance of something that would show and tell them what they wanted.

Because Ferdinand and Imelda worked so closely together in getting him elected to office, they could conceive of the public sphere of politics as being coextensive with their private lives. Singing together on stage, they turned their private lives into a public spectacle, staging a stylized version of their intimacy. That intimacy was formalized to a remarkable degree and made over into a staple element of the Marcos myth, particularly in their respective autobiographies, whether officially commissioned or otherwise. Indeed, the interviews granted by them after their overthrow and exile dwell invariably with a kind of formulaic wistfulness on the events pertaining to the beginning of their romance.[6]

Prior to meeting Imelda in 1954, Ferdinand is described in his biography as being a sexually active bachelor: "The young Representative was immensely popular, especially with the ladies . . . There were whispers that men introduced their sisters and daughters to him at their own risk, a reputation which caused him trouble." Society pages in Manila daily newspapers referred to him as the "Number One Bachelor."[7] Ferdinand was often linked romantically to other women from prominent families, including the daughter of former president Manuel Quezon. Though potentially disturbing, Ferdinand's libidinal energy was regarded nonetheless as an indubitable sign of his virility.

But this also meant that a woman of special qualities, specifically destined for him, was needed in order to sublimate his sexuality: "You remember how we used to tell you that the girls you went with were not right for you?" Ferdinand, then thirty-one years old and preparing to run for Congress, is asked by his neighbor, Mrs. Servera Verano. "You remember how we used to ask, 'How would she be as First Lady?' You must be even more careful now when you choose a bride, because a man's wife is very important in politics; she can ruin him. You have a special mark, Andy . . . Don't scar yourself with the wrong woman."[8]

Ferdinand seemed never to have entertained any doubts about Imelda. She had first come to his attention through photographs in newspapers in connection with her involvement in a Manila beauty contest. Seeing her eating watermelon seeds at the cafeteria of the former Congress building, Ferdinand was seized by desire: "He stood motionless for a moment, an action which did not go unnoticed by canny politicians present, whose eyes miss nothing unusual. Other members of the House drifted in. Marcos asked to be introduced to the fair stranger."[9] He was convinced that she was the "Archetypal Woman," the "wife that he had been waiting for all his life . . . who in this case appeared to have all in a woman to make matrimonial alliance . . . simply ideal." As Ferdinand said later, meeting Imelda for the first time "made me feel as I never felt before." It was as if "I had her in mind many times before, but who she is and where she is, I (didn't) know—now, here she is."[10]

The striking thing about the various narratives of the Marcos romance is the way in which they all indicate the presence of others watching the process of the matrimonial alliance develop. These include Ferdinand himself, who first sees Imelda's photograph in the papers, and is then stirred by her unexpected appearance at his side. It is as if her appearance confirmed what he had in mind all along but could not quite articulate. Similarly, the canny politicians present in the cafeteria recognized the scene as unusual, something set apart from casual meetings. Throughout Ferdinand's pursuit of Imelda, a third party was invariably made to witness the courtship. The position of this third party, however, was taken by neither of the couple's parents, as might be expected in lowland courtship rituals; instead, it was occupied by other politicians, journalists, or the "public." For example, the couple was introduced by a congressman, Jacobo Gonzalez; a journalist friend of Ferdinand, Joe Guevarra, seemed to be present at every moment of the eleven-day courtship in Bogiuo that led to the couple's marriage. Indeed, Ferdinand's mother never figured in the romance, and Imelda's father was informed of the couple's marriage only after the civil ceremony was performed by a local judge in Trinidad Valley. Just as Ferdinand had first discovered Imelda in the newspapers, so Imelda's father, Vicente Orestes Romualdez, first learned of Ferdinand from "articles in old magazines" which featured him as one of the outstanding congressmen of the year. Parental authority is thus marginalized or, more precisely, subsumed into a larger category which includes the "public" as it is constituted of newspaper readers. The relationship between Imelda and Ferdinand seemed from its inception to have been a part of their official history; rather than being held back from view, it was exposed for all to see, an integral moment in the unfolding of his future as president and hers as First Lady.

The chronicling of the Marcos romance, like the identification with the legend of Malakas and Maganda, was part of the larger attempt of Ferdinand and Imelda to manufacture their pasts. The biographies of Imelda and Ferdinand rework their respective pasts to make it appear as if they were always meant to be the First Couple. Ferdinand's commissioned biography, for example, opens with the sentence, "Ferdinand Edralin Marcos was in such a hurry to be born that his father who was only eighteen years old himself had to act as his midwife."[11] Having dispensed with the burden of paternal influence, the narrative quickly focuses on the son's life. Its portrayal of Ferdinand's past is relentlessly and monotonously one-dimensional. His "destiny" is never in doubt. Every detail of his life—from schoolboy to law student, from guerilla fighter to congressman, from lover to father—is seen from a single vantage point: his future as president of the Philippines. It is as if everything that has happened in his life was meant to happen. Accused of murdering his father's political rival in 1939, Marcos turns the trial into an opportunity to gain national attention. He defends himself while studying for the bar exams, which inevitably he passes with honors.[12] "Ever since his escape from the youthful murder conviction, the Ilokanos have said . . . that this favorite son would one day be President."[13] Minor incidents are seen as auguries of greatness. As a young boy, Marcos, punished by his father for some mischief, is made to work in the mines and there learns how to use dynamite. This knowledge then becomes useful years later when Ferdinand battles the Japanese during the war.[14]

One gets the impression from this biography, therefore, that everything in Marcos's life always has been accounted for, all outcomes foretold from the start. Biography merely confirms destiny, so that the past simply becomes another version of the future. Personal and public history converge predictably so that events occur in ways that could not have happened otherwise. The point here is not the accuracy or objectivity of the biography. Indeed, many details in official accounts have been shown to be spurious, particularly the stories of Marcos's war record.[15] Marcos's biography is yet another instance of his characteristic tendency to revise the past in the interests of projecting a spectacle of personal prowess. His notion of "destiny"—which I take to mean a kind of transhistorical, and thus natural, right to rule—is made to function as the unassailable context, determining not only *his* past but that of other Filipinos as well.

In contrast to accounts of Ferdinand's life, Imelda's biographies stress the element of luck in her climb to power. While his past is always and everywhere made to bear the marks of an inescapable future, hers seems to have left the future to chance. It is well known that Imelda's family—the Romualdezes of Leyte—was part of a class of landed elite whose privileges were largely sustained by an American colonial machinery. Imelda's uncles rose to prominence in local and national politics after World War II, though her father, a lawyer by training, was weak and feckless in the care of his family. For this reason, Imelda's childhood was spent in relative poverty. Educated in Leyte, she went to live with her rich uncle in Manila and worked first as a music store clerk and later in the public relations department of the Central Bank of the Philippines. She came to the public's attention after being chosen Miss Manila in 1953 and appeared on the cover of a weekly news magazine. Her life was thus marked by a series of transitions, from relative poverty to relative wealth, from countryside to city, from clerical obscurity to cover-girl prominence. Until she met Ferdinand, her involvements with other men seem to have had no certain trajectory, least of all towards marriage. One reads about Imelda's past only to conclude that things indeed could have been different.

The possibility of such difference, however, is figured by her biographers as the operation of "fate." Carmen Navarro-Pedrosa is explicit: "Imelda Romualdez Marcos more than anything is a child of fate. Her life . . . is a Cinderella story . . . for her fairy godmother visited her on the evening of April 6, 1954, and with the magic wand, brought her into the life of Ferdinand E. Marcos."[16] She then quickly comes under his tutelage and works as his "secret weapon" to deliver the votes. Imelda becomes "The Other Marcos, beautiful, tender and appealing."[17] "It was she who filled the gap—the need to make her husband more popular—because she was not just a woman but a special kind of woman whose natural charms were lethal."[18] Imelda's "potency" is thus linked to her difference from Ferdinand. Whereas his claims are couched in the idiom of an irresistible destiny, her power is a matter of projecting a certain kind of natural charm. Of what did this charm consist? As the other Marcos, Imelda is also the other of Ferdinand. He takes over the direction of her life in the same way that she is said to "fill a gap" in his. Thus, Imelda provides Ferdinand with an occasion to display his mastery: he in turn converts her into an avid campaigner and a good student of politics by teaching her to defer to his authority. "She adopted his ways."[19] Through Ferdinand, Imelda discovers politics as a means of articulating her ambitions in ways which would not have been possible otherwise. In so doing she came to see her power as the result of submitting to the destiny of her husband.

Mere submission to male ambition, however, does not account for the potency of her charm. Charm suggests the ability to fascinate, to compel the attention of others as if by magic. Its Latin root, *carm* (song or magic formula), points to the necessarily performative, even theatrical nature of that which is charming. Thanks to its association with ritual magic, the power to charm can in one sense be understood as the ability to present oneself both as source and object of desire. As various accounts indicate, Imelda's voice and body forced people to watch and listen in rapt expectation. A woman journalist and admirer of the Marcoses writes the following description of the workings of Imelda's "lethal charm" during a political rally in 1965:

> Led to the microphone, she touches it, and prepares to sing her winning repertoire: *Dahil sa Iyo, Waray, Dungdunguen can to la unay.* She has lost weight considerably, her bones show through her torso—it is a slight and vulnerable back that rises above the scoop of her neckline. But this is not the girl from Olot anymore, not this woman tonight; her face is drawn, fatigue sits on those shoulders, but she looks triumphantly at the scene. . From the convention floor at the Manila Hotel nine months ago, to this stage tonight, stretch innumerable miles and countless lessons, and she has learned each one very well. . . . She knows

the excitement of power. The crowd waits, like a trapped and unresisting prey, for Imelda to begin using that power; this is the secret they share, the crowd and Imelda, Imelda and the crowd. She will smile and flick those wrists and sing her little songs. . . . She bends and barely sways, beating time glancing at the guitar and then lifts her face to point with her chin at the night bright with neon lights and a moon—the old charisma, with its look of suffering, potent tonight as never before, the brilliance of beauty commingling with the brilliance of pain, the haunted, agonized, tragic look encircling the plaza and holding her audience in thrall.[20]

This passage recalls the difference between Imelda and Ferdinand of which I spoke earlier. The juxtaposition of contrasting qualities— "fatigue" and "triumph," naiveté and cunning—in the person of Imelda evokes the transitions she has negotiated. Power excites her precisely because she did not always expect to possess it. In this case, her power came less from her husband's destiny than from her ability to turn herself into an image recalling a sense of shared loss among those who watch her. The crowd willingly submits itself to her charm like an "unresisting prey." In a political rally, it is put in the position of spectators, included in the fantasy of loss that Imelda plays out. The secret she shares with them resides in her ability to stir a desire in them to see without being seen, to hear without being heard.

Imelda's charm was lethal to the extent that it was able to provoke and feed the wish for a kind of depoliticized community, one which would make the hierarchy between leaders and followers seem thoroughly benign. Through a series of stylized gestures and a standard repertoire of love songs in the vernacular, she created an atmosphere of generalized melancholia, a melancholia which was but one of the effects which her charm was calculated to generate. Other sensations doubtless-ly grew out of seeing her, for her charm compelled others to stop thinking and start looking. Ferdinand himself is said to have fallen prey to her allure. When he saw her for the first time in the flesh, he stood "motionless." A journalist wrote that "Imelda was such a simple girl then and she had a way of making even the eloquent Congressman tongue-tied."[21] During the early stages of Marcos's first run for the presidency in 1965, "the oft-heard remark about the prospect of a Marcos victory was 'Well, whatever kind of president he will make it is certain that if he wins, we will have the most beautiful and the

56

youngest First Lady.'"[22]   During the inauguration of Marcos, the crowd was less concerned with the message of the speeches than with the appearance of Imelda,

> as if to say, "If there is anything the incoming administration can boast of it is having the fairest and youngest First Lady." "Just to see, just to see!" they screamed in mob fashion. It was very little they asked . . . most people who had gone to the Luneta grandstand that morning were merely there to see the celebrated beauty of the new First Lady of the land . . . Even as they heard the President declare "This nation can be great again," a marvelous slogan calculated to impress the public mind, they preferred the soft smile of the Lady by his side.[23]

What the public wanted was thus not the message of his speech but the sight of her smile. It was as if the people saw political gatherings as an occasion for them to constitute themselves as an audience, in a spectacle whose central figure was the First Lady.

It is, however, important to note that her primacy was thought to stand in relation to his destiny.   The mythology of the Marcos romance underlined not only the lethal charm of Imelda, but also Ferdinand's conquest of that charm. He married her; he taught her; he drew her into his future; and, in doing so, he turned her into his secret weapon. Rather than disrupt his ambition, her charm worked as an instrument for its realization.   Imelda's difference became useful in depoliticizing the encounter between the candidate and the crowd. Converted into voyeurs, the people took in her feminine charm, but at the price of acknowledging its masculine owner.

On one level then, narratives of the Marcos romance are about the domestication and deployment of sexual and historical differences in the realization of one man's ambition. Stories of Ferdinand's eleven-day "coup-courtship" of Imelda reformulated her difference as an asset that redounded to his credit. Her charm was the feminine surplus which she brought into their marriage alliance and which was put into circulation during political campaigns and throughout Marcos's tenure as president. This surplus was constituted, as we have seen, by the power to elicit interest and thereby set the stage for the exchange between her husband and the public.   Imelda's striking presence thus allowed power to circulate between Ferdinand and the crowd.   While she reduced the people to spectators, he overwhelmed them with slogans and speeches

57

with his "booming voice." They looked at her while he spoke to them. To employ Imelda, the "Archetypal Woman," is thus to control the conditions of possibility for the circulation of authority, just as in the courtship stories such employment also requires a representation of the past from the perspective of a single, totalizing male ego. Imelda thus makes visible the link between history and circulation. By domesticating her, Ferdinand establishes symbolic dominance over both.

Film and Female Ambition

Imelda Marcos's deference to her husband's ambitions was in some ways entirely traditional and expected. Previous First Ladies had done no less. Beginning with Mrs. Aurora Quezon, First Ladies involved themselves in such ostensively apolitical activities as the Red Cross, the Catholic Women's League, and various charities and civic projects. Others, like Mrs. Esperanza Osmeña and Mrs. Evangelina Macapagal, played active roles in redecorating the palace and "beautifying" national parks. Living largely in the shadow of their husbands, they seemed to have accepted their place without qualm. As one writer put it, "All were out to be real helpmates to their husbands and each did it loyally and in the context of what their husbands set out to accomplish."[24]

Imelda's spectacular difference lay, however, in the degree of attention which she attracted and cultivated. Her "cultural" projects refashioned the landscape of metropolitan Manila. Her active participation in her husband's campaigns, her role in projecting an international image for the Philippines, the innumerable rumors of her extravagance, and her own political ambitions, all placed her constantly in the public eye. By the late 1960s and early 1970s, that public eye, however, had become accustomed to the spectacle of women acting out their ambitions. The rise of a new kind of First Lady coincided with the emergence of a new *image* of woman, that of the *bomba* star. Bomba literally means "bomb," and it was a popular way throughout the 1960s of characterizing impassioned political rhetoric. It was also a synecdoche for charges and countercharges of graft and corruption by politicians in Congress or during political campaigns. As Philippine newspapers and magazines of this period make clear, for a politician to "hurl" or "explode" a bomba was to reveal something to the public about another politician that the latter would have preferred to keep secret. By exposing what was once inaccessible to the public eye, whoever explodes a bomba gains a privileged visibility. That is, he or she is able to stir public interest at the expense of his or her rival. This interest was directed as much at the nature of the other's crime as at the fact that it had come to light. What was once hidden is now exposed for everyone to see and hear.

Bomba thus referred to the sudden yet motivated emergence of scandal, that is, of what was new and out of place. In this way, it allowed for the imaging of scandal as spectacle not only in the domain of national politics but also in other contexts. For example, *bomba* came to refer to the wave of soft- and hard-core pornography which swept over the Philippine movies of this period. More precisely, *bomba* connoted the specific scenes in the movies in which women exposed their bodies to the camera for the audience to see. It also pertained to lurid scenes of simulated sexual intercourse. Such scenes were tenuously related to the narrative of the film and often arbitrarily inserted (*singit*) into it.

Women who appeared in these movies achieved a degree of notoriety guaranteeing further exposure on magazine covers, on television talk shows, and in gossip columns. Indeed, most magazines in the Philippines, from the gossip sheets to the respectable weeklies, such as *The Philippines Free Press* and *The Weekly Graphic*, often featured bomba stars on their covers to increase sales. Their photographs provoked others to look in expectation. One magazine which featured a bomba star on its cover printed the following caption to her photograph: "Besides the ability to peel off her clothes in a provocative manner, what other attributes should a bomba star possess? Annabelle Rama, our cover girl for this issue, and the rest of her kind come up with very startling and exciting revelations."[25]

These "revelations" consisted of a kind of double exposure: that of the woman revealing her body to the camera and that of a largely male audience viewing scenes removed from everyday life. The audience in a bomba film—indeed in any film—identifies in the first place with the camera because the viewer's gaze is welded to the mechanical facility of the camera and so sees things that would normally be unobserved or inaccessible.[26] For this reason one writer was able to describe the bomba scene from the film *Igorotta* in the following way: "In the opening scene, a group of Igorotte maidens are shown bathing *au naturel* in a stream and every now and then, the camera zooms in on bosoms and behinds for intimate close-ups" as the writer and the audience gaze.[27] The camera thus stands for—as well as extends—the audience's eyes. In this way, bomba movies sustain the interests of a predominantly male audience by mechanically reproducing the "explosion" of female bodies on the screen.

Bomba movies were tremendous commercial successes. They often played to capacity crowds in Manila and provincial cities. The Board of Censors occasionally banned such movies or cut some of their more lurid scenes. The effect of government action, however, was to further incite people to see these movies, and the excised versions were either amended with "bonus" scenes or restored in prints that circulated in the provinces.[28] A movie producer said, "Bomba is bombshell at the box office. Working on the proposition that sex almost always sells, local movies have more and more caught on to all the world's sin-erama [sic]."[29]

But bomba movies sold images of women, not the women themselves. What viewers saw on the screen and read about in magazines were understood to be the simulation, not the actual occurrence, of violence and sex. For instance, it was common for bomba scenes to begin with the rape of a woman. "The rape scene . . . became more and more realistic with the entry of such cuddly pussycats as Bessie Barredo, Gina Laforteza, and Menchu Morelli."[30] The men who portrayed the rapists were usually typecast as *kontrabidas* (villains) or "bomba specialists" who were expected to give in to their urges. Here, the "realism" of rape had to do with the way in which it led to fulfillment of expectation. Indeed, audiences were prone to yell *harang* (foul, cheat) at the screen when bomba scenes that were promised never emerged. Hence, the scandal precipitating the exposure of women was neutralized, or, more precisely, bomba movies generated both scandal and its containment insofar as what appeared on the screen were mechanically reproduced images existing in a space and time irreducibly separate from that of the viewers. More important, they were also made to seem the product of the intentions of others. We get a sense of this in other more benign but no less tendentious versions of the "revelation" of women in bomba movies. "The sexpots in local movies showed appetizing glimpses of their superstructures in swimming pool scenes where they donned itsy-bitsy, teeny-weeny bikinis which often—oops— got detached in the water, or in the bathroom scenes where their only covering was a curtain of water."[31] Movies were invested here with the capacity to motivate accident and to intend surprise. Shock was thus aestheticized as the product of a prior set of calculations. Perhaps this was the reason bomba movies could engage in the most graphic violence against women and yet project them as "reasonable" people seeking to realize their ambitions apart from their roles as victims. For example, the trajectory of one bomba star's career was described as follows:

> "It was only of late that I've consented to appear in bomba scenes," Mila del Rosario, 23, admits. "In my first twelve pictures, I never thought I could be so daring. . . ."

> Mila started exploding in *Pussycat Strikes Again* when Bino Garcia, one of moviedom's most hated villains, undressed and attacked her in one scene, kissing her torridly and pawing her. In *The Gunman* she had a torrid love scene in bed with Van de Leon. In *Ligaw na Sawimpalad* (The Wayward Unfortunate), she was one of several girls victimized in a brothel. She had another love scene with Henry Duval in *Vice Squad*.

> "I only consent to appear in a bomba scene if such a scene is extremely necessary to the plot and story. After all, European and Hollywood pictures have infinitely more salacious scenes."

> Before she entered the movies, Mila was an art model. She insists that all the bombas she explodes are done in good taste and with finesse.[32]

Here the bomba star is given a voice with which to speak rather than simply a body with which to act. She is depicted not as a passive victim of male intentions but as one who consented to, and actively participated in, the making of bomba scenes. She thus comes across as "reasonable": open to negotiation and able to express her opinions. It is as if her complicity in the explosion of her own body makes those scenes the product of a prior contract among the star, director, producer, and consumer of these films which includes the writer and readers of magazine articles about them. Framed in this way, the explosiveness and exploitativeness of bomba movies could be legitimized as part of a network of market transactions including Europe and America. As such, viewing bombas in cinemas or reading about them in magazines was conventionalized, made part of a larger ethic of consumption correlated with female ambition. The scandal of male violence against women is reformulated in terms of the "bold" and "courageous" yet "taste[ful]" acts of women in exposing their bodies.

61

In bomba movies, women acted out their ambitions in full public view; thus, such movies established a new context for articulating female desire as a function not only of male desire but also of the interests of an anonymous mass of movie viewers and magazine readers.

Imelda Marcos in some ways personified the notion of female ambition which the bomba movies seemed to project. She saw her own desire not simply as a function of her husband's but also as a matter for public display. "She dressed to please Ferdinand . . . she lived she said to see him look at her. 'I want to stand out in his eyes.'"[33] Just as his destiny validated her fate, so her existence was given form for everyone to witness through his gaze. "Politics was his life and Marcos was hers—since she lived for Marcos, she would live for what Marcos lived for . . . Her days rose and fell by the Marcos sun."[34] Driven by his destiny, she found a way of expressing her ambition by responding to his desire "[t]o revive national pride and curb national weakness." So while he governed, "she would inspire" and "sow beauty where she could . . . 'Culture and art and a taste for the beautiful must lead to goodness,' she said."[35]

This peculiar mix of ambition and deference on Imelda's part recalls the coupling of boldness and vulnerability among bomba stars. The notion of bomba could furnish a means of conceptualizing what was new and thus potentially unsettling about the First Lady. This was so partly because of the workings of mass circulation media, which brought together into sharp juxtaposition formerly disparate objects, people, and events. For example, it was not uncommon for magazines to feature bomba stars on their cover with stories and photographs of Imelda Marcos on the inside one week, then to reverse the order of appearance in the next. Since the problematic position of the First Lady could thereby be imagined in conjunction with the explosive appearance of women in the movies, the ambivalent representations of Imelda came to share in the conditions of reception of bomba movies. Visualized beyond the public stage of electoral politics, her images, like those of bomba stars, created an audience which came to expect the political style of Ferdinand. For just as she appeared to move back and forth between traditional roles and unexpected prominence and accessibility, so her husband sought to project a new postcolonial, nationalist appeal which at the same time capitalized on an older ethos of clientage and factionalism.

What allowed for this reconfiguration of sexual with political imagery in ways that anticipated, and so constructed, the terms of their popular reception in the 1960s? To answer this question it is necessary to consider the larger historical context within which power was rendered as spectacle: the breakdown of traditional patron-client ties in the face of an expanding capitalist market that characterized the dynamics of postwar Philippine politics. We must first turn to this history if we are fully to appreciate Imelda's role in the manufacture of Ferdinand's "destiny."

The Simulation of Politics

Imelda's numerous attempts to spread beauty and culture were of a piece with Ferdinand's nationalist pretensions of "making this nation great again." As recent studies have shown, Marcos succeeded in monopolizing the resources of the country by joining a modernizing nationalist pose to a parochial, factionalist-oriented politics. As with previous presidents, Marcos turned the state into an instrument for asserting his factional hegemony over the country's competing elites. However, he was also scrupulous in articulating factionalism in terms of a vocabulary of modernization and nation-building. This language left its most visible marks on the country's landscape by way of new schoolhouses, extensive roads, and expansive bridges—more were built under Marcos than under any other president, thanks largely to his ability to secure foreign loans.[36]

Imelda's cultural projects were logical extensions of Ferdinand's attempts to leave traces of his power everywhere. He sought to instrumentalize nationalism by embarking on development projects which also served as occasions for the expansion of patronage and pork barrel, and by appointing technocrats to his cabinet, thereby gaining control of a new elite with no prior bases of influence. She sought to complement these moves by turning state power into a series of such spectacles as cultural centers, film festivals, landscaped parks, five-star hotels, and glitzy international conferences, which seemed to be present everywhere yet whose source was infinitely distant from those who viewed them. These spectacles cohere less around egalitarian notions of nationhood than around the fact that they all originated from her and reflected her initiatives, which in turn had been sanctioned explicitly by the president. Whether on the campaign trail for Ferdinand or as First Lady, Imelda was in a unique position to rework Philippine culture into the sum of the traces left by the regime's patronage. National culture was construed as a gift from above bestowed upon those below.

Imelda's role in imaging culture as state munificence cannot be understood apart from the vicissitudes of a notion of patronage which pervades the history of Philippine politics, a notion which assumes that power is synonymous with the ability to provide for all the discrete and multifaceted needs of *specific* others. Patronage implies not simply the possession of resources but, more important, the means with which to stimulate the desire for and the circulation of such resources. In a political context ruled by a factional rather than class-based opposition, patronage becomes the most important means for projecting power. While it rests traditionally on the benign assumption that a long-standing hierarchy (usually measured along generational lines) will be the guarantee of benefits from above to those below, it is also meant to confirm that those above are the natural leaders of those below. Patronage thus mystifies inequality to the point of making it seem not only inevitable historically speaking but also morally desirable; power is recast in familiar and familial terms. As such, the display of patronage is meant to drain the social hierarchy of its potential for conflict. Ideally, conflict is thought to occur among factions (rival patrons and their respective clients, as in elections, when only those with sufficient means may aspire to have purchase over others), not between patrons and their clients.[37]

The ideology of patronage determined to a large extent the shape of postwar political discourse in the Philippines. However, the economic and social basis for realizing traditional patron-client ties had been eroding steadily well before the war. Indeed, as Benedict Kerkvliet has so brilliantly shown, the intensified penetration of capitalist modes of production into the countryside around Manila which began around the 1930s resulted in the trend towards wage labor, mechanization, and absentee landlordism. Such developments led to the subversion of the economic and social basis of patronage, while at the same time encouraging peasants to frame their demands ever more forcefully in terms of traditional reciprocal indebtedness. However, such demands, ultimately culminating in the Huk rebellion from the late 1940s to the early 1950s, did not result in the restoration of precapitalist forms of personal relationships but in the further institutionalization of impersonal contractual, money-based relationships among peasants, landlords, and their local agents. Under the sponsorship of the Philippine state, which in turn was heavily dependent on military and financial support from the United States, the material and moral matrix of traditional notions of patronage rapidly dissolved.[38]

These developments in the Philippines—of which Central Luzon and the Manila areas are only the most notable examples—amounted to the consolidation of a capitalist economy by the mid-1960s which did not at the same time lead to the widespread establishment of ideas and practices of class-based politics. Instead, a generalized longing for a notion of patronage seemed to persist, harking back to more traditional concepts of hierarchy which relied simultaneously on money to forge and sustain instant patron-client ties. National and local elections became the privileged venues for playing out this desire for patronage, as vertical alliances reminiscent of traditional patron-client ties were contracted, consolidated, or redrawn.[39] Such ties were deeply problematic, because they tended to be determined less by the exchange of moral obligations than by the circulation of money. Money had the effect of turning patronage into a commodity. Investing the ideal of patronage with money made it possible for a candidate running for national office to accumulate a clientage beyond any specific locality over a drastically shortened period of time. These clients, however, remained largely anonymous to the candidate. The exchange of money for votes—a practice almost universally commented upon by those who have written about postwar Philippine politics—turned elections into markets.[40] Elections were seen neither in the liberal-democratic sense of expressing one's will on matters of political representation, nor as rituals for the reiteration of reciprocal indebtedness between leaders and led; instead, in a society increasingly governed by commodity exchange, elections became moments for the *simulation* of patronage. The extremely common practice of buying votes recreated the sense, and the sensation, of patronage as wealthy men distributed money through their agents, thereby giving the impression of being in control of circulation; yet, the treatment of votes, like patronage, as commodities also undercut the moral and ethical basis of traditional patron-client ties. While money made it possible to have instant access to a mass of anonymous clients, it also enabled such clients to switch patrons readily and to evade their influence. In short, money attenuated the moral force of reciprocity by trading on the desire for patronage with its calculated imaging.

Philippine politics in the 1960s was caught up in the profound contradiction between the ideology of patronage and the material and social conditions set forth by capitalism, between an apparently generalized wish for social hierarchy, stabilized by traditional idioms of reciprocity, and a national state whose links with various localities were

65

mediated by money. It was precisely at this historical juncture that the Marcoses emerged into the national scene. Their success was a function of their ability to seize upon—rather than resolve—the central contradictions of postwar Philippine politics. Ferdinand and Imelda played on them, seeking to utilize money and what it could buy in order to simulate patronage and the imaging of benevolent power (inexhaustible "strength" and eternal "beauty") at the top of the national hierarchy. Herein lay one source of their early popularity: they seemed to be able to furnish a way of conceiving the "new" and the alienating changes it implied in the familiar and familial terms of patronage.

The Marcoses deployed a cultural repertoire ranging from the narrative of virility and romance to spectacles of nationalist vigor and feminine allure, all appearing to evoke change while simultaneously eschewing the imperative of social reform. They seized upon the crisis of authority generated by the traumatic changes in colonial regimes and postcolonial upheavals: they sought to project the aura of patronage by resorting precisely to the very means which guaranteed its disintegration, thereby calling forth its repeated simulation. Converted into grand public gestures and discrete forms of commodities, patronage could in this way blur the difference between popular and mass culture, between the ambitions of one couple and the history of the nation. Thus did the projection of state power in the early Marcos years also dictate the ideological conditions under which they were to be received.

Imelda's biographies give an idea of how the Marcoses simulated patronage. She styled herself as the consummate patroness of the Philippines. As she tells one of the biographers: "People come to you for help. They want jobs . . . or roads or bridges. They think you're some kind of miracle worker and because of their faith, you try to do your best."[41] In this regard, she also saw herself as a privileged mediator between the rich and poor. Rather than reverse or abolish the difference between the two, she sought to drain it of its tension, "officiating at the marriage of public welfare and private wealth."[42] She is characterized not as moderately but as exceedingly generous. Forever besieged by callers of all sorts, from mayors to fashion models, ambassadors to barrio folks, she comes across as a dynamo on the move:

> Day after day, at the stroke of 9 a.m., undeterred by lack of sleep, fainting spells, miscarriages, low blood pressure, kidney trouble, bad teeth, the brutal barrage of newspapers, and the ire

of Benigno Aquino, she sits upright in a French sofa, receiving callers.

Forty callers, on lean days; fifty on the average; a hundred when they come in delegations. . . .

She eats a late lunch. "I take no siesta," she says. In the afternoons, before she goes out to "cut a ribbon, maybe," inaugurate a hospital pavilion, attend the opening of a hotel, or launch a tanker, a book, or a painter, she has two or three free hours. "I sit down and am quiet."

No one disturbs her while she runs mentally through a list, checking and cross-checking what she could have done and failed to do.[43]

Virtually impervious to adversity, Imelda was seen as the symbolic origin of all activity, from ribbon-cuttings to book-launchings. Nothing escaped her, for she kept a running account on things which had been and were yet to be accomplished. Thus we get the fantasy of a panoptic consciousness wedded to a body that, like money, is in constant circulation. This image of inexhaustible patronage was one that stirred a deal of interest from people.

Then before I go to sleep, I have to go through the correspondence I received during the day . . . usually 2,000 letters a day. This one asking for a job, that one telling about a child that had to be hospitalized, this one asking for a picture, that one for an autograph. It takes me one or two hours just signing letters: they all want your real signature.[44]

This is to say, "They all want a part of me. They cannot help but think of me." They ask not only favors but for the real marks of her person: her photograph and signature. The circulation of her patronage and, by extension, that of her husband was thus conjoined to the dissemination of their images.

Imelda was acutely conscious of the link between patronage and its imaging. For example, it was common for visitors to the presidential palace to be presented with souvenirs which included "pictures, small bottles of perfume, bound copies of a favorite Marcos speech. Who before her ever took the trouble and the thought to make each palace visit [into] An Occasion?"[45] By converting such moments into an occasion for the display of patronage, the giving of souvenirs thus was not only to commemorate the simple fact of having been in the presence of the Marcoses but also provided the means for memorializing the distance separating the benefactor from his or her client long after the visit had occurred. The status of such objects as souvenirs lay precisely in their ability to convey the aura of their source to the extent that they forged a relationship of indebtedness between their source and recipients. In so doing, such objects were meant to ensure that the latter continue to keep the former in mind. Souvenirs as tokens of patronage prompted reciprocation and thus acknowledgement of the power of their provenance.

However, as fetish objects images of patronage also invoked their character as commodities, especially when they appeared in mass circulation newspapers and magazines. Mechanically-reproduced images of patronage simultaneously denied and confirmed the workings of money at the basis of national politics. One focal point of this tension was the figure of Imelda herself. As suggested earlier, she shared a kind of spectacular displacement with bomba stars, whose public display was thought to be desirable as much as it was ultimately disempowering. The following examples should illustrate Imelda's explosiveness—in a sense, the real meaning of her lethal charm—which recalls patronage, even as it mystifies its breakdown *and* simulation. Shortly after the reelection of Marcos in late 1969, the *Philippine Free Press* published photographs of three oil portraits of Imelda.[46] These paintings were given to her by the artists themselves and hung, along with her other portraits, "above stairwells and along corridor walls where they startled."[47] An anonymous commentary accompanies the reproductions and helps us to anchor our reading of these portraits. Although the paintings were done by academically trained painters and were accompanied by a commentary in English, their reproduction appeared in an influential weekly usually purchased by educated readers inside and outside of Manila. Hence, these documents, which are not necessarily representative examples of mass response to the Marcoses, nonetheless can be seen as symptomatic of precisely the kind of reception which the Marcoses would have wanted to generate among the nation's population. They provide us with an instructive moment in the history of the Marcoses' attempt to encourage and contain the complicity of those whose cultural and social influence was considerable.

Ferdinand Marcos as *Malakas* (Strong)

Imelda Marcos (painted by Claudio Bravo)

Imelda Marcos (painted by Federico Aquilar Alcuaz)

Imelda Marcos "A-Go-Go" (painted by
Antonio Garcia Llamas)

The commentary notes that the artists were trying to express the real Imelda in a way which would adequately sum up her many roles as a "figure of state, a politician, a housewife and mother, a fashion pacesetter, a civic worker, a connoisseur of good living, a patroness of the arts."[48] We can see that both the artists and the commentator were seeking to come to terms with what seemed to be a new dimension to Imelda: she exceeded the traditional categories associated with being a woman and a First Lady. Imelda provoked attention because, as with bomba stars, she exposed herself in novel situations and made her body available for all to see; but while the bodies of bomba stars bore the signs of the marketplace, Imelda's body served both as focus and mystification of the history of patronage in the midst of the marketplace.

The first portrait, by Claudio Bravo (fig. 2), shows Imelda seeming to glide past some mysterious landscape. The accompanying commentary is worth quoting at length, for its attempt to match the allusiveness of the paintings.

> [T]he figure moves in a line that never was on sea or land. The details are precise: that parasol tugs at the hand and is tugged by the wind blowing a skirt into rich folds. Yet the landscape is not so much seen as felt: a seaside, early in the morning, on a cool day. And the figure seems not to walk but to float on the stirred air. The expression on the face is remote; this is a woman beyond politics and palaces, a figure from dream or myth. It's the pale ivory color that makes the scene unearthly, as though this were a frieze from some classic ruin. Just beyond the frame will be sirens choiring, the swell of a striped sail and, across the perfumed seas, Troy's burning roof and tower.[49]

The remoteness of the figure, combined with its pale ivory color, gives this portrait an uncanny quality. One looks at it feeling that, although one can recognize Imelda's features, one cannot quite establish a context for them. Indeed, just as the figure seems to float on the stirred air, so the mind that contemplates this painting drifts outside of the frame towards thoughts of a distant Greek epic. Because this figure seems so removed from the world of politics and exists as in a dream, its precise details cannot but take on a hallucinatory quality: they set the mind in motion, inducing it to think of that which is not there. This painting leads one to perceive not simply the likeness of Imelda but, as with bomba films, the possibility of seeing something which is out of place transformed into an object to be seen. At stake here is the imaging of patronage as something to which one may lay a claim, because it is shaped by one's own gaze. The figure is compelling, not only because one feels one can see through and past it, but also because one is reminded of the unbridgeable distance which separates one from the source of power that the portrait represents. The viewer is haunted by the absence that the figure makes present.

This sense of being haunted is even more apparent in the second portrait, by Federico Aquilar Alcuaz (fig. 3). Again, it is instructive to cite at length the accompanying commentary.

> [here] the scene is definite enough. Malacañang is in the background; so this must be the park across the river. . . . Nevertheless, it's not the Palace or park, certainly not the city that we feel here. This is provincial verdure, pastoral ground. And the figure in old rose is a country girl . . . of whom kundiman and balitaw sing. Indeed the melancholy of our folk music is in her wistful face. She has been sniffing at the white flower in her hand and it has stirred a memory. She herself stirs memories in us . . . Her quiet dignity evokes a nostalgia for childhood's vanished countryside and its lovely simple girl.[50]

Again, the painting evokes the sense of the familiar sliding into something strange. What looks like the presidential palace and its immediate surroundings is conflated with memories of pastoral grounds, folk music, and childhood's vanished countryside. Thus, it summons the imaginary scene of patronage untainted by the complexities of the marketplace. Symbolic of this is the figure of the woman in deep reverie. What is curious is that although we are never told about the contents of her thoughts we, nonetheless, are invited to reminisce with her. Recalling her childhood, the viewer may also be drawn to look back upon another time and place, in which women were simple and presumably knew their place. In this way, the figure calls forth something no longer present. The nostalgia-inducing effect of this second painting is not very different from the hallucinatory quality of the first; both lead the viewer to think of something absent and to expect its appearance.

A notable contrast with these two portraits of Imelda, however, is the third painting, by Antonio Garcia Llamas (fig. 4). Here the figure of Imelda is backlighted in such a way as completely to obscure any

74

sense of place. The background exists as mere shading, serving to highlight the foreground. The figure is erect and so made to seem wholly autonomous, its sovereign appearance underlined by the absence of details on the dress and the centering instead of distinctive features on the face. The effect of this composition is to lead one to focus on the figure's gaze.

> A poised modern woman looks us over. It's not we who eye her, we can only respond to her glance. She is definitely of the city and of our day, as lustrous with nervous energy as the powerful cars she rides or the go-go committees she chairs . . . The glance we respond to flashes across the muddled cityscape we must unravel to get where the white-on-blue decorum is, the promise of a civilized society.[51]

In this portrait, we are confronted with a somewhat jarring reversal of the relationship between the subject and the object of spectatorship. Unlike the other two, which exist as objects for our gaze, this figure "looks us over" and so causes us to take notice of her and to reflect on the fact that we are doing so. Her glance is what makes up the condition of possibility of our sight. We experience the painting as the presence of a powerful eye that sees all, yet we only apprehend flashes of this pervasive glance; and in doing so we feel ourselves to be part of a civilized society constituted by the modern state. The power of her gaze is seen in association with the nervous energy of cars and go-go committees which can operate at all times of the day and night. Thus can we account for what seems initially a puzzling discrepancy between what we first see of this gaze and what the commentator is led to see. Although Imelda does not, in fact, look directly at the viewer but off to the side, the commentator claims that she looks at us, as if our position as viewers has been split into two: we are at once in front of the portrait, yet also at the margins of the frame—spectators to the extent that we have been incorporated into a prior and largely invisible spectacle. Just as the audience in bomba movies comes to sense its subjection to the staging of revelations intended by others, the viewer of the painting is made to realize his or her other identity as one who sees, a realization which results from his or her already having been seen by someone else.[52]

Taken together with the Marcos biographies, these paintings suggest some of the ways in which assumptions about patronage can work to aestheticize and so dehistoricize politics. Since the relationship between ruler and ruled is converted into fantasies about seeing and being seen, the viewer then imagines himself or herself as alternately the subject and object of the intentions of the other. Imelda's privileged visibility resulted from her use of Ferdinand's name in carrying out projects meant to enhance both of their positions as national patrons concerned with the needs of the country. Her visibility, however, corresponded to a pervasive invisibility, as indicated by the third portrait. Constructing her role as a patroness meant that, like money, she had constantly to be in circulation: her photographs in newspapers confirmed her ability to seem to be everywhere. Thus, they could and were construed to be traces of a ghostly presence whose gaze, except for flashes, remained essentially hidden from our sight. This is perhaps why Ferdinand referred to Imelda over and over again as his secret weapon. Given the foregoing discussion, we might take this to mean that she served as his favored bomba, exploding her lethal charms for an audience grown habituated as much to the staging of scandal as to the commodification of politics. In both politics and the movies, women were made to represent instances of larger intentions at work, galvanizing the interests of people while demarcating their identity as mere viewers of spectacle.

NOTES

1. Revised version of an essay first published in *Comparative Studies in Society and History* 32/2 (April 1990).

2. *Malacañang, A Guidebook* (Quezon City: Kayumangi Press, 1986), 13. For various lowland versions of this myth, see Francisco Demetrio, S.J., *Myths and Symbols Philippines* (Manila: National Bookstore, 1978), 41-43. See also Remedios F. Ramos et al., *Si Malakas at Si Maganda* (Manila: Jorge Y. Ramos, 1980). I am grateful to Doreen Fernandez and Ambeth Ocampo for bringing the commissioned rewriting of the legend to my attention.

3. Numerous accounts of the Marcoses on the campaign trail can be found in various Philippine magazines and newspapers. For this chapter I have relied on the following: the series of essays by Kerima Polotan in *The Philippine Free Press [FP]*: "Marcos '65: The Inside Story of How Marcos Captured the Presidency," 29 March 1969, 2-3, 50-60; "The Men, The Method," 15 April 1969, 4, 54-62; "The Package

Deal," 12 April 1969, 2-3, 46-51. See also Carmen Navarro-Pedrosa, *The Untold Story of Imelda Marcos* (Manila: Bookmark, 1969), chap. 15; Napoleon G. Rama and Quijano de Manila, "Campaigning with Marcos and Osmeña," *FP*, 30 August 1969, 2-4, 181-82; and Filemon V. Tutay, "Marcos VS Osmeña: Nakakahiya," *FP*, 20 September 1969, 2-3, 64-72.

4. Rama and de Manila, "Campaigning with Marcos," 2.

5. Pedrosa, *The Untold Story*, 216.

6. For accounts of the Marcos romance, see Hartzell Spence, *Marcos of the Philippines* (New York: World Publishing Co., 1969), 237-67. Originally, this book appeared as *For Every Tear a Victory* (New York: McGraw Hill, 1964). See also the biographies of Imelda Marcos: Pedrosa, *The Untold Story*, chaps. 11-12; Kerima Polotan, *Imelda Romualdez Marcos* (New York: World Publishing Co., 1969), 79-82. For interviews of the Marcoses from exile in Hawaii, see "Marcos Remembers," *Asia Week* (5 July 1987), 28-33; and "Imelda and Ferdinand Marcos," *Playboy* (August 1987), 51-61. The romance between Ferdinand and Imelda was also of central importance in the Marcos campaign movies, *Iginuhit ng Tadhana* (Drawn by Destiny) in 1965 and *Pinagbuklod ng Langit* (Joined by Heaven) in 1969. Unfortunately, I have been unable to locate copies of these films. See Napoleon G. Rama, "The Election Campaign in Review," *FP*, (15 November 1969), 5.

7. Spence, *Marcos*, 217.

8. Spence, *Marcos*, 207.

9. Spence, *Marcos*, 240.

10. Pedrosa, *The Untold Story*, 153-54.

11. Spence, *Marcos*, 5.

12. Spence, *Marcos*, chaps. 3-6.

13. Spence, *Marcos*, 194.

14. Spence, *Marcos*, 28.

15. See, for example, Charles C. McDougald, *The Marcos File* (San Francisco: San Francisco Publishers, 1987), 5-108.

16. Pedrosa, *The Untold Story*, xv.

17. Polotan, "Marcos '65," 59.

18. Pedrosa, *The Untold Story*, 203.

19. Polotan, "Marcos '65," 56.

20. Polotan, "The Men, The Method," 59-60.

21. Joe Guevarra, cited in Pedrosa, *The Untold Story*, 156.

22. Pedrosa, *The Untold Story*, 216.

23. Pedrosa, *The Untold Story*, 222-23.

24. Rosario Mencias Querol, "What Are First Ladies For," *Weekly Graphic* (February 1965), 87.

25. *Weekly Graphic*, (30 December 1970), 1.

26. I owe a great part of my discussion of film to the work of Walter Benjamin, "The Work of Art in the Age of Mechanical Reproduction," in *Illuminations*, ed. and trans. Harry Zohn (New York: Schocken Books, 1969), 217-52.

27. Jose A. Quirino, "Another Kind of Bomba," *FP*, 6 December 1969, 18.

28. Petronilio Bn. Daroy, "The New Films, Sex and the Law on Obscenity," *Weekly Graphic*, 30 December 1970, 7-9.

29. Cited in Quirino, "Another Kind of Bomba," 16.

30. Quirino, "Another Kind of Bomba," 18.

31. Quirino, "Another Kind of Bomba," 18.

32. Quirino, "Another Kind of Bomba," 36.

33. Polotan, *Imelda*, 87.

34. Polotan, *Imelda*, 86, 220.

35. Polotan, *Imelda*, 184.

36. See, for example, the work of Primitivo Mijares, *The Conjugal Dictatorship of Ferdinand-Imelda Marcos* (San Francisco: Union Square Publications, 1976), 129-75, 400-411; Gary Hawes, *The Philippine State and the Marcos Regime* (Ithaca: Cornell University Press, 1987), especially chaps. 1-5. See also John Bresnan, ed., *Crisis in the Philippines* (Princeton: Princeton University Press, 1986), chaps. 4-7.

37. The literature on the history and structure of patronage in the Philippines is enormous and of uneven quality. The more significant works include Mary Hollnsteiner, *The Dynamics of Power in a Philippine Municipality* (Quezon City: University of the Philippines Press, 1963); Theodore Friend, *Between Two Empires* (New Haven: Yale University Press, 1967); Carl Lande, *Leaders, Factions and Parties: The Structure of Philippine Politics* (New Haven, Yale Southeast Asian Studies, 1964); Onofre D. Corpuz, *The Philippines* (Englewood Cliffs: Prentice-Hall, 1965), esp. 93-140; K. G. Machando, "From Traditional Faction to Machine: Changing Patterns of Political Leadership and Organization in Rural Philippines," *Journal of Asian Studies* 33/4 (August, 1974): 523-47; Amando Doronilla, "The Transformation of Patron-Client Relations and Its Political Consequences in Postwar Philippines," *Journal of Southeast Asian Studies* 16/1 (March 1985): 99-116; Reynaldo Ileto, *Pasyon and Revolution* (Quezon City: Ateneo de Manila University Press, 1979); Benedict Kerkvliet, *The Huk Rebellion: A Study of Peasant Revolt in the Philippines* (Berkeley: University of California Press, 1977); Resil Mojares, *The Man Who Would be President: Serging Osmeña and Philippine Politics* (Cebu City: Maria Cacao, 1986). For the vicissitudes of patronage under the colonial regime of the United States see the essays in Peter Stanley, ed., *Reappraising an Empire: New Perspectives on Philippine-American History* (Cambridge: Harvard University Press, 1984), and Ruby Paredes, ed., *Philippine Colonial Democracy* (Quezon City: Ateneo de Manila University Press, 1989). My own discussion of the historical origins of patronage and notions of reciprocity in the early Spanish colonial era is found in Vicente L. Rafael, *Contracting Colonialism: Translation and Christian Conversion in Tagalog Society Under Early Spanish Rule* (Ithaca: Cornell University Press, 1988), 110-35.

38. Kerkvliet, *The Huk Rebellion,* 1-25, 250-60, and 266-69. See also the works of Lande, Steinberg, Friend, Machado, and Mojares cited above.

39. See Lande, *Leaders, Factions and Parties,* 15-19, 24-25, 62-68, 72-75, 79-81, 111-14; Machando, "From Traditional Faction to Machine"; Glenn May, "Civic Ritual and Political Reality: Municipal Elections in Late 19th Century Philippines," in his *A Past Recovered* (Quezon City: New Day Press, 1987), 30-52, which suggests that the commodification of patronage was a process with roots in the latter half of the Spanish colonial period, just as different parts of the country were going through a more thoroughgoing transition to a capitalist economy. The indispensable guide to the economic and social processes entailed by such a transition is Alfred McCoy and Ed. J. de Jesus, eds., *Philippine Social History: Global Trade and Local Transformations* (Quezon City: Ateneo de Manila Press, 1982).

40. See especially Mojares, *The Man Who Would be President,* 71-81, for a succinct summary of the importance of money in Philippine politics.

41. Polotan, *Imelda,* 195.

42. Polotan, *Imelda,* 195.

43. Polotan, *Imelda,* 233-34.

44. Polotan, *Imelda,* 235.

45. Polotan, *Imelda,* 237.

46. "Three Images of Imelda," *FP,* 13 December 1969, 92-94. By the latter half of 1970, the *Philippine Free Press* became increasingly critical of the Marcoses. Its editors came to be convinced that Ferdinand intended to stay in office beyond his constitutionally mandated second term, which was due to expire in 1973. There were widespread rumors that Imelda was going to be fielded as a candidate for the presidential elections and that her election would maintain her husband as de facto president. The fear of a Marcos dynasty was compounded by reports in 1971 of secret plans for the declaration of martial law, the declaration of such a law in 1972, and the shut down of the *Free Press* along with other media critical of the Marcoses.

47. Polotan, *Imelda,* 212.

48. "Three Images," 92-93.

49. "Three Images," 93-94.

50. "Three Images," 94.

51. "Three Images," 94.

52. The theoretical issues informing my account of patronage and spectatorship in postcolonial Philippines owes a great deal to the closely related essays of Stephen Greenblatt, "Invisible Bullets: Renaissance Authority and its Subversion," *Glyph,* no. 8, (1981), 40-46; Christopher Pye, "The Sovereign, the Theater and the Kingdom of Darknesse: Hobbes and the Spectacle of Power," *Representations,* no. 8 (Fall 1984), 85-106; and William Flesch, "Proximity and Power: Shakespearean and Cinematic Space," *Theatre Journal,* 38/3 (October 1987), 227-93.

THE CHRIST STORY AS THE SUBVERSIVE MEMORY OF TRADITION: TAGALOG TEXTS AND POLITICS AROUND THE TURN OF THE CENTURY

Jose Mario C. Francisco, S.J.

Studies in Philippine history, as well as contemporary events (the so-called EDSA Revolution, for instance), suggest that the Christ story is the narrative frame for lowland Philippine society.[1] The pioneer among them, Reynaldo Ileto's *Pasyon and Revolution*, occupies a special place for undertaking a history "from below" through the use of vernacular sources such as narrative poems and songs.[2] He analyzes social movements from 1840 to 1910 in the light of a Tagalog text of the Christ story chanted during Holy Week and arrives at the conclucion that "during the Spanish and colonial eras, these images [from the text] nurtured an undercurrent of millenial beliefs which, in times of economic and political crisis, enabled the peasantry to take action under the leadership of individuals or groups promising deliverance from oppression."[3]

Ileto's basic insight has provided the impetus for subsequent significant works like Vicente Rafael's *Contracting Colonialism*.[4] Focusing on the earlier colonial period, Rafael sees translation as the root metaphor for the exchange between the Spanish and the native. This, however, does not negate Ileto's insight into the social significance of religious narrative. In fact, Rafael's comments in the chapter entitled "Paradise and the Reinvention of Death" confirm the centrality of narrative: "The popularity of these devotional writings attests to the fact that by the nineteenth-century conversion had become commonplace, its discourse of paradise a vital part of Tagalog tradition."[5]

Thus Ileto's study continues to be a seminal work in Philippine history. It has given a new perspective to local historiography and, at the same time, opened directions for research. For example, Holy Week rituals related to the Christ story appear to have served two functions: (1) "to inculcate among the Indios loyalty to Spain and Church," and (2), probably unintended by the friars, "to provide lowland Philippine society with a language for articulating its own values, ideals, and even hopes of liberation."[6] His analyses of the different social movements support this, but there is no further explanation of how the narrative text of the Christ story could have achieved its contrary functions as colonial tool and as language for liberation. In response to one of his critics, Ileto simply mentions "that a text is capable of generating multiple meanings in relation to audience or context."[7]

The present essay will be concerned with this particular question, how Tagalog narratives of the Christ story gave rise to different and even conflicting social responses. As popular mediations of the Christ story, these narratives did not only describe events, but also prescribed behavior for their audience. The essay locates its answer in the nature of an authoritative story and therefore draws from the current discussions about the elements of narrative, beginning with Fredric Jameson's discussion of the traditional Christian hermeneutic.

Within this perspective, the essay analyzes a wide range of Tagalog narratives of the Christ story from the nineteenth and early twentieth centuries. These vary from the different versions of the *pasyon*, generally "a type of religious verse which narrates the life of Jesus Christ the Saviour,"[8] and the narratives about holy people popular during the later part of the Spanish colonial period to the propaganda pamphlets and the socialist novels produced during the first decade of the American occupation.

The Christ Story and Its Interpretation

In the preface to *The Political Unconscious*, Fredric Jameson states his project in the following way: "to restructure the problematics of ideology, of the unconscious and of desire, of representation, of history, and of cultural production, around the all-informing process of narrative, which I take to be (here using the shorthand of philosophical idealism) the central function or instance of the human mind."[9] The project begins with a critique of how these issues were addressed by

Christian historicism which produced "the first great hermeneutic system in the Western tradition."[10]

The basic tenet of this historicism lies in the self-understanding of Christianity as a historical religion. Here "historical" means that the beginnings of Christianity are related to certain events in history, essentially those in the life of Jesus of Nazareth. This sequence of events, henceforth referred to as the Christ story, is told and retold in both oral and written forms. Prominent examples of these narratives are the four Gospels in Christian Scriptures and the professions of faith from the early patristic period. Under the light of Christian historicism, interpretation takes a form correlative to this genesis of narrative texts from a single story. To borrow the words of Jameson, interpretation becomes "an essentially allegorical act, which consists in rewriting a given text in terms of a particular interpretative master code."[11]

This view of interpretation developed into the highly complex system of medieval exegesis, when the relationship of the Christ story to the other realms of human life was established. This was made possible through Irenaeus's notion of "salvation history that focuses on the story of the incarnate Word of God but relates that story to the Word's activity in creation and in the history of Israel."[12] This understanding of Jesus Christ and his place in history provided the basis for the four levels of meaning in medieval exegesis—the literal, the allegorical, the moral, and the anagogical.

Jameson explains the relationship among these four levels and shows their political significance in interpretation. The literal and allegorical levels actually correspond to the two testaments in Christian Scripture, with the Old interpreted as a prefiguring of the New: "the transindividual dimensions of the first narrative [Israel's history] are then 'reduced' to the second, purely biographical narrative, the life of Christ." This "reduction" gives rise to further interpretative levels which make the political dimension explicit. As Jameson says, "the interpretation of a particular Old Testament passage in terms of the life of Christ . . . comes less as a technique for closing the text off and for preparing aleatory or aberrant readings and senses, than as a mechanism *for preparing the text for further ideological investment*" (italics mine).[13]

This occurs because the subsequent moral and anagogical levels are generated by the application of the Christ story to the other realms of human life:

On the third or moral level, for example, the literal and histori-
cal fact of the bondage of the people of Israel in Egypt can be
written as the thralldom of the believer-to-be to sin and to the
preoccupations of the world ("the fleshspots of Egypt"). . . .
But this third level of the individual soul is clearly insufficient by
itself, and at once generates the fourth or anagogical sense, in
which the text undergoes its ultimate rewriting in terms of the
destiny of the human race as a whole.[14]

Thus Jameson correctly describes the moral and anagogical levels as
corresponding to the realm of the psychological (individual subject) and
the political (collective "meaning" of history) respectively. The
traditional Christian hermeneutic then is able to encompass all reality
from the beginning of history, through the history of Israel, to personal
and social experience.

Although Jameson points out its theoretical limitation as a general
framework, this hermeneutic remains a useful tool for understanding
nineteenth- and early twentieth-century Tagalog narrative texts. These
texts, after all, have been generated by the same Christ story which is
the basis of this hermeneutic.

The Pasyon and Its Revisions

The Christ story came with the other implements of Spanish
colonization and took its first Tagalog form with the translation of the
so-called Apostles' Creed in *Doctrina Christiana* (1593).[15] The
schematic narrative in the creed, describing the sequence of events from
the Incarnation to the Second Coming of Christ, grew with the increas-
ing "Christianization" of the Tagalog-speaking lowland regions. The
Christ story was expanded and expounded through the various cultural
productions, such as *devocionarios* and *vocabularios*, written by the
Spanish missionaries and their native collaborators.

Through these works and the missionary activity of the Catholic
church, the Christ story remained alive in Tagalog society; but its fullest
expression would come in the tradition of the pasyon. The first text
appears at the beginning of the eighteenth century as an appendix to a
translation of a Spanish book of prayers commending the dying.
Written by the prayers' translator, Gaspar Aquino de Belen, and entitled
Mahal na Passion ni Jesu Christong Panginoon Natin sa Tola (1703),

it tells the story of Jesus from the Last Supper to the martyrdom of Longinus.[16]

The next Tagalog narrative of the Christ story comes a century later, in 1814. Commonly called *Pasyong Henesis* (because it opens with the creation story) or *Pasyong Pilapil* (on account of Fr. Mariano Pilapil, wrongly thought to be its author but actually its ecclesiastical censor), this text would become the primary text of the pasyon tradition because of its enduring popularity and influence up to the present.

Such significance comes from its consolidation of eighteenth-century literary tradition and the scope of its theological vision. Javellana writes that "[its] achievement lay in being able to pull together disparate strands of tradition and to synthesize these into a pleasing exposition of the meaning of Jesus' Passion."[17] The text consists of 2660 stanzas in the *quintilla* form used by Aquino de Belen, and draws from both Spanish and indigenous literary sources.

However, it is the breadth of its textualization of the Christ story which accounts, in greater part, for its significance. The narrative covers the following sequences: (a) from Creation to the Deluge, (b) from Mary's conception to the Annunciation, (c) from the infancy of Jesus to his Death, Resurrection, and Ascension, (d) Mary's death and Assumption, and (e) Empress Helena's discovery of Christ's Cross, and the Last Judgment. Javellana spells out the import of this breadth:

> The expanded spatial and temporal frames of the reworked Passion story are both cut out of one piece. By expanding the spatial frame, the poet is now able to work out his story on three levels, hence creating the impression that his story happens within eternal space—for much of the action begins in heaven, continues on earth, and ends in heaven. By expanding the temporal frame, the pasyon of Aquino de Belen, which concerned itself primarily with personal and individual salvation, now becomes an exposition of universal salvation.[18]

The 1814 pasyon is clearly then the classic expression in Tagalog of the all-encompassing historicism in the Christian tradition. This is reflected in its complete title, *Casaysayan nang Pasiong Mahal ni Jesucristong Panginoon Natin na Sucat Ipag-alab nang Puso nang Sinomang Babasa* (Story/History of the Holy Passion of Jesus Christ Our Lord Which Inspires the Heart of Whoever Will Read It).

Not long after the publication of the *Casaysayan* follows another Tagalog text with a Pampangan cognate, both from Aniceto de la Merced, a native priest of Norzagaray, Bulacan, and the vicar forane of Candaba, Pampanga. The Tagalog version was submitted for ecclesiastical approval in 1843 and published in 1852 as *El Libro de la Vida/Historia Sagrada con Santas Reflexiones y Doctrinas Morales para sa Vida Cristiana en verso Tagalo* (The Book of Life/Sacred History with Pious Reflections and Moral Doctrines for Christian Life in Tagalog verse).[19] The text departs from the *Casaysayan* in using the dodecasyllabic quatrain for the sections prior to Christ's life, and in adding prayers at the end of each homiletic section.

Although other texts like the so-called *Pasyon Guian* are mentioned in the literature, the *Mahal na Passion*, the *Casaysayan*, and *El Libro de la Vida* constitute the backbone of the pasyon tradition in Tagalog. This is so partly because they are all extant in complete form, but, in greater part, because their textualization of the Christ story reflects the concrete conjuncture of social forces during their time.

This conjuncture of social forces manifests itself in the continuing multiplication of pasyon narratives, both oral and written. Between the publication of Aquino de Belen's narrative and the *Casaysayan* other texts—aside from the missing *Pasyon Guian* (dated 1740)—appear to have been circulating. Javellana's reconstruction of the textual history of the *Casaysayan* through four Manila archbishops indicates a convoluted line of editions bearing family resemblances of many kinds.[20] This multiplication persists even after Aniceto de la Merced, and well into contemporary Tagalog renditions of the Christ story.

While some of these textual variations were a result of the process of oral transmission or publication, the major changes represented a conscious effort at rewriting preceding texts through revision and expansion. *El Libro de la Vida* meant to improve the *Casaysayan* in the same way that *Casaysayan* meant to expand and rework Aquino de Belen's narrative of the Passion, Death, and Resurrection of Jesus.[21] Even the different editions of the *Casaysayan* were directed toward arriving at the definitive pasyon text.

The specific grounds for rewriting earlier pasyon texts were literary and theological. On the literary level, Tagalog had changed in orthography, pronunciation, and vocabulary during the century between Aquino de Belen's *Mahal na Passion* and the *Casaysayan*. Prior to the printing of his *El Libro de la Vida*, de la Merced went to the extent of publishing his criticisms of the *Casaysayan* and claiming that it no longer conformed to the lofty canons of current literary style.[22]

More important than the literary were the theological grounds for rewriting earlier texts. All printing presses were owned by religious orders, and thus concerned with orthodoxy or what was perceived to be more in conformity with it. In the *Casaysayan*'s use of Aquino de Belen's text, stanzas were reworked for greater clarity and precision lest any erroneous interpretation arise.[23] De la Merced criticized the *Casaysayan* for its faulty scholarship and senseless moral lessons.[24]

It is within this overt literary and theological rationale for rewriting that one discovers the signs of "the political unconscious."[25] First, one finds the dialectic between narrative impetus and closure. Narrating a story produces an oral or written text; each retelling yields a text different from its predecessor on account of its having been simplified, expanded, or otherwise changed. The Christ story continued to be retold not only through the multiplication of Tagalog pasyon texts but also through the development of social contexts within which the texts were performed. These contexts centered around the *pabasa*, the antiphonal chanting of the text in front of a makeshift altar during Lent and funeral wakes, and the *sinakulo*, the folk dramatization of the Christ story based on the narrative text. The folk quality of these rituals opened the pasyon tradition further, accentuating the inherent narrative impulse towards continuing revision.[26]

Nevertheless, there was also concern for closing the narrative process through control of the text and the contexts in which it was used. Though the Comision Permanente de Censura was yet to be formed in 1856, the production of the *Casaysayan* itself, the efforts to win ecclesiastical approval, and the complex genealogy of its editions all indicated the obsession with the definitive text, superceding other texts. Similar efforts to suppress the pabasa were common during the nineteenth century. They alleged that this practice encouraged heresy, provided occasions for trysts between young men and women, and generally led to public disorder.[27]

Significantly, this concern for closure came from agents of the ecclesiastical institution, namely the Spanish clerics. As early as 1827, there were letters from parish priests to bishops or from church authorities to the Spanish government urging a ban on the pabasa.[28] At the same time, travelers took note of how popular the chanting of the pasyon was with the *indios*.[29]

What is unmasked, then, in this dialectic between narrative impulse and closure is the struggle for control over the Christ story. By "contracting colonialism," which included the encounter with Spanish Christianity, the people appropriated the Tagalog texts and contexts of the Christ story, making use of them in ways often denounced by the agents of the ecclesiastical institution. Thus, the clerics were anxious to produce a definitive text—one that clearly did not give rise to "heretical" ideas and behavior—and to forbid its chanting as an occasion for sin. This is the first manifestation of political interests at work in the pasyon tradition.

The second appears in the inherent gap between narrative sequence and homiletic application. In the pasyon texts, narration of key events such as the Last Supper precedes the section called *aral*, which draws out the lesson from that particular narrative sequence. Often Jesus is presented in the narrative as an exemplar, and the homiletic section explicated how the Christian is supposed to imitate him. However, the logic from narrative to application, from what Jesus did to what the Christian must do, is not straightforward. It is in moving from one to the other that political interests again emerge.

A comparative study of the texts may illustrate the point. For instance, in the aral following the flogging of Jesus, Aquino de Belen emphasizes the vanity of all physical beauty, whereas the *Casaysayan* would also include the vanity of honor. A more profound difference between the two is reflected in the way the final stanza of the homiletic section is changed in the later text:

Mahal na Passion

Ang buhay mo,y, dili iyo	(Your life is not your own
and maganda,y, ingatan mo	what is good is to be careful
minsang mamatay dito,y,	once you die here
di na moling maguin tauo,t,	you will not live again
ang daratnan pa,y cun ano?[30]	what will happen to you?)

Casaysayan

Ang maganda ay ingatan	(Better care for
and caloloua mong iyan,	that soul of yours
marahil minsang mamatay,	for should it die once
mahirap muling mabuhay	it is hard to live again
sa gracia nang Dios na mahal[31]	in the grace of the holy God.)

89

The focus here clearly has shifted from physical to spiritual death; this shift is consistent with the sociohistorical context of the two pasyon texts, one concerned about how to die like Christ, and the other about how to live like Christ.

But it is from the *Casaysayan* to Aniceto de la Merced's text that the shift is most pronounced, where the gap between narrative and application becomes most instructive. To take but one example, their accounts of the finding of Jesus in the temple are similar. But the homiletic applications they draw from the event are diverse. The *Casaysayan* exhorts children to be obedient, by emphasizing that they can do nothing whatever to repay the debt owed to their parents.[32] The lengthy aral in de la Merced is a whole series of precepts for parents and children, first scolding children for their vices then addressing parents about their obligation to take care of their children physically and morally; it tells parents to scold without cursing, to be strict and not negligent, to teach Christlike temperance, and to be prudent in arranging the marriage of their children.[33] In another example from de la Merced, the aral after the raising up of Lazarus and the dinner at Simon's house lists moral precepts regarding debt obligations, stealing, what to do when one finds lost items, and so forth.[34]

This process of spelling out the moral from a narrative sequence results in a greater preoccupation with particular precepts. Each application becomes increasingly difficult to justify on the basis of what is narrated. Thus, the relationship between what is narrated and what is prescribed tends to be tenuous; put conversely, the gap between narration and application increases, making way for political interests.

For instance, the episode with the Magi offering precious gifts to Jesus provides de la Merced with a gratuitous opportunity to discuss poverty and riches:

Ang mag hirap at yumaman
ang tauo sa pag buhay
Dios and may calooban
at siya ngang nababagay
sa manga pinamigayan.

(People's becoming poor and rich
in life
it is God who wills
and God makes it appropriate
to whoever is given.)

May yumamang di nag hangad
sucat and ugaling sicap
may di quinusang nag hirap
Dios ay siyang may tatag
dapat ipag pasalamat.[35]

(Some became rich without desiring
a measure of industrious nature
some became poor without wanting
God establishes
one should be grateful.)

90

Here, one's social status is ideologically explained as part of God's will. This becomes the basis for analyzing situations of poverty and wealth. Voluntary poverty is praised, but poverty due to laziness, vice, or carelessness is severely censured. The rich are warned against avarice and commanded to be charitable. On the surface, these moral precepts appear harmless. Put in the context of nineteenth-century Tagalog society, however, they supported a world view which domesticated natives and underlay the colonial establishment.

This development of the pasyon tradition is one instance of narrative as a socially symbolic act. The *Casaysayan* provided an all-encompassing view of reality based on the Christ story as master code. It thus gave a Tagalog form to the anagogical sense of Christian historicism. In contrast, Aniceto de la Merced's text focused on the moral sense, by way of detailed prescriptions.

The Moralization and Individualization of the Christ Story

De la Merced's emphasis on the moral sense of the Christ story, the third level of meaning in the traditional Christian hermeneutic, was by no means an isolated phenomenon. It was but one manifestation of a whole cultural ethos, characteristic of the later half of the nineteenth century.

The roots of this ethos, historians point out, lie in economic and political developments in the archipelago as well as Spain. The local ports were opened for general commerce, thus encouraging increased economic activity, especially in agriculture. The political tenure of liberalism in Spain, though brief, brought more liberal colonial administrators and allowed the possibility of higher education through the Royal Decree of 1863. The net result of increased economic prosperity and greater political space was the cultural desire for *urbanidad* among that social class created by these developments.[36]

Certainly there were earlier signs of this desire for urbanity. But only in the second half of the nineteenth century would it intensify. Likewise, the literature which refracted and strengthened this desire proliferated only during this time. This literature consists of two kinds of texts which continued, in different ways, de la Merced's emphasis on the moral sense of the Christ story. First are narrative texts aimed at telling the Christ story, but no longer featuring Christ as the hero but another person, established as *alter Christus*. The other species of

91

literary texts belong to the broad category of anatomies of conduct based on the Christ story.

The narrative texts vary in length and are written either in prose or in any of the traditional verse forms. Among the examples of the short forms are lives of saints which, according to Resil Mojares, are "of a lesser order than the pasyon but composing a sizeable segment of early printed literature."[37] However, as one moves on in the nineteenth and even into the early twentieth century, the greater number of these narrative texts come to concern the lives of ordinary but exemplary people, with the lives of depraved people for counterexamples.

The common form of these longer narratives is the metrical romance and its dramatized cognate known as the *comedia*. The romance itself was either a *corrido* or an *awit*, the two being distinguished with respect to the number of syllables per line and the manner of reading. Though many of their story lines came from European literary sources as early as the seventeenth century, the metrical romances took root on native soil, as Damiana Eugenio asserts in her comprehensive study of the Philippine metrical romance.

> Spain brought to the Philippines the genre and subject matter of the traditional romance: the Carolingian, Arthurian, and classical romances; the *libros de caballerias*; and the noncyclic Oriental romances. But after the genre had become well established in the country, it was put to a great variety of uses, perhaps by the Spanish writers at first and then by the local poets, after they had become thoroughly familiar with its mechanics and conventions. These latter used it to narrate saints' lives, Bible stories, conduct books, fairy and folk tales, and even debates.[38]

It is not surprising then that the nineteenth-century metrical romance would be, in the words of Lumbera, "the consolidation of tradition."[39]

These romance forms are often called "secular" or "profane." They are thereby made to herald the advent of secularization in Philippine literary history. This view needs to be qualified. They can be so called only if the pasyon tradition is used as reference point. Certainly they were not about Jesus Christ, nor were their texts subjected to imprimatur. Whatever their subject matter, one finds them informed by a basic Christian worldview. Eugenio writes "that the most dominant theme developed in the traditional corrido is the theme of

92

Faith, expressed through the conflict between Christians and Moors, with the former inevitably vanquishing the latter in a demonstration of the superiority of Catholicism."[40] She proceeds to enumerate the manifestations of this basic Christian worldview: an invocation to God or a saint at the beginning, the pious nature of many heroes and heroines, the usual conversions of Moors, the incidence of miracles and even of direct communication with God.[41] Under no circumstances is it true to say that these narrative texts eschewed the Christ story.

The second set of literary texts popular in the late nineteenth century consists of the anatomy of conduct, whose basis is the Christ story. Mojares lists many forms in this set, such as the *epistolario*, *ejemplo*, *dialogo*, and *tratado*—all of which he discusses in relation to the development of the Filipino novel.[42] Each of these forms has narrative elements, but the nature and focus of these elements vary greatly. For instance, the events in *Urbana at Feliza* (1864) are narrated through an exchange of letters, while in *Si Tandang Bacio Macunat* (1885), they are framed in a series of narrators. What is evident in these various forms is "the didactic impulse [which] so rules Philippine literature during the Spanish period that one can say that the 'book of conduct' is the most representative specimen of this literature," and "a quintessential expression of the spirit of the times."[43]

As in de la Merced, there is in both the narratives and anatomies of conduct a dialectic relation between narrative sequence and homiletic application. This is manifest in apparently opposing tendencies between illustration and representation. On the one hand, they serve to illustrate morality based on the Christ story; on the other, they have to represent this morality in local contexts familiar to their audience. Mojares, for instance, points out that "undoubtedly, local or contemporary elements must have entered into these hagiographical narratives—the citation of local miracles, or the stress on values that appear to the writers to be the most called for by the times."[44] This is also true of many of the metrical romances which "took on a Philippine coloring."[45] In the case of the anatomies of conduct "because they deal with the norms of ordinary, day-to-day life, one also finds the 'mimetic' impulse at work."[46] Thus, these kinds of literary texts represent the two aspects of the same problematic inherent in de la Merced's pasyon.

But each of them goes beyond de la Merced. Each resolves the problematic by emphasizing one side of the dialectic relation. The narrative texts focus on sequence, while the anatomies of conduct on homiletic application. The result is a dual reduction, a tendency to individualize and to moralize the Christ story.

The first reduction of the Christ story consists in its individualization. Both in the narrative texts and anatomies of conduct, Christ is no longer the main literary character as in the pasyon. At the center are humans, whether saints, exemplary persons, or counterexamples of unchristian behavior. Moreover, these texts circumscribe the life of the individual, demarcating it as the realm in which the Christ story must play itself out. The life of the individual character, then, must be told in such a way as to make it appear as an epiphany of the Christ story:

> From the dense thickets of dogma (such as those that fill the pages of *Barlaan at Josaphat*), the ornate, artificial world of corridos, and the rarefied atmosphere of meditations and novenas, one is transported into the freer ground of day-to-day living in the native community.[47]

The focus on the everyday life of the individual is not without political consequence. In many of the nineteenth-century texts under consideration, the wider sense of the Christ story—the anagogical sense, in medieval vocabulary, and the political/historical, in Jameson's terminology—is suppressed.

This suppression of the political sense of the Christ story takes, as I have suggested, yet another form. By underscoring homiletic application, these literary texts reduced the Christ story to moral prescriptions to be carried out by the individual. What Mojares writes of a Cebuano *lagda* applies as well to these Tagalog texts:

> This collection of maxims sets down detailed, specific injunctions as to how a good Christian must conduct himself from the time he rises in the morning till he retires at night. The stress is on the performance of Catholic duties and the cultivation of habits of cleanliness, obedience, modesty, honesty and moderation. The reader is also instructed in moral vigilance in avoiding occasions of sins, which include among others such festivities as dances and the comedia. What runs through the entire work is a passion for the "orderly" life.[48]

The political implications of this dual reduction through an individualization and moralization of the Christ story appear in the congruence of faith and proper manners, "made manifest in a decorous and ceremonious life that turned on the axis of obedience to God and His Church," and the further indentification between the good Catholic and the perfect colonial.[49]

A classic example of this congruence of faith and proper manners is *Urbana at Feliza* (1864) by a secular priest, Modesto de Castro.[50] Written as an exchange of letters between sisters—Urbana ("urbanity") studying in Manila and Feliza ("happiness") staying in rural Bulacan—it discusses matters from cleanliness to holiness with equal gravity. One discovers, further, which virtues are celebrated: purity and its cognates, modesty, humility, and trustworthiness in material things. This concern with sexuality, reputation, and possession is then subsumed under the rubric of *pakikipagkapwa-tao* (being human to each other), a concept with profound roots in Tagalog culture which, in this case, is reduced to abiding by approved manners. Moreover, more social rules for moral behavior are directed to women, suggesting the low status of women in colonial society.

One exception to the predilection for women and at the same time an indication of the identification of the Catholic and colonial is Fr. Juan Dilag's narrative, *Caaua-auang Buhay nang Magsusugal at Nacamumuhing Asal ng Lasing* (1883).[51] As its title indicates, the episodic corrido tells the miserable life of a gambler and the hateful behavior of a drunkard. Typically, it chides the men about the evils of vice. But what is of greater interest is its aral concerning attendance at mass on days of obligation:

> Sapagca,t, sa di nating pagsisimba sa mga nasabing arao nagbubuhat ang pagpapadala na Panginoon Dios ng mga parusang salot, tuyot, pagbabaca luctong at pagcacamatay ng ating mga hayop; sapagca,t, ang hindi magsimba sa mga nasabing arao ay ang casalanang hayag ng bayan caya ito namang parusang hayag sa bayan ang ipinarusa ng P. Dios. Capatic co: cun icao ay isa sa mga sauing palad na dili nagsisimba tantoin mo na icao ay isa sa mga caauay ng bayan mo na pinagagalit ang Dios at ng parusahan ang iyong bayan ng mga parusang ating madalas maquita dahil sa di pagsisimba natin sa mga arao na catungculan nating isimba.[52]

> (On account of our not going to church on these days, the Lord God sends punishments like pestilence, drought, locusts, and the

death of our animals; because not going to church is a public sin of the people, so its punishment is also a public one for the people. My brother, if you are one of those miserable ones who do not go to church, realize that you are one of the enemies of the people who anger the Lord God, and when our people are given those punishments we frequently see because of our not going to church on days we should.)

Here, going to church is equated with civic duty, so that one who does not go to church is designated an enemy of the people and exposed to censure.

What these nineteenth-century narratives and anatomies of conduct did was to treat all mundane matters with equal seriousness and to attach them directly with following the Christ story. This reduction of the Christ story to moral minutiae for personal life suggests a total "Christianization" of life rather than its secularization.

Yet, it is precisely on account of this reduction that subversion is possible. As Rafael points out, *reducir* has multilayered definitions: "to reduce a thing to its former state, to convert, to contract, to divide into small parts, to contain, to comprehend, to bring back into obedience."[53] Its application in different contexts makes reduction/translation for the Tagalogs "a process less of internalizing colonial-Christian conventions than of evading their totalizing grip by repeatedly marking the differences between their language and interests and those of the Spaniards."[54]

This, in fact, was what some enlightened natives did, even within nineteenth-century literary tradition. In his *Florante at Laura* (1838), Francisco Baltazar retold the Christ story through a narrative of Christians and Moors bound by *katwiran* (reason/righteousness)—a concept which will be fully explored by the socialist writers at the turn of the century.[55]

The Critical Appropriation of the Christ Story

The individualization and moralization in late nineteenthcentury literary texts underscored the need for retrieving the anagogical sense of the Christ story. Many metrical romances and anatomies of conduct were confined to the moral sense of the story, for they considered the Christ story to be definitive, its meaning in the undisputed keeping of the church. Hence, their preoccupation with homiletic application,

96

whether by narrating an exemplary individual's virtues or by offering moral prescriptions. What was needed, therefore, to break out of this preoccupation was to continue the story and focus on narrative sequence.

It is no coincidence, then, that the critical appropriation of the Christ story emerged within two broad historical movements in the early twentieth century: the establishment of the Iglesia Filipina Independiente (IFI), and the rise of socialist ideas.

These two movements have a common origin in the figure of Isabelo de los Reyes, writer and publisher.[56] Sympathetic to the aims of the Propaganda Movement, De los Reyes ended up in prison, first in Manila and then Spain. His stay in Europe from 1897 onward brought him into contact with socialist and anarchist ideas and enabled him to work against American aims in the Philippines as a member of the Malolos government in exile. Furthermore, he made common cause, even before his return to the Philippines in 1901, with those among Filipino clergy who wanted to take over parishes from friars. It is, therefore, not surprising that in the following year, he founded with Hermenegildo Cruz the first labor union, Union Obrera Democratica and later proclaimed the Iglesia Filipina Independiente even before Fr. Gregorio Aglipay agreed to be its bishop. Though connected in origin through de los Reyes, these two movements developed separately under the pressure of historical events. Likewise, the literary texts they inspired are fundamentally different. The literary texts associated with the establishment of the IFI were traditional forms, containing critical material. Like nineteenth-century texts, they emphasized the homiletic application of the Christ story. But it was a new application, given the changed, and changing, historical situation.

Some of these texts came as pamphlets like *Justicia ng Dios* (1899) and *Lilim ng Dalawang Batas mula sa Paraiso* (n.d.), both in the dodecasyllabic verse of the awit but with a clearly different content.[57] The first, written by the journalist Mariano Sequera, opens with an invocation to "Inang Filipinas" and chronicles how a Spanish friar preyed on a mother and a daughter. The friar wanted to win the daughter's hand though favors; but when she refused, he had their house set on fire, in which the mother perished. The daughter was finally able to escape through the help of a Filipino secular priest, who brought the friar to justice and told him "you should not be called God's minister" (icao nga'y di dapat tauaguing/ ministro ng Dios).[58]

In presenting the Spanish friar as a counterexample of Christ, this narrative clearly illustrates a different moral. It condemns the Spanish friars and exhorts the Filipino clergy to action. Moreover, Sequera uses the illustration explicitly to undermine ecclesiastical and colonial authority: *"At cung sacali nga'y susulat na muli tungcol din sa* fraileng *pilipit ang budhi,/ hindi rin titiguil, cahi ma't mumuhi,/ sa aquin ang* papa, cardenal *at* hari" (And if I have to write once more to about wicked friars, I will not stop even though the pope, cardinal and king hate me).[59]

The second example, *Lilim ng Dalawang Batas*, has less narrative and more moral ideas and application. With the exception of a few scattered episodes, Joaquin Manibo's pamphlet is a moral tract in verse about the laws of God and of country and the struggle between Christ and evil. Both laws serve to defeat the evil side, where one finds the local *caciques* (power holders), politicians, judges, and, of course, the friars and the pope, whom he identifies with Caiaphas and Anas. Manibo ends by calling Filipino priests to action: *"Maniuala cayo paring cababayan/ sa sabi cong itong may catotohanan/ yamang panahon pa y inyong pagsicapang/ ang 'Pananarili ng Templo sa bayan'"* (Priests who are fellow countrymen, believe in the truth I speak, since it's time that you work for "Freedom of the Temple in the country").[60]

The most significant literary text of the IFI is its pasyon called *Patnubay ng Binyagan* (2d ed., 1935), written by Pascual Poblete, born and educated Catholic but drawn to the new church by his nationalist sentiments and through close association with de los Reyes.[61] Here is a clear attempt to continue the pasyon tradition, and at the same time, to revise it in the light of the historical situation. Thus Poblete's text retains the form of de la Merced but identifies the villains in the Christ story with the Roman pontiff and his followers in the Philippines.

The main revison in this text is in the area of moral application. For instance, in the section where Jesus curses the fig tree, Poblete's narration and aral are practically the same as de la Merced's. In the aral more stanzas are added, which are critical of Roman Catholicism:

Ang imbing pangangalacal
sa Religiong caniyang lalang
na guinagawang paraan,
upang cayamana'y camtan
guminhawa yaong buhay.

(The wicked commerce
of the Religion he created
he used as a means
to accumulate wealth
for a comfortable life.

98

Inyo ngang alalahanin	You should then remember
sa tagalog na narating	what happened to the Tagalog
sa pagbiling lico't linsil,	in his wrong and wicked buying
ng cuintas, correa't calmen	of necklaces, cords, and scapulars:
tagarito'y inaalipin.	the natives were enslaved.
Ang mga fraileng castila,	The Spanish friars
budhing malabis ng sama,	with truly evil souls
yumaman ng di cawasa,	became rich easily
ang tagalog ang naaba	the Tagalogs suffered
naamis at naguing dukha."[62]	were oppressed and became poor.)

In the end, the text exhorts the readers to think critically: *"Caya ngayo'y ating bucsan/ ang isip sa pag-aral,/ sarisaring carunungan,/ ng muling hindi na naman/ maraya ng mga hunghang"* (Let us then open/ our minds to examine/ different kinds of knowledge/ so we will no longer/ be fooled by the wicked).[63]

The most far-reaching critical appropriation of the Christ story is in literary texts associated with the rise of socialist ideas. Unlike those related to the Iglesia Filipina Independiente, these texts were not content with changing the moral application. They aimed at nothing less than a radical revision of the Christ story. This required a corresponding change in literary form; and so it was that the appropriation of the Christ story by socialism took modern narrative forms—the Tagalog novel and prose drama being most suited for this purpose.

The best examples of this appropriation are the play *Bagong Cristo* and the novel *Pinaglahuan*, both dated 1907 and written by educated nationalists, Aurelio Tolentino and Faustino Aguilar, respectively.[64] Each narrative uses for its main protagonist a Christ figure whose name incorporates the honorific title *Gat*, meaning "great." In Tolentino's three-act play, the hero is openly identified by his name, Jesus Gatbiaya, and his title, meaning the new Christ. In Aguilar's novel, the identification is not as open; only at the end is Luis Gatbuhay referred to as "a new God who, in those last moments of the afternoon and in the midst of the mellow rays of the sun, manifests his full power" (isang bagong Diyos na sa mga huling sandaling iyon ng hapon at sa gitna ng malamlam na sinag ng araw, ay nagpapakita ng boong kapangyrihan).[65]

The plot of both narratives centers around the nexus of events involving these Christ figures. In *Bagong Cristo*, Jesus appears as an itinerant preacher, whose basic message is the equality of all humans as children of God. He attracts followers, especially among workers and peasants, by criticizing the rich for opprevive practices and the poor for their addiction to gambling. The rich finally plot against him and though their leaders—Magdangal and Capitang Berto—are exposed and punished. Jesus is stabbed at the close of the play.

In the novel, the primary conflict is between Luis and Rojalde over the love of Danding. Luis wins Danding's love but she is forced to marry Rojalde in exchange for her father's gambling debt. Not content with this, Rojalde plots to destroy Luis by arranging to have him dismissed from work at Mr. Kilsberg's factory, and imprisoned through a frame-up. The novel closes with a great conflagration in Manila; Luis dies because of an explosion, but Rojalde discovers that he is not the father of Danding's son.

The use of these Christ figures suggests, in both narratives, the critical appropriation of the Christ story mentioned earlier. While characters in the nineteenth-century literary texts tend to be simply illustrative of moral ideas and ideals, Jesus and Luis appear as characters whose lives are a representation of the Christ story. What accounts for this is not the particularity of their characterization, but what Robert McAfee Brown calls "the dialectic of similarity and dissimilarity" between stories.[66]

The story of *Bagong Cristo* obviously is patterned after the Christ story. Jesus Christ and Jesus Gatbiaya both preach; their teaching attracts followers from among the poor, but also antagonizes the powerful, who eventually kill them. The similarity between the story of Luis in *Pinaglahuan* and the Christ story is more subtle; both are about a poor person who is oppressed but finally vindicated in death.

But there are differences. Even in *Bagong Cristo*, which is closer to the Christ story, events are altered to avoid making the play simply a reprise of the original story. For example, Jesus Gatbiaya does not die at the crucifixion-like scene in the second act, but later when he is stabbed. The dissimilarity in relation to *Pinaglahuan* is easier to see; Luis's love for Danding has, for instance, no analogy in the Christ story.

Aside from these differences, there are others which stem from a deeper source. That source is the socialist influence in the two narratives. One finds in both certain socialist motifs which resemble the utopian socialist views of Robert Owen and Fourier: the equality of all individuals as children of God, the existential struggle between the

100

oppressed and the powerful, the moral priority of labor over capital, and the critique of clericalism and establishment Catholicism. Such motifs are reflected both in the speeches of the Christ figures as well as in the narrative plot.[67]

On the level of proclamation, the motifs crystallize around katwiran (reason/righteousness), a word with deep roots in Tagalog discourse and generally meaning the rational ground for human existence. Jesus begins his very first speech thus:

> Ang lahat ng tao sa sanglibutan ay nanggaling sa isang ama, sa makatwid ay magkakapatid na lahat. Sa makatwid ay dapat sanang tayong lahat ay magmahalang parang tunay na magkapatid, at magdamayan sa lahat ng hirap at kaginhawahaan.[68]

> (All human beings in the world come from one father; therefore all are brothers/sisters. Therefore we should love one another like true brothers/sisters, and help each other in all suffering and comfort.)

Sa makatwid, which literally means "following from reason," takes the substantive form at the end of the speech: "*Mabuhay ng katwiran, mabuhay ang Bagong Cristo!*" (Long live Reason; long live the New Christ!).[69] This same emphasis on katwiran is reflected in the conversations of Luis in Aguilar's novel, especially as he is identified as a Christ figure:

> Sapagka't sa ikapagtatgumpay ng alin mang layon, sa ikabibihis ng katauhang dinudusta, at sa ipagwawagi ng Katwiran laban sa lakas ay kailangan ang dugo, kailangan ang buhay, kailangan ang luha, ang apoy na panunog.[70]

> (For the accomplishment of any aim, the transformation of oppressed humankind, and the victory of Reason over Power, there is need for blood, there is need for life, there is need for tears, the fire that burns.)

Katwiran then appears as the rational foundation of the moral order governing personal and social existence.

The socialist motifs are reflected equally in the plot of both works. In Tolentino's play, events are propelled by the conflict between the *maguinoo* and the followers of Jesus, who include those rich who have thrown their lot in with the poor. The integration of socialist motifs is more complex in *Pinaglahuan*. The enemies of Luis are actually representatives of social forces—the Spanish mestizo Rojalde, the American capitalist Mr. Kilsberg, and the Filipino elite parents of Danding. This struggle versus Luis unfolds against the backdrop of the contemporary historical situation; the first scene in the novel describes a public meeting on the question of Philippine independence.

The cumulative effect of similarity and dissimilarity between the Christ story and the narratives of Tolentino and Aguilar is to re-present the Christ story in early twentieth-century Tagalog society. In telling the stories of Jesus and Luis, these narratives retell the Christ story, which once again is situated as a personal life within history. The anagogical sense of the Christ story is hence retrieved.

The Subversive Memory of Tradition

This essay has discussed Tagalog texts of the Christ story in the light of the traditional Christian hermeneutic whose theological basis, Jameson indicates, we can no longer presume. Nevertheless, this hermeneutic is useful in showing how an authoritative story functions, and why the political perspective is the horizon of interpretation.

It is in this context that the Christ story can be said to function as the subversive memory of the narrative tradition constituted by these texts. Such description is based on the nature of narrative, whose "multiplicity of meanings is not a product of excessive critical ingenuity," but "one of the necessary features of narrative as such."[71] What this implies will be explained, first in relation to the two elements of narrative mentioned above—the dialectic between narrative impulse and closure, and the gap between narrative sequence and homiletic application—and second, in terms of the political horizon of interpretation.

As the memory of this narrative tradition, the Christ story generates numerous texts, many of which are themselves revisions. This process of generation continues because of the inherent impulse in an authoritative story to move forward. At the same time, there is a heuristic and practical necessity for closure. Generated within a particular historical context, each narrative is itself an attempt at closure. As Paul Ricoeur explains, "to follow the story is . . . to apprehend the episodes which are themselves well known as leading to this end."[72] Thus closure—the path to an ending—can only be relative; it is but the "re-treading" of the Christ story in a specific context, never for all situations.

This dialectic between narrative impulse and closure is exemplified in the development of the nineteenth- and early twentiethcentury Tagalog literary works discussed. No sooner had a text of the Christ story been finished than another retelling or revision appeared. This applied not only to the pasyon for which the clerics wanted definitive closure in the form of an approved text, but also to the other literary texts grounding themselves in the Christ story. Not only did these narratives continue the Christ story, they "closed" it by explicating what following the story demanded in, for instance, the aral or the speeches of a socialist Christ figure.

Closure then is related to the second element of narrative, the gap between narrative sequence and homiletic application. Narratives based on an authoritative story describe events *and* prescribe behavior on account of these events. However, the link between sequence and application is not straightforward, nor is the homiletic application demanded by a narrative ever univocal. Even when imitation is the operative logic, it is invariably necessary to choose what to imitate. Thus each narrative mediation of the same Christ story proposes its own social response.

Comparison of the different narrative texts analyzed and the kinds of moral prescription they give bears this out. It is in the homiletic application of narrative sequences that de la Merced places reactionary views coated in pious language, or where *Patnubay ng Binyagan* inserts the call against Roman Catholicism and the Spanish friars. The anatomies of conduct reduce the following of the Christ story to obeying moralistic minutiae. Even in narratives which have no separate section for homiletic application, the *alter Christus* exemplifies the kind of behavior set up for imitation. For instance, in the works of Aguilar and Tolentino, the exemplar is clearly the worker-organizer who preaches socialist ideals.

The diversity of the social responses proposed in these texts appears intrinsic to the nature of an authoritative story. The Christ story, as memory of tradition, then, may be described as subversive; it could not be closed definitively, any more than its application might be reduced to one plan of action or political program. This explains why particular narrative mediations of the Christ story could fulfill contrary functions as colonial tool and as language for liberation.

The Christ story is the subversive memory of Tagalog narrative tradition in a second sense. According to Jameson, the traditional Christian hermeneutic is "particularly suggestive in the solution that it provides for an interpretative dilemma . . . that of the incommensurabilty of the private and public, the psychological and the social, the poetic and the political." This is most evident at the fourth or anagogical level where "[the historical or collective dimension] is attained once again," and "has been transformed into universal history and the destiny of humankind as a whole."[73] Here, as Jameson insists, the political inescapably asserts itself as the horizon of all reading and interpretation.

The development of the nineteenth- and early twentieth-century Tagalog narratives discussed confirms this. As Ileto's study has shown, the *Casaysayan* articulated the anagogical sense of the Christ story: "For one thing, the inclusion of episodes relating to the Creation of the World, the Fall of Man, and the Last Judgment makes the Pasyon Pilapil an image of universal history, the beginning and end of time, rather than a simple gospel story."[74] In contrast to it, the later pasyon texts, most of the metrical romances, and the anatomies of conduct limited the master code to the moral level, and, therefore, merely served to perpetuate the colonial status quo. Only with the socialist appropriation in fiction and drama would the Christ story recover its anagogical sense, expressed in terms of the socialist reading of history. Thus the subversive quality of the Christ story persists as long as the anagogical level is neither ignored nor suppressed.

This quality of the authoritative story must be kept in mind if one is to understand contemporary struggles for liberation. For, as Stephen Crites rightly observes, people desiring liberation today are attracted toward "abstraction in which images and qualities are detached from experience to becaome data for the formation of generalized principles and techniques" or toward "constriction of attention to dissociated immediacies: to the particular image isolated from the image stream."[75] What this concretely refers to is an activism either imprisoned by rigid ideology or based on pure spontaneity.

The same is true for later twentieth-century Philippine society. While new developments in society at large and within religious traditions have taken place, signs of the Christ story continue to appear in significant events and movements for change. The most dramatic, of late, has been the 1986 EDSA Revolution—a singular conjuncture which involved Filipino and American interests, political forces and military

104

factions, church and state, institutional religion and native religiosity. Today, its singular achievement remains, though many of its promises have been betrayed. Both its achievement and betrayal can be understood, I suggest, only if the event in EDSA is seen within the tradition discussed in this essay: "what is called for is a narrative understanding of the February Revolution which is integral to this cultural history yet leads towards practical action for the future."[76]

NOTES

1. This essay follows the distinction between story and narrative which Seymour Chatman makes in *Story and Discourse: Narrative Structure in Fiction and Film* (Ithaca: Cornell University Press, 1978), 23: "Story is the content of the narrative expression, while [narrative] discourse is the form of that expression."

2. Reynaldo Clemena Ileto, *Pasyon and Revolution: Popular Movements in the Philippines, 1840-1910* (Quezon City: Ateneo de Manila University Press, 1979).

3. Ileto, *Pasyon and Revolution*, 19.

4. Vicente L. Rafael, *Contracting Colonialism: Translation and Christian Conversion in Tagalog Society under Early Spanish Rule* (Quezon City: Ateneo de Manila University Press, 1986).

5. Rafael, *Contracting Colonialism*, 170.

6. Ileto, *Pasyon and Revolution*, 15-16.

7. Reynaldo C. Ileto, "Critical Issues in 'Understanding Philippine Revolutionary Mentality,'" *Philippine Studies* 30 (1902): 94.

8. Rene B. Javellana, S.J., ed., *Casaysayan nang Pasiong Mahal ni Jesucristong Panginoon Natin na Sucat Ipag-alab nang Puso nang Sinomang Babasa*, 1882 ed. (Quezon City: Ateneo de Manila Press, 1988), 3.

9. Fredric Jameson, *The Political Unconscious: Narrative as a Socially Symbolic Act* (Ithaca: Cornell University Press, 1981), 13.

10. Jameson, *Political Unconscious*, 18.

11. Jameson, *Political Unconscious*, 23.

12. Rowan A. Greer, "The Christian Bible and Its Interpretation," in *Early Biblical Interpretation*, with James L. Kugel (Philadelphia: Westminster Press, 1986), 156.

13. Jameson, *Political Unconscious*, 30.

14. Jameson, *Political Unconscious*, 30-31.

15. *Doctrina Christiana* (1593), facs. ed. (Washington: Library of Congress, 1947).

16. Rene B. Javellana, S.J., ed., *Mahal na Passion ni Jesu Christong Panginoon natin sa Tola ni Gaspar Aquino de Belen* (Quezon City: Ateneo de Manila University Press, 1988).

17. Javellana, *Casaysayan*, 40.

18. Javellana, *Casaysayan*, 33.

19. Aniceto de la Merced, *El Libro de la Vida/Historia Sagrada con Santas Reflexiones y Doctrinas Morales para la Vida Cristiana en verso Tagalo* (Manila: J. Martinez, 1906?). (The stanzas of this text are not numbered; hence references to verses shall be in page numbers.)

20. Javellana, *Casaysayan*, 13-14.

21. Javellana, *Casaysayan*, 15-23.

22. Aniceto de la Merced, *Manga Puna na Sinulat nang Pbro. D. Aniceto de la Merced* (Manila: Limbagan nina Fajardo at Kasama, 1907).

23. Javellana, *Casaysayan*, 22.

24. De la Merced, *Manga Puna*, 59, 77.

25. Jameson, *Political Unconscious*, 20.

26. Nicanor G. Tiongson, *Kasaysayan at Estetika ng Sinakulo at Ibang Dulang Panrelihiyon sa Malolos* (Quezon City: Ateneo de Manila University Press, 1975).

27. Sinibaldo de Mas, *Informe sobre el estado de las Islas Filipinas en 1842* (Madrid: n.p., 1843). Trans. in Emma Blair and Alexander Robertson, *The Philippine Islands* (Cleveland: Arthur H. Clark Co., 1903-9).

28. Censorship Notes ("Senor Juez Provisor"), *Casaysayan nang Pasiong Mahal ni Jesu Christong Panginoon Natin na Sucat Ipagalab nang Puso nang Sinomang Babasa* (Manila: Imprenta de los Amigos del Pais, 1882), 2.

29. Juan Alvarez Guerra, *De Manil a Tayabas* (Manila: Establicimiento Tipografico, 1878), 2.

30. Javellana, *Mahal na Passion*, stanza 236.

31. Javellana, *Casaysayan*, stanza 1280.

32. Javellana, *Casaysayan*, stanzas 399-408.

33. De la Merced, *El Libro de la Vida*, 62-64.

34. De la Merced, *El Libro de la Vida*, 98-100.

35. De la Merced, *El Libro de la Vida*, 56.

36. Bienvenido L. Lumbera, *Tagalog Poetry 1570-1891: Tradition and Influences in its Development* (Quezon City: Ateneo de Manila University Press, 1986), 61.

37. Resil B. Mojares, *Origins and Rise of the Filipino Novel: A Generic Study of the Novel until 1940* (Quezon City: University of the Philippines Press, 1983), 56.

38. Damiana L. Eugenio, *Awit at Corrido: Philippine Metrical Romances* (Quezon City: University of the Philippines Press, 1987), xxxvi.

39. Lumbera, *Tagalog Poetry*, 83-111.

40. Eugenio, *Awit at Corrido*, 64.

41. Eugenio, *Awit at Corrido*, xxxii-xxxiii.

42. Mojares, *Filipino Novel*, 80-99.

43. Mojares, *Filipino Novel*, 80.

44. Mojares, *Filipino Novel*, 57.

45. Eugenio, *Awit at Corrido*, xxxvi.

46. Mojares, *Filipino Novel*, p. 80.

47. Mojares, *Filipino Novel*, 80-81.

48. Mojares, *Filipino Novel*, 81.

49. Mojares, *Filipino Novel*, 80.

50. Modesto de Castro, *Pag susulatan nang Dalauang Binibini na si Urbana at ni Feliza* (Manila: J. Martinez, n.d.).

51. Juan Dilag, *Caaua-auang Buhay nang Magsusugal at Nacamumuhing Asal ng Lasing* (Manila: J. Martinez, 1907).

52. Dilag, *Caaua-auang*, 76.

53. Rafael, *Contracting Colonialism*, 90.

54. Rafael, *Contracting Colonialism*, 211.

55. See Jose Mario C. Francisco, "Di Tuwid ang Katwiran," and other recent studies on *Florante at Laura*, in *200 Taon ni Balagtas*, ed. Soledad S. Reyes (Quezon City: Balagtas Bicentennial Commission, 1989).

56. See Mary Dorita Clifford, B.V.M., "Iglesia Filipina Independiente: The Revolutionary Church," in *Studies in Philippine Church History*, ed. Gerald H. Anderson (Ithaca: Cornell University Press, 1969), 223-55.

57. Mariano Sequera, *Justicia ng Dios: Mga Ilang Bagay na Inasal dito sa Filipinas nang mga Fraile* (Manila: Limbagan ni Chofre y Comp., 1899). Joaquin Manibo, *Lilim ng Dalawang Batas mula sa Paraiso* (Manila: J. Martinez, n.d.).

58. Sequera, *Justicia ng Dios*, 19.

59. Sequera, *Justica ng Dios*, 24.

60. Manibo, *Lilim ng Dalawang Batas*, 41.

61. Pascual H. Poblete, *Patnubay ng Binyagan: Kasaysayan mula ng lalangin ang Sanglibutan hanggang sa Pasiong Mahal nang Ating Panginoong Jesucristo*, 2d ed. (Manila: Dia Filipino Press, Inc., 1935).

62. Poblete, *Patnubay ng Binyagan*, 89.

63. Poblete, *Patnubay ng Binyagan*, 89.

64. Aurelio Tolentino, *Bagong Cristo*, in *Aurelio Tolentino: Selected Writings*, ed. Edna Zapanta-Manlapaz (Quezon City: University of the Philippines Press, 1975), 143-219.

65. Aguilar, *Pinaglahuan*, 300.

66. Robert McAfee Brown, "My Story and 'The Story,'" *Theology Today* 32 (July 1975): 166.

67. It is difficult to prove how direct the influence of the utopian socialists was on the Tagalog writers. One can point out similarities in views. See Timoteo S. Melliza, "A Study of Early Filipino Socialism as found in *Banaag at Sikat* and *Pinaglahuan* in the light of Catholic Social Teaching" (M.A. thesis, Ateneo de Manila University, 1990).

68. Tolentino, *Bagong Cristo*, 148.

69. Tolentino, *Bagong Cristo*, 151.

70. Aguilar, *Pinaglahuan*, 300.

71. Wallace Martin, *Recent Theories of Narrative* (Ithaca: Cornell University Press, 1986), 187.

72. Paul Ricoeur, *Time and Narrative*, vol. 1 (Chicago: University of Chicago Press, 1984), 67.

73. Jameson, *Political Unconscious*, 31.

72. Paul Ricoeur, *Time and Narrative*, vol. 1 (Chicago: University of Chicago Press, 1984), 67.

73. Jameson, *Political Unconscious*, 31.

74. Ileto, *Pasyon and Revolution*, 18.

75. Stephen Crites, "The Narrative Quality of Experience," in *Why Narrative? Readings in Narrative Theology*, ed. Stanley Hauerwas and L. Gregory Jones (Grand Rapids, Michigan: William B. Eerdmans Publishing Co., 1989), 85.

76. Jose Mario C. Francisco, S.J., "Interpreting the February Revolution," *Branches: Pacific and Asian American Journal of Theology and Ministry* (Fall-Winter 1986), 18.

4

ON THE ANVIL: REALISM AND REVOLUTION IN A CONTEMPORARY PHILIPPINES NOVELIST

D. M. Roskies

"One of the immemorial ways of praising a writer," it has been observed, "that is, by saying that he or she is true to life, has become obscurely tabu, as if it involved some fundamental misconception of the nature of literature and the world."[1] A trawl through the periodical shelves of any respectable university library in Western Europe or in North America, or a glance at recent specialist monographs in literary criticism (not excluding criticism of Southeast Asian literatures), inescapably leads to this rather sombre conclusion.[2] Critics in the future will without doubt see the literature of our age as being peculiarly obsessed with a perverse version of imitation. They will have no trouble classifying its tendencies, or attributing them to the waning influence of nineteenth-century doctrines. They will note that many of their immediate forerunners bent over backwards to point out that the whole thing was a deception, that literature, of no matter what kind, can never be in the smallest degree like life but only like other examples of literature. The paradox may briefly amuse them. They may conclude that whereas writers—particularly novelists—were instinctively conditioned or inclined in principle to make reading seem like living, critics were programmed in the opposite direction, to point out that all was artifice.

What follows is far from lending support to this line of critical revision. It is to be understood as being in animated conversation with other points of view put forward in this volume (with, for example, that of Paul Tickell, who explores Putu Wijaya's departures from verisimilitude). The demurrer which my analysis represents rests on two

111

assumptions. The rationale of each is too extensively and too conscientiously spelled out elsewhere to require more than succinct review here.[3] The first assumption is that the most important and arguably the most honorable function of a novelist remains that of bearing witness: volunteering the truth of things as he or she finds them in his or her time and place. Thus the novelist is at liberty to do as much by virtue of discretionary policy as at the bidding of external compulsion by deploying the appurtenances of character, tempo, and sequential plot, all of which convey an interest in motives, aspirations, and reversals, belonging to what is sometimes referred to (not without condescension) as "secretarial realism."[4]

The second assumption is that nowhere is this liberty more splendidly or purposively exercised than in the polities of the so-called Third World.[5] This is so, notwithstanding such "magic realists" as Gabriel Garcia Marquez of Colombia or, more pertinently, Iwan Simatupang in Indonesia (for instance in his 1968 novel *Merahnya Merah* (The Red of the Red). Lu Hsun, China's most admired and respected writer, comes immediately to mind also, as does Pramoedya Ananta Toer. In mainland Southeast Asia one would want to include within the scope of such a judgement Thailand's master storyteller Kukrit Pramoj (in his two novels *Si phaendin* [Four Reigns] and *Phai daeng* [Red Bamboo], both published in 1953) and Burma's Theein Hpei Myint, whose novels *Thabeik-hmauk Kyaung-tha* (The Student Boycotter), *Lanza poow-bi* (The Way Out), and *Ashei-ga nei-wun htwet-thipama* (As Sure as the Sun Rising in the East), published respectively in 1937, 1949, and 1958, depicting the anti-British nationalist movement which burgeoned during the years 1936-47, have secured his reputation as one of his country's most widely read and influential writers in the realist mode.

It is most strikingly in this dimension of expression and of geopolitical experience that one sees the nature of the case to be made. Far from being always what it is sometimes alleged to be, a bulwark of the status quo and a repository of repressive values, representational realism, in its many inflections and deployments, is alive and kicking and capable here of sustaining a progressive idiom and outlook. (That this idiom and outlook may be inherent, as Lukàcs insists, is an associated argument and one still worthy of consideration.) The point stands little chance of being taken if, as sometimes happens, a critic dogmatically insists upon realism as merely a species of automatic writing or as an immature device to which a writer sometimes resorts for want of imaginative hardihood.[6] Representational realism is easier to accept when one recalls that, considered precisely from a historical point of view, narrations of lifelikeness have specialized in telling the truth—not all of it, certainly, but an important part of it, and that part wonderfully. They have been worked aforethought to epitomize, to convey what Benjamin calls a pregnant or charged moment of historical recognition in which one can find condensed in a text a whole life and in a life a whole epoch.[7] In the African and European traditions, as Soyinka and Balzac suggest (to take but two examples), representational realism is in fact a form most fecund within crises exfoliating from barbarous disproportions of scale.   In the Philippines, who can doubt that the decade and a half preceding People Power was constitutive of such a crisis, brought to so spectacular a head? Doreen Fernandez has shown that realist drama reacted powerfully in just this way.[8]

The name of Linda Ty-Casper, while scarcely one to conjure with, will be familiar to students of contemporary Philippine letters in English. Nor will it be entirely unknown to observers of the Philippine cultural scene generally. Historical fiction is her metier, fiction which recuperates the moral and political genealogy of a country pinioned on the anvil of revolution and perturbed by severe structural stress. Her first novel, *The Peninsulars* (1958), vouchsafed a critical view of eighteenth-century Manila under the Spaniards; her two recent novels, *Awaiting Trespass* (1985) and *Wings of Stone* (1986), distil to perfection the atmosphere in the capital, the ecology of sordid factionalism, squalid maneuvering, and widespread disillusion bred under the New Society. They are valuable if for no other reason than that they foreground with a striking fullness of registration the period framed by the events of 21 August 1983 and February 1986.

This is of course not to say that there are no other reasons for valuing them.   Before noting them, however, some preliminary observations are in order. At the outset it needs to be said that Ty-Casper's way with language has an edifyingly circumscribed quality to it. It is a quality not unrelated to her being a citizen of the Philippines long domiciled in the United States. Though they cannot be the focus of what follows, such shortcomings have much to do with her status as a Filipina writing in English and in a condition of uneasy expatriation, and very little with the fact that she (although a graduate of the University of the Philippines and of Harvard University who has on more than one occasion been Writer-in-Residence at the University of the Philippines and the Ateneo) is simply not up to the job. Insofar as they spring from an imposition of American on Filipino attitudes, these lapses are worth remarking for the way they manifest an economy of utterance as "dependent" as is the national economy. If anything may be said to vitiate these novels, it is the kind of parasitism in the cultural field against which the historian Renato Constantino has so eloquently inveighed. The difficulty—one that is by no means hers alone—is with a style that has been kidnapped by a rhetoric of fancy creative-writing-school-course prose. It is a style written under the impression that this is how good writers write, and which enjoys intermittent currency in her country of residence. The citations adduced in the pages to follow will bear this out, and evaluation of her work which is going to be mealy-mouthed about this aspect of it is sure to come to grief.

Yet skill with words is not the only qualification for being taken seriously. Of equal importance is to have written an inclusive kind of fiction which attempts to convince as a sustained and unflagging exploration, the discovery, which Rizal made, of a significant subject. That Ty-Casper occupies a place in the pantheon in which Rizal himself is the chief exhibit is very much to the point. For it has been an argument running through this volume that what is eccentric to a corpus of "major" texts, or is otherwise tacitly deemed surplus to requirements, can command a degree of interest comparable to that elicited by the central components of the corpus. While these components are not necessarily an instrument of oppression, they do presume some system of inclusion and exclusion. In virtue of their centrality, they are implicated willy-nilly in the establishment, determination, and reinforcement of standard options of taste and social understanding. The contrast (always awaiting concrete demonstration) is with writing at the margin, where a desire to disturb and requalify legitimating presences is found inscribed with special boldness and where a covert, even idolatrous agenda may be glimpsed backing into view. Ty-Casper, unlike N. V. M. Gonzalez or Carlos Bulosan or even Nick Joaquin, is an author of this sort. She occupies a place in recent Philippine writing in English analogous to that held by such Tagalog writers of the late 1960s as Efren Abueg, Edgardo Reyes, Rogelio Sikat, and Amado V. Hernandez.[9] Like them, she writes in the teeth of a genteel tradition of romantic documentary fiction and is dismayed by political injustice. Unlike them, however, she is interested not in a working-class pastoral but in a psychopathology of everyday life amongst a rentier class, the foundations of whose existence are in the process of being eaten away from within. (In this, she keeps company with another interesting

114

novelist, Jessica Hagedorn, whose *Dogeaters* (1991) is almost identical in theme and in choice of subject.)

Restriction of social domain, together with possible misgivings as to a conditioned waywardness of style, form the debit side of her account. But her credit side is healthy. Without making exaggerated claims for them, her novels are remarkable on several counts. They are noteworthy for their inwardness with various states of disfranchisement. They deliver a very interesting political critique, a critique informed by an attention to the particularities of gender and by a horrible fascination with tensions within a cacique. They are buoyed up by a prescient topicality of theme. The prescience and the topicality, in my view, are sufficient to rescue them from relegation to the decent secrecy of footnote. They are also an invitation to trouble. That the author was at risk of incurring the odium of the powers-that-be is therefore not to be wondered at. To be sure, neither of the novels just mentioned was the object of an outright banning order. But it needs no great insight to see that plans for publication in the Philippines at the time of the books' conception amounted to so much wishful thinking. Ultimately they appeared under the imprint of Readers' International, publishers headquartered in London and pledged, according to the dust jacket, to "conserving literature in danger." And a good thing, too. Their indictment is of the sort at which authority under challenge is bound to look askance; the danger to the author of being had up on a charge of sedition plainly was no laughing matter.

Ty-Casper is a "committed" writer, where commitment, in the Philippine context as elsewhere, implies one of two things. In the weak sense, it suggests a reluctance to endorse a setup in which private gains are regularly achieved at the expense of social losses. In the strong sense it signifies an uncompromisingly insurrectionary outlook. Either formulation may mislead by suggesting a more programmatic stance than is in fact on display here. Engagée Ty-Casper most certainly is, in the Sartrean sense of asking, Where do I stand? For whom am I speaking? With what practical effect in view? Her work is shot through with such questions.[10] But the specific nature of her commitment lies elsewhere. It is to be found in the dexterity with which she lights upon internal correlatives for external turmoil. Public and private dilemmas are observed in stereoscopy, leaving her readers without the usual incentive to consign each to its sealed and separate compartment. Hence the value possessed in particular by her two latest novels for anyone interested in the genesis of EDSA.[11] This value, I want to argue, is a function not only of their putative status as forecast or documentary, but also of the difficulties placed, sometimes challengingly, in the way of any tendency to draw a rigid line of demarcation between the personal and the political.[12] Their virtue—a very traditional one—is to have united them without trading crassly on the belief that "everything is politics." *Wings of Stone* will serve for illustration.[13]

Its central figure (hero is the wrong word, in respect of one so eaten up with qualms and prevarications) is witnessed at the start returning home to Manila not long after the fatal day in August 1983. The historicity of the narrative is thus immediately and effaciously established through its chronological range: Johnny Manolo had migrated to the USA on 21 August 1971, the very day when a bomb hurled at a Liberal party rally at Plaza Miranda in Quiapo had killed and maimed many opponents of Ferdinand Marcos. Like any expatriate, but perhaps more than most, he is a man without a shadow, well on the way towards deracination by years of residence in America, many of them on downright unlawful terms. He swings aimlessly in a moral and psychic limbo, his loyalties and affections put into deep freeze. He has come back, in fact, on a lark: "simply to take off, to be free of the earth" (3).[14] Bereft of any firm sense of purpose or direction, he finds himself, in Manila in the autumn at the time of Ninoy Aquino's murder as in Boston during the preceding ten years, a castaway in the designer wilderness that is his life, lapped by the usual creature comforts but scandalized by a vacancy within. "Running and dodging, practised for almost a lifetime, kept him on the edge, . . . were his lifelong confidants . . . he laughed at himself. Who, seeing him in Dior shorts and Ralph Lauren slacks, would guess that he had these doubts rotting inside?" (5).

Physically and emotionally, then, Johnny is in pretty bad shape. The novel interests itself in forensic analysis of his condition. His life in the American suburbs had been a rackety affair, a thing of scaled-down expectation, of chance intrusions and stimuli. It was a life lived sedulously in the interstices, made possible by a marriage of convenience to an unloved girl and actuated for his part by *delicadeza*, by the desire to "be congenial, . . . to get everything decided and settled" (147). He is a capable and alertly intelligent young Filipino but skittish, and dying of inanition. His difficulties lie chiefly in the effecting of spontaneous transactions with reality and in the maintenance of sexual relationships. He drifts in the void created by a bad conscience towards a wife in name only ("What exactly *did* he owe her?") (5), enveloped,

116

moreover, by a sense of the falsity of his position as an interloper in the USA. The author is at pains to point out that he is doubly denatured, as a citizen and as a lover. For the United States has been haven but not home for Johnny, and a treacherous haven at that inasmuch as he finds himself at the mercy of an exploitative superior at work on laser research (a token in the text for the enlightenment in which he is seen to be wanting?). The novel, then, discovers him in a phase of exhaustion: remote from the controls of his life and painfully dislodged within it. He is the man for whom Andre Gide's fastidiously formulated saying seems to have been made to measure: "to free oneself is nothing; to live in freedom, that is the difficulty."

Wings of Stone takes the force of this negative distinction. By disciplined gradations, it accommodates the character of the hero to the central trope of the title, whose denotations are of still life and petrifaction. Johnny is shown, accordingly, to have assembled for himself a form of life which is safe and bounded and therefore quite inert, purged of prospects. It is, of course, a sanitized, apolitical existence, engineered to the principle of looking out for Number One. It acknowledges no imperative other than the short-term hedonism and careerist frenzy customary in the world left behind on the banks of the Charles River. So the crisis precipitated by his return to Manila and to his ageing father's house is seen to have to do with a moral and affective minimalism. At the same time, it is felt to have been long in the making. It gestates in a universe progressively eclipsed from within and from without, where a sense of desperation is struggling for coherence.

What, precisely, is Ty-Casper driving at, her eye firmly trained on the sordid vicissitudes of her country in the late 1970s and early 1980s? For an answer, it may be helpful to think of the novel as a gloss on the meaning, and on the sorry dislocation in the meaning, of the linked terms *pater, patria,* and *patrimony.* For this, unmistakably, is the etymology in which the book's imagination of things is couched. A minatory syllogism is on view throughout: the man who betrays his fatherland for a cushy berth overseas (though, as it happens, one nothing like as well-upholstered as he had hoped) is the man who will encounter formidable difficulty in communicating with his beloved parent—the same man, again, who is at a loss to identify, never mind fully to enter into, possession of the ancestral inheritance which the father is prepared to bequeath. The inheritance in question is revealed by stages in its subjective and objective aspects. Subjectively speaking, and as personified by Johnny's father, it is an affair of the heart, of moral

117

contract, of consistency of feeling; it appears to be composed of small unremarkable acts of daily attentiveness, of consideration, and of personal dignity. Speaking silence is its natural mode, affection for the dead (especially for Johnny's mother, whose funeral he could not bother to attend) its cardinal strength.

Indeed, it is not for nothing that the father's Tagalog Christian name is Magtanggol—one who defends. His defense is, first, of the memory of his wife, for whom the house has become both shrine and mausoleum, and second, of the chivvied and downtrodden in the neighboring *barangay* whose cause Dr. Manolo is quietly championing by proposing to erect on its site a clinic to service the inhabitants. The contrast formed is with his son, in whom exile and self-estrangement have conduced to the belief that "history was only someone's memory, never true" (3). Objectively speaking, the father's inheritance consists of a liberalism which has yet to be articulated into credo. It is by definition prearticulate, having little to do with doctrine or injunction and nothing at all with this or that party's political platform. It is the expression of a whole way of being, lived by a community for whom the social, in the last analysis, is not a theatre for fleeting gratifications of sexual, financial, or professional appetite, but a summons to contractual obligation and discharge of duty—to *utang na lo'ob*.

The inheritance from which Johnny Manolo is dissevered is, in other words, mainly a matter of instinct and experience, not of codified belief. For this reason, perhaps, it is exposed to threat and is vulnerable to erasure. At the very least, it is susceptible to important modification, by change for the worse in the manners of a class or thanks to a bedrock shift in a settlement segmented along fault lines of class. The inheritance, we see, is in the process of being nullified, prevented from being formed into legacy, by several people in the hero's immediate vicinity. There is Martin, Johnny's younger brother, a smooth executive with a glib tongue and a flair for appearances, his fingers in every commercial pie. He is the sort who takes corruption in stride as being justified on pragmatic grounds, "as long as you learn to grab your share" (34). There is Sylvia Mendez, a beautiful young thing (though actually not so young) with whom Johnny has, as he thinks, fallen in love. Her name has been put forward for the opposition list in elections impending for the National Batasan. But her loud misgivings about the state of her country are given the lie by her plutocratic excesses. She is, in fact, a member of that far-from-endangered species, the salon radical, flirting with *gauchiste* activism but inclined to populist sentimentality and apt to bolt at the first sign of trouble.

Above all, the inheritance is in process of being traduced by Johnny himself, discounting for the future and clinging to the conviction that "politics is not my game" (63). Force of habit has inclined him to a brittle insouciance when faced with demands for wholehearted involvement, earlier in sexual dalliance, latterly in the life of his adopted land, now in the political cockpit of his sundered homeland. Now this detachment is turned corrosively against him and proves to be ludicrously inadequate in dealing with "the poor people of Macario, Pete Alvarez, the rich cronies carting off millions in government funds to invest in foreign nest eggs" (116). An engulfing skepticism threatens, augmented by news of his brother's defection from his wife and children (lured by the charms of Sylvia Mendez's sister) and leading him to choose self-delusion as the best opportunity for self-fulfillment.

Ty-Casper is too perspicacious a novelist to wish on her characters a factitious resolution of difficulties or to organize for them a facile disabusing of illusions. There is to be an awakening on the part of Johnny Manolo, but it is not, in the first instance anyway, an awakening to any positives. It amounts, instead, to a grasp of the circumambient nature of the evil abroad in his country in general and to a registration of disease among the Makati bourgeoisie. He comes to, as it were, in a milieu where everything "seemed a kind of violation" (50). This is as it should be. Surrounded in the posh clubs his brother frequents by talk of "capital investment declines, . . . of economic stewardship which reduced business confidence because . . . foreigners were permitted to exploit the country in exchange for private deals," he feels at first that "this made no difference" (30). In so saying, he is convicted out of his own mouth of an innocence which is consequentially as culpable as almost everyone and everything in his environment. For one thing, he feels that the facts of the case are to be none of his concern; when thrust upon him, he remains wilfully immune to their significance. For another, he is given to excessive self-exculpation, in which the onus for actions taken or evaded is shuffled off and knowledge of any untoward consequences qualified out of the consciousness.

Wings of Stone, then, visits a young man in extremis and during a moment of collective disintegration. It takes a humane but, in the last resort, a dim view of his lugubrious melancholy and of his tendency to be mesmerized (but only mesmerized) by questions of duty and obligation. His education out of these propensities is—we are being encouraged to feel—long overdue. Once underway it is subversive of what can be fairly described as a curatorial husbanding of energies. Though it proceeds by fits and starts, it requires for its completion a transvaluation of values. In the sexual sphere there is supposed to be achieved in the company of Sylvia Mendez "an intimacy he had not felt with Rose Quarter," his pitied and pitiable American wife (7). (I say supposed, because Ty-Casper favors telling, not showing, and the inner progression of events is not always convincingly established.) More persuasively, his moral and emotional retreat from accidie takes for its catalyst the murder of Pete Alvarez, the opposition organizer, a killing in which Johnny suspects his brother of having had a hand. Pity replaces glacial contempt for Martin, the ultimate victim, who puts him in mind of the emblematic "blue jay fledgling he had found pushed out of its nest one rainy spring, . . . no longer able to hold its head upright . . . it claws tightly curled, feathers dull and rent" (85). Bestirred from indifference, he feels himself to be "implicated," the stimulus the slaughter in full public view of a priest at the hands of a *barangay* captain, whose henchmen, it transpires, have buried the corpse of Alvarez, the opposition activist, in the foundations of Dr. Manolo's new clinic.

   Wings of Stone bids farewell to its hero with a metaphoric flourish. Regarding him through the prism of the central simile, it leaves him on the point of release from indolence and selfishness into affective life. As a novel it succeeds by showing the character mobilized not for direct action but, more convincingly, for entry into a cognitive involvement with the destiny of the Philippines on the grim terrain of the present. We are left in no doubt that this destiny is now annexed to a personal fate. More: it is to be understood as a personal fate writ large. Another novelist might have seized with alacrity the windfall occasion for propaganda offered here and made a meal of it for hortatory purposes. Ty-Casper, to her credit, does not take the easy way out. She does not steer her hero towards the barricades and help him to mount them; no proletarian novel, this, partial though it may be to allegory. Instead, we see the glimmering forth of knowledge that enables acknowledgement, and which may—or then again may not—come to serve as the presentiment of action. Having been taken to task, an individual and a society are shown in readiness, and after much distress, to take charge of their own affairs, equipped, in distinct but related ways, to become not patient but agent of them. Whether the one or the other remains genuinely open to question. As befits a novel written to a formula of veracity and privileging conventions of openendedness, what is possible is not, for that very reason, probable. In the fiction, as indeed in fact, all bets on the future are off.

Ty-Casper's penultimate work inspects the progress of a single character through a manifold of difficulties, whose assimilation to the political is primarily a means of characterizing them. *Awaiting Trespass*, with which it forms a diptych, treats in like manner of psychic and political emergency.[15] Psychic emergency has, this time, a far more audacious root, a more sensational parallel, in the political fortunes of the Philippines. The national community is shown to be (as in fact it was, at the time of writing) at sixes and sevens with itself. Unambiguously, if a trifle mechanically, it is identified as the locus of individual disturbance. Family (together with its assorted hangers-on) and the state are in this novel the cynosure, never lost to sight. And what a family it is. There is great-aunt Maria Esperanza, forever boasting of "serving better *pancit molo* than they do in Iloilo. And [her] stuffed *moron* should be served to the Holy Father when he comes in February" (7). A *monstre sacrée*, she is conscientious but devoid of conscience, thus earning her place in the novel's gallery of grotesques and far from alone in seeing and hearing no evil—dismissing for instance as "blasphemy" talk of the Westinghouse nuclear plant in construction on requisitioned barrio land in Bataan. There is Sol, one of the president's cronies, whom one has only to "tell . . . what you need and he'll get it for you. Name the park in front of your church after Imelda and you will get a cathedral" (62). There is schemer and fixer Aurelio Gil, hot for subsidizing the erection of a perimeter fence to obscure from the eyes of the papal motorcade the slums along its route, and who "never charged for his ministrations—'thank you's were mostly what he got" (104).

The occasion for their disobliging scrutiny is the wake of Don Severino Gil, sexual athlete, loyal friend, everybody's rich uncle, epitome of *compadrinazgo*, the absent center of the story, vengefully and contradictorily present in the mourners' midst. The circumstance of his death is the proverbial mystery enshrouded in an enigma: his coffin has been sealed, prompting discomfiting questions on the part of his relations, obsessed to a man (and woman) with keeping up appearances at any cost. Was he, when alive, jealous of his privacy after death and anxious to cock a snook at a society that abetted his indulgences? Or is the old devil still alive but in hiding? Sensibilities are outraged when the catafalque, prised apart, discloses a brutally assaulted corpse.

121

Yet the "trespass" of the title which we are being asked to credit refers not only to the impious mutilation of a corpse. By imaginative projection, it advertises the wholesale violation of the polis. Dead, Don Severino is the synecdoche for the abused collectivity, his manhandled body the emblem of encroachments upon personal liberties licensed by the regime, symbol of the government-driven terrorism which is the chief manifestation of martial law. It is the values he and his kind live by, and the effect these have wrought, which are also being called into question by the device of part standing for whole. As before, a connection is being proposed, and as before more or less subtly worked, between the components of the cant phrase "body politic"; the fiction is busy taking a long hard look at the semantics of both words.

At the center of the narrative there is made to stand—a little unsteady on her pins—Telly, favorite niece of Don Severino. She is an Americanized Filipina, shipwrecked by mental trouble and by a botched suicide and weighed down in the upshot with a hypertrophied capacity for reflection. At the center of the narrative is installed also Don Severino's son Sevi, a doubting padre who is hard put to respond to others' torments in proportion as he registers them with immobilizing intensity. Son and niece share a plight, which in turn is clearly metonymic of a greater difficulty. Each is prone to anguished retrospection and to much wringing of hands for sins of omission and commission. As well, Sevi is exercised by suspicions of his own illegitimacy, which, confided through authorial voice-over, take on sinister overtones:

> He is wary of confrontation, having had enough with his father and with himself. Afraid of his anger, of breaking apart because of the hurt that has lived inside him, he cannot face the doubt that he is Don Severino's son, because he cannot reconcile being that son and looking up at the windows of that house, at which his father sometimes appeared, called for him to come up and receive a coin. If he is the heir, then he must be his son; but if he is the son why did he live in the hut. (62)

It is an arresting passage in at least two ways. First, it posits a predicament with obvious metaphoric resonance, the disturbance in the bond of father and son serving as analogue for disturbed, because humiliatingly stratified, relations in the New Society. Second, it is inflected towards schism and insult, phenomena here meant to be grasped by the reader, I think, at the level of feeling and idea. The

122

feeling, as experienced by one of the two main characters in the book ("If he is the heir, then he must be the son; but if he is the son, why did he live in the hut?"), is so imperfectly under control as to be susceptible, under further stress, to detonation. The idea is of a stifled seditiousness rising explosively to the surface, a volcanic resentment seeking any outlet to hand. These things lie at the heart of the novel's recension of the moment of Marcos; they are there by transparent intention. So much is apparent from the author's prefatory note, to the effect that "the agonies in this novel are those of nation and family, the result of usurpations that have turned Filipinos into exiles in their own country."

Father Sevi is the avatar of such internal emigrés. He is on the periphery of a crazily ordered world, where it is the rich who are the oppressed (if their gossip round the barbecue, relayed by free indirect speech, is anything to go by) "because their profits are down and someone else who had nothing on his back before Martial Law was declared now buys P900 shirts at Rustan and rides in a Mercedes or Cadillac Seville" (168). His cousins stalk the corridors of the (ostensibly) grieving household, twittering on "about their condos, export zone regulations, weekends in European cities" (66). His revulsion from this spectacle deepening, it is as much as Sevi can do to propose to turn the house into a hospice for the terminally ill. His managing aunt, the preposterous Maria Esperanza, grasping, egotistical, emptily chattering, will have none of it. Nor will Sandoval, a friend of the family perennially on the take, who extenuates official depravity on the doubtful rationale that Malacañang does not know and even if it does its chief occupant is "too busy with matters of policy and grave concern to us all" (168). In intercourse with such vicious types, Sevi is meant to be seen as having sustained mortal damage as it were to the internal organs, most especially to the faculties responsible for judgement and friendship. His talent for relationship, constrained at the best of times by ecclesiastical ordinance, has now been put into suspension; standing before his uncle's bier he "feels nothing." So in this novel, too, psychology is morbid. But the dynamic that drives psychology, the mainspring of the work's representation of personal relations, is not politics in the abstract but the virulent, grubby politics of the cacique variety. Watching attorney Sandoval congratulate himself on having practiced what he preaches ("you have to learn to take care of yourself. No one else will do it for you"), Sevi senses the iron entering his soul (120). Faced with cant, hypocrisy, vaulting ambition, bureaucratic pigheadedness, plain inefficiency, what is a good man and a patriot to do?

So, chafing at his irrelevance and quietism, he has to contend with surreal conformism and with the deeply insecure complacency of the Gil clan. As a man of the cloth, he is, for them, at best a ghost at the feast. At worst, he is a colossal nuisance, since, though "nothing is going right in the country—they are prosperous—They see the Pope's coming in terms of minor European aristocracy—who help the administration inaugurate resorts" and "speak of the poor as if they are diseased private parts that have to be excised" (123). Father Sevi's self-castrating surrender to this universe of discourse takes the form of a cynicism with sensational equivalents in the public sphere. His failure of nerve bears testimony to larger failures of command and confidence: violence in street and in Ayala Avenue boardroom is distantly echoed in and—by a reticulated chain of cause and effect—related to the violence of one man's feelings. It is replicated in the discord and embittered competitiveness of his family, whose members vie with one another in cattiness and in conspicuous consumption:

> Sevi tries to pray, while around him people continue to talk. Their words burst and ricochet, travel like gunfire. . . . Here are relatives from Tarlac, from Bicol and Antique; from all the provinces to which the Gils have scattered, intermarried and returned; each one speaking in the accent and pattern of his region, totally appealing and charming in diversity which in point of sound makes of the wake something of a high festival with the flowers entirely covering the casket and reaching up to the altar like medallions. In this family, he thinks, one has to be beautiful, or rich, or close to those in power, . . . in order to be admired. (79)

Sevi, it is disappointing to find, is as humorless a character as is his creator in the guise of implied author. (There are no really good jokes in this novel.) But allowances might just possibly be made both for the sentiments to which he gives vent and for their exacerbated delivery ("totally appealing and charming"), if the accusative nature of the text is taken into account. The overheated goings-on meditated through this introspection have much to answer for. Lubricity, cupidity, pique, brute indifference, brutal calculation—all the vices of a metropolitan oligarchy turned in upon itself—get a showing in the gossip and noises ricocheting

124

round the funeral obsequies. All are projected through Sevi's appalled and becalmed observation from the sidelines.

Observation, notice, is in stereoscopy here. Its burden is distributed equally between hero and heroine. Telly's unsparing arraignment is of an action which, confined to one day in one house, severely observes the unities. Her understanding of the dismal nexus of microcosm and macrocosm is antiphonal to Sevi's anguished ruminations. Nonetheless, there is an elective affinity. Her life, like his, is an incommunicado battle for survival; like him, she inhabits the curious calm that comes from keeping emotions in cold storage. Shortly before the inception of the plot, Telly had been prostrated by a nervous breakdown, product of the discovery of her former husband's philandering, her world having in consequence been turned upside down. That Quiel's faithlessness should then be gleefully represented to her by her kin as proof, if proof were needed, of manliness, and thus as a sort of grace abounding, is entirely in keeping with the novel's understanding of patriarchal values in a community historically bound by the prerogative of the male and by his sexual priority. It illustrates, too, what happens when the moral capital of a governing class has been expended; the ambience of the Manila bourgeoisie under Marcos, or at any rate of one significant subsection of it, is an unfolding drama of valuelessness where "words do not mean anything any more, . . . the government calling its dictatorship a 'revolution from the top'" and where everything might easily be something else (99). It is within such a polity, within this ambience, the novel dramatically shows, that discriminations are to be made under circumstances where the social categories are shifting (when they are not arbitrary or nonexistent) in accordance with the vagaries of situation, caste, or time.

Time most especially: collective historical time, domain of political shame and of the well-merited comeuppance; and solitary, private time, realm of mortified conscience. Both dimensions of time unite in the lacerated mind at the center of the novel. Standing along in the azotea, listening to the voices in the hall, she thinks of how in the New Society,

> We will be like the rest of the world, which knows nothing about us because we, too, will know nothing about ourselves: we cannot remember what we are, what we wanted to be, we will accept whatever happens to us, . . . like streets that cease to be

landmarks after their names have been changed repeatedly. (111-12)

This is the point at which the text contrives to be of signal interest. We are being encouraged to acquaint ourselves in some depth with a sensitive scion of the Manila business and propertied classes caught in a web of private hurts and erotic jealousies. But the manner in which she is so caught, and her way of attempting an extrication, sets up stronger resonances without quite telescoping story into parable. Symbolically and emotionally, it makes available for consideration the enmeshment of an entire country in the matrix of deceit overseen by Ferdinand and Imelda Marcos. By the same token we are being invited to adjudicate the qualified success—imminent for the heroine, proleptic for the Republic—of the attempted disengagement. I call the success qualified, on account of the ambiguous nature of the heroine's private life. This life, intensely reflective and richly imagistic, is being presented serially as a drawback and as a resource. A drawback at first inasmuch as it shores up a sterile self-regard, a pusillanimous inclination to cut one's losses, to venture nothing in the belief that "the important thing she must keep in mind is that she must not love" (99). A resource, at last, because empowering analysis. At the end Telly is seen to be in a state of taut anticipation, in which the readiness is all: released through understanding from the shell of herself into a dedication to her own recovery, which is to be a recovery not only of herself. A regeneration in time to come is on the agenda, and there is already in operation a retrieval of time past through memory, and on behalf of the dead, the dying, and the as yet unborn:

> She thinks she will write after all about the family, gather them together; . . . she will write it as a tale of what happens when men mutilate justice in their own country. It will be about her uncle, too; it will be for him. In remembrance . . . she will let the word in her mind out into the world. . . . She has a choice . . . with breathtaking clarity she is seeing him through what others have remembered of him during the wake . . . the sky is no longer dark to her; it looks like an empty tree that is beginning to fill with new life, brightening with leaves and promises in an unenclosed garden. (177)

Ty-Casper subtitles her novel a *pasion*. However, I do not think she means it to be read as a straightforward imitation, in the (European) form of the novel, of the indigenous Tagalog vernacular genre so brilliantly investigated by Reynaldo Ileto. Nor is propagation of a melioristic outlook the object of the exercise, albeit that Tagalog *pasyon* exhibits millenarian tendencies redolent of its origins in Christian liturgy. The point to make is that *pasyon* is not so much mimed here as intertextually quoted.

In other words, it is realized in the fabric of the narrative as a conceit, a temperamental bias. It sponsors a disposition of storytelling in which a redemptive transformation is sensed by readers slowly to have taken place, fruit of the sustained striving of a beleaguered and deprived consciousness. The note of didactic strenuousness sounded toward the end is to be judged a lapse only on an assessment of the novel as an Anglo-American exemplar of the genre, only if it is seen as intended for consumption by a Western readership conditioned to place such resolutions under embargo on grounds of sentimentality and tendentiousness. If the action is observed, as I think we are asked to observe it, through the optic of *pasyon*, then a conventionally unsuccessful exemplar of The Novel is what this novel is most decidedly *not*. It is not simply that it is unafraid of sentiment, particularly where sentiment is geared to the idea of resurgence, but that it is not truly didactic. For it does not teach, it prophesies.

So the sense of an ending in *Awaiting Trespass* is formally consistent with resolutions permitted in European realisms, in which the pathos of a trapped passivity is exchanged, often at tragic cost, for the operations of a directed individual will. But the *values* associated with such metamorphosis in this novel are fundamentally different, essentially local. Setting and action, above all the moral-political construction to be placed upon action, are autochthonously Southeast Asian. Sense and sensibility, too, are indigenous and are to be read against the grain of impositions foisted on them. It is part of the novel's way to make us see and feel that all these elements—setting, action, the sense they make and the sensibility they embody—could only have been generated from within the particular context of the archipelago and from within the historical conjuncture which was to lead, two years after the novel's publication, to Corazon Aquino's accession to office, and out of no other. Its author is not clairvoyant; she has no need to be, she simply sees straight ahead.

I have suggested that Ty-Casper's novels are deficient in certain respects and that these deficiencies, encoded into the texture of her prose, make a sitting duck for criticism both literary and cultural. To this might be added a tendency to attitudinize, natural to fictions which have designs upon their readers. But then a contingent overearnestness, of tone and of speech, is not exactly in short supply in Rizal's novels either.

Yet nobody is disposed to dismiss *them* out of hand. The flaws in both cases are specific to any colonial or neocolonial literature of protest, and evince its more or less uneasy relationship with the tradition of the former metropolis. The difference, in degree and in kind, will be obvious. So is the similarity, which lies in the fact that the failings can be condoned readily for the sake of the truths which ring through, in this case truths not so readily available within the mainstream of prose fiction in English in the Philippines since the 1970s. What is admirable about these novels of Manila under the dictator is the ability of their creator, writing at her best, to sum up with great density of specification the material and moral life of a subsociety, part of a nation moving steadily towards its contention, while at the same time cathartically evoking pity and horror for its members. She writes tendentiously, but at times shrewdly and absorbingly, dramatizing what Gramsci calls "an interregnum," the moment when, as "the old is dying and the new cannot be born . . . there arises a great diversity of morbid symptoms." In a Philippine context, the interregnum is fixed with dreadful accuracy, the symptoms here discovered, as is the wherewithal, in the form of a many-sided accession of self-confidence, required to dispel the disease which is the cause.

NOTES

1. A. D. Nuttall, *A New Mimesis* (London: Methuen, 1983), vii-viii.

2. An invidious example is on offer in Tineke Hellwig and Marijke J. Klokke, "Focalization and Theme: Their Interaction in *Orang-Orang Bloomington*," *Bijdragen tot de-Taal-, Land-, en Volkenkunde* 41/4 (1985): 423-40.

3. The nomenclature is Frank Kermode's, as quoted in General Graff, *Literature Against Itself: Literary Ideas and Modern Society* (Chicago: University of Chicago Press, 1979), 186.

4. The most spirited and almost certainly the best informed apologia for realism, after Nuttall's *A New Mimesis*, is Raymond Tallis, *In Defence of Realism* (London: Edward Arnold, 1988), to which the discussion below is in debt.

5. See Barbara Harlow, *Resistance Literature* (London: Methuen, 1987), a book as stimulating as it is badly written. The assumption forms the basis of Jack Yeager's *The Vietnamese Novel in French: A Literary Response to Colonialism* (Hanover, N.H.: University Press of New England, 1987).

6. This is the position taken by Catherine Belsey in her lucid and succinct account of some of the arguments against realism, *Critical Practice* (London: Methuen, 1980), and by Michael Boyd in his *The Reflexive Novel: Fiction as Critique* (Lewisburg: Bucknell University Press, 1983).

7. See his "Thesis on the Philosophy of History," in Walter Benjamin, *Illuminations*, trans. Hannah Arendt (London: Fontana, 1973).

8. See her important contribution "The Asian Theatre of Communion: A Look at Contemporary Philippine Theatre," in *Change and Continuity in Southeast Asia*, ed. Roger A. Long and Damaris A. Kirschhofer, Centre for Asian and Pacific Studies, Southeast Asia Paper No. 23 (Manoa: University of Hawaii, 1982), 69-83.

9. On this tradition of Philippines fiction, see Milagros C. Guerrero, "Proletarian Consciousness in Philippine Literature, 1930-70," in *The Writer and Society in Asia*, ed. Wang Gungwu, M. Guerrero, D. Marr (Canberra: Australian National University Press, 1977), 67-76.

10. Enunciated in Jean-Paul Sartre's *What is Literature?* trans. B. Frechtman (New York: Philosophical Library, 1949).

11. For an explanation of EDSA see p. 44, n. 56.

12. The fidelity to fact of the novel both in its many references passim to contemporary events and in respect of its unquantifiable but unmistakable period "feel," can be gauged by consulting, for example, articles by Jeffrey Race, "Whither the Philippines?" Institute of Current World Affairs, 30 November 1975; Belinda Aquino, "The Philippines Under Marcos," *Current History* 18/474 (1982): 160-63; and Robert Shaplen,

"Letter from Manila," *New Yorker* (26 March 1979): 56-101. See also John Bresnan (ed.), *Crisis in the Philippines: The Marcos Era and Beyond* (Princeton: Princeton University Press, 1986). What the novelist has imagined and recreated has received scholarly attestation by Rober Stauffer in "The Philippines Political Economy: (Dependent) State Capitalism in the Corporatist Mode," in *Southeast Asia: Essays in the Political Economy of Structural Change*, ed. Richard Higgott and Richard Robison (London: Routledge & Kegan Paul, 1985), 241-65.

13. Linda Ty-Casper, *Wings of Stone* (London: Readers International, 1986). All page numbers cited below refer to this text. The temporal chronology of the two novels discussed below is not in the order of their dates of publication. Historical chronology has determined the sequence in which the works are discussed.

14. Linda Ty-Casper, *Awaiting Trespass: A Pasion*, (London: Readers International, 1985). All page numbers cited below refer to this text.

15. Antonio Gramsci, "State and Civil Society," in *Selections from the Prison Notebooks of Antonio Gramsci*, ed. and trans. Quintin Hoare and Geoffrey Nowell Smith (London: Lawrence and Wishart, 1971) 276.

5

BOREDOM IN BATAVIA: A CATALOGUE
OF BOOKS IN 1898

H. M. J. Maier

Albrecht & Co: a book and print store opposite the Landraad, downtown Batavia, at the end of the nineteenth century.[1] Business was good. In 1898 the firm published yet another free catalogue, a list of books in stock and samples of the various printing techniques it was capable of handling.

Eighteen ninety-eight was an eventful year in the history of the Dutch East Indies, as full of events as any year, some casting their shadow forward, others confirming processes set in motion in previous years. In retrospect, only the coronation of the young Wilhelmina as the new queen of the Dutch empire—the lavish ceremony in Amsterdam was supplemented by all sorts of festivities both in the motherland and the colonies—may be regarded as a memorable event that stands by itself; it would be difficult to name anything else that was to play as strongly upon people's imagination that year. At all events the minds of the Dutch Indies administrators were almost set to accept the Ethical Policy. More and more full-blooded Dutch arrived in the Indies to begin a new life. Inhabitants of Chinese descent in the colony showed an increasing curiosity for the land of their ancestors. The first native journalist-to-be, Tirto Adisoerjo, allegedly sat musing over the portrait of his queen that hung on the wall of his room. The journalist-novelist P. A. Daum died during a visit to the motherland.

In all, Albrecht's catalogue of 1898 offered some 750 titles for sale; most of these were in Malay, but books in Javanese, Sundanese, Minangkabau, and Dutch also were available in the store. The books were of all sorts, from collections of tales to poems, from horoscopes to treatises on religion and law books, from cookbooks to novels, from dictionaries to books on etiquette. Some three years later business was still good enough to publish another catalogue, a less extensive one this time, mainly covering the Malay titles and serving perhaps as an illustration that Malay books were the ones best appreciated by the group of literates Albrecht had managed to reach. The titles offered this time were essentially the same as those in the previous catalogue, with only a few additions. Could this mean that business was not going well after all? Precisely the same phrases of commendation were used, exactly the same prices charged—repetitions which read like remarkable offenses against the rules of capitalism which slowly were invading life in Batavia.

Albrecht & Co not only sold books, it published and printed them as well. A considerable number of the books listed in the catalogues were the company's own products and were among the ones elaborately praised. The catalogue's inclusion of models of various printing techniques shows that the firm produced more than just books; samples of ornamented wrapping paper and fine letterheads which clients could use to impress colleagues and friends suggest that the firm covered a considerably wider terrain of activities.

Albrecht was bookstore and printing plant, a combination which was certainly not unique in the Dutch Indies in those days. The company had to cope with stiff competition in Batavia. M. H. Van Dorp and G. Kolff deserve mention; both primarily served a public which spoke and read Dutch. Then there were companies like Goa Hong & Co, Tjoe Toei Jang, Yap Goan Ho, and Tjong Eng Lok which apparently reached for the same public as did Albrecht: Eurasians, Chinese, natives.

Selling stationary was another activity of Albrecht's. Pens and paper served very well to make a profit, as did the big picture of Queen Wilhelmina, printed in commemoration of her coronation and an object of admiration alike among government officials and native intellectuals. The 1898 catalogue must have given the clientele a good impression indeed of what was for sale opposite the Landraad.

Companies like Albrecht had one thing in common: they all operated within a socioeconomic system which was increasingly ruled by the power of money and profit. These were entrepreneurs in culture, so to say; selecting their products on the basis of possible commercial value rather than idealistic considerations, they sold them wherever they could. That is why the books they published could be found not only in their own bookstore and in those of their competitors beside paper and pens, but also in emporiums next to towels, rattles, gloves, umbrellas, and cigars.[2]

Good management implied that the commercial risks were to be spread. Albrecht also published a newspaper, *Pemberita Betawi*. It had fifteen hundred subscriptions, "more than any other Malay newspaper," its editor, Wiggers, proudly claimed in the *Almanak Priaji* of 1898. No doubt it was an important source of revenue. The publication of this *Almanak* itself was, by the way, yet another highly successful enterprise of Albrecht's as was its series of Malay translations of the laws and regulations which the government fabricated in growing numbers in its efforts to keep society under control. Albrecht was a very active company, in short, with a great diversification of products. The risks involved in publishing printed materials in Batavia in the last decades of the nineteenth century certainly should not be underestimated. Technical and logistic problems initially were many and varied. In order to overcome the inevitable growing pains any newly introduced product would experience, entrepreneurs needed considerable starting capital.

Publishing was a gamble for yet another reason in those years. The population of Batavia, and of the Dutch Indies as a whole, was going through a period of considerable hardship because of economic problems. Books certainly formed no part of the primary necessities of life, and the fact that the economic crisis did not prevent cultural entrepreneurs from publishing a steadily growing number of texts alone may serve as an indication of a growing demand for reading materials. To put it in different terms, in spite of all sorts of problems, the literate public in the metropolis of the Indies continued to grow.

In the expanding Dutch sphere of influence, Batavia had always been a rather unusual place, different from anywhere else. Ever since its foundation in 1619 it had played a central role in administration and trade and had become in consequence a gathering place for representatives of all sorts of ethnic groups, for people of all walks of life. Even though there was a strong tendency to live with other members of one's ethnic background, a person could not avoid meeting representatives of other nations and had to come to term with them, if only for the sake of survival. More than any other urban center in the archipelago, Batavia had taken on the traits of a plural society, in which extremes were mitigated and assimilation took place within the social hierarchy. There were Europeans and Chinese with a fluent command of the Malay and Javanese languages who immersed themselves in local culture, some of them disappearing in the *kampoeng* (native residential area) to live with their beloved in the native way. European masters behaved like native rulers and had themselves protected by yellow umbrellas, the sign of royalty. European women used native herbs and preferred rice to potatoes. Natives in their turn tried to learn Dutch, wore glasses, smoked cigars, started to read newspapers and almanacs, and attended performances of the Chinese opera.

In this interaction of cultures and languages, the tools of reception and prediction of another person's thought and conduct had to be rich and elastic, shock-proof, as Moretti calls it in his stimulating discussion of the urban personality.[3] By way of more or less intensive contacts with representatives of other nations and classes, new rituals and habits were created and vistas opened up to new discourses and ideas. To put it in more technical terms, new signifying practices emerged, which had to find a place within discursive forces already operating. In this process, a new configuration of rules and regulations rose slowly but steadily alongside those which were already available. Various ethnic groups clung to traditions more or less consciously in order to retain their cultural identity in an uneasy world of diversity and extremes. Batavian society had assumed the contours of a mestizo-culture, a complex of values, customs, and regulations which were shared and appreciated by people of all races and classes, regardless of distinctions in legal status, irrespective of differences in social position in the colonial hierarchy, regardless of distinctions in ethnic background.

In the closing decades of the nineteenth century these develop-ments were accelerated by a rather sudden concatenation of elements and events: printing techniques were beginning to be used on a wider scale, railway networks were being laid out over Java, educational facilities were expanded, and the economic system underwent enormous changes following the privatization of plantation ownership in the seventies. Dutch immigrants began to arrive in growing numbers and the Dutch Indies army became emphatically present. Altogether an enormous energy was set loose.

This energy found its outlet in one language in particular: Malay. For centuries, Malay had been the predominant language in the contacts among members of the various ethnic groups in the archipelago. Experiences and ideas were exchanged by way of Malay; because of this, Malay had always been the language associated with novelty and innovation. It comes as no surprise to find that in an urban area such as Batavia, Malay was also the language par excellence in which new signifying practices were explored; here lived together a great variety of people who were forced to accept one another. Forms of Malay pidgin had developed which had gradually turned into creoles for those who had been living in the town for generations. In the wake of this process, Malay also had become the language of which most Dutch administrators made use in their day-to-day business at the local level.

Malay Language Texts

The sort of Malay in use in Batavia not only differed from the Malay in use in other urban centers such as Menado, Makassar and Palembang, it also differed from the various forms of Malay that were used in the heartland of the Malay nation: the east coast of Sumatra, Riau, and the Peninsula. The influences of Chinese, Javanese, Sundanese, and those of Balinese, Portuguese, and Dutch, had made it a special variety, an instrument primarily of conversation, shaping itself to practical needs, tending to give priority to the signified over the signifier so as to create for those who used it the order and sequence needed to keep afloat. Although within the town itself differences may have been considerable owing to its division in to numerous kampoengs and neighborhoods, developments seemed to indicate that this creole kind of Malay was sufficiently strong so as to serve as an integrative force of some importance.

During the last decade of the nineteenth century, at the time Albrecht's catalogues appeared, the Malay textual system in Batavia had a configuration that was radically different from the Malay culture that had been supported for so long by Malay nobility and commoner in Penyengat and Alor Setar, in Jambi and Kota Bahru. In certain sections of the metropolis, too, *hikayat* (Malay tales in prose) and *sjair* (four-line rhyming verses), manifestations of the heritage, were still being sung and recited in the very way they were done in the Malay heartland, and Malay *kitab* (works on Islamic topics in Malay or Arabic) still found an avid appeal in certain circles. Yet the cohabitation of so many ethnicities had led to a diversification and enrichment of Malay discursive forces, giving rise to all sorts of elements inconceivable and untenable in such places as Penyengat or Alor Setar.

Even in a place such as Batavia, the strongly auditive and commemorative cultures which the various ethnic units supported tended to regard a text as part of a whole and thus as authoritative; each of them had for long managed to retain its own distinctly communal experience, its *Erfahrung* as it is called by Benjamin: "experience is indeed a matter of tradition, in collective existence as well as private life. It is less the product of facts firmly anchored in memory than of a convergence in memory of accumulated and frequently unconscious data."[4] In the course of time, however, it became increasingly difficult for these language units to let things develop within their own cultural framework; each of these ethnicities was subjected constantly to pressures from all sides and of all sorts, pressures in which Malay played a predominant role.

The dispossession of the communal spirit, and the concurrent loss of memory, had started among those who enjoyed the privilege of some formal education and those who sustained extensive trading links. Here, information in Malay was substituted for traditional knowledge in the "traditional" language, and isolation and uneasiness were taking the place of a feeling of belonging.

No doubt, the Malay textual system was radically reshaped by the introduction of a great variety of novelties. Yet it would be incorrect to describe developments around 1900 in terms of a "great divide": the heritage did not disappear all of a sudden but rather was pushed gradually to the margin by pressures exerted by the new structure of feeling. It was to continue its life up to the present day, albeit received in different forms not only in Batavia but in Leiden and Paris as well. Radical breaks seldom occur in a textual system, not even in one so complicated as the Malay, in which so many non-Malays always had been active, constantly introducing novelties and adding new forms. The introduction of Arabic script in the thirteenth century had not resulted in a radical disappearance of oral traditions. The tentative use of print and of another script at the beginning of the nineteenth century had not led to a radical demise of manuscript authority. Similarly, the sudden expansion of the number of people writing and reading in Malay, resulting from the spread of printed materials and education facilities at the end of the nineteenth century, was not to silence Malay work up to then which had been preserved and transmitted, even though pressures may never have been stronger.

Newspapers and almanacs, pamphlets and catalogues, translations and adaptations of Western and Chinese works appeared in Malay. These texts relied upon the dynamics of supply and demand rather than the instructions of patrons and community leaders and were distributed through commercial channels rather than because of aristocratic or religious benevolence. Concepts and events presented in this newly begun era of mechanical reproduction were no longer to affect a person's inner life as they had done in the time of participatory production; fragmentation and discontinuity were substituted for the spirit of community, opening up modes of knowledge which were to lead to that blurred dichotomization between referentiality and fiction.

> Man's inner concerns do not have their issueless private character by nature. They do so only when he is increasingly unable to assimilate the data of the world around him by way of experience. Newspapers constitute one of the many evidences of such an inability. If it were the intention of the press to have the reader assimilate the information it supplies as part of his own experience, it would not achieve its purpose. But its intention is just the opposite, and it is achieved: to isolate what happens from the realm in which it could affect the experience of the reader. The principles of journalistic information (freshness of the news, brevity, comprehensibility, and above all, lack of connection between the individual news items) contribute as much to this as does the make-up of the pages and paper's style. Another reason for this isolation of information from experience is that the former does not enter "tradition."[5]

Newspapers that is, those "one-day best-sellers of ephemeral popularity."[6] More than anything else, newspapers were the instruments that initiated a shift in Malay textual activities in Batavia: a commodity, a discursive force, a source of information which did not need to be assimilated actively by its public. *Pemberita Betawi* and *Bintang Betawi* passed over in silence the knowledge that had for so long been transmitted through tradition, stripping authoritative texts of their prestige, detaching their public from a communal life which had kept the various ethnic communities relatively separated for so long. By crossing the strict ethnic boundaries newspapers became manifestations and harbingers of the newly imagined community which was taking shape by way of Malay.

Newspapers could be seen as an emblem of the discontinuity in the Malay textual system, as initiated through the new printing culture of Batavia. They were fragmentary both in content (items of variable informative content were linked together at random) and form (various genres [advertisements, poems, reports, and government statements] were arbitrarily brought together, in spite of their differences in style, diction, and vocabulary). Here no face-to-face contact and participatory rituals but advertisements of invisible companies, statements about faraway facts, articles by unknown editors, and contributions from anonymous authors—disparate chunks of amusement and information which were isolated from the realm in which they could affects its public's experience, and which did not therefore need to be memorized, suggesting a kind of stability inconceivable in the mainly oral communications preceding it.

It was not only the *Pemberita Betawi* which gave expression to the new structure of feeling spreading through Batavia; the same might be said of the books of laws and rules in the Malay language which had begun to be published in the nineties. They, too, overturned existing ethnic hierarchies in their attempts to silence oral gossip and unwritten *adat* (traditional law) rules. They, too, evoked a new sort of stability and order. From now on, political and cultural manipulation was indeed to be continued on another level. The Dutch were to make their presence emphatically felt, and commercial thinking was a new phenomenon.

Malay Language Poetry and Prose

The same structure of feeling expressed itself in the books of prose and poetry in Malay which began to appear in Batavia. Each text might be seen as an individual concretization of tradition, restating the conventions of the tradition, reformulating its formulas, rules and regulations, commenting upon the hierarchy of the discursive forces which operate within it and without. Considered historically, there are periods in every language community when tradition is stronger than the individual text: the latter professes, implicitly or explicitly, allegiance to the rules in which it claims to operate, thus aiming at the maintenance of traditional authority. That is how Malay tradition, with its strongly auditive and participatory character, came to develop a distinct set of regulations: works were transmitted anonymously; there were frequent references to earlier narrators of texts, and to stories of old; and the authority of God's Word was confirmed again and again by means of a rather limited set of linguistic devices. All of these features converged in Malay "memory" and preserved the Erfahrung of those who felt they belonged to the Malay world.

Where a textual system is concerned, however, there are also periods when authors try to escape from the rules and regulations imposed upon them by tradition. If they succeed in these efforts, discursive forces begin to undermine authority which is consequentially no longer able to keep them under control. That is what happened in Batavia in the period during which Albrecht & Co published its catalogues, its newspaper, its almanacs, its law books.

As with any cautious government, Dutch authorities kept a careful eye trained on cultural developments in Batavia, the better to ensure that nothing could take them by surprise. In the course of the nineteenth century they had become increasingly aware of the importance of Malay for the effective maintenance of their administration; already in the early 1860s competitions were organized for the writing of textbooks which could be used in schools, another source of growing care and worry. The aggressive criticism which flared up over these books may have been disturbing to some people's peace of mind. Far more disconcerting, however, was the growing corpus of printed materials which appeared and which lay beyond the government's direct control. Authorities started to feel concerned and driven by that strange mixture of sentiments so characteristic of every colonial government: sheer curiosity, desire to interfere in the name of progress, fear of losing control. Heated debates arose among administrators, missionaries, and scholars in Batavia: what is the correct Malay? Which species of Malay should be taught in school? Which script used? Which spelling taken for a standard? In which variety of Malay should textbooks be composed?

For the Dutch East Indies government, one thing was beyond question: the language should be domesticated. Equally self-evident was the necessity that the standard Malay-to-be should not be the Malay heard in the streets and alleys of Batavia. Unable to appreciate the distinct richness of pidgin and creole varieties and the cultures they sustained, the Dutch were apt to describe Batavian Malay as "low Malay," "gibberish Malay," "incorrect Malay," a hybrid, impure variety beyond control, in short, and that is a prospect that any colonial power should loathe—was there not the possibility that order and stability would be shaken? They preferred to look at what was assumed to be the cradle of Malay culture, the Riau archipelago. There, in almost everyone's view, the "original" Malay was spoken and the "real" Malay was written. There, respected scholars like Klinkert and von de Wall had been sent to collect manuscripts and other materials which they had subsequently used as the basis of their solid and admirable dictionaries, essential if authorities wanted to establish a standard. Back to the roots, to purity, to origins. From a purely political perspective, it was not such a bad idea to start from a place so far away. Sheer distance could be basis for creating the authority for an official language policy in Batavia.

The first step to be taken was to substantiate the notion of "high Malay," as it was called, a standard Malay, a correct Malay. Grammars were written, spelling lists composed, discussions held about all sorts of linguistic problems, both in Holland and in the Indies, usually without regard for those who used Malay from day to day.[7] Rather than conscientiously collect and study the printed books and pamphlets distributed in Batavia, Dutch literary scholars focussed their attention on the heritage. This attention found a glorious climax in van Ronkel's *Catalogue der Maleische handschriften in het Museum van het Bataviaasch Genootschap van Kunsten en Wetenschappen*. The available elements of the heritage were organized neatly around solid catchwords such as *verhalen* (stories), *Mohammedaansche legenden* (Muhammadan legends), *geschiedenis* (history), and *Inlandsche wet en adat* (native law and adat). With its seemingly precise descriptions, written in a Dutch voice preserving a soothing balance between praise and derogation, the book breathes a feeling of control: everything is knowledgeable, this is what Malay written heritage is all about, and this is the basis on which developments of language and literatures should be measured and continued.[8]

Malay Language Textbooks

Dutch language politics were most directly concretized in the form of the textbooks which were published and distributed in growing numbers by the Landsdrukkerij in Weltevreden, not far from Batavia, so as to provide schools with reading materials acceptable to the Dutch East Indies government and which would serve as the standard for those natives who were to take up roles in the bureaucracy. The Landsdrukkerij published catalogues similar in nature to those of Albrecht & Co; the *Daftar dari Goedang Kitab Goebernemen di Weltevreden* appeared around the turn of the century as regularly as those of its competitors on the free market. What is most striking at first glance about the *Daftar* of 1898 is that it opens with a list of Malay titles although their number is not as large as the number of the Javanese and even Sundanese titles available. The language used in this catalogue, as well as the language of the majority of the Malay books recommended, is intriguing: a form of language standing midway between the Malay of Riau and that of Batavia. An artificial language, in short, alien, new to everyone in the Indies except perhaps the Dutch themselves. No matter how artificial, here was another discursive force and one which, backed as it was by the authorities, was to play a leading role in developments to come.

One of the Landsdrukkerij's publications was the *Daftar besar dari toko boekoe dan kantor tjitak Albrecht & Co.* Like the *Daftar dari Goedang*, the *Daftar besar* of Albrecht's catalogue opens with a list of Malay titles, and like the *Daftar dari Goedang* it has sections with titles of books in other languages (Javanese, Sundanese, and Dutch), illustrating clearly that in Batavia, Malay had not only to reconcile internal tensions among its various versions but had to come to terms with other languages as well. Different from the Landsdrukkerij's *Daftar*, however, is the way in which titles are organized in sections as if to suggest that a distinction should be made between the "new" texts—the various collections of poetry and the translations—and those forming part of the heritage, that is, religious books in Arabic script (mainly by Snouck Hurgronje's favorite, Said Uthman) and the government-commissioned storybooks which were being published in Weltevreden. As has been remarked already, not all the books offered for sale in the Landsdrukkerij's *Daftar* can be found in Albrecht's catalogue; the criteria Albrecht used in its selection remains unclear. There are omissions which may be even more surprising.

As with the other publishing houses in Batavia, Albrecht was apparently uninterested in the work of Muhammad Bakir, a professional Malay author who had written a large number of texts playing upon the conventions and rules of Malay heritage; Bakir had a lending library of his own manuscripts aimed potentially at the same public as Albrecht's, Malay-speaking Chinese, natives, Eurasians.[9] It is an omission that still awaits a satisfactory explanation. No less intriguing is the absence of lithographs and prints of works of the heritage published at the time in Singapore and Pinang and which must have found their way to Batavia. It is reasonable to conclude that in the configuration of discourses presented by Albrecht the Malay heritage assumed an ambiguous relevance; as a whole, obviously it was no longer able to operate as an integrative force for the Malay-speaking community of the metropolis. Neither the temporary popularity of poetry collections by Malay-speaking urbanites nor the halfhearted efforts of the Dutch with their artificial textbooks was sufficient to turn the tide.

141

The rapidly expanding demand for textbooks could have been a gold mine for Albrecht, but this part of the book market was almost completely controlled by the government's publishing house in Weltevreden. It forced the company opposite the Landraad to try its luck in other directions. It is tempting of course to describe those efforts in terms of subversion, but it is all too easy to do so when dealing with the publication and selling of newspapers, almanacs, law books, and poetry. New elements may carry the seeds of subversion indeed, but sooner or later even elements which question authority in the most provocative manner run the risk of becoming commercialized, and of losing their sharpness and capacity to raise questions.

Albrecht's activities as a publisher were primarily led by these very commercial considerations, or so it seems. There was presumably little idealism attached to the company's efforts to explore the tastes of the rising number of readers. It was a matter of gain and loss, debit and credit. The courage to undertake exciting and potentially subversive experiments in a new kind of literature was safely combined with a shrewdly businesslike attitude towards the commissions given by (semi-) government bodies to print all sorts of rules and regulations. It was a matter of survival, which leaves unanswered the question whether selling books published by the Landsdrukkerij for prices higher than those demanded by the Landsdrukkerij itself was a good way of doing business.

Albrecht's and Batavian Cultural Life

Based on the now available picture of Batavia at the turn of the twentieth century, Albrecht's safely can be assumed to have played a trend-setting role in the cultural life of the town. In publishing and selling newspapers, law books, almanacs, poetry, and novels with a strong emphasis on things Malay, it aimed at an as yet rather undifferentiated public of literati who may have had only one thing in common: a passion for printed letters. The 1898 catalogue reads like a sensible starting point for an exploration of the discursive practices at the time which should be seen as the initial phase of modern Malay literature, i.e., the first phase of the era of mechanical reproduction in which the basis was laid for a division into "high" literature and "low" literature which were to have a complicated interplay up until the present day.

The 1898 catalogue has no fewer than 135 pages and a number of appendixes in which samples of envelopes and paper-headings are shown. The titles of the books in stock are given with their prices, if possible with the name of the author and translator. Indicative the importance of Malay is the fact that the first part is entirely used for the listing of titles of Malay books, often accompanied by all sorts of explanatory comments as to why and how these should be read. The catalogue itself is preceded by two pages of well thought-out rules about how those who could not walk into the shop could obtain books through the mail. The sophistication of these rules is such as to suggest that by setting up a commercial distribution system, Albrecht's had been able to identify a clientele not only in Batavia but elsewhere in the colony.

Catalogue titles are arranged in sections and according to type, as though they are dealing with genres with clear-cut conventions and rules. Most of the "newly created" texts are printed in Western script (*hoeroef Olanda* or *letter Olanda*). The first few sections describe texts which students would later refer to as literature *(sastra)*, a cultural category for which the catalogue itself did not yet have a term. The accompanying explanatory notes added to some of the Malay titles state explicitly that they are written in "low Malay" *(Melajoe rendah)*, and that this would enhance the pleasure of reading *(tertjaritakan di dalem bahasa Melajoe renda memang sedap di batja)*. From the same notes it can be deduced that most of these books were meant for a varied public: Chinese, Eurasians, Javanese, and administrators *(prijaji)*. Remarks of the same purport can be found in some poems as well, for instance, Oey Peng Long's introductory remark in his *Boekoe sair roepa-roepa*: "This book is printed in Dutch letters, in it there are all sorts of *sjairs*, youngsters like to read them, of all nations, without distinction" *(soerat di tjitak letter Olanda/sekalian sair semoeanja ada/jang soeka batja sekalian amat moeda/sekalian bangsa tiada berbeda)*. In Tan T. L.'s *Boekoe sairan* a similar remark can be found: "respectful greetings to the readers of all communities" *(membrie tabik dengen lah hormat/kepada pembatja semoewanja oemat)*.

Malay must have been an integrative force of importance, and Malay books meant for anybody who knew Malay; for commercial reasons, however, in Albrecht's catalogue one community was singled out. Malay books based on Chinese originals were treated in a separate chapter and were meant for Chinese alone. The catalogue states, "Most of the Chinese in the Indies, that is the *peranakan*, do not really know the stories of days of yore from China where their ancestors were born" *(kebanjakan orang-orang bangsa tjina di tanah India, ia-itoe peranakan sini tiada taoe betoel tjerita-tjerita doeloe-doeloe kala dari negri tjina*

143

tempat lahirnja toewa-toewanja jang doeloe). It was about time this changed. Probably people of Chinese descent were the most important clinetele for companies like Albrecht's; their special treatment may serve as a strong indication—but the question of how far these books managed to overcome their Chinese stamp and were actually read by non-Chinese remains unanswered.

Poetry

Relatively speaking, much space is given to the presentation of books of poetry in the two most important poetic forms which the Malay heritage managed to perpetuate in printed form: *pantoen* and *sjair*.[10] Of course, this was not without reason. Poems had always been popular among Malay-speaking people, and so they were among the new group of readers at the time. Poems appeared in all kinds of forms in newspapers and almanacs alongside news about Japan, the rise and fall of coffee prices, timetables of trains, and lists of government officials. Albrecht must have realized that there was a market for separate publications too. As it turned out, the company was right: some of the collections of pantoens and sjairs offered for sale went through various editions within a relatively short period of time.[11]

On the basis of available sources it is impossible to trace the genealogy of this printed poetry. Forms, images, and themes suggest direct links with the heritage retained in oral forms and manuscripts in the Malay heartland. It remains a matter of speculation, however, as to how authors in Batavia had become sufficiently intimate with the Malay heritage such that they could follow its poetic conventions so closely. On the other hand, the terms *sjair* and *pantoen* became used more and more indiscriminately to refer to any verse form, the language that is used quite different from that used in manuscripts. In Batavia, this poetry as a whole attracted a more varied public than in the Malay world itself. In all, a fundamental departure from Malay traditions was initated here.

Not only such purely formal features as rhyme scheme and number of words per line, but also the metaphors and images which were used link Batavia with Malay tradition. The descriptions of flowers, bees, birds, gardens, and the often ambiguous use of language which can be found in such works as de Queljoe's *Timpalan Sair Mengimpi* and Tan Teng Kie's *Sair Binatang* read like plays upon a solid knowledge of the heritage. So do the frequent references to *sindir*

144

(innuendo, insinuation). Across the subject matter of these poems falls the shadow of Malay tradition as well: feelings of desire, for instance, and of longing for the beloved (in particular expressed in pantoens like those collected in Boenga Mawar's *Boekoe pantoen pengiboer hati* and Tan T. L.'s *Boekoe pantoon*); and historical events based upon either personal observation or reported information (mainly expressed in sjairs like Tan Teng Kie's *Sair Perdjalanan Kreta Api* and numerous poems in almanacs such as Tang Tjook San's *Siair akan perpoedjian dan kehormatan bagei Sir Baginda Maha Radja Wilhelmina* in the *Almanak Bahasa Melajoe* of 1898). Malay tradition appeared in linguistic playfulness in poems with a very loose story line or no story line at all, for example, Tan Teng Kie's *Sair Kembang* and Oey Peng Long's *Sair Anak Moeda.*

Of the verse forms that operated within the Malay heritage, only sjairs were committed to paper, and insofar as pantoens were written down at all, this happened mainly as insertions in sjairs in the scenes where two lovers, hero and heroine, feel compelled to give expression to their feelings for one another. Insertion of pantoens in sjairs can be found in the printed sjairs as well. But more intriguing is the fact that in the metropolitan culture of Batavia the distinction between the terms *pantoen* and *sjair* was no longer very clear. In circles of those familiar with print, confusion was already being felt in the 1850s; witness the title of a booklet written by *Sa-orang jang bangsjawa* for beginning readers in Batavia: *Boek saier oetawa terseboet pantoen* (A book of sjairs, or in other words pantoens). Toward the end of the century the indiscriminate use of the two terms grew apace. Did it mean that tradition was losing ground? Or should it rather be formulated in positive terms, and is it another indication that Malay poetry was entering a new phase from the very moment print was introduced? Or should this development be formulated in more positive terms and did Malay poetry enter a new phase?[12]

So far as the language was concerned these poems were radically new: full of words and grammatical forms that were derived from low Malay. Consider for example the following four lines: *Apa inie siboengah mawar/sedeng terboeka aroem baoenja/saia denger kabar di loewar/sedeng adinda bloen ada jang poenja.* For Batavians this must have sounded very familiar indeed; to a public in Riau it was a form of Malay that was undoubtedly hard to understand at all.

As for the third departure from Malay heritage, it can be safely assumed that printed poetry reached a much more varied public than its oral predecessors ever had. In Batavia it was shared and enjoyed not only by ethnic Malays but by people of a variety of other communities as well—another illustration of the integrative potential of Malay. Chinese lady singers, for instance, sang a mixture of pantoens and sjairs accompanied by a little orchestra called *gambang* and used the booklets printed by Albrecht and its competitors as a mnemonic device.[13] Eurasians incorporated Malay poetry in the hybrid form of theatre called *Komedi Stamboel* which had developed in the urban areas around the Java Sea on the model of Malay *bangsawan* and European forms of theatre.[14] Youngsters of all communities and classes loved to sing poetry, accompanied by guitar or violin, if only as a way of passing the time, preferably on lonely nights when girls were listening in their homes.[15]

These ways of presenting Malay poetry were in part a mere continuation of past transmissions of the heritage, at all events so far as sjairs are concerned. Within the Malay heritage recitals of these longer poems usually were based on manuscripts, and in terms of presentation this was not so very different in Batavia, where apparently they were recited on the basis of printed materials. Somehow, sjairs managed to maintain themselves for several decades before becoming relegated to secondary status. The way pantoens were dealt with in Batavia was a far better manifestation of the new structure of feeling that was taking hold in Malay-speaking circles: distinct from sjairs, pantoens could be placed on a par with newspapers and textbooks; concurrent with the spread of printing techniques they directed the shift in the Malay textual system.

Within Malay tradition, pantoens had been the form of language par excellence used to express personal emotions by way of traditional means. They were used to convince opponents in political and religious debates, but were most of all associated with love. Would-be lovers were supposed to create these four-line poems on the spur of the moment, in a play of witty repartees meant to impress the object of their affection. In these efforts to express their deepest emotions they followed the rather strict rules of tradition, operating on the basis of experience in the Benjaminian sense of that word quoted in the above: "the convergence in memory of accumulated and frequently unconscious data." Pantoens were supposed to vanish into thin air; they were to not be written down, let alone be printed.

In the form of the booklets which Albrecht and his competitors had started to publish, this highly personal character of this communication was given up. These pantoens, too, may have been created by individuals, but in this printed form no longer were they supposed to come from the heart. Nor were they meant to affect a flesh-and-blood listener, challenging him or her to formulate a witty answer. Rather, they offered some handy tools to be used to maintain oneself in an uncanny world. People were to consult these printed poems and learn them by heart, without feeling personally involved in what they were to say. The introduction to the poem chapter of Albrecht's catalogue clearly plays on this: "any young man who likes to go out should buy one or two of these pantoen books; they are cheap and he can please the heart of others, the more so when he is singing them in company among young ladies."[16] Directed to everybody and to nobody, available to be memorized by anybody, these playful phrases were no longer necessarily born from emotion but, rather, from paper. Ready-made emotions, conventional, artificial, interchangeable, they missed the point pantoens belonging to the heritage tried to make. No longer individual reactions to concrete circumstances, but examples for memorization, ready for use as and when called for by the situation. No individual outbursts of emotions, but prearranged sentences. The fact that pantoens were so easily mistaken for sjairs, and that the two genres were so often regarded as one kind of literary expression, made Malay poetry as a whole diverge even more from the heritage. No longer was there participatory communication but soothing and impersonal print. Very cheap indeed.

Impersonality and Boredom

This tendency to impersonality, or should we say alienation, is confirmed by the fact that a number of the new artists preferred to hide their identity behind a pseudonym such as Boeng Hindrik, Nohah Boto, or Boenga Mawar. It is as though they wanted to keep a distance from their own texts, as though they refused to accept responsibility for their own deeds. Others, so it seems, made a conscious effort to overcome this alienation; leaning on traditional phrases, they reflected explicitly upon their authorship. "This is a newly written poem," writes Tan T. L. in *Boekoe sairan dari tjeritanja Samphek, Ing Tan.* "This is no imitation, no emulation. If you want to write, think first and whoever wants to borrow this, do not just imitate" *(ini sair karangan baroe/tida menoelar tida meniroe/mau menoelis di pikir dahoeloe/siapa jang pindjam jangan meniroe).* Tan Teng Kie appears to be equally self-

147

conscious in the introduction to his *Sair Kembang*: "This *Sair Kembang* has a certain order. I wrote it myself, and used my own ideas. I sat down in patience" *(Sair Kembang poenja atoeran/mengarang sendiri dengan pikiran/ doedoek menoelis dengan kesabaran)*.

This claim for originality and novelty is also expressed in the images and key words recurring in the remarks poets make about the craft of writing at the beginning or the end of their verses. Rather than claim allegiance to traditions of yore, looking to examples from Riau, harking back to stories of elders, the Lord, or the Koran, authors now claim to have drawn new ideas *(tjari pikiran* or *tjari ingatan)* from their own heart *(tarik dari dada)* which they have ordered *(atoer)* into poems. Tan T. L. summarizes this new creative process as follows:

> *Kapan waktoe moelaie mengarang*
> *Dodoek sendirie jang sepie orang*
> *Tjarie ingetan jang sampek terang*
> *Biar bahasanja tiada jang koerang.*
> *Waktoe mengarang poen tiada brentie*
> *Tarik ingetan die dalem hatie*
> *Atoer bahasanja dengen setitie*
> *Biar pembatja moeda mengertie.*

> (When the time came to write,
> I sat down all by myself,
> I looked for ideas until they were clear
> Lest the language would be less appropriate.
> I did not stop once I was writing,
> I drew ideas from my heart,
> Carefully organized the language
> So that the reader could easily read it.)

Authors claim to be motivated by a feeling of tedium *(iseng)*, and from the frequency with which the term is used we may conclude that iseng had become a ruling obsession in circles of Batavian literati. "I wrote this *Sair Kembang*," Tan Teng Kie tells his public, "after I sat down in *iseng-isengan.*" Albrecht's catalogue offers a handy definition of the word: "not to know what should be done" *(tiada taoe apa misti di bikin)*. Time and again, poets admit to being haunted by this tedium. More than that, they assume that their public is in a similar state of mind. "I am writing poems and articles that can be read if one feels

148

bored" *(Saja menoelis sair dan karangan/boeat di batja iseng-isengan).*
In older Malay, the word *iseng* does not occur; its use in *Boek Sair* by
Sa-orang Bangsjawa published in 1857 may serve to indicate how closely
this notion of boredom was related to print and to the modes of
knowledge that arose around it.[17]

Iseng is dangerous; people who give in to it open their hearts to
all sorts of temptations *(penggoda)*, to gambling, for instance, to card-
playing, and to neglect of the household. Of course there are various
ways to avert this danger. Working hard may be the best *pharmakon*
for this disease, and writing poetry may well be one of them, too. De
Queljoe wrote in his *Timpalan Sair Mengimpi* of 1884 as follows:

> *Kaloe di toeroet penggoda setan*
> *Tamtoe sadja ilang ingatan*
> *Doekoek memoelis mengarang sair*
> *Sair ditoelis dengan berpikir*
> *Ingantan banjak djadi terlachir.*

(If one gives in to the devil's temptations
Of course thoughts will vanish
When one sits down to compose a sjair
And the sjair is carefully written down
All sorts of thoughts are born.)

Reading poetry is a way to fight boredom; after all, dealing with
language in a poetic manner, poets assure as again and again, will make
one's heart happy *(senang* or *gembira)*, and well-written poetry will
certainly please the heart *(hiboerkan* or *hiboerin ati jang kesal/enak
dibatja atas bangsal).* Albrecht's catalogue gives an intriguing
description of this phenomenon in the introduction to one of the prose
sections. It is worth a lengthy quotation not only as an illustration of the
remarks that are added to the catalogue's title-descriptions, but also
because it offers a fascinating glimpse into the language used to solicit
the public's attention.

> *Apakah sebabnja orang-orang perampoewan di dalem roemah
> kaseringan soeka pegi bermaen kartoe atawa laen hingga
> kabanjakan kali tinggalin roemah tangganja? tiada laen tjoema
> dari sebab pengoda. Adapoen bagimana pengoda itoe dapat
> masoek di dalem hatingja? pengoda dapat masoek dari sebab*

149

perampoewan itoe terlaloe iseng tiada taoe apa misti di bikin.
Tjoba dari bermoela-moela ia berlaki isteri, si Soewami ladenin
dan toentoen betoel isterinja nistjaija tiadalah djadi tjilaka.
Tjoba si Soewami kadang-kadang batjain boewat isterinja
berbapa hikajat jang enak di dengar dan gampang di mengarti,
tentoe si isteri tiada bisa djadi iseng, dan kaloe dia bisa batja
maka ia nanti maoe batja sendiri hikajat jang bagoes-bagoes
itoe, kapan si Soewami tiada ada tampo. Bagimanakah pengoda
bole timboel di ati jang senang, kerna itoe baiklah, hei sobat-
sobat pilih sadja hikajat-hikajat jang ada terseboet di bawah ini,
semoewa pilihan betoel enak di batja.

(What is the reason that women in the house so often go out and
play cards or do other (bad) things so that they all too often
neglect their household work? The only cause is temptation.
How can temptation enter their hearts? Temptation can enter
because the women are bored and no longer know what to do.
Really, if from the start of their marriage the husband serves and
takes care of his wife, nothing bad could happen to her. Really,
if the husband would now and then read some hikajats to his
wife, lovely to listen to, easy to understand, then his wife would
not feel bored, and in case she herself can read, she soon enough
loves to read those beautiful hikajats by herself whenever her
husband does not have time for her. How could temptations
arise in a contented heart? For that reason, my friends, it is
good to choose from the hikajats that are mentioned in the
following. Whatever you choose, it will be pleasant to read.)

Of course such a quotation tells us a great deal. It suggests that
the new texts were meant to be read aloud as well as to be read in
silence, just as were manuscripts in the Malay tradition. It associates
women with lust and boredom, an idea equally strongly reminiscent of
the heritage. In this connection, the most relevant point may be that
notions like *iseng* and *enak di batja* are not restricted to poetry alone;
reading prose, too, seems to have been a good way of spending one's
leisure time, one of the basic conditions for the rise of literature as a
special category of culture.

This is not to say, however, that in the newly emerging
discursive configuration, prose and poetry can be lumped together
without further ado: differences between the two in terms of individual-

ity and originality are far too great for that. As has been suggested, links between Batavian culture and the poetry of the Malay heritage are obvious and undeniable. Very careful research, however, is needed to determine what contacts existed among Batavia, the Malay heartland, and other areas where Malay was used as an important language and to ascertain how people in Batavia had become as familiar as they were with some of the predominant features of Malay tradition. As for prose, almost the reverse could be said: most of the prose texts advertised in Albrecht's catalogue are clearly translations of European and Chinese texts, yet here it is hard to determine the practical links with the Malay heritage.

There are some prose texts which might be regarded as mediations between tradition and modernity. In particular A. F. von de Wall, the son of H. von de Wall who spent many years in Riau to collect materials for a Malay dictionary, wrote a number of books meant as adaptations (or emulations) of works of the Malay heritage. They are written in a curiously hybrid form of Malay, which is neither low Malay nor the Malay that can be found in manuscripts from Riau and allegedly used by the Dutch as the standard for their concept of "classical Malay." An arbitrarily chosen example will suffice for illustration: the first sentences of his *Hikayat Bachtiar*.

Ada seorang radja, terlaloe besar keradjaannja daripada segala radja-radja. Sjahadan maka baginda pon beranak doewa orang laki-laki, terlaloe amat baik parasnja, gilang-goemilang, dan sikapnjapon sederhana. Hata maka berapa lamanja, dengan kodrotoe'llah soebhanah wata'ala, maka baginda pon hilanglah.

These sentences may contain numerous echoes of the Malay heritage, but they never hit the right tone: an unbalanced use of *maka*; an uneasy description of the young prince; a strange use of the term *kodratoe'llah* an unnecessary duplication of *raja* after *segala*. It makes one wonder if such a text should be described as an expression of the new structure of feeling that was taking hold of Batavia or rather as an effort to continue the authority of the Malay heritage in the form of a printed version; in either interpretation it failed.

In Albrecht's catalogue as well as in the *Daftar* of Weltevreden, texts which may be read most effectively against the background of the Malay tradition are relatively few: *Hikajat Indra Bangsawan, Hikajat Masjhoedoe'llhak, Hikajat Hang Toewah,* and *Hikajat Poetri Beloekis.*

151

Just like *Hikajat Bachtiar*, these are contemporary adaptations of Malay classics, composed to government assignment by Eurasians such as von de Wall and Gerth von Wijk, in a style and language modelled on Riau Malay without really imitating it. The same failed imitation of Riau Malay can be found in the text books inspired by stories from the European heritage: *Hikajat Robinson Cruse*, and *Kesah pelajaran Nachoda Bontekoe* are equally hybrid, equally ambivalent, equally artificial.[18]

Dutch educational policy made these books obligatory reading material at schools, and no doubt von de Wall and Gerth von Wijk were more than pleased to see that their hybrid creations went through a number of reprints: it was a good way of making money. They must have had a considerable influence upon the ideas which the new group of literates developed about Malay, but, as it turned out, there was no guarantee that they would play a predominant role in the changes taking place in the textual system of Batavia as a whole. In the expanding market of printed materials there was not only fierce competition from newspapers but also from translations and adaptations of novels and stories from Chinese or European literature, composed in a kind of Malay which, closely leaning on newspaper language, must have sounded considerably more familiar to their public: *melajoe renda* (low Malay) as Albrecht's catalogue consistently tells its readers. W.N.J.G. Clasz's translations of Jules Verne's novels are a pleasure to read *(sedap di batja)* indeed, and easy at that, as the cover of the Malay version of Dumas's *Conte de Monte Cristo* states: *"Bahasa Melajoe rendah dengan menoeroet djalan jang gampang."* Apparently, the novels of Jules Verne and Dumas reached a public big enough to take the risk of publishing several of their books in translation. The same could be said of the other novels which in Europe itself connoisseurs and critics alike treated as popular literature.[19]

The European heritage as transmitted through Dutch next to the Riau heritage is a second line in the genealogy of the modern textual system. But even more important probably for the rise of a modern literature as a distinct cultural practice, however, is the link with the Chinese textual system.

The ethnic Chinese who had lost contact with the land of their ancestors and now used Malay as their first language seemed to have played a crucial role in this reformulation of Malay literature. By the eighties, an impressive number of Chinese works already had been translated and adapted into the kind of low Malay with which Chinese in the urban areas of the archipelago were familiar.[20] In a separate chapter, Albrecht's catalogue of 1898 alone offers some sixty titles of various genres for sale, all presented as *salinan* (adaptations) which were meant for a quite distinct public: the Chinese who no longer knew Chinese. "Only after Chinese people have read these," is the catalogue's promise, "will they understand how China became so great" *(kaloe orang batja itoe maka baroelah di ketahaoeinja sebagimana negri tjina itoe bole djadi begitoe besar).*

For readers who had been taught to read from the textbooks by von de Wall, these books must have been a source of wonder, much as were books inspired by European examples. In terms both of form and of content they represented novelty. Written in a language much closer to day-to-day conversations in Batavia, these narratives presented topics that opened access to worlds hitherto unreachable and inconceivable. On the one hand, China, France, and Russia must have once more constituted never-never lands for readers, just as those encountered in the hikajat and syair of tradition. But read against the background of the fragmentary and discontinuous information from newspapers, these writings must have had a strong reality effect, an effect which could only be confirmed by the beautiful pictures with which these books often were adorned.

It can be said with confidence that books such as Verne's *Rumah asep* (The Steam House) and *2000 mijl di dalem laoot* (Twenty Thousand Leagues under the Sea) created a feeling of liberation and exuberance in the hearts of their public no less than did newspapers, law books, and almanacs. Liberation, however, never comes alone: manipulation and exploitation appear soon enough. Works of art? Commodities? Almost unrelated to the heritage, and appearing in an intellectual vacuum, this new prose had the capacity to develop in every direction and initially did just that, albeit hesitantly. Most texts may have been meant to amuse and to inform—the better to fight boredom and create a new kind of experience—but soon there appeared an occasional text which was more political in tone and content, criticizing and questioning the socioeconomic order, written in a language which made authorities raise their eyebrows. The short stories of Kommer may have irritated some; the same could be said of the activities of journalist Tirto Adisoerjo.[21] Just like *Rumah asep* their work too set itself up for imitation and emulation by admirers, and for the same reason it invited more or less open intervention on the part of those in power: printing regulations could be changed, the Landsdrukkerij could receive some additional financial or logistic support, and censorship always remained. In retrospect, however, it should be said that this literature in low Malay followed the spirit of Albrecht's, remaining closely associated with commerce and money rather than with ideals and concepts. Conflicts between idealistic radicals and modern-style capitalists are as a rule decided in favor of the latter; literary life in the Indies followed this pattern.

The texts advertised in Albrecht's catalogue made an important contribution to the downfall of the Malay heritage; more precisely, it was prose rather than poetry that pushed the Malay heritage aside. Should we say that the beauty of manuscripts and oral performances was simply superseded by the efficiency of print? At all events, it was through this new prose rather than through the new poetry that the idea of imaginative writing became manifest for the first time, unbidden but disturbing, the beginning of the concept of "literature," enclosed it its own distinct linguistic space. It was only with the rise of its complement, criticism, after the Declaration of Independence in 1945, that the terms *kesusastraan* and *sastra* entered Malay discourse and the bifurcation into high and low literature was completed. The new beginnings so emphatically advertised by Albrecht & Co had been so promising that it is rather surprising to realize that during the next eighty years, with the expansion of the new Malay culture, literary life did not crystallize sufficiently to the point of determining the role high literature was to play in Indonesia. Or is this delay rather a cause for rejoicing?

NOTES

1. I wish to thank James Siegel and Gijs Koster for some inspiring conversations through the years.

2. *Allerhande soorten van winkels of "toko's," waarin men alles kan krijgen wat men noodig heeft. In diezelfde "toko" koopt men een bundel poezie en een stel handdoeken, om de tranen weg te vegen, die deze gedichten mochten opwekken. Tegelijk een rammelaartje voor uw jongste spruit, een paar handschoenen en een parasol of "pajoong" voor mama en een kistje manilla's voor den gelukkige huisvader* (H. Werumeus Buning, *In en om de Kampong—Oost-Indische schetsen* [Utrecht: Boele, n.d.] 74).

3. See chapter 4 of Franco Moretti's *Signs Taken for Wonders* (London: Verso, 1988).

4. See Walter Benjamin, *Illuminations* (New York: Schocken, 1969), 157.

5. See Benjamin, *Illuminations*, 158-59, and, for a wider context, Jonathan Arac, *Critical Genealogies—Historical Situations for Postmodern Literary Studies* (New York: Columbia, 1989), 177-214.

6. See Benedict Anderson, *Imagined Communities* (London: Verso, 1984), 39.

7. Hoffman seems quite correct in the conclusion of his fascinating article on Dutch discussions about the use of Malay: "When developing administrative needs demanded standardization of Netherlands Indies Malay, this was done at the beginning of the Twentieth Century in terms of Dutch ideas." J. Hoffman, "A Foreign Investment—Indies Malay to 1891," *Indonesia* 27 (1979): 92.

8. It is no irony that this book, too, was published partly under the responsibility of Albrecht in Batavia. It was another way of making money, and money is what counted for the company.

9. Compare H. Chambert-Loir, "Malay Literature in the XIX Century—The Fadli Connection," unpublished paper, Leiden, 1987.

10. A *pantoen* consists of four lines, two lines of a more general character (usually referring to phenomena in nature) followed by a second pair of lines that is more or less explicitly addressed to a particular person; its rhyme scheme is fixed: *a b a b*. A *sjair* is a longer or shorter series of four-line rhyming verses (*a a a a*) usually presenting some narrative. The lines of both types of poetry consists of four to six words.

11. E.g., *Boekoe pantoen pengiboer hati*, written by Boenga Mawar, and *Rodja Melati, ja-itoe boekoe pantoen roepa-roepa* by Si Nonah Boto. It seems well possible that there were more "bestsellers" like these published elsewhere.

12. This point was made by Sykorsky in his article "Some Additional

Remarks to the Antecendents of Modern Indonesia Literature,"
Bijdragen tot de Taal-, Land-en Volkenkunde 136 (1980): 489-516.

13. See, e.g., the frequent references to this in Boenga Mawar's *Boekoe pantoen pengiboer hati*; a derogatory description of this kind of amusement can be found in J. A. Uilkens, *Indische Schetsen* (Amsterdam: Peet, 1885), 127-29.

14. See, e.g., the booklet entitled *Pantoen sindiran* by Nona L...; for a short description of the Komedi Stamboel, see R. Nieuwenhuys's *Oost-Indische Spiegel* (Amsterdam: Arbeiderspers, 1973), 302-5.

15. See the description in Victor Ido's novel *De Paupers* (reprint) (The Hague: Thomas & Eras, 1978), 68-74.

16. *Siapa djoega anak moeda jang soeka berplesiran baik ia beli dowa tiga dari itoe boekoe-boekoe pantoen; harganja moerah, maka ia bisa membikin senang orang poenja ati apa lagi djika ia berkoempoel menjanji-njanji di antara orang-orang prampoewan moeda.*

17. *Perbatjaan nja boewat orang moeda/beladjar saier seperti bido-enda/iseng iseng lah aken bertjanda/barang ijang hasiel simpoel didada.*

18. Von de Wall's *Hikajat Sinbad* deserves special mention here as an exemplary case of how "popular" literature wanders around the globe just as the themes in popular music. It is a Malay adaptation of a Dutch version of a story which was widely spread in the Middle East.

19. Once again, it is hard to get a complete picture of what was available to the reading public in Batavia; no doubt there was more available than Albrecht offered.

20. See Claudine Salmon's *Literature in Malay by the Chinese of Indonesia* (Paris: Archipel, 1981).

21. See, of course, Pramoedya Ananata Toer's *Sang Pemoela* (Jakarta: Hasta Mitra, 1982).

6

THE METAMORPHOSIS OF A JAVANESE ARISTOCRAT: THE MEMOIRS OF PANGERAN ACHMAD DJAJADININGRAT

C. W. Watson

Reconstructions of the late colonial period suffer from the dénouement of decolonization in a double way: first because nationalism appears to be the most significant trope for understanding events—after all, the nationalists won and the task of historical interpretation is to explain how and why—and second because the unpicking of anticolonial rhetoric, appearing as it does to be the most pressing of the tasks of historical analysis, often restricts the scholar's vision of a period. There are, of course, exceptions, and recently there has been a shift away from a history of national movements to a history of colonial institutions and the reactions to them, but the very powerful historical constructs of a strident nationalist movement, belaboring a defensive and increasingly insecure colonial government, continue to dominate the popular imagination. Part of the reason for this lies in the cult of historical personality, fostered both in the imperial and the postindependence interpretations of events. Gandhi, Nehru, Aung San, Nkrumah, Kenyatta, Sukarno, Nasser, and Ho Chi Minh, not only stood synec-dochically for the nation, they also were symbols for a history which was, inevitably, a nationalist history. Hence to understand them, their lives and their projects, is metaphorically to (re-) possess the history. It is true that, once in possession, the scholar continues to extend that history and to modify it, and there is a dialectical evolution through which a study of other personalities or other colonial institutions leads to new perceptions. These new perceptions, however, only rise from

157

the initial framing of an argument in terms of its challenge to, or incorporation within, a version of nationalism.

This, at least, is how the writing of modern Indonesian history seems to have taken place. Significantly, the point now reached in the reconsideration of nationalism has been to present the cases for other significant nationalists to be seen as contributors to, if not as images for, the cultural ethos of the nation. Thus, Ben Anderson has made cases for Dr. Soetomo and Tan Malaka, and recently there have been publications of major biographical works on Sjahrir and Hatta.[1] Soetomo's autobiography has appeared in English translation as has Tan Malaka's autobiographical masterpiece.[2] In Indonesia itself, the last decade has witnessed the publication of innumerable volumes of memoirs and biographies of "nationalist" figures. Yet the crucial observation here is that they are all "nationalists," or at least aspire to that status: the agenda of scholarship still appears to be written in accordance with this paradigm, and its significance to the student lies in its contribution to the accepted account. This framing of historical problems is partly self-conscious, as when the historian decides to set the record right or provide a better-balanced perspective. However, it is largely unmeditated or taken for granted, as when the historian's selectivity is unconsciously determined by a consensual view of which events metonymically constitute the history of the period. Moving away from the central figures of nationalism, the historian's glance first falls on those who are different yet comparable. Rarely does he or she consider the person who, observed through the glass of nationalism, appears to have faded into historical insignificance.

Achmad Djajadiningrat is one such figure. Not being part of the nationalist movement, being, indeed, on the contrary a strong supporter of Dutch-Indonesian cooperation which he himself practiced so assiduously during the course of a long civil service career, he has been somewhat overlooked by historians. There is good reason, therefore, to recall that his memoirs are not only, as Du Perron remarked in an early review, an excellent source of historical information but also offer us a rare opportunity to step back from an interpretation of history over-dependent on nationalism and view a historical landscape of different dimensions from those to which we have become accustomed.[3]

Achmad Djajadiningrat (1877-1943)

Compared to what was provided for the indigenous elites of India and the Philippines, access to European education came very late to the Indonesian elite. With the exception of a few people (such as the painter Raden Salleh and the schoolteacher Willem Iskandar), who fortuitously found their way to Holland in the nineteenth century, there was no attempt before the twentieth century to formulate a policy designed to open up Dutch education to the indigenous inhabitants of the Indonesian archipelago.[4] So much so, that in 1900 there were in Java only four Regents—Regent being the most senior position in the native administrative service (Inlands Bestuur)—who could converse in and understand Dutch. One of them was Achmad Djajadiningrat.

It was not that the Dutch colonial government felt that education was unimportant: it had set up schools for senior native administrators in the middle of the nineteenth century. There was, however, a strong feeling that Dutch and native administrative services should be kept quite separate, and that for the performance of their tasks the Regents would have found a Dutch education inappropriate.

At the turn of the century, however, there were signs that attitudes were beginning to change. A new breed of colonial official, encouraged by the energetic liberalism of individual politicians in The Hague, was advocating in public and sponsoring in private a Dutch education for the Javanese aristocracy. This progressive group, known as the Ethici, included journalists and teachers as well as politicians. Its position met strong opposition from colonial administrators who leaned on a crude version of Social Darwinism and said that the Javanese, however aristocratic, were not ready for such education. The Ethici maintained that for practical reasons (efficient administration in the transition to modernization) and on moral grounds (the aristocracy were capable of deriving the highest benefit from these opportunities and could be held up as examples) Dutch education should be made available to the native aristocracy. It was an argument which drew for support on the successful example of the British in India. Indeed, it has been suggested that it was the desire to emulate British achievement which led European circles to the posthumous promotion of Raden Ajeng Kartini as an enlightened Javanese aristocrat who not only wrote in Dutch but shared the same philosophical outlook as her liberal European friends.[5] The publication of her letters, dramatically entitled *Door Duisternis tot Licht* (From Darkness to Light), presented a powerful case for demonstrating how the benighted native aristocrat with an inherent sensitivity and cultural refinement could, through a sympathetic induction into Durch culture, be transformed into an intelligent European liberal.

Ultimately the Ethici won the argument, but it was a partial victory. The doors of the Dutch educational establishment were not flung wide open but they were opened sufficiently to allow a thin trickle of native students into schools previously reserved for Dutch and Indo-Europeans. The majority of students, if they did seek to pursue a modern education, were persuaded into schools specifically established for the native population. The expatriate community still had a very strong resistance to integration at any level, a resistance which in some ways grew stronger as an influx of new Dutch expatriates, including women, put great pressure on the colonial community to retain a sense of separateness on formal, professional occasions. It discouraged informal associations and liaisons as well as practices of dress and habit deriving from native custom. So strong did the sense of separateness become that language itself was used as a social marker. The use of Dutch by a native when addressing a Dutchman in public was considered offensive, an impertinence. The degree to which change was occurring within rigid racial conventions, including a sensitivity to the issue of language, is well brought out in Pramoedya Ananta Toer's novel, *Bumi Manusia.*[6]

The movement towards changing attitudes and developing skills in native society, although it gathered pace after the Dutch queen's policy speech from the throne in 1901 which announced a new emphasis on irrigation, emigration, and education, did so only slowly, and more because of a perceived demand for new managerial and bureaucratic skills than because of any strong conviction of the merits of enlightenment. In 1906 the inevitable point was reached when individual Javanese with appropriate higher educational qualifications applied for admission to the Colonial Administration (Binnenlands Bestuur). Opposition to the integration of the two services was still too strong, and again the Javanese were directed into the non-European service.[7]

The principal advocate for a policy of integration, or an association policy, as it was called, was Christiaan Snouck Hurgronje, then Adviser for Native and Arab affairs, a man whose liberalism was attacked bitterly by the Dutch community, but who had the ear of the governor-general. In addition to the arguments put forward by Dutch liberals Snouck suggested another cogent reason why it was imperative to open up Dutch education for a native elite. There was a danger that, with the deeper penetration of Islamic ideas among the population at large, opposition to colonial government would grow. To preempt this, and to facilitate the progressive development of the country, required a strategy of winning hearts and minds. This, in turn, meant persuading the influential leadership of native society to cooperate in the joint endeavor of developing the country. Such persuasion could be successful only if the native elite saw themselves as equal partners with commensurate responsibility. Again it was an argument which received a lukewarm reception from Dutch society at large, but which, nonetheless, found favor in the higher circles of the administration. One of the beneficiaries of Snouck's advocacy, and indeed one of the best examples of the realization of the association policy, was Achmad Djajadiningrat.

Achmad was eight years old when he first met Snouck. The latter, impressed by his manner and by his enthusiasm for Dutch education, decided to become the boy's patron. His family belonged to the minor Javanese aristocracy in West Java known to be favorably disposed to Western ideas. Achmad's father had held a succession of posts in the native civil service and was destined for a Regent's post. In the normal course of events after obtaining a rudimentary primary education in a religious school, and with the aid of a tutor, Achmad might have been expected to go to the Regent's school and from there to enter the native civil service, in his father's footsteps. Thanks to Snouck's intervention, Achmad was sent to Batavia where he was found lodgings with a Dutch family and where he went to a Dutch primary school (Europeese Lagere School—ELS). From the ELS he went on to middle school (Hoogere Burgerschool—HBS). Throughout his schooling he remained in constant touch with Snouck Hurgronje, at whose house he dined regularly of a Sunday afternoon.

After graduation from the HBS the intention was that he should proceed to further education in the Netherlands. This plan, however, was thwarted by his father's untimely death. The latter had at the time been serving as Regent of Serang, a district difficult to administer in northwest Bantam, having taken over the Regency from his brother, who had also died in office. Under these circumstances Achmad was obliged to remain in Java to act as head of the family and assist his brothers and sisters. The obvious career open to him was in the native civil service, but this posed problems. On the one hand, he was too highly educated to commence at the bottom rung of the administration. On the other hand, he was insufficiently experienced for the senior position of Regent. Ideally the family would have liked him to replace his father in Serang and, given the Dutch encouragement of the principle of hereditary office this did remain a possibility. Ultimately, the colonial government compromised and appointed an acting Regent while Achmad served two years of apprenticeship in official posts elsewhere in the region. After the two years he was appointed at the unusually young age of twenty-two to be Regent of Serang.

He served as Regent for twenty-five years, during which period he was several times appointed a member of important government commissions. He also became involved in Regents' organizations set up to promote the position of Regents and take on greater responsibility for the social welfare of the native population. In all these activities he worked especially closely with the two or three other Regents who, like him, had received a Dutch education. When the Volksraad, the quasi-representative legislative assembly, was set up in 1918, he was one of the first elected members.

In 1926, after what appears to have been a period of some difficulty in relations with the Dutch Resident, Achmad was appointed to head the new Regency of Batavia, a post he held until 1928, in which year he retired, again after experiencing some hostility from the senior Dutch administrators. Following his retirement he was appointed to represent the colonial government in a conference in Switzerland, and thus in 1933 he made his first trip to Europe. On his return to the Indies he was appointed member of the Raad von Indie, the Council of the Indies, the most senior advisory body in the colony. He retired from the Raad van Indie in 1935 for reasons of ill health, and wrote his autobiography shortly afterwards. He died in 1943, shortly after the Japanese took control of Indonesia.

It is not with these superficial details of his career, however, that we need to be concerned, but with the relationship of his ideas to the intellectual climate of his times. A proper understanding of his position should confine itself neither to the particular kinds of public service in which he was employed, nor to the explicit statements which he made in relation to historical events and developments. For a more comprehensive insight one must turn to his autobiography, *Herinneringen*, published in 1936.[8] From the structures of this book a view of the world can be elicited which, while not necessarily representative, contains within it shared perspectives which were historically influential.

Herinneringen: The Form

The ostensible form which Achmad's autobiography takes conforms to the expectation of the record of the life of the distinguished civil servant. It is chronologically ordered, beginning with the birth of the writer and with remarks and observations on his family, proceeding to an account of his childhood and youth, and concluding with a narrative of his years of public service. That it is clearly the latter which is stressed is indicated by the chapter divisions, each of which takes its heading from particular periods in the writer's career: "Memories from the time when I was Assistant-*Wedana* in Bodjonegara"; "From the early years of my Regentship"; "From the time of my Regentship of Batavia"; and so forth. Clearly, self is being defined, at least for the purposes of the autobiography, as a public self, and it is this public self, it would appear, which constitutes for the autobiographer the ego of the narrative.

Within the narrative, then, it is the accomplishments and achievements of public life which are privileged for description and discussion. But we need to be cautious here because the printed text of 363 pages is apparently only half the original manuscript. Hence there may be grounds for arguing that textual omissions forbid our reconstruction of the original stresses of the writer, however explicit the claims that neither the original style nor the nature of the contents has been distorted. Certainly we have to reckon with this, but there is sufficient within the published text to indicate that it is indeed the res gestae of a career in public service which is at the heart of the autobiography. Achmad's earliest memory as a child is that of escorting his mother in a period of food shortage in her walks round the market, trying to save the lives of abandoned children. The final passage describes a tour of Europe as a representative of a commission to investigate the position of the middle class within Indonesian society with a view to making practical suggestions for development. In between he has caught thieves and robbers, exposed charlatans, laid drainage systems, participated in debates in the Volksraad, sat on numerous welfare committees; in short, he has led a life of exemplary public service.

Yet, proud as he is of these accomplishments, it would appear to be not so much the deeds themselves, but the symbolic significance of the offices held to which he chooses to draw his reader's attention. The appointment to a new commission, the chairmanship of the Regentenbond, the bestowal of an honor, are significantly marked out for the reader in a way which almost obscures the res gestae themselves. There are two possible reasons for this: the reluctance to expatiate on one's own merits common to both Western and Eastern notions of decorum and reticence; and the need to indicate the trajectory of a career by significant signs, again not so much for self-aggrandizement but for the representativeness of events, since at these points the actor of the autobiography is being projected deliberately to the reader as representative. At every such point there is, it seems, an implicit collusion with the reader, as though at the level of subtext the writer were stating, "Look, here is what is possible under enlightened colonial government. Ignore what I have just been saying about my personal trials and tribulations and observe how a person born in native society acquired a Dutch education and entered the civil service, rising to a position of honor within the society." The collusive nudge is never explicit, but it is there. Take for example an occasion in 1920.

Achmad describes how he was asked to give a speech at the opening of the famous Technical High School in Bandung by Governor-General van Limburg-Stirum. He mentions having shivered with nervousness before his speech, without being able to understand why, since he was used to public speaking. The description continues:

> Toen ik mij met geweld trachtte te beheerschen merkte ik, dat ik inderdaad van aandoening zenuwachtig was; ik dacht daarbij terug aan mijn onderwijzer in de Nederlandsche taal, die plotseling in een naga was veranderd. Ik dacht verder aan den tijd, toen ik Willem van Bantam heete en tot een behoorlijke Europeesche lagere school werd toegelaten. Ik was mijn aandoening bijna niet meer meester, toen ik onder de pas ingeschreven studenten van de openen hoogeschool een Inheemschen jongeling zag met een hoofdoek op en een kaen aan. . . . Ik was daarbij zoo vol dankbaarheid: ik had niet kunnen denken, dat wij toen reeds een hoogeschool hier te lande zouden hebben. (305)

> (When I tried to pull myself together with an effort, I observed that indeed I was nervous with emotion; I thought back then to my teacher in Dutch who had suddenly changed into a dragon. I thought further to the time when I was called Willem van Bantam and was admitted to an outstanding European primary school. I was almost unable to control my emotions, when

among the students newly registered for the college which was about to be opened I saw a young native student with a head-cloth and wearing the traditional *kain*. . . . I was then so full of thankfulness: I had not been able to imagine that by then we would have a University college in this country.)

It is easy to cringe at the expression *vol dankbaarheid* (full of thankfulness), dismissing it as an indication of just how sycophantic the native civil servants had become, in consequence of the warping effect of Dutch education and patronage which caused them to see the foundation of an educational establishment as a beneficent extension of privilege to the colony. Nonetheless, one should not be so distracted by such considerations as to fail to observe the movement of the text at this point.

Clearly, it is an emotional moment for Achmad. At the same time, this emotion coincides with, indeed is caused by, an event of historical importance in the development of the period: the opening of the college. At this point the autobiographer recalls the uniqueness of Achmad's position. Here he is on this important occasion, a native being asked to present a public speech in Dutch. The honor has been extended to him as an individual; yet at that very moment consciousness of his selfhood impels him to reflect on the significant experiences which have constituted that particular notion of self, a notion in which a consciousness of two identities, Dutch and native, is implicated. There then arises a memory of the boy at school, Willem van Bantam, almost fortuitously the early personality of Achmad himself, here presented as a third person. This contemplation of self is immediately complemented by the observation of the native student sitting in front of him, a single student, yet also representative. It is a moment of clarity, of vision, of self-understanding; it is perhaps the nearest one comes in the autobiography to *lacrimae rerum*.

Through charting his career in this way, by constant reference to a set of upward stages in a career, the autobiographer makes of himself as much an emblem as an individual. There is a readily observable teleological structure underlying the progress which the reader is obliged to note in the passage from innocent child to member of the Raad van Indie. That is, however, only one element within the formal composition of the autobiography which contains further explicit points of thematic reference. These can be seen, for example, in the record of significant events of the period in which Achmad participated, either centrally (the setting up of the Volksraad and the introduction of the ethical policy) or peripherally (the founding of Boedi Oetomo, and the setting up of the Sarekat Islam), as well as in the observation of social and economic change (the replacement of carriages by motorcars) and the evaluation of personalities.

Of the recording of events and of Achmad's reactions to them, little needs to be said. The autobiography has already been used extensively by historians as a source. However, one salutary instance of how history can never be a record of the facts but is always an interpretation may be worth a comment.

In her book *The Making of a Bureaucratic Elite*, Heather Sutherland spends some time on a crucial meeting of the Regentenbond at the time of the setting up of the Volksraad where the major issue for discussion was the role which the Regents should play in the coming session of the Volksraad.[9] Achmad, Sutherland informs us, argued hard that the Regents should play an active role as leaders of native society and that they should become politically involved. To this end he advocated membership in the NIVB, a multiethnic party which in advocated an association policy and gradual devolution of responsibility to the Indies. He was, however, opposed by the chairman of the meeting, his friend the Regent of Djapara, Koesomo Oetoyo, who, after having chaired the meeting rather unsatisfactorily (this at least is the account of the Dutch observer Mr. Schrieke), swung the opinion of the Regents against Achmad. The Regents' decision to remain uncommitted was crucial, according to Sutherland. It had been their last chance, if not to capture the leadership of the nationalist movement, then at least to be influential within it. After the meeting the opportunity was lost, and progressive nationalist opinion dismissed the Regents henceforth as tools of the Dutch.

The meeting is also described in the autobiography, and the different opinions of Achmad and Koesomo Oetoyo are rehearsed there too. It is remarkable, however, that nowhere does the writer attach the significance to the decision that the historian does. For the writer it is an instance of a particular event in which he participated, important historically because leading to the neutrality of the Regents. Yet, had that decision been as critical as Sutherland suggests, one would have expected the autobiographer, with the hindsight of eighteen years, to comment further. This might, after all, be said to be the raison d'être of political autobiography, setting the record straight for posterity. Indeed, Achmad avails himself of the opportunity on numerous other

166

occasions. How, then, are we to interpret his silence here? Is he unwilling to be critical of his friend? Or is it that he simply does not give the weight of interpretation to the decision that Sutherland does? The point is not altogether trivial, since it involves an assessment of the role and influence of the Regents in native society at an important historical juncture.

My own impression is that, by 1936, when he came to write the autobiography, Achmad was able to perceive that the nationalist momentum had gathered such a pace in the years between 1920 and 1934 that, even had the Regents spoken out and been politically committed to moderation, they would have been ignored by the radical elements. His description of his meeting with radical Perhimpoenan Indonesia students in Leiden in 1929 certainly suggests a realistic appraisal of this kind. Of that meeting he wrote as follows:

> wilde ik wagen een enkel woord tot die studenten te zeggen, al kon ik, met het oog op hetgeen mede door anderen op dat gebied was verricht, wel verwachten, dat ik daarmede als een Don Quichot zou handelen. . . . Contact kreeg ik wel met die studenten het bleek mij echter spoedig dat het vechten was tegen de bierkade. (353)

> (I wanted to risk saying a few words to the students, although, observing what others had tried in that respect, I could anticipate that I would be treated like a Don Quixote. . . . Although I had some contact with the students, it soon appeared to me that I was beating against a brick-wall.)

In 1936, he could well adopt this tone of condescension, not just because he was an elder statesman, tolerantly critical of hotheaded youth, but, more important, because historical events, not recorded in the autobiography, had already appeared to vindicate the moderate approach. The radicals had been arrested and sent to Boven Digoel internment camp in West New Guinea, in 1934 the nationalist parties had been crushed by a repressive colonial government, and the principal nationalist leaders were all in prison. The question of the appropriate direction for the Regents to have taken in 1920, then, appeared in hindsight to be academic. Sutherland, however, viewing the situation forty years later, brings to it an awareness of nationalist triumph; in this perspective, 1934 was simply a temporary suspension of inevitable success. The dangers of such unconsciously teleological explanations of the history of this period have been outlined suggestively by O'Malley.[10] With respect to the specific question of the Regentenbond meeting, however, no interpretation can be definitive, and the autobiographical account simply alerts one to the pitfalls of interpretation and the judicious use which must be made of autobiographical narrative in historical reconstruction.

The two other categories of experience which form part of the immediately observed narrative are the description of change and the placing and evaluation of personalities. I want to say more about the description of social change below, when I come to consider the writer's perception of what is historically significant in the period which he chronicles. The treatment of individual personalities within the narrative, however, should be considered briefly here.

The individuals who are mentioned in the text can be classed readily into three categories. The largest comprises people with whom Achmad has had some dealings in his public life; second come family members; and, finally, come people who only incidentally have crossed Achmad's path but who are considered worthy of mention because of their roles in the history of the period. In this last category one finds figures such Tjipto Mangoenkoesomo, whom Achmad knew from the time when the former was a student in the Dokter Jawa school. He comments on him as follows:

> Reeds als jongen toonde hij niet alleen buitengewone verstandelijke gaven, doch ook een zelfstandig en onafhankelijk karakter te bezitten. Die zelfstandigheid sloeg later, helaas, telkens over in revolutionaire uitingen, zoodat hij zijn gaven van hoofd en hart tenslotte niet heeft kunnen benutten in het belang van zijn land en volk. (278)

> (Already as a young man he had demonstrated not only remarkable gifts of intelligence, but also that he possessed a self-assured and independent character. This self-assuredness later led, alas, often to revolutionary actions, so that ultimately he has never been able to use his gifts of head and heart in the interests of his land and people.)

This short critical evaluation of the man is a good example of the brief sketches found throughout the book, which indeed form an

168

important element in its overall composition. It is also, of course, revealing as much for what it says about the author as for what it says about Tjipto. In the nationalist record Tjipto stands out as one of the most vigorous and principled opponents of the colonial government, yet also he is one of the few nationalists to speak out unequivocally against Japanese intentions in Southeast Asia. In 1936, however, Tjipto's anti-Japanese sentiments were yet to be expressed, and Achmad, aware of Tjipto in exile and detention, could therefore write again with regret for the waste of talent. That historians have not agreed with this assessment is, again, a function of the dominance of the nationalist paradigm.

The treatment of members of the family and family occasions within the autobiography is mixed, revealing what seems at certain points to be a lack of sureness or an ambivalence about the autobiographical enterprise. The question whether this is to be an autobiography of public life or an autobiography of personal experience, which in other areas of the book seemed to have been so firmly resolved in favor of the former, appears to be reopened in he discussion of family life. The autobiography begins with the classic account of parents' origins and ancestors, and a pedigree is produced, legitimating the persona which the autobiographer is creating of himself. The same reiteration of claims to status through associations of kinship is part of the continuous narrative of the book. Within a slightly different perspective, but again one still designed to illuminate aspects of public life, Achmad mentions the closer relatives with whom, over the period of public service, he came into frequent contact. In connection with this, as if anticipating objection, he gives a brief account of the accusation of nepotism frequently levelled at his family. This accusation Achmad, with his democratic principles, finds difficult to rebut although he understands why nepotism continues to operate.

The incidental mention of family members is thoroughly consonant with this type of public memoir, as indeed is the simultaneous omission of much reference to close family life. There is, however, one significant exception here: constant reference to Achmad's mother, and the frequently mentioned memory of her reciting Sundanese maxims to him. Such references serves as a leitmotif in the autobiography, to remind both reader and writer of the latter's closeness—despite his Western education—to his Sundanese heritage and to signal what is omitted from other mentions of family life, the emotional bond between close relatives. He records the deaths of close members of the family in almost the same register as he chronicles significant external events.

The reader thus obtains no sense of the emotional weight of a family occasion. In describing the premature death of his brother Hasan in 1920, for example, he simply remarks that the latter's service as chairman of the Bantam branch of the Sarekat Islam had not gone unnoticed and that, had he lived, he would certainly have become a member of the Volksraad.

The nearest he comes to acknowledging that important family events are not a matter of emotional indifference to him is in a passage entitled *Vreugde en leed in de familie* (Joy and Sorrow in the Family), in which he records the occasion on which the same day brought news of the death of his eldest sister's first child and of his brother's success in an examination in Leiden (274-75). This combination of good and bad news he describes as follows:

> Wanneer men op hetzelfde moment of op denzelfden dag vreugde en verdriet ondervindt, dan zegt man "soeka-doeka," *soeka* beteekent vreugde en *doeka* verdriet. Ook ik heb eens soeka-doeka gehad. (275)

> (If one at the same moment or on the same day experiences joy and sorrow, then one says "*soeka-doeka*"; *soeka* means joy and *doeka* sorrow. I too once had soeka-doeka.)

There is something curiously detached about these remarks, the effect of which is to objectify a personal experience by making it an illustration of a general phenomenon. There is almost greater interest in explaining the term *soeka-doeka* than in describing the events themselves. A similar uneasiness is to be found in the description of his marriage. He and his brother married two sisters, a practice which was frowned upon by the wife's family and regarded as ill-fated. In fact his wife did die prematurely after a few short years of marriage, and her death was followed by that of his brother's wife. In neither case, however, does he mention the personal relationship of the spouses. When he notes the death of his brother's wife, once more he refers to superstition: "*De oudere familieleden zeiden natuurlijk: 'daar ziet men weer het gevolg van het overtreden van een voorvaderlijk verbod' (ngagempoer awi sadapoer)*" (The older family members naturally said, "There one sees the consequences of transgressing an ancestral prohibition"). The effect of his introducing this remark is to distract attention, displacing it away from the events themselves and onto the curiosity of the superstition.

The understandable reticence about the public disclosure of what is regarded within Javanese society as intensely personal and intimate, in a culture where, even more strongly than in England, any display of emotion is regarded as improper, is not the central issue here. It is the deliberate deflection of interest away from the event which, having been singled out for recording, should in the reader's eye be given more prominence. Instead, it is undermined by being treated in association with a separate and relatively trivial matter—the quaintness of indigenous belief.

This ambiguity in discussion of his family seems to spring from an uncertainty not simply about how to deal with an aspect of his life in which the public and the private face are not easily separable. At a more profound level, there is uncertainty about who exactly his intended readers are. We shall come back to a consideration of the projected readership of the autobiography below. Here I want to register that in these passages where Achmad takes the trouble to explain a custom or describe a ritual, it is clear that the implied reader is a European, one essentially sympathetic to liberal ideas, but not necessarily conversant with life in the Indies. For such a person an explanation of *soeka-doeka* is required. For Achmad's friends, it would not be. It is, then, the consciousness of a *totok* audience which occasionally constrains and determines his style of presentation. This is particularly true, as I have suggested, in his rendering of the experience of family. Anxious to maintain an appropriate distance between the reader and the experience described—which would not have been the case if he had been writing solely for friends and family (compare Soetomo's *Reminiscences*, which were not designed for sale)—Achmad goes too far in the direction of objectification, simply leaving the reader perplexed at what seems the undervaluing of family experiences.

Writer and reader may be uneasy in relation to the absence of a feeling of family life—which, incidentally, seems all the more paradoxical, since the text itself is illustrated by photos of family members—but there is no mistaking the sureness of tone when Achmad describes the Europeans with whom he has had dealings. One is, indeed, initially surprised by the number of Dutch people who are prominent in the text. It would be wrong to attribute that prominence to any snobbishness on the author's part, or even, to put it another way, to a deliberate decision made in the light of an imagined Dutch readership. Rather, what we must be aware of here is the dual purpose of self-justification and self-explanation. Both these purposes are mediated through the description of Dutch character.

The necessity for self-justification is adequately described within the text (and confirmed in historians' accounts, for example Williams's). Clearly Achmad was a controversial figure in his day, meeting with hostility both from Indonesian nationalist leaders and from conservative Dutch officials. It is with regard to the latter that he feels self-justification to be necessary. Again, this is because he sees them as more formidable opponents in the context of the times, certainly the opponents with whom he has had most to contend. Consequently, there is throughout the text a strong defensive undercurrent, occasionally breaking through to the surface when history requires some explanation of particular disagreements with individual Dutchmen.

A good example of this is the difficulties he experienced in his final years as Regent of Serang when it appears that he was constantly clashing with the Dutch Resident. Achmad describes at length one occasion when the Resident's nose was put out of joint during a short stopover by the governor-general at a railway station. Achmad upstaged the Resident, without deliberately intending to do so, by providing refreshments. The Resident rebuked him for not having consulted him first before doing so and there was bad feeling about the incident. The last sentences concerning the episode run this way:

> In 1926 achtte men het noodig in een officieel rapport te vermelden, dat ik als Regent van Serang zooveel botsingen met de Residenten had gehad. Ik vroeg mij af of de pas boven omschreven kwestie al dan niet tot die botsingen werd gerekend. (295)

> (In 1926 it was considered necessary in an official report to remark that I was Regent of Serang had had a lot of clashes with the Residents. I wondered whether the incident just described above was not counted as one of these clashes.)

Clearly the incident rankled, and given its location in the narrative, the reader is invited to regard it as typical of the difficulties Achmad encountered.

In a way even more significant, however, than the recalling of specific scenes is the general remark occurring almost gratuitously in the body of the text, since the indication is that, in recollection at least, Achmad's sense of being embattled must have been a constant source of distress. In a poignant chapter on his year as Assistant-Wedana in Bodjonegara just prior to his becoming Regent, he describes that period as perhaps the happiest of his official career (*Het is voor mij de beste tijd geweest van mijn geheele ambtelijke loopbaan* [118]), a startling admission since he had in fact just joined the civil service and was to go on as an official for another thirty years. There is perhaps something of a nostalgia for lost youth in his description of his exploits during that year, but he later makes it clear that the reason it was, in retrospect, so enjoyable was that it was not blighted by the petty disputes of later years.

In a carefully worded passage in which he sums up his experiences as Assistant-Wedana, the unpleasantness of the later years bubbles up into his memory. The passage is worth quoting in full:

> Ik had volop gelegenheid het leven en denken van de breede massa van mijn volk grondig te leeren kennen; de bij de aanraking met de bevolking opgedane kennis is mij mijn gansche leven steeds van nut geweest. Helaas heeft die kennis mij niet veel geluk gebracht, want door het bezit van die kennis heb ik mij bij de beoordeeling van zaken, de Inheemsche bevolking betreffende, ten rechte of ten onrechte, gevoeld de meerdere te zijn van de Europeesche bestuurambtenaren, die het in den regel niet dulden konden, dat ik het leven en denken van den Javaan beter begreep. Spijt heb ik er echter niet van, dat ik heb moeten strijden. Tenslotte had ik dan toch niet allen de bestuurambtenaren te dienen, doch ook, evenals zij, mijn volk. (184)

> (I had a lot of opportunity to get to know thoroughly the life and thought of the broad mass of my people; the resulting knowledge which came from contact with the people has always been of use to me throughout my life. Alas this knowledge has not brought me much luck, since through the possession of this knowledge I have felt, rightly or wrongly, in the course of things, that in what concerns the native people, I am superior to the European civil servants, who in general could not bear the fact that I understood better [than they] the life and thought of the Javanese. I have never, however, regretted that I have had to fight.

Ultimately, after all, I was not only supposed to be serving the civil servants, but, as much as they, my own people.)

Achmad's writing of the autobiography and the justification of his actions against criticisms which he received must, then, in the light of this passage be read as part of continuing struggle. It is a matter of getting down his version of events in the face of those who would wish him ill. The constant presence of the Dutch in the narrative cannot, however, be explained by this alone, since, relative, to those unnamed individuals with whom Achmad crossed swords, there is more frequent mention by name of Dutch people for whom Achmad clearly felt respect, warmth, and friendship, among them Snouck Hurgonje himself, but above all Residents Hardeman and Overdijn. Photographs of all three illustrate the text.

One way of accounting for the descriptions of these individuals, who—Achmad is at pains to stress—were liberal and enlightened, and had the interests of the people at heart, is to suggest again that what we find here is a form of vindication, not a vindication of particular attitudes or actions, but of Achmad's general weltanschauung. To that extent self-explanation might be the more appropriate term. As he constantly stresses, he became convinced at a very early age of the correctness of the association policy and the need to work cooperatively with enlightened Dutch minds for the betterment of the country. His life's work, as reflected in the autobiography, can be regarded as an articulation of commitment to these ideals. That enterprise, that total commitment, could only be justified, however, if there was a genuine reciprocal desire on the part of the Dutch to commit themselves in equal measure. It had been a lifetime disappointment to find that there were many influential and educated Dutchmen who did not share his ideals, and who lent credence to the hard core of the nationalist movement who rejected the possibility of any form of cooperation. It was, therefore, doubly necessary to signal that there were sympathetic Dutchmen, first as substantive justification for the political approach with which Achmad had identified himself so closely, and second to indicate to the skeptics that, for all the petty opponents one encountered, there were to be found, in greater numbers, men of honesty and integrity, and to work in conjunction with them offered the best hope for the future. If, then, the critical remarks he makes of certain individuals are to be read as a rebuttal to his Dutch critics, the encomia for his Dutch friends should be taken as a riposte to the nationalists and as an encouragement to his political sympathizers.

So far, however, we have concerned ourselves with the surface structure of the text, what it ostensibly announces itself to be. We need to look somewhat deeper if we wish to provide a more comprehensive account of the consciousness which informs that text.

Herinneringen: The Project

In the foreword to the autobiography Achmad is explicit about his intention.

Nadat ik's Lands dienst met pensioen had verlaten, rieden mijn vrienden, zoowel van Europeesche als van Inheemsche zijde, mij aan om memoires te schrijven, omdat ik, zooals sommigen hunner het uitdrukten, een belangwekkende periode in de geschiedenis van Nederlandsch-Indie in de laatste decennia had medegemaakt, de periode n.1. van overgang van oud naar nieuw. Aan die instigatie meende ik gehoor te moeten geven, omdat het in het belang de verdere ontwikkeling dezer gewesten zoowel voor de bestuurders als de bestuurden kan zijn, dat terzake ook eens een stem van Inheemsche zijde wordt gehoord. (foreword)

(After I had left government service with a pension, my friends, as much my European friends as my Native friends, advised me to write my memoirs, because, as some of them expressed it, I had lived through an important period in the history of the Netherlands Indies over the past decades, namely the period of the transition from old to new. I thought that I should pay heed to their prompting because it may be in the interest of the further development of these regions, as much for the administrators as for the administered, that for once a voice from the Native side be heard.)

It was at the prompting of his friends that Achmad came to write his autobiography, and to that extent the work is for them. It was also for them in that they would constitute some of the potential readership; having lived at least through some of the events and changes described, they would find in the autobiography a sharing of memories and perhaps some enlightenment on matters in which they, too, were intensely involved. There is a consciousness on Achmad's part, then, of this constituency of his readership, and, as I have suggested, the manner in which he represents the characters of personalities in the text seems particularly addressed to a specifically Dutch audience within that readership.

Beyond simply acceding to the request of friends, he had a general intention, as he puts it, to give an account of events from the Native side which, for both the administrators and administered, might be in the interest of the further development of the Netherlands Indies. The autobiography, therefore, is also to serve a didactic function, not only describing what has happened, but trying to draw general conclusions which will be of use to a younger generation. This consciousness of a continuity of service is echoed in the last sentence of the book: *"Al moge er nu in deze moeilijken tijd voor land en volk heel wat te doen zijn, met een gerust hart kan ik die taak aan anderen en jongeren laten"* (Although now there may be a lot to be done in these difficult times for the country and the people, with an easy mind I can leave this task to other and younger people).

In addition to being simply a memoir, the book was intended also for those who can profit practically by learning and reflecting on its contents. It was, of course, written in Dutch—an Indonesian translation was, however, shortly to appear—and among Indonesians its potential readership was limited to those with a Dutch education. Within that circle, although by implication there is an attempt to engage in a debate at the level of the subtext with nationalist sympathizers, the underlying assumption is of a readership sympathetic to Achmad's general outlook on Dutch-Native cooperation.

Within its didactic mode the autobiography is exemplary at different levels. At one level, the book is intentionally rhetorical and persuasive. It makes the argument that an association policy, wisely and judiciously pursued by the good and the great on both sides (and one notes here that there is already a polarization of Dutch and Native) is the proper course for the country's future. Achmad constantly intervenes in the narrative to substantiate that argument and to make the relevant rhetorical points. He suspends the chronicle and takes up the argument, either in the course of a comment on a historical event or in one of the passages dealing with personalities. It is an argument in which the reader is expected to engage and acquiesce.

The interventions and the rhetoric, however, are minor strategies in the overall context of the book, since Achmad's intention is to persuade not so much by argument as by example: the triumphal progress of the hero of the autobiography himself. The story is not one of the rags-to-riches of the self-made man whose successful career is offered as a model for the young reader, although there is an aspect of this: here there is an invitation to the Native reader to emulate what Achmad has achieved, an invitation he makes explicit again in the closing sentences of the book where he conjures up the image of a future ex-council member no longer a Native (Inheemsch), but, significantly, an Indonesian (Indonesische). It is not so much as a moral tract that Achmad offered the book, but as an example of the successful realization of the political views which he holds: his achievements, his position in society, the progressive march of history which he describes are all to be read as evidence of the rightness of his ideas. And even though unconsciously that project may be seriously undermined by incidents which he relates of checks and rebuffs, we are in no doubt that the final accolade of *Pangeran* (Prince), the award of which is triumphantly described at the very end of the book, is to be understood not only as a personal victory over sometimes adverse circumstances but the triumph of a particular political vision. This, again, is signalled very explicitly for the reader in Achmad's reflections:

Daarbij dacht ik het meest aan mijn politieke vrienden, H. C. Kerkamp en S. J. Aay, die, wanneer ik al te zeer verdacht werd gemaakt, mij plachten te zeggen: "Houd maar goeden moed, eens zal men toch moeten erkennen, dat je bedoelingen altijd zuiver zijn." Toen de plechtigheid afgeloopen was, dacht ik neit zonder voldoening: Eind goed, al goed! (363)

(Moreover I thought particularly of my political allies, H. C. Kerkamp and S. J. Aay, who, whenever I came under too much suspicion, used to say to me, "Keep in good spirits; ultimately it will have to be recognized that your intentions were always honorable." When the ceremony was over, I thought not without satisfaction, all's well that ends well.)

The final sentence is trite and there is a sense of bathos about it, but the meaning to the reader is clear enough: "You see: I was right."

The autobiography should, therefore, be read as a political statement about engagement in the world, incorporating argument and example. We need to consider now how Achmad articulated, through several textual strategies within that statement, the relevant issues which form the substance of the debate. For convenience we may distinguish three: first, the presentation of his career, that is, the rather elaborate curriculum vitae in which a description of the stages of education is followed by a description of offices held and the honors received; second, the general observations regarding both specific issues and events relating to more amorphous perceptions of social change (these observations are sometimes separate from the ongoing narrative of the hero's life and sometimes interwoven closely with it); finally, there are specific opinions and comments made with reference to incidents and events throughout the book. Of the last, enough has been said above of the way in which opinion intrudes into a discussion of personalities; further examples would not add substantially to the points made there. (One might, however, note that frequently, when discussing native institutions such as child marriage or going on the pilgrimage to Mecca, Achmad apparently is trying to engage sympathetic friends in a discussion of such institutions rather than argue the case for a specific proposal or present a justification, as is the case elsewhere.) A little more needs to be said, however, of the representation of the curriculum vitae and considerably more about the way in which observations function as a strategy within the text.

Within the autobiographical rehearsal of the lifestory of the narrator there are two parallel movements of metamorphosis which concern reader and writer: the transformation of the *pesantren* pupil, Achmad, into the council member Pangeran Ario Adipati Achmad Djajadiningrat, and the transformation of the Sundanese minor aristocrat into the respected quasi-Dutch gentleman. The first of these is by no means unusual or even exceptional: there were many others who made successful careers for themselves by pursuing the logic of the possibilities of Dutch education at an early age, but the degree of accomplishment is worth noting, and Achmad takes pains to draw it to the reader's attention. In addition to the need to make his career function as a model, however, he has a further purpose in the demonstration: the vindication to his critics, a point strongly made within the context of the narrative since he immediately follows the description of contretemps and the specific details of disputes with Dutch officials with accounts of his elevation in office. These elevations provide the psychological encouragement which prompt him to persevere. As he notes at one point vis-à-vis a Resident with whom he was having trouble,

Zoo heb ik ook vaak op het punt gestaan om dien Resident, op het Officierskruis van Oranje-Nassau Orde, dat mijn borst sierde, wijzende, te zeggen: "Het kan mij niet schelen, dat U mij niet vertrouwt, omdat ik weet, dat H.M. de Koningin mij wel vertrouwt." (319)

(Similarly I too have often been on the point of saying to this Resident while pointing to the Officer's Cross of the Order of Orange-Nassau that decorated my breast, "It makes no difference that you distrust me, because I know that H.M. the Queen does trust me.")

This curriculum vitae which reveals the public acknowledgment of a civil service career honorably and assiduously executed is, therefore, an important part of the autobiographical project, yet it is not what makes the *Herinneringen* so fascinating for the contemporary reader. Almost atemporal within its own terms, the curriculum vitae can be read off as representative of a general bureaucratic career (much as *Hikajat Kadirun*, the novel by Semaun, can be read as representative of the radical alternative available to those who also enjoyed a Dutch education).[11] The fascination lies with the unique and temporally aware description of the other metamorphosis.

The distinctiveness of this latter metamorphosis lies in the circumstances arising from its being the first of its kind. To return to an earlier point, European education came late to the Javanese. In the Philippines and in India by the end of the century one was already speaking of a second and third generation of Natives educated in the European tradition. Autobiographies could look on a tradition of family Europeanization stretching back into the first half of the nineteenth century. What their autobiographies chronicled, therefore, was not the process of metamorphosis which had already been accomplished in previous generations, but the idiosyncratic twists that personal fortunes had taken.[12] For Achmad and his generation, however, the experience of Europeanization was entirely novel. Prior to the pioneering efforts of the Tjondronegoro family in East Java and the Djajadiningrats in West Java, acquaintance with European culture had been limited to the ersatz life-styles of the European senior officials whose collections of furniture, clocks, and fancy goods were purchased at the well-known *vendutie* (auctions at the end of service). In later years, of course, in particular after greater, although still much restricted, access to the

European primary schools was available, the process of metamorphosis was to be repeated in the lives of different individuals, but by that time there were differences in the experience, not the least of which was the awareness that other natives had preceded them. Hence there was a model, a structure, to follow or, in some cases, particularly in relation to the decision to join an administrative elite, to avoid. In Achmad Djajadiningrat's case, however, the situation was entirely novel, and in following his experiences, observing his strategies, and puzzling over his reflections, we are provided with a unique opportunity to analyze and interpret the growth of an original yet ultimately representative mentality.

From a very early age Achmad became acutely conscious of his unusual position, and his decision to record episodes in his life when that consciousness was forced upon him indicates how sensitively alive to the issues he remained to the end of his career. For example, among the incidents which he singled out for description are the scorn and ridicule with which, as a young boy, he was treated when he offered his hand to a Dutchman upon being introduced to him, and a Dutch official's refusal to speak to him in Dutch when he first entered into a civil service career. He also recollects being called a black ape behind his back by someone in a restaurant who thought he could not speak Dutch; being required as a junior native official to sit on the floor in the presence of Dutch officials; and being allowed to appear in European-style clothing before a particularly ethically minded Resident.

What is remarkable here is not so much the incidents themselves: interesting though they are in terms of the historical record, they could be multiplied several times over in other accounts of the general ethos of the period. It is that Achmad chooses to recount them and to emphasize his own reaction to them. These are not anecdotes for occasional retelling, but significant events within a lifetime which have shaped awareness and perception of the social environment. One or two examples can illustrate this.

When he was first taken to Batavia to board with a European family and to be placed in a European primary school by Snouck Hurgronje, Achmad first underwent a metamorphosis in appearance.

> Nauwelijks was ik aan Mevrouw KAMPSCHUUR overgegeven of ik onderging een geheele gedaanteverwisseling. Eerst moesten mijn lokken eraf, daarna kreeg ik afgedragen kleeren van haar oudsten zoon aan, die mij pasten.

Toen de Heer KAMPSCHUUR en zijn reeds schoolgaande kinderen thuis kwamen, leek ik niet meer op een Bantamschen jongen, doch meer op een Ambonees of een Indo-Europeaan. (66)

(Scarcely had I been given over to Mevrouw Kampschuur than I underwent a whole metamorphosis. First my hair had to be cut, and then I put on the clothes that her eldest son had grown out of, which fitted me.

When Heer Kampschuur and his children who were at school returned home, no more did I look like a young Bantanese, but more like an Ambonese or an Indo-European.)

The physical change was complete, but his Dutch at that stage was still rudimentary, and this caused difficulty in school. In a short time, however, as a result of playing with the children of the household, his Dutch improved. He was then moved to another school. On entering it the headmaster informed him that "*Voortaan heet je niet meer Achmad, maar Willem van Bantam*" (Henceforward you are no longer to be called Achmad, but Willem van Bantam). At this new school he describes how he was totally accepted:

Op mijn nieuwe school waren mijn medeleerlingen voor mij veel aardiger dan die op de vierde school. Ik had geen last van plagerijen en werd zelfs nu en dan op huiselijke feestjes uitgenoodigd. Dit, zooals mij later bleek, was toe te schrijven aan het feit, dat niemand van mijn medeleerlingen wist, dat ik geen Europeaan was. (Misschien was het den heer KRUSEMAN ook hier om te doen geweest, dat hij mijn naam veranderde). (68)

(At my new school my fellow pupils were far nicer to me than at the Fourth school. I had no trouble with teasing and I was even invited to household parties now and then. As it later seemed to me, this was attributable to the fact that none of my fellow pupils knew that I was not European. [Perhaps this had also been Heer Kruseman's intention in changing my name.])

181

It is worth remarking that, at that period at least, the Indo-European child was very easily able to assimilate into Dutch status, and that, although the social and cultural division between mixed and pure-blood Europeans was growing, it was not immediately apparent then. For this reason, Achmad, taken to be an Indo(-European), had no problem in passing.

This relatively quick metamorphosis was, however, the first and last time there was exact congruence in the perceptions of Achmad and his fellow Dutch of his European status. Complete acceptance within the European community was clearly a status and an identity which Achmad relished; one is reminded of the similar experiences of Indians brought up in British public schools (or preparatory schools, perhaps). It is, however, inevitably a transient experience, not simply because the status once afforded is withdrawn by the European community, but because the boy growing up perceives his roots and responsibilities to lie within indigenous society.

The disenchantment and rejection for Achmad, however, was a painful experience which occurred when he went to the HBS, the Dutch secondary school.

Voor het afleggen van het toelatingsexamen voor de H.B.S. moest ik wel mijn waren naam opgeven. Zoo werd ik op de H.B.S. weer ACHMAD genoemd; alleen thuis bij de familie MEISTER bleef ik nog steeds WILLEM heeten. Nauwelijks had ik mijn vermomming afgeledge, of mijn Europeesche vrienden, vooral vriendinnen, keerden mij den rug toe.

Voor velen hunner was ik weer "de Inlander." Hoe vaak voelde ik mij diep gegriefd als meisjes met wie ik dikwijls had gedanst of schaatsen had gereden, niets meer van mij wilden weten. Eens voelde ik mij door die behandeling zoo diep bedroefd, dat ik het betreurde, dat ik een Inlander was.

De leerlingen van de H.B.S. te Batavia hadden n.1. een gymna-stiek-vereeniging. Lycurgus genaamd. Ik werd bij mijn toetre-ding als leerling van de H.B.S. lid van die vereeniging. Eenmaal in het jaar gaf die vereeniging een uitvoering, gevolgd door een soiree dansante. Eens werd daarbij geen gewoon, maar een gecostumeerd bal gegeven. Zoolang ik een masker voor had don ik lustig met elk miesje, dat ik ten dans vroeg dansen, doch nauwelijks was het demasque of het was met de pret gedaan. (75)

(For the purpose of taking the entrance exam to the H.B.S. [European Secondary School] I had to register my real name. Thus at the H.B.S. I was again called Achmad; only in the Meister family home was I still called Willem. Scarcely had I thrown off my disguise, than my European friends, especially the girls, turned their backs on me.

For many of them I was again the "Native." How often did I feel aggrieved that girls with whom I had once danced or skated had decided that they wanted to know nothing more of me. Once I felt so deeply upset by this experience that I regretted that I was a Native.

The H.B.S. pupils in Batavia had a sports association called Lycurgus. I was on entering the H.B.S. a member of this association. Once a year the association held a performance followed by a dance evening. On one occasion not an ordinary ball but a masked ball was arranged. So long as I had a mask before me, I could happily dance with any girl I asked, but as soon as the unmasking was done my game was up.)

It is an instructive account, again for both the historical recording of an experience which is different from the racism and prejudice experienced by the Indian, the Filipino, or the Burmese, and for the light it sheds on the autobiographer. It takes a certain courage to write *ik het betreurde, dat ik een Inlander was*, yet at the same time the act of self-revelation here is surely ironic and indicative therefore of a mature consciousness of self, prepared to mock the idle pretensions of youth and rest secure and content in being an Indonesian. To commit the sentiment of youth to the public domain of print is, perhaps, one way of exorcising the older man's complicity in having shared that sentiment.

Metamorphosis, it seems, cannot be durable or permanent. At best there can be only pretence, only a temporary disguising. Whether the reader is meant to understand this as metaphor, or whether the symbolic nature of the example is only unconsciously intended, the description of the masked ball captures exactly the dilemma for those who would wear a disguise. From this point in the narrative, however,

183

and from that point in adolescence onwards, Achmad remains conscious that he is not Dutch, and that the struggle must be not to become Dutch, but to achieve equal legal status for the Dutch and the Native.

Indeed, this is the political and social goal which becomes increasingly important to him in the middle years of his career, the obstacles to which he learns to perceive lucidly on the occasions when his identity as a Native is deliberately brought home to him. One of the most revealing of these was at the time of the celebration of the Queen's Jubilee in 1922. Feeling that his position as Regent was being threatened by the Resident, Achmad took the opportunity of going to see the chief secretary to the governor to express his unease. The secretary's reply was that "*Wij Europeanen zouden in dit geval dit doen: wij zouden naar den Resident gaan en hem vragen of hij iets tegen ons heeft. Ik behoef niet te zeggen, hoe vreemd de uitlating 'Wij Europeanen' mij aandeed*" (321) (We Europeans should in this case do this: we should go to the Resident and ask him whether he has anything against us. I need not say how strange the expression "We Europeans" struck me).

For Achmad the secretary's manner of expressing himself is redolent of the attitudes he is having to contend with in the Resident— whom he describes as a "*vurig voorstander van het dualisme*" (ardent champion of dualism)—and he returns to Serang from Batavia with forboding. There he finds that, under the Resident's instructions, preparations are going ahead to hold celebrations which will keep the Dutch and Native communities separate. On this he comments as follows:

> Ten aanzien van de viering van het 25-jarig Regeeringsjubileum van H.M. de Koningin had de Resident zijn doel bereikt: gescheiden samengaan; maar het verschil van deze feesten met die van 1898 en van 1909, de geboorte van de Prinses, is in het bijzonder in het oog van de Inlanders groot. (321)

> (With respect to the celebration of the Queen's Silver Jubilee the Resident achieved his end: separate participation; but the difference between these celebrations and those of 1898 and 1909—for the birth of the Princess—was particularly marked in the eyes of the Natives.)

The way forward lay not in the separation of the two communities, but in their merger: not the merger into a nondescript uniform society but into an association of political and legal equals who maintain their distinctive cultural identities with mutual respect.

So powerful is this particular political and personal vision that, in fact, it does shape the construction of the *Herinneringen*, even in the documenting of incidental observation, and this is where we must look for further insight into the nature of Achmad's autobiographical project. Within the text, progress is measured implicitly by the degree to which the Native is visibly allowed to come to resemble the European. Such outward showing, at least in the early stages of political development, is a sign of a deeper structural *gelijkstelling* (equality of non-Europeans with Europeans), while *ontvoogding* (detutelization), to which much of the narrative is devoted, is a less visible but more formal aspect of the same process.

It is in noting the history and development of these visible signs, in particular in the areas of language and dress, that Achmad is at pains to generate within the narrative a sense of the passing of time and—as it seems to him—the march of progress. The illustrations accompanying the text make this point visually. The early photographs of the native aristocrat families portray individuals in native dress; the photographs of the middle years show the extent to which they adopted European dress, particularly in the clothing of the children. The final photographs show Achmad as a member of various commissions, indistinguishable from the Europeans in the three-piece suit he is wearing. These last photographs are the visual correlative of the culmination of his career and at the same time assertive statements supporting his general argument.

The importance of the rituals of dress as an indicator of social change needs some explanation. Throughout the nineteenth century, in trying to devise an appropriate administrative system based on a dualism between a European and a Native civil service, the Dutch had struggled to preserve the native aristocracy's status in the eyes of the population at large, at the same time as they effectively whittled away the power of that aristocracy. What the Dutch wanted was a scheme to make visible to the people the reality of Dutch power, while at the same time conserving a respect for tradition. The solution was to draw up a very rigid set of protocols in relation to public ceremony and ritual which would graphically demonstrate the political points while appearing consonant with native tradition. Thus, not only did the Dutch draw up

185

regulations with respect to the appropriate forms of dress and decoration for European and Native officials, they regulated footwear, entitlement to retainers, symbols of office, horses, the appropriate language of official exchange between European and Native officials, and even the posture of Natives in the presence of European officials. With respect to the latter, for example, only the most senior Native officials were allowed to sit on chairs in the presence of Europeans; others had to crouch or sit on the floor. By the end of the nineteenth century these rules and regulations had been rigidly cast into a very strict code of practice which Native officials found both irksome and offensive. The gradual abandonment of these practices can be and indeed was taken as a very real visual index of changing attitudes on the part of the colonial government. While little might have changed in terms of the realities of power, the shift in attitudes certainly heralded changes in the style of administration which found tangible expression in the decentralization laws of 1906, and in the concept of *ontvoogding* (detutelization), which extended greater autonomy to native officials.

It is these matters which are quite central to the *Herinneringen*. Achmad had already noted the importance of dress at an early age. The embarrassment in relation to the hand-shaking incident had arisen, in Achmad's account, because he had had the temerity to appear in European dress in front of a man *"die blijkbaar behoorde tot die Europeanen, die van meening waren, dat het in het belang van den Javaan is, dat hij zich in alle opzichten zoover mogelijk van een Europeaan afhoudt"* (121) (who apparently belonged to those Europeans who were of the opinion that it is in the interest of the Javanese that in all respects he distinguishes himself from a European as far as possible). When Achmad was next to meet the man, he wore native dress to avoid further ridicule.

At a later date, in the two-year period of apprenticeship before being appointed Regent of Serang, Achmad came across another Dutchman with similar views. To understand the full implications of this encounter, it is necessary to recall that Achmad by this time had successfully completed a Dutch secondary education. In terms of general learning he was the equal of any Dutchman his age. Describing the taking up of his appointment as Assistant-Wedana, a relatively senior post, he remarks on one of his Dutch seniors as follows:

Mijn tweede Europeesche chef was de Adspirant-Controleur. Deze was ongeveer van mijn leeftijd, zoodat ik een stille hoop had, dat hij mij min of meer vriendschappelijk zou behandelen, al was het slechts om daardoor in de gelegenheid te zijn mijn kennis van de Nederlandsche taal te onderhouden. Ik werd daarin echter teleurgesteld; nooit heeft hij mij b.v. gevraagd om bij hem op een stoel plaats te nemen. Als ik een dienstzaak met hem te behandelen had, moest ik steeds voor hem op den grond zitten. (121)

(My second European head was the Adspirant-Controleur. He was about my age, so I had a tacit hope that he would behave towards me in a more or less friendly fashion, even though that might be only here and there, giving me the opportunity to keep up with my knowledge of Dutch. I was, however, disappointed in this. He never, for example, asked me to take a chair in his presence. If I had to come to him with an official matter, then I had to sit on the floor in front of him.)

Achmad later contrasts his position as Assistant-Wedana with the news of his appointment as Regent. On that occasion, along with fellow Native officials, he had to attend a conference and was with the others seated on the floor, with the only native official on a chair being the Patih (a Regent's deputy). The Patih received a telegram, and, having read it, got up from his stool, moving deferentially across the floor, and kissed Achmad's foot in a token of submission, at the same time offering his best wishes, all to the great embarrassment of Achmad. This first visual sign of his change in status was followed by the official ceremony of his installation as Regent, the regulations concerning which he quotes at length. These governed the clothes that he was entitled to wear, the style of trousers with piping and gold braid, the epaulettes, pins of office, style of kris, details of headwear, and so forth. In addition, written instructions indicated how the Regent should deport himself when standing by the Dutch Resident, never with his back to him, and always with his head facing in half-profile.

Acutely aware of the symbolic importance of this ritual and its significance for an understanding of Dutch-Native relations, Achmad incorporates it within his autobiography to indicate what we might call the *mentalité* of the period. The subsequent advances which he describes in the nature of interpersonal relationships, and the incremental changes he observes, are to be measured against the overelaborate and ossified ceremonial of the late nineteenth century. The changes did not

187

occur overnight. When they did, their significance was not lost on him. Thus, although he notes the issuing of the famous hormat circular in 1911, which officially acknowledged that ritual and ceremony had been carried to absurd extremes and advising the abandonment of the more offensive and humiliating of the practices, he comments that it was some time before the *hormat* circular was generally implemented. On the other hand, he remembers with approval the occasion on which the Dutch Resident Hardeman finally suggested to him that they should speak Dutch rather than Malay together, and that Achmad should not bother with native dress when he appeared before him.

Achmad, however, was fully alert to the fact that the removal of these formal barriers to social intercourse between Europeans and senior Native officials also betokened a changed role for the latter. There is a slightly self-mocking description of how the great days of the Regent have come to an end, and how the grand tours in horse-drawn carriages accompanied by retainers are a thing of the past. On the other hand, he appreciated this change in style as being a move towards the profession-alization of the senior civil service, a move which becomes consciously articulated in the shift in policy away from hereditary office. It is a shift which, despite his emotional attachment to the notion of an aristocracy, Achmad ultimately approves as being conducive to development.

It is not political events at the national level, let alone interna-tional events, which provide the historical frame of the *Herinneringen*. Indeed, dates are significant by their absence. Instead what we read is an account of the steady progression of a career in which the significant moments the official appointments and the changes in administrative roles. That, at least, is one movement within the narrative. The other trajectory is to record an impression of social change, and this, as we have just seen, is accomplished by a concentration on the changing nature of Dutch-European relations.

Achmad's account of history differs substantially from that of the radical nationalists, for whom the period is marked by successive confrontations and the increasingly vociferous demands for indepen-dence. Nonetheless, we should not let the aftermath of decolonization obscure the significance of Achmad's perceptions of historical change. It is only hindsight which relegates his position to the status of an alternative while raising nationalism to that of orthodoxy. Furthermore, to ignore Achmad's view of things would be to ignore a tradition which continues into the present history of Indonesia and contributes actively to it. Despite appearances, the liberal democratic notions which implicitly inform the autobiography are still recognizable in formations within Indonesian society today. It is wise, therefore, to insist that there is no uniform assessment, no accepted consensus, and that each single interpretation leaves its traces in the evolution of complicated and sometimes inconsistent multiple views of the encounter between Europe and Asia.

NOTES

1. For Tan Malaka, see Benedict R. O'G. Anderson, *Java in a Time of Revolution: Occupation and Resistance, 1944-1946* (Ithaca: Cornell University Press, 1972); and for Dr. Soetomo, his "A Time of Darkness and a Time of Light: Transposition in Early Indonesian Nationalist Thought," in *Perceptions of the Past in South-East Asia*, ed. Anthony Reid and David Marr (Singapore: Heinemann, 1979).

2. Soetomo, *Towards a Glorious Indonesia: Reminiscences and Observations of Dr. Soetomo*, edited, annotated, and introduced by Paul W. van der Veur, translated by Suharni Soemarmo and Paul W. van der Veur, Monographs in International Studies, Southeast Asia Series, no. 81 (Athens, Ohio: Ohio University Center for International Studies, 1987). Tan Malaka, *From Jail to Jail*, trans. Helen Jarvis, Monographs in International Studies, Southeast Asia Series, no. 83 (Athens, Ohio: Ohio University Center for International Studies, 1991).

3. E. du Perron, *Indies Memorandum* (Amsterdam: De Bezige Bij, 1946), 220-25.

4. For Raden Salleh, see Harsja W. Bachtiar, "Raden Saleh: Aristocrat, Painter and Scientist," *Majalah Ilmu-Ilmu Sastra Indonesia* 6/3 (August 1976): 31-79. For Willem Iskandar, see Tamar Djaja, *Pusaka Indonesia*, vol. 2 (Djakarta: Bulan Bintang, 1966), 529-38.

5. See Pramoedya Ananta Toer, *Panggil Aku Kartini Sadja*, vol. 2 (Djakarta: Nusantara, 1962), 197.

6. Pramoedya Ananta Toer, *Bumi Manusia* (Jakarta: Hasta Mitra, 1980). The work was published in English by Max Lane as *The Earth of Mankind* by Penguin Books Australia in 1982.

189

7. Heather Sutherland, *The Making of a Bureaucratic Elite: The Colonial Transformation of the Javanese Priayi* (Singapore: Heinemann Education Books, 1979), 50-51.

8. P. A. A. Djajadiningrat, *Herinneringen* (Amsterdam: G. Kolff, 1936). All page references which follow refer to this text.

9. See Sutherland, *Making of a Bureaucratic Elite*, 77-80. For the use of the autobiography as historical source, see Akira Nagazumi, *The Dawn of Indonesian Nationalism: The Early Years of the Budi Utomo, 1908-1918* (Tokyo: Institute of Development Economics, 1972); Michael C. Williams, *Communism, Religion and Revolt in Banten*, Monographs in International Studies, Southeast Asia Series, no. 86 (Athens, Ohio: Ohio University Center for International Studies, 1990).

10. W. J. O'Malley, "Second Thoughts on Indonesian Nationalism," in *Indonesia: Australian Perspectives*, ed. J. J. Fox, R. G. Garnault, P. T. McCawley and J. A. Mackie (Canberra: Australia National University, 1980).

11. For the *Hikajat Kadirun*, see H. Maier, "Geschreven in het licht van de gevangenis: de Hikajat Kadiroen van Semaoen," in *A Man of Indonesian Letters: Essays in Honour of Professor A. Teeuw*, ed. C. M. S. Hellwig and S. O. Robson, Verhandelingen van het Koninklijk Institut voor Taal-, Land- en Volkenkunde 121 (Dordrecht Foris Publications, 1986).

12. Compare the experiences described in an Indian Civil Service autobiography, S. Bonarjea, *A Nation in the Making: Being the Reminiscences of Fifty Years of Public Life* (Bombay: Oxford University Press, 1963). First edition 1925.

7

THE EARLY FICTION OF
PRAMOEDYA ANANTA TOER, 1946-1949

Keith Foulcher

Among the earliest writing of Pramoedya Ananta Toer there is a short reminiscence entitled *Kenang-Kenangan Pada Kawan* (Memory of a Friend), written in 1947 after the execution of a young Indonesian freedom fighter charged with terrorism by the Dutch.[1] In the early months of the Indonesian revolution, Pramoedya's "friend" (the character in his story) had commanded a unit of people's militia forces (*lasykar*), working in uneasy coalition with what was to become the regular Indonesian Armed Forces (Tentara Nasional Indonesia—TNI). On one occasion before his enforced demobilization by the regular army, the friend had challenged a senior regular army officer over the condition of the soldiers in his unit. Characteristically, Pramoedya's sympathies in the situation he is describing lie with the underdog; they are antihierarchical, anti the power that results from privilege and social position, and on the side of a visionary enthusiasm that rests on skill, courage, and a sense of responsibility. A key passage in the exchange runs as follows:

> Suatu kali kekesalan hatinja memuntjak. Ia protes pada kepala staf—perlakuan kurang baik, kesehatan seksinja tak terdjaga. Dan ia mendapat djawaban jang pahit, "kepandaian jang harus kita pakai sekarang bukan sadja kepandaian mempertahankan tanah-air sebaik-baiknja, tapi djuga kepandaian mengatasi kesukaran dan kekurangan diri sendiri." Djawaban jang buatnja hanja rangkaian perkataan jang indah dan enak untuk diucapkan sambil minum kopi. Sebab, badan orang jang dihadapinja itu

merupakan *kapstok* setelan Amerika setengah wol, arlodji-tangan
waterproof, vulpen atom dan sepatu mengkilat oleh kiwi.[2]

(On one occasion the annoyance he was feeling reached a peak.
He protested to the chief of staff—poor treatment, inadequate
attention to the health of his men. The reply he received left a
bitter taste in his mouth: "The skills we need now do not only
involve the defense of our homeland to the best of our ability,
but also the skill of overcoming our own individual difficulties
and shortcomings." It was for him a reply which was no more
than a string of beautiful words, something nice to say over a
cup of coffee. Because the body of the man he was facing was
in fact no more than a coat hook for a 50 percent woollen suit
from America, a waterproof wristwatch, a cartridge fountain
pen, and shoes polished up with Kiwi.)

The description is arresting, and it contains some of the
suggestive power of Pramoedya's best writing. For not only does it
encapsulate a sense of the social tensions which beset the Indonesian
revolution (and, indeed, remind us that it is an awareness of social
inequalities which drives Pramoedya's writing from its very beginning),
but it is also a thought-provoking statement about the nature and power
of rhetoric. It is words, and the combination of words, which shape our
sense of reality, which give tangible form to experience, and which are
the means by which the reality they form is then communicated, so
creating "the past." Here the specific reality being foregrounded is the
experience of the Indonesian revolution. The officer's words are on the
one level to be taken as mere hypocrisy, but they also suggest a
conception of the revolution where the defense of the nation stands
alongside the struggle of the individual over the limitations of time and
circumstance. For readers of Indonesian literature, especially Indone-
sian literature of the revolution, this formulation of the meaning of the
revolution has an uncanny, almost eerie familiarity about it. For taken
out of context, the officer's words so easily could evoke the vision of
the revolution toward which a great deal of literary rhetoric has been
directed.

One thinks, for example, of Mochtar Lubis's much-admired
novel of the revolution, *Jalan Tak Ada Ujung* (A Road with No End),
with its central concern being the struggle of the individual for
psychological maturity in circumstances of terror and uncertainty,

192

"overcoming [one's] individual difficulties and shortcomings." The statement is a reduction, though not necessarily a distortion, of the "humanism" of the two figures often seen as the pioneers of the literature of the revolution, Chairil Anwar and Idrus. In the work of both these writers, the circumstances of revolution are seen to provoke an inner questioning, and it is this introspection, directed at understanding the nature of "humanity," which is then set against the outer events of the "defense of the nation" to create the characteristic literary picture of the revolution.

What Pramoedya's friend does in this passage is to remind us of the rhetoric of representation. The literary pictures we obtain are "*rangkaian perkataan jang indah*" (a string of beautiful words), put together in precise ways by precisely defined and located individuals. In any given writer, we can trace both the process of construction and the location of the vision. Just as the regular army officer and the lasykar fighter will construct different word pictures of the revolution, each for his own purposes, so too will different writers, or even different works by the same writer, attempt to change our viewpoint on the nature and meaning of a particular reality.

In what follows, I aim to explore the particular modes of literary representation which characterize the earliest writing of Pramoedya Ananta Toer, all of it completed before the end of the revolution and most of it written in Dutch prisons between 1947 and 1949. Apart from perhaps the novel *Keluarga Gerilja* (A Guerilla Family), Pramoedya's writing of this period is today little known and little read. It represents, however, the formative period of modern Indonesia's greatest prose writer, and for that reason alone deserves to be better known. Moreover, for both the student of literature and the student of the Indonesian revolution, it is an extremely rich and valuable set of documentary material, based on the author's direct personal experience of the revolution in and around Jakarta between 1945 and 1946. It is the work of a young man not yet twenty-five years old, writing prolifically in a language which is not native to him, a language which seems to have been liberated by the times in which he was alive. The documents—all creative prose works of varying length—constitute a series of different combinations of language and experience, as Pramoedya the writer explores the possibilities of Indonesian literature or literature in Indonesian. Interestingly, as these different modes of representation emerge, so too does Pramoedya's shaping of experience move in, out, and around the dominant humanist ideology which underlies most of what is now seen as the literature of the Indonesian revolution.

Pramoedya appears to have begun writing late in 1946, at the end of a period of almost one year with units of the civil defense group known as the Badan Keamanan Rakjat (People's Security Body—BKR), and its successor, the Tentara Keamanan Rakjat (People's Security Army).[3] In the latter half of this period, he headed a unit of sixty soldiers fighting in the Kranji-Bekasi area outside Jakarta, then left the army, once rationalizations began to take place, at the beginning of January 1947.[4] Returning to live in Jakarta, he joined The Voice of Free Indonesia, the publishing section of the Indonesian Republic's Information Service. It was this body which published his first literary work, sometime in 1947. This was the novelette *Krandji dan Bekasi Djatoeh* (The Fall of Kranji and Bekasi), the middle section of a much longer work, which must have been written during or immediately after his time with the army. Later, in 1951, the Jakarta publisher Gapura brought out the first part of the complete work under the title *Ditepi Kali Bekasi* (On the Banks of the Bekasi River). The remainder of the novel was never published. It was lost after Pramoedya's arrest and subsequent imprisonment by Dutch marines in July 1947. Thus, apart from a few short stories, only one of which was later republished,[5] it is *Ditepi Kali Bekasi* and its sequel *Krandji dan Bekasi Djatoeh* (although published in reverse order) which provide us with our first glimpse of the writer Pramoedya was to become. And what an extraordinary "glimpse" it turns out to be.

Ditepi Kali Bekasi and *Krandji dan Bekasi Djatoeh* relate, in a fast-moving and vivid third-person narrative, the experiences of Farid, a seventeen-year-old youth who leaves a secure life in Jakarta to enlist with the youth militia fighting against the British and Dutch forces trying to extend their control outside the city itself at the end of 1945. His experiences, which come to center around his adventures as a unit commander, are obviously a creative reworking of Pramoedya's own experience at the time, and as such the novel acquires a distinctly authentic "insider" viewpoint on the *pemuda* (revolutionary youth) world. From its opening pages, the novel's location within pemuda experience is clear. Farid's decision to leave the security of home and family in Jakarta for the adventure, idealism, and danger of the struggle is presented quite explicitly as a deliberate exchange of value systems. As Farid and his two friends, Soerip and Amir, leave behind the city and head for the battle zone, they see themselves exchanging the *tjita-*

tjita kemadjuan (ideals of progress) represented by the city, along with thoughts of family, neighbors and *kampung halaman* (childhood home), for a new reality, embodied in pemuda rhetoric, *gelora hati masing-masing, gelora hati pemuda berdarah panas* (the tumult in the hearts of each of them, the tumult in the hearts of hot-blooded revolutionary youth).[6] Farid's father, a figure reminiscent of the father of Mochtar Lubis's pemuda fighter Hazil in *Jalan Tak Ada Ujung*, acknowledges sadly that present-day pemuda have replaced "parents" with the new sources of authority and devotion, *tanahair, bangsa dan kemerdekaan* (homeland, nation, and independence). Despite the genuine affection between father and son, they are now divided irrevocably by their location in different periods of history. Later in the story, they both experience the pain in this division when Farid returns excitedly to Jakarta for one week's leave, only to discover that his father has become an employee of the Dutch civil administration, the hated NICA. Jakarta itself then becomes the object of pemuda rage, as Farid cries in a fit of anger and despair,

> "Djakarta hantjur. Saja ingin melihatnja rata dengan tanah. Dan saja ingin melihat segala jang ada disini djadi debu sama-sekali. Saja ingin mendengar bangsa saja sendiri berteriak dari lautan api: ampunilah kami, wahai pahlawan. Padamkan api itu dan biarlah kami bersudjut pada kakimu."[7]

> (Jakarta destroyed. I want to see it level with the earth. And I want to see everything here reduced to nothing but dust. I want to hear my own people cry out from a sea of fire: forgive us, you heroes of the struggle. Extinguish this fire and let us kneel before your feet.)

From the point of view of Indonesian literature, this passage acquires an added meaning. The representation of the revolution in literature is itself largely a product of Jakarta, one in which the voice and the rhetoric of the pemuda rarely finds expression.

Yet *Ditepi Kali Bekasi* and its sequel are not simply paeans to pemuda rhetoric and ideology, as the above might tend to suggest. The reader's perception of the pemuda world emerges through a range of events, interchanges between characters, and reflections which circumstances provoke in the mind of Farid. It is a self-assured, arrogant, and explicitly male-oriented world, in which the major female character, the

195

Eurasian girl Nanny, is the recipient of male action throughout and is largely denied the privilege of self-determination, the principle which guides the experience of the male characters.[8] Yet it is also a world of deep and genuine intimacy, where people are brought together feeling themselves to be participants in a great moment of history, able to take risks, both physical and emotional, that in another age they may have foregone.

Near the beginning of Farid's story, there is a brief but moving exchange between himself and a young woman on the overcrowded train leaving Jakarta. Unable to secure a foothold, even on the steps of the carriage in which Farid is travelling, the woman ties herself with a sarong to an outside fixture on the carriage wall. When Farid cautions her from the window against the danger she is courting, the woman replies simply with a grin, and the words *Berdjuang, bung* (These are times of struggle, brother). Farid does not react, and looks away to try to ignore the danger, but the reader is left with a visual image that encapsulates the spirit of the times, the sense of adventure, of history, overriding personal safety and security. It is a fleeting image, but it is also one of the few moments when the spirit of the ordinary Indonesian people—the *rakyat*—has been fully captured in literary representation: the grin on the face of the young woman, and the words of spirit and resilience. (Shortly after on the train journey, after Farid has been joined by Amir and Soerip, the woman does in fact fall, and is dragged along by the train, badly injuring her hands and feet, and almost being caught in the carriage's wheels. She is rescued by other passengers clinging to the steps, but falls again, fortunately this time as the train is slowing down to enter a station, where young women of the Indonesian Red Cross are able to assist her.)

Throughout the story, events are portrayed according to their meaning within the world of the pemuda and the armed struggle for Indonesian independence. Humanism of the "every man is my brother" kind is explicitly rejected, as in the aftermath of a vicious battle at Cikampek, when enemy soldiers, Sikhs and Dutch, are buried with scorn by the local people. The narrator's voice, speaking on the collective behalf of the people, asks if it "was for this that God gave life to these men, to come from far away to shatter the happiness of the Indonesian people, men whose nations enjoyed their own freedom, only now to be destroyed by the bamboo spears of Indonesia's youth."[9] The struggle for independence is uncompromising in its definition of the enemy and of its acceptance of the realities of armed combat. In another incident, the pemuda forces are inspecting a train bound for Bandung and loaded with RAPWI (Repatriation of Allied Prisoners of War and Internees) supplies, enforcing Indonesian demands that such trains be free of armed guards or arms supplies. They are provoked into combat by a trigger-happy Gurkha guard, and a short but violent exchange ensues in which a number of Gurkhas are killed, some murdered by local people as they try to escape.[10] The description is gruesome and ugly, with the brutality of the situation undisguised. Yet the outcome of the clash is presented unequivocably as a victory for the pemuda, resulting in a year's supply of food for the troops of the Greater Jakarta region.

We are most keenly aware of the novel's basis in pemuda ideology in its presentation of a series of events recorded in other historical sources of the period. This is the story of the burning of the town of Bekasi by British forces, in reprisal for the killing of British aircrew and Indian soldiers aboard a British plane that made an emergency landing near Bekasi on 24 November 1945. The day following the crash, the Republican authorities in Jakarta acted quickly in an attempt to ensure the safety of the plane's passengers and crew, but they later declared that the local people, feeling themselves to be at war and having seen the burning of villages in the area by foreigners, had immediately exerted a brutal justice of their own.[11] In the novel, however, the people approaching the stricken plane do so only in order to help the crash victims, and are provoked into violence when fired upon by Gurkhas from the plane.[12]

Whatever the facts of the historical situation, it is important to note that once again the novel has directed our attention to the innocence and suffering of the Indonesian people. The focus is on the aftermath of the killings, dealt with in detail before reference to the original incident itself. In fact, the horror of the burning of Bekasi, and the death and destruction it caused, is one of the lasting images implanted by the novel. Once again, it is a horror not of war itself, but of the actions of specific people directed against the Indonesian people and their fight for independence. In the midst of Farid's wanderings through the devastated town come the words of an old woman's song, in the Malay dialect of the region:

> Sajang-sajang tjutju nenek tjumah seorang,
> Bapak djadi Heiho baru pergi ke Birma,
> Aduh tjutjuku udah ora ada ibumu,

197

Inggeris-India membakar segala-galanja.[13]

(I have but one grandchild.
Her/his father became a Heiho and left not long ago for Burma.
Alas my grandchild, your mother is no more.
The English-Indians have burned everything there is.)

Almost in anticipation of the later debate in Indonesia on whether humanism could be universal, Farid comments to himself that the song is an illustration of the *kemanusiaan* (humanity, or here, humanitarianism) brought to Indonesia by the Japanese and the British. As he surveys the ruins around him, again he remarks bitterly on the humanitarianism of the British.

The novel's focus on the justice and heroism of the pemuda cause, and its rhetoric on behalf of the pemuda view of reality, do not mean that it avoids the issue, so important to other writers of revolution literature, of violence perpetrated by Indonesians against other Indonesians, either real or suspected enemy spies. The killing of the haji suspected of collaboration with the British, the same event which later was used as the basis for the weirdly surrealistic story "Dendam" (Revenge),[14] figures also in this story, with less emphasis on the haji's magic invulnerability to pain and death than on the sadistic and inhumane methods used to wring life out of him. Farid is appalled at that to which he bears witness, for although he accepts that war means the killing of the enemy, he rejects torture and the inhumanity it represents.[15] Elsewhere, Soerip tells Farid of an occasion where, but for his intervention, Nanny herself would have been killed by women of the Barisan Srikandi fighting brigade, who had apprehended her merely on suspicion of her Western features and the red, white, and blue pattern she was wearing.[16] Farid himself knows of fellow Indonesians wrongly accused and summarily executed.[17] He recognizes that he lives in *jaman kebinatangan* (an age of animalness) where "anyone with a gun feels the king of anyone without a gun."[18] Neither Farid nor the narrator of his story has any answer to the moral dilemmas provoked by this recognition of brutal reality. The important point, however, is that while incorporating it as a part of pemuda reality, Pramoedya here does not follow the path of other revolution writers (or indeed, later examples of his own work) in finding it a cause for distancing himself from "engagement." The novel remains totally engaged, with the external enemy and the heroism of the struggle constantly the main focus of

198

attention. What the novel demonstrates may be seen, in fact, to have links with the philosophy of the *wayang*. The moral dilemmas are ever present, however just and necessary it may be to act out the struggle itself.

Just as the narrative voice undercuts heroism with ugly reality, so too does it relieve seriousness and high-minded devotion to the cause with flashes of irony and humor. On one occasion Farid and his men have arrived at nightfall in Bekasi and are staking out a disused hospital in search of shelter. The people of Bekasi, after the terror of the burning of their town and the killing of many of its inhabitants, are fearful and suspicious of any outsiders; the occupation of the hospital must proceed with great caution. A noise is heard, and after much stalking, a frightened local inhabitant is captured, confessing himself to belong to the Bekasi police. A candle reveals that he is naked, clutching a rolled up pair of pants to his genitals. Farid's questions elicit nothing more informative than a frightened stream of "No, sir's," and the man finally is dismissed, leaving Farid and his men surprised and confused. There is of course some tension in the scene, surrounded as it is by images of warfare and terrible violence, and the reader fears for what may still be waiting in the hospital building's shadows. All that a search does reveal, however, is another naked person, not a man this time, but a woman. In the midst of death, Farid and his men have uncovered the persistence of life, adding an unexpected variation, even a degree of humor, to the tone of the narrative.

This sudden shift to earthy detail later becomes a characteristic of some of Pramoedya's best writing, but even at this stage, it can function as a device to pull the narrative back from "romantic" display. After Farid's early return to the fighting zone from his planned leave in Jakarta, he and Nanny wander as sweethearts through the rice fields as he tells her of his experiences. They come to a small stream and stop on a bridge. The choice of words seems conventionally sentimental:

Dua pasang mata memandang air jang deras dibawah sambil menjandarkan dadanja dipagar djembatan. Setangkai bunga mawar hanjut dibawa air.

(Two pairs of eyes watched the fast-flowing water below, as they leaned against the railing of the bridge. A single rose passed by, swept along by the current.)

But directly following these sentences comes

> Menjusul bangkai ajam. Tahi orang. Sebatang kaju djambu.
> Silih berganti pemandangan jang mengisi air itu.[19]

> (A chicken carcass followed. Human feces.[20] The branch of a
> *jambu* fruit tree. The sights which filled the water kept on
> changing, one after the other.)

As in the water flowing under the bridge, the views in the narrative
itself are designed to subvert conventional expectations of any kind.

The *Ditepi Kali Bekasi* series represents one of the modes of
literary representation which Pramoedya employed in his writing during
the period of the revolution. It is an uncluttered narrative mode, highly
visual and constantly in movement, with a minimum of direct authorial
commentary. The narrative moves mostly by action and dialogue, a
technique Pramoedya himself declares he learned from Steinbeck's *Of
Mice and Men*, which "freed action from interpretation."[21] The words
are an apt description of the narrative style of *Krandji dan Bekasi
Djatoeh*, in particular, where, as in *Of Mice and Men*, filmic dialogue
is the main technique of representation. In *Ditepi Kali Bekasi* and
Krandji dan Bekasi Djatoeh, the technique is used to convey an
experience of the revolution which is highly specific, localized, and
personal, which stands in sharp contrast to the dominant tendency of
revolution literature towards abstraction and universality. Later,
Pramoedya was to reuse this mode of representation in other contexts,
but before this occurred his work also was to move in other, different
directions.

If it was Steinbeck who taught Pramoedya a technique which
"freed action from interpretation," curiously, it was another American
who helped him evolve a second mode of representation which worked
in quite the opposite direction. This was William Saroyan, whose *A
Human Comedy*, Pramoedya says, taught him "how the most basic
human feelings are the quickest bridge to communicate with one's fellow
human beings," such that Saroyan steered his sentences "towards scenes
in which those basic human feelings could be displayed."[22] Characters
in *A Human Comedy* in fact are steered very tightly by their creator
towards such scenes and are given to serious, sometimes moving, but
rarely realistic monologues on the nature of human existence, such as it
is seen by the writer and his characters at a time when Americans are

fighting and dying amid the horrors of the Second World War. This style, in which the authorial intention stands fully revealed and in which statements on the nature of human existence form a distinct part of the narrative, probably also has affinities with traditional Javanese modes of rhetoric, making it all the more easily assimilated into Pramoedya's experiments with an "Indonesian" literature. It forms the basis of much of his writing completed between 1947 and 1949, while Pramoedya was imprisoned in Bukitduri in Jakarta and the island of Edam in the Bay of Jakarta.[23] Significantly it is also the basis for the writing which has drawn Pramoedya most of his recognition as a writer of revolution literature and which has given him a place in the established "canon" of Indonesian literature.

This second mode of representation makes its first significant appearance in the story "Blora," the first of Pramoedya's prison writing to appear in print. Along with other manuscripts, "Blora" was smuggled out of Bukitduri prison by Pramoedya's long time friend, the Eurasian lawyer and scholar Prof. Mr. G. T. Resink, sometime in 1948-49.[24] In 1949, before Pramoedya's release, it was published both in the journal *Indonesia* and in Dutch translation in the journal *Orientatie*.[25] The editors of *Orientatie*, in introducing the Dutch translation, commented that the story would for many

> lie heavy on the stomach, because this direct human protest against the struggle, against war as such, acquires something of an oppressiveness, an oppressiveness which, as we hope, leads to the awareness that everything shall be better than this tormenting obsession, this psychic cramp, that a human being can be exposed to by war and imprisonment.[26]

Writing years later, H. B. Jassin commented that

> Novel *Blora* sekaligus mengharumkan nama Pram. . . . Novel ini terutama menarik perhatian karena kemanusiaan yang memancar dari dalamnya, hasrat seorang tawanan pada kemerdekaan, pengalaman dalam angan-angan apa yang akan dilakukannya sesudah merdeka.[27]

> (The novel *Blora* at the same time gave Prameodya a fine reputation. . . . It attracted attention primarily because of the humanity which shone from within it, the desire of a prisoner for

freedom, and the imagined experience of what he would do after he was free.)

Professor Teeuw, in his *Modern Indonesian Literature*, recalled that "this story, because of its heart-rending poignancy, did not fail to make a deep impression."[28]   Clearly, the publication of "Blora" marked Pramoedya's debut as a writer whose appeal had moved beyond the "localized" context of *Ditepi Kali Bekasi*.

Compared to *Ditepi Kali Bekasi*, "Blora" is an elegantly crafted and composed literary work, carefully paced within its thirty-odd pages and enclosed within a conventional literary device, that of the dream that stands for reality.   The story is told in the voice of the first person narrator, initially relating the experience as though in direct conversation with the reader, later receding into the background to allow other characters in the story to continue the narrative through dialogue among themselves.   The opening paragraph sets the tone of the writing:

> Saudara! Engkau tahu apa jang ditjita-tjitakan oleh tiap tawanan? Engkau pasti tahu! Keluar—mendapat kebebasan kembali, hidup bergaul dengan kawan, saudara dan sesama manusia.   Buat saudara mungkin perkataan "keluar" itu tak memberi kesan apa-apa.   Tapi buat tawanan dan bekas tawanan kata itu alangkah merdu menggairahkan. Sama saktinja dengan lagu kebangsaan.[29]

> (Friend! Do you know what every prisoner dreams of? You must know! Getting out—regaining his freedom, living in communion with friends, relatives, and his fellow human beings. Maybe for you the words "getting out" don't leave any impression at all.   But for a prisoner and a former prisoner what a sweet and stirring sound those words have. They have the same magic as the strains of a national anthem.)

Immediately we recognize Saroyan, and his attempt to steer the reader towards "basic human feelings," rather than Steinbeck and his "action freed from interpretation." "Blora" is unreal, not simply because it is a dream, but because it proceeds not out of lived experience, as is the case with *Ditepi Kali Bekasi*, but from an idea, the degradation of humanity by war. The narrative, and the characters who act in it, are so constructed as to give expression to this underlying moral concern. As "morality," rather than "narrative," is the basis of the story, the seriousness is unrelieved by incongruity and irony; each detail is crafted into position to lead the reader towards the "oppressiveness" identified by the *Orientatie* editors.

The story itself relates Pramoedya's (the author names himself as the narrator) dream of release from prison and return home to Blora in the midst of the torment and brutality of the revolution. Contact with friends and family illustrate the devastation which has occurred, and prompt the remarks directed to the reader (*saudara*) on the inability of human beings to withstand the external forces that are brought to bear on their lives. The horrors seem endless: an old friend now a soldiers' whore, a grandmother begging on the streets, a visit to the grave of mother and sister both dead with the coming of the war, one younger brother lame, another captured by the Dutch. Finally the narrator is brought face to face with what seems the ultimate horror: the hideously wounded brother who, though without legs, is still the local revolutionary commander in the district. The final agony is even yet to come, however, because the narrator must ultimately accept the order of this "revolutionary commander" to kill the youngest of the family, because he threatens to betray the revolution by his enthusiasm for telling all he meets about the things to which he is witness. Jassin remarked that "many people" were disappointed by Pramoedya's adoption of the "it was only a dream" ending, because they saw it as representing a failure to recognize that the devastation which the story portrayed was in fact the reality of the revolution.[30] Yet it is clear that along with the adoption of the changed literary mode, Pramoedya has moved into a much more recognizably humanist conception of the revolution, in which, in contrast to *Ditepi Kali Bekasi*, there is no clear external enemy, for the enemy is war itself and what it can do to humanity.

Both the crafted literary mode and the humanist ideology which first appear in "Blora" were also the basis for Pramoedya's two long works written in prison, *Perburuan* (The Fugitive) and *Keluarga Gerilja* (A Guerilla Family). Like "Blora," *Perburuan* was taken up by agents other than its author and became one of the means by which Pramoedya's status as a writer was established. From Professor Resink the original manuscript found its way to Jassin, who entered it in a 1949 writing competition being held by Balai Pustaka. The novel won first prize. On Pramoedya's release from prison in December 1949, he found to his surprise an unexpected gift of Rp. 1000, which covered the expenses of his approaching marriage.[31]

Unlike Pramoedya's other writing of this period, *Perburuan* is set before the outbreak of the revolution itself, at the very end of the Japanese occupation.[32] It is a short novel, only about half the length of *Keluarga Gerilja*, but like the latter the story is concentrated in an extremely short time frame, one twenty-four hour period. In this, both the hand of the literary craftsman and the influence of his American model are evident. But whereas Steinbeck's three-day period in *Of Mice and Men* was localized in space and characters, *Perburuan* reaches back into the past to encompass a range of experience belonging to different characters in different times and places during the Japanese period. The narration proceeds not so much through an interchange of dialogue as through dialogue serving as a means for lengthy descriptions of past events or speculations on the meaning of those events. More than one quarter of the novel (56 of the 202 pages in the 1955 edition) is given over to a meeting between the novel's protagonist, the fugitive PETA commander Den Hardo, and his father, both of whom have lost their former social positions and are now outcasts of society. For the purpose of the narrative, the father must fail to recognize his son during this meeting, and despite the fact of failing eyesight, it becomes difficult for the narrator to retain the novel's realism during an interchange of this length between the two. As a result, the novel takes on a stylized, even contrived literary air.

The expectation of realism for a time seems to be misplaced; the single night seems endless and strangely dreamlike. For some readers, the writing may appear a confusion of genres; for others it may hold its own fascination. Yet undeniably, although the story is based on an actual historical event, the PETA revolt in Blitar in February 1945, *Perburuan* is more a novel of ideas than a historical novel.[33] As in "Blora," each character is assigned a particular role in the construction of a statement about human behavior under the most extreme of conditions. This time the central ideas revolve around notions of fear and courage, betrayal and revenge. Only in the final section of the narrative, as the news of the declaration of Indonesian independence alters the course of events, do the outer and inner worlds seem to be brought into contact, and the characters become historical actors reminiscent more of Farid and his companions than the devasted family of "Blora."

In *Keluarga Gerilja* the mode of representation common to "Blora" and *Perburuan* finds its most elaborate expression. Again the time frame is restricted, this time to a period of two-and-a-half days, and the actors themselves are largely confined to the members of a single family. Yet the scope which the novel seeks to encompass is enormous, as it aims to be a statement on the nature of the revolution itself and of its meaning in the lives of individual human beings. For the first time the writing is unrestrainedly sentimental and the drama of the revolution is represented as melodrama.[34] Jassin remarked that the novel appeared to be an answer to those who regarded "Blora" as failing to present the ugliness of the revolution as reality, for it showed the extent to which a man might be prepared to commit evil for the sake of humanitarianism in the future.[35] Neither Jassin nor Pramoedya as narrator raises the moral dilemmas inherent in this outlook, but everything about the novel stresses its attempt to blend sentimentality and crafted melodrama with a humanist ideology. In a key exchange in the narrative, Saaman, the condemned freedom fighter, confesses to his captor that he has murdered his own father. The issue is the same as that encountered in "Blora"—the revolution chooses its own victims, and Saaman as the agent of the revolution knowingly sacrifices his own humanity to its cause, for the sake of its ultimate victory. The humanity lost to the revolution is in fact partly recovered in the interaction of its individual antagonists. For the first time in Pramoedya's writing, we find the "universal humanist" concern with the "goodness in the enemy" theme, as Saaman discovers kindness, help, and even sympathy for his cause in his Eurasian jailer.[36]

It is not my purpose here to contest the superiority of the "engaged" pemuda view of the revolution or the distanced humanist view which the works just discussed share with most of the literature of the Indonesian revolution. What I wish to draw attention to is the shift in literary mode which accompanies the shift in ideological outlook, from authentic "insider" narrative to an elaborately constructed, more distanced and abstracted conception of the same reality.[37] It is likely, of course, that this change came about as the result of the circumstances of imprisonment, for indeed, Pramoedya's own reality had changed. The adventure, enthusiasm, and *semangat* (spirit) of 1946 had been replaced by captivity, enforced contemplation, and no doubt a need for a reassessment of experience. Yet "Blora," *Perburuan*, and *Keluarga Gerilja* do in fact represent only one side of Pramoedya's prison literature of this period. There was yet another literary mode which he was to explore, one which preserved the vivid authenticity, earthiness, and irony of his earliest writing and combined it with a broadly based engagement on behalf of the need for equality and justice which was to underlie all his subsequent writing. This is the mode of representation Pramoedya adopted in a number of the short stories from prison collected as *Pertjikan Revolusi* with which we began this discussion.

In this third mode of representation, Pramoedya again relies directly on personal experience as a basis for literary construction. This time, personal experience appears less mediated than in the *Ditepi Kali Bekasi* writing, as it is presented in the form of first-person recollections. As such, it would seem to have some affinities with "Blora," but the choice of the first person narrator is in fact not what determines the characteristics of this literary mode. The difference is immediately apparent if the opening paragraph of "Blora," as quoted above, is compared to the opening paragraph of "Gado-Gado," the long set of personal recollections of arrest and imprisonment, interspersed with historical reflections, which begins the *Pertjikan Revolusi* collection:

> Sudah lama aku ingin menulis. Terasa kepalaku penuh sekali oleh bahan-bahan tulisan. Aku ingin membuat buku roman jang menarik hati. Tetapi sudah lama kutjoba-tjoba mentjari pahlawan dan pendjahat untuk tjeritaku itu, ah, tiada djuga bisa dapat. Djadi bahan tulisan itu kubuat sedjadi-djadinja sadja—suatu tjampur-aduk jang tak tersusun dan tak berentjana.[38]

> (I've been wanting to write for a long time. My head has felt full of material for writing. I would like to put together a novel that would be of interest to readers. But I've looked around for ages, trying to find heroes and villains for this story of mine, and I just can't find them. So I'm writing up all this raw material I've got just as it comes out—an uncomposed and unplanned mixture.)

Whereas "Blora's" evocation of the reader, with its impassioned appeal to his or her "basic human feelings," marks the carefully crafted and composed, "Gado-Gado" has once again a specific, localized, and authentic character. Significantly also, the playfulness has returned, as the narrator confesses his inability on this occasion to craft a work of literature, complete with heroes and villains, and announces that he is settling instead for something "as it comes," uncomposed and unplanned. The rhetoric is self-conscious and ironic, of course, because by positing an implied reader with certain expectations and addressing that reader in direct conversational terms, the writing immediately announces itself as imaginative, or "literary" in some form or other. The tone continues in the following paragraphs, as the writer only somewhat less playfully goes on to hope that this series of uncomposed recollections may altogether acquire some of the taste delights of a gado-gado salad, or the strange beauty he has heard in Western music that at first seemed ugly and unfamiliar to his ears. The "story" progresses in this tone for seventy-six pages, as we follow the experiences of Pramoedya as narrator through the Japanese occupation, the war, and his arrest. His reflections on experience roam into universal questions but they remain fixed in a localized context:

> Perang! Ini semua akibat perang. Perangnja sendiri hanja menimbulkan luka, rusak dan binasa. Tapi akibatnja djauh-djauh menjalari seluruh kehidupan manusia digaris belakang. Diudjung-udjung djalan raksasa dibalik bumi, orang sibuk mendjaual koran dan berteriak adjaib. "Perang berketjamuk di Djawa dan Sumatera." Dan semua koran diseluruh dunia menggemborkan peristiwa ini.

> (War! All of this is the consequence of war. War itself brings nothing but wounds, damage, and destruction, but its consequences range far and wide, touching every aspect of life for those people at the rear lines. On the corners of huge thoroughfares on the other side of the world, people are busy selling newspapers and shouting out their amazing headlines. "War is raging in Java and Sumatra." All over the world all the newspapers are proclaiming this event.)

The irony is felt again:

> Perusahaan koran dan katjung-katjung koran didjalan raja itu mendapat keuntungan berlebih daripada biasanja. Kantor berita diseluruh dunia bangga karena mendapat kabar penting, sebangga modiste mendapat mode gaun jang tak ada taranja.

> (The newspaper publishers and the newsboys on the streets make a bigger profit than usual. News agencies all over the world feel proud at getting hold of important news, just as proud as the owner of a fashion boutique who obtains a gown that no one else can match.)

Those who die belong to specific nations, and again, Indonesia is fighting for its freedom and self-respect:

> Tapi di Indonesia sendiri—disini darah bertetesan. Pemuda-pemuda dari Friesland dan propinsi-propinsi disekitar laut Utara berdebar-debar menghadapi maut. Dan seorang demi seorang dagingnja tembus dilalui peluru penembak tersembunji. Dan gadis-gadis kekasihnja akan sedih sebentar, kemudian mentjari kekasih baru. Dan bangkai-bangkai kekasih dulu dilupakan. Dan inilah perang. Perang! Suling, ketjapi jang merdu, tak lagi menidurkan puntjak-puntjak pegunungan di Pasundan. . . . Puntjak-puntjak gunung tak tidur lagi—bangun. Berbondongan peluru menggantikan gamelan jang mendaju-daju. Pemandang baru jang menimbulkan sesak dada akan timbul.[39]

(But in Indonesia itself—here everywhere the blood drips. Young men from Friesland and the provinces around the North Sea feel their hearts pound in the face of death. And one by one their flesh is shot through by a sniper's bullet. And their sweethearts back home feel sad for a little while, then go looking for new boyfriends. And the corpses of their former sweethearts are forgotten. And this is war. War! The flute, the lovely sound of the Sundanese lute, no longer lull the mountaintops of Pasundan. . . . The mountaintops do not slumber any more— they are awake. A hail of bullets replaces the soft sonorities of the *gamelan*. New sights will arise, sights that cause the breath to catch in the chest.)

The injustice perpetrated between nations, which underlies this view of the Indonesian revolution, has its counterpart in other stories dealing with different forms of oppression. In the story "Kemelut" (Crisis), the dramatic description of a railway accident Pramoedya himself survived, it is not armed struggle in the name of national freedom, but the exploitation of the weak by the strong which is the driving ideological force in the narrative. What moves Pramoedya in his telling of the events is the ability of profiteers—those with economic means—to turn human tragedy to their advantage, making full use of the innocent generosity of the poor. The engagement this time is on behalf of social reform; there is no faith in a humanist solution.[40]

The variation in tone which Pramoedya achieves within this personal recollection mode is one of its chief characteristics. "Kawan Se-Sel" (My Cellmate) is the novelist's observation of a character with whom for a time he shared a prison cell. The moral basis of the story is outrage at the torture and imprisonment of a deaf man, simply because his disability prevented him from being alert to danger and being able to explain himself in words. The story is among the most blackly funny of all Pramoedya's writing. The "cellmate" is described in all the fine detail of his eccentricity, as it presents itself to the writer's eye. His initial defining feature comes as a surprise, to writer and reader alike:

> Sel ini terlalu sempit untuk kami . . . mengeluhlah aku. Siksa dikamar sempit jang tak tertahankan. Karena, kentut kawanku itu tak ditahan-tahan lagi. Tak gampang dielakkan dengan usaha jang praktis. Tjelaka! Dalam sepuluh setengah djam selama dalam kuntjian, paling sedikit ia kentut limapuluh kali. Anehnja, baunja mengandung aroma jang orisinil. Siksaan baru.[41]

> (This cell was too small for us. . . . I groaned. The torture in this small room was unbearable. Because I just couldn't take any more the smell of my cellmate's farts. It wasn't easy to avoid by any practical means. Damn! In the ten-and-a-half hours we were locked up he would fart at least fifty times. The strange thing was, the smell had a very original aroma to it. A new form of torture.)

The cellmate's farts, with their "original aroma," punctuate the remainder of the story. But the joke is finally on the narrator himself. The cellmate is released, but the aroma remains:

> Kalau aku ingat padanja, tersenjum sebentar, turut melihat tjakrawala dimalam hari, memandangi alam bebas merdeka. Namun bau kentutnja jang mengandung aroma jang orisinil itu tak hilang-hilang djuga. Dan barulah aku tahu kini, bahwa bukan si Gagu jang dulu kentut selalu, melainkan gas kakus jang naik dari bawah sel.[42]

> (Whenever I thought of him, I smiled a moment, looking at the night sky, watching the world of nature, free and unfettered.

But the smell of his farts, with their original aroma, still hadn't disappeared. And it's only now that I know, it wasn't old Gaga farting all the time, but the smell of the gas that built up from the covered earth toilets rising up from under the cell.)

Pramoedya could have written of this figure with all the seriousness and emotion which attached to his person and his condition. Elsewhere such tragic figures did receive this sort of attention in his work. But the story of the hapless cellmate indicates a different literary possibility, one that belongs within the conversational, earthy framework of the personal recollection mode of representation.

The one case in which the characteristics which define this mode—direct, conversational narrative, interspersed with irony and black humor, and based on an awareness of injustice and inequality—do not appear in the form of personal recollection is the final story in the *Pertjikan Revolusi* collection, "Djongos + Babu." This story in fact belongs stylistically with the best of Pramoedya's mid-1950s writing, collected in *Tjerita dari Djakarta*, where indeed it is reprinted.[43] It is perhaps the most complex of all Pramoedya's writing of the revolution, savagely ironic and deeply political, and yet on the surface light-hearted and funny, even playfully innocent. It is again a story of oppression, this time the internalized oppression which is one outcome of imperialism. It is an oppression which destroys individuals, psychically and culturally, yet those who are so destroyed are shown to have adapted successfully to the ways of the world. The narrative allows them the material prosperity which is the reward for their own internal oppression.

The story concerns a brother and sister, Sobi and Inah, living in Jakarta at the time of the revolution. They are the last in a long line of servants to foreign masters, all of whom have not been just any old servants but *hamba jang tak tanggung-tanggung—setia sampai bulu-bulunja* (slaves of no half measure—loyal from top to toe). A quick run through the family genealogy alights on the grandmother of the present generation, the first of the family to have "a delicate facial glow" (as the result of a lung disease), and thus the first whose slavery to a European also involved sexual slavery.[44] From this union was born Sobi and Inah's mother, a woman who knew how to profit from her servant status by exercising a politics of "divide and surrender." Sexual promiscuity with the master class meant that she was able to claim compensation from a number of European "fathers" on the birth of each of her two children. As a result, Sobi and Inah have grown up in material prosperity, but are still faithful to their family tradition, *djongos dan babu dari karat tertinggi* (houseboy and maid of the highest quality). History demands of them the skill to turn their slave mentality to advantage in the conditions of the revolution. It is Sobi who gets the first break. He finds employment with a Dutch family, responding enthusiastically to the needs of the young woman of the house for massage and sex, disposing of the resulting unwanted child, and preparing himself for making the wondrous transition to a European through his envisaged marriage to her. His sister Inah has not yet fully absorbed the fantastic possibilities that the slave mentality can arouse:

> "Aku mesti ingat sama adikku. Kalau aku sudah bisa kawin sama non Mari, aku mau masuk Belanda. Lantas minta mobil sama tuan besar gubernur-djendral. Kalau pagi plesir ke Tjilingtjing sama non Mari dan bertelandjang-telandjang dipesisir."

> "Tapi kulitmu sudah terotol bekas kudis dan panu. Engkau taku malu, kak?" Tanja adiknja lebih sedih.

> Sobi tertawa tinggi. "Kalau aku sudah masuk Belanda bekas kudis dan panu mesti hilang dengan sendirinja. Kapan tak ada orang Belanda jang panuan? Jang kena kudis tjuma orang Indonesia."[45]

> ("I won't forget my little sister. Once I get married to Miss Mary, I intend to become a Dutchman. Then I'll be able to ask the Governor-General for a car. In the mornings I'll go driving with Miss Mary and we'll run around naked on the beach."

> "But your skin is all covered with the marks of scabies and white blotches. Won't you be embarrassed?" his sister asked, rather sadly.

> Sobi laughed loudly. "Once I've become a Dutchman, the scars and blotches will go away automatically. When did you see a Dutchman with white blotches on his skin? It's only Indonesians who get scabies.")

Sobi berates his sister for her failure to seize the opportunities her pretty face sends her way, for after all, *Perempuan tak usah tahu apa-apa. Kalau sudah tjantik seperti engkau ini—semua akan gampang djadinja.* (Women don't need to know anything. If they've got a pretty face, like you, everything comes easy to them). There is in fact not much one needs to learn in order to become Dutch:

> "Kalau kita sudah djadi Belanda kita tidak boleh malu. Kita harus berani telandjang. Kita harus berani mabuk. Kita harus berani menggertak orang pakai 'godperdom.' Djuga kita harus selalu bilang begini 'Djepang memang binatang.' Tuan ku djuga berbuat semua itu. Semua perbuatannja aku perhatikan dan aku hafalkan. Rupa-rupanja gampang sadja untuk djadi Belanda. Kalau orang tjukup tjerdik seperti aku memperhatikan dan menirukan, dalam tempo seminggu djuga bisa djadi Belanda."[46]

> ("Once we are Dutch people, we mustn't be bothered by feelings of shame. We musn't be afraid to go around naked. To get drunk. We'll have to be able to snap at people and say, 'God damn you.' And we must always say this, 'The Japanese were animals, you know.' My master does all of that. I'm paying attention to everything he does, and I'm learning it all by heart. It seems it's quite easy really, to become Dutch. If you watch and copy carefully, like I do, you could be Dutch within a week.")

Sobi has lined up an agent for Inah to move into the Dutch world, and the narrative closes with her sexual surrender to the married "Tuan Piktor." Beyond the story, of course, Sobi and Inah are both going to fall flat on their faces into a most terrible nightmare they will never understand, that of an independent Indonesia. The narrative itself, however, does not compromise their innocent amorality and the rewards of their oppression. It is from within the playfulness that we read the irony, and within the irony that we are confronted by the political comment, whether we take it specifically as a reference to the condition of the "Indo," or more generally, in relation to a politics of cultural independence.

Pertjikan Revolusi was first published in 1950, with an introduction by H. B. Jassin, dated 13 January, just after the transfer of sovereignty and Pramoedya's release from prison. The terms in which

Jassin describes the stories claim the collection on behalf of the emerging universal humanist tradition and its view of the revolution:

> Apa kebebasan? Apa siksaan? Apa mati? Apa keadilan bagi rakjat djelata? Apa bahagia? Apa fungsinja uang? Apa tjinta? Apa kepuasan? Bagaimana berdjuang tjara gerilja? Bagaimana perdjuangan tjita-tjita dan perut? Suasana Djakarta sesudah aksi militer jang pertama. Bagaimana perasaan orang disel? Apa kemanusiaan? Apa keluarga? Soal Indo. Persahabatan.
>
> Semua ini djadi buah renungan dan perhatian bagi Pramoedya, bukan sadja sebagai penonton, tapi djuga sebagai orang jang turut mengalami pada tubuh dan djiwa revolusi dan segala akibatnja. Buah renungan jang tidak tjuma gelembungan, tapi adalah hidup sendiri, djelas, tadjam, disana-sini mengkirikkan bulu roma karena kedjamnja, penuh pertentangan baik dan buruk, djelek dan bagus, memperlihatkan manusia dalam kesungguhannja, kepalsuannja, kekuatannja, kelemahannja, keseluruhannja.[47]

> (What is freedom? What is torture? What is death? What is justice for the common people? What is happiness? What is the function of money? What is love? What is satisfaction? What is guerilla warfare like? What is it like to struggle for ideals and struggle for everyday necessities? The atmosphere in Jakarta after the first Police Action. How does someone feel in a prison cell? What is humanity? What is family? The problem of the Eurasians. Friendship.

> All of this was a source of contemplation and interest for Pramoedya, not just as an observer, but also as someone who experienced in body and soul the revolution and all its consequences. A source of contemplation that was not just bubbles in the air, but life itself, clear, sharp, here and there making our hair stand on end because of its cruelty, full of the conflict between good and evil, beauty and ugliness, showing mankind in his sincerity, his deceit, his strength and his weakness, his entirety.)

By the time he wrote these stories, however, Pramoedya clearly saw a more divided humanity than Jassin saw or cared to acknowledge in them. He saw injustice and the oppression of some human beings by others. In these stories, he used the most sophisticated, and yet at the same time the most lively mode of representation so far evolved in his writing to implant the notion of divided humanity in the literature of the Indonesian revolution. Criticism, however, chose to see it otherwise, and Pramoedya's work was interpreted and valued along the lines of the evolving universal humanist tradition.

The dominance of the universal humanist approach in Indonesian literary history has had important consequences for the subsequently received view of Pramoedya's early writing. It has meant that Pramoedya has been remembered primarily for the writing which has been identified in this discussion as the second narrative mode, his experimentation with a type of narrative where immediate experience is subjected to moral purpose, and lively description gives way to sentimental abstraction, in conscious pursuit of universal human truths. Yet as this discussion has suggested, this mode is the least successful of all Pramoedya's literary experiments during this period. It is also the least characteristic the writer Pramoedya's later work has revealed him to be. For in his post-1950 writing, this particular narrative mode drops away and is replaced by variations on what have been identified here as the first and third modes.   These styles encompass lively, realistic narrative based on observed experience, together with a taste for irony and satire, often found in brilliantly drawn caricature and culturally subversive parody.

It is in this type of writing, so startlingly developed in his *Tjerita dari Djakarta* of 1957, that Pramoedya's stature as a writer has been revealed most fully. Importantly, it is also this writing with which Pramoedya's outlooks have been most at odds with conservative or universal humanist understandings of social and cultural realities. Satire and caricature in Pramoedya is historically and socially, rather than universally, based. As such, it has not been accommodated easily with notions of literary value informed by the dominant universal humanist paradigm. The tradition which this paradigm represents has preferred to value that writing where Pramoedya, in his apprenticeship as a writer, came closest to its own values and outlooks. The price, however, has been the relative obscurity of the best of Pramoedya's early writing.

We began this discussion by suggesting that modes of literary representation are related to rhetoric and the power of words to create reality. As contemporary literary theory reminds us, however, the realities formed by words are always in flux, threatening even as they

214

acquire form to shift into new and different realities. Yet within these shifts we locate our experience, knowing it has form, though we may fail to grasp and define it, or pin it to the words that are our only means of communicating it. Pramoedya knew this too, as he sat writing, awaiting what freedom would bring, in 1949. At the end of his set of "Gado-Gado" recollections, he returned to his opening metaphor of the gado-gado salad, using words to illustrate their own limitations:

> Kalau kita menjelidiki rasanja gado-gado, akan tahulah kita bahwa seperti djuga makanan lain, riwajat rasanja hanjalah antara bibir dan tenggorokan. Dan tak ada seorangpun didunia ini bisa mengatakan bagaimana rasanja. Hanja lidahnja djua jang kuasa menerangkan. Pengalaman—hanja dengan pengalaman. Namun, disamping itu semua, adalah suatu rasa jang bertaburan sebagai awan berarak ditempurung langit dalam kenangan kita.
>
> Gado-gado ini demikian pula adanja. Ia akan hilang setelah lepas dari pantjaindera. Tapi ia akan hidup pula sebagai awan berarak ditempurung langit dalam kenanganku.[48]

(If we examine the taste of gado-gado, we are aware that, like other foods, the history of the taste lives only in the distance between the lips and the throat. And no one in the world can say what that taste is. It's only the tongue itself that has the power to explain it. Experience—only by experience. Yet, despite all of that, there is a taste scattered across our memory like clouds passing across the canopy of the sky.

This gado-gado of mine is the same. It will disappear completely once the senses let go of it. But it will live on in my memory, just like the clouds making their journey across the canopy of the sky.)

NOTES

1. My thanks to Anton Lucas, who provided me with first edition copies of some of the material discussed in this article. Thanks are due also to Ben Anderson, whose remarks and suggestions so often pointed to new discoveries, and whose comments and corrections have reduced the number of errors in what follows.

2. Pramoedya Ananta Toer, *Pertjikan Revolusi* (Outcomes of Revolution) (Djakarta: Gapura, 1950), 147.

3. See Robert Cribb, "Jakarta: Cooperation and Resistance in an Occupied City," in *Regional Dynamics of Indonesian Revolution, Unity from Diversity*, ed. Audrey R. Kahin (Honolulu: University of Hawaii Press, 1985), 182-88.

4. For details of Pramoedya's biography at this time, I am following the information provided by the author himself to Professor Teeuw in 1959. (See A. Teeuw, *Modern Indonesian Literature*, vol. 1 [The Hague: Martinus Nijhoff, 1979], 164.) More detailed information from the same source is available in Savitri Scherer, "From Culture to Politics: The Writings of Pramoedya A. Toer 1950-1965" (Ph.D. thesis, Australian National University, 1981), 15-24.

5. This is the story "Kemana??" (Whither??) published in *Pertjikan Revolusi*, 78-84. The precise dating of all Pramoedya's early short stories remains an issue for research. For details of their first appearance in published form see Ernst Ulrich Kratz, *A Bibliography of Indonesian Literature in Journals: Drama, Prose, Poetry* (London: School of Oriental and African Studies, 1988), 534-35. The short stories discussed in this article are drawn only from the *Pertjikan Revolusi* collection, all of which are known to have been written before the end of the revolution. Parts of the collections *Mereka Yang Dilumpuhkan* (The Paralyzed Ones) and *Tjerita dari Blora* (Stories from Blora), first published in 1951 and 1952, respectively, were also written at this time and are consistent with the picture presented here.

6. Pramoedya Ananta Toer, *Ditepi Kali Bekasi I* (Djakarta: Gapura, 1951), 31. Compare the description of pemuda values in Benedict R. O'G. Anderson, *Java in a Time of Revolution: Occupation and Resistance 1944-1946* (Ithaca: Cornell University Press, 1972), 185-86.

7. Pramoedya, *Ditepi*, 31.

8. Nanny is even subject to Farid's directions on how to dress. See Pramoedya, *Ditepi*, 148-49.

9. Pramoedya, *Ditepi*, 96.

10. Pramoedya, *Ditepi*, 56.

11. See the discussion of this incident in the sympathetic and largely sensitive account of the early months of the revolution in Java by the ABC correspondent John Thompson, *Hubbub in Java* (Sydney: Currawong Publishing Company, 1946), 68-99.

12. Pramoedya, *Ditepi*, 171-72.

13. Pramoedya, *Ditepi*, 86.

14. Published in Pramoedya Ananta Toer, *Subuh, Tjerita-Tjerita Pendek Revolusi* (Dawn, Short Stories of the Revolution) (Djakarta: N. V. Nusantara, 1961), 52-83. See also the discussion of this story in Ben Anderson's essay on the politics of language in Java, "Sembah-sumpah, politik Bahasa dan Kebudayaan Jawa" (Sembah-sumpah, The Politics of Language and Javanese Culture), *Prisma* 11 (November 1982), 69-96, and the same author's suggestive and wide-ranging "Reading Pramoedya's 'Revenge' (1978-1982)," in *Writing on the Tongue*, ed. Alton L. Becker, (Ann Arbor: University of Michigan, 1989), 38-73.

15. Pramoedya, *Ditepi*, 61.

16. Pramoedya, *Ditepi*, 151-52.

17. Pramoedya, *Ditepi*, 152-53.

18. Pramoedya, *Ditepi*, 160.

19. Pramoedya, *Ditepi*, 139.

20. This was originally altered to *shit*, following Ben Anderson's comment that *feces* was a mistranslation of the Indonesian *Tahi*. The point is precisely the shift from the idealized to the earthy reality.

21. See Pramoedya Ananta Toer, "*Perburuan* 1950 and *Keluarga Gerilya* 1950" (trans. Benedict Anderson), *Indonesia* 36 (October 1983): 41. This recollection by Pramoedya of the circumstances surrounding the writing of these two works offers a fascinating insight on Pramoedya's own view of the creative process.

22. Pramoedya, *"Perburuan* 1950," 41.

23. According to Pramoedya's own account, published in the story "Gado-Gado" (see below), his arrest was occasioned by the discovery of a letter he was carrying which opened with the revolutionary greeting, *"Merdeka"* (Pramoedya, *Pertjikan Revolusi*, 42). Teeuw refers only to "papers which' the Marines regarded as incriminating" (Teeuw, *Modern Indonesian Literature*, vol. 1, 165).

24. It is Resink's role in these events which adds poignancy to Pramoedya's dedication of the first of his Buru prison novels, *Bumi Manusia*, to him, with the words *"Han, Memang bukan sesuatu yang baru. Jalan setapak ini memang sudah sering ditempuh, hanya yang sekarang perjalanan pematokan"* (Han, this is indeed nothing new. I've travelled this narrow path many times; it's just that this time I'm marking out the ground).

25. *Indonesia* was originally a publication of the government printer, Balai Pustaka, which first appeared in 1949 under the editorship of Idrus. *Orientatie* was a cultural affairs journal set up in occupied Jakarta on the initiative of Dutch authorities at the end of 1947. Its editorial staff included Henk de Vos and Rob Nieuwenhuys, who at the time worked for the Dutch Ministry of Cultural Affairs. Reference to both journals may be found in Teeuw, *Modern Indonesian Literature*, vol. 1, 116, 118).

26. *Orientatie* 26 (November 1949): 2 (Dutch original).

27. H. B. Jassin, *Kesusastraan Indonesia Modern dalam Kritik dan Esei PT II* (Jakarta: PT Gramedia, 1985), 76.

28. Teeuw, *Modern Indonesian Literature* vol. I, 169.

29. Pramoedya, *Subuh*, 7.

30. Jassin, *Kesusastraan*, 78.

31. Pramoedya, *"Perburuan* 1950," 42.

32. It is also to my knowledge the only one of Pramoedya's works of this period to be translated into English. See Pramoedya Ananta Toer, *The Fugitive*, trans. Harry Aveling (Hong Kong: Heinemann, 1975). A more recent and readily available translation is that by Willem Samuels (New York: William Morrow, 1990, and Penguin, 1992).

33. On the PETA revolt, see Anderson, *Java in a Time of Revolution*, 36. In his introduction to his English translation of the novel, Aveling stresses the idea content rather than the historical background to the novel and relates it specifically to wayang plots and characters.

34. It is in *Keluarga Gerilja* that the influence of the third of the foreign models Pramoedya identified in his "*Perburuan* 1950 and *Keluarga Gerilya* 1950" recollections would seem to be felt most clearly. This is the Dutch novel *Moeder, Waarom Leven Wij*? (Mother, Why Do We Live?) by the Flemish writer Lode Zielens, first published in 1937. More so than either of Pramoedya's American models, Zielens' writing appears highly emotional, sentimental, and overblown, characteristics which are more easily related to *Keluarga Gerilja* than most other writing of Pramoedya from this period.

35. Jassin, *Kesusastraan*, 76.

36. Pramoedya Ananta Toer, *Keluarga Gerilja* (Djakarta: N. V. Nusantara, 1962), 152-54.

37. I am suggesting, of course, that the former is the more vigorous, interesting—and in that sense more "valuable"—literature. The lack of authenticity and the preference for the more distanced and "crafted" construction is a characteristic of much early postwar Indonesian literature, which probably has its roots both in the distance of the Indonesian language from authentic everyday experience at this time and in the selectiveness exercised by criticism. Jassin, the single most influential figure in the world of Indonesian literary criticism, made the extraordinarily revealing comment that in reply to a later query by Pramoedya about the possibility of republishing *Krandji dan Bekasi Djatoeh* he had rejected the idea because the story was "too localized" and lacking a "grand idea." See Jassin, *Kesusastraan*, 75.

38. Pramoedya, *Pertjikan Revolusi*, 9.

39. Pramoedya, *Pertjikan Revolusi*, 34-35.

40. Compare Teeuw, who leans to a "humanist" description of the story: "The main theme of human interest in the book [*sic*] is the contrast between the villagers at the scene of the accident, wretchedly poor and sickly but nevertheless very human, and the *tukang tjatut* (black marketeers) from the town who were involved in the accident, and who, although they seemed to be the victims, in fact were not. These latter professed the *Tuhan jang bisa dikantongi* (the God who can be pocketed), while the miserable villagers had the (true) *Tuhan diatas Langit* (the God above the Skies)." Teeuw, *Modern Indonesian Literature*, vol. 1, 168-69.

41. Pramoedya, *Pertjikan Revolusi*, 129-30.

42. Pramoedya, *Pertjikan Revolusi*, 141.

43. Pramoedya Ananta Toer, *Tjerita dari Djakarta* (Djakarta: Grafica, 1957), 5-18.

44. See also the discussion of the opening paragraphs of the story in Anderson, "Sembah-sumpah," 87-88.

45. Pramoedya, *Pertjikan Revolusi*, 189.

46. Pramoedya, *Pertjikan Revolusi*, 193.

47. Pramoedya, *Pertjikan Revolusi*, 8. (The "his" in the final lines of the translation is chosen advisedly, in the spirit of the original.) The comment is repeated in Jassin, *Kesusastraan*, 98.

48. Pramoedya, *Pertjikan Revolusi*, 76.

8

LITERATURE, CULTURAL POLITICS, AND
THE INDONESIAN REVOLUTION

Keith Foulcher

Introduction

In the conventional view of modern Indonesian literary history the term
Angkatan 45, the "Generation of 45," is a standard designation for those
writers active during the 1945-49 national revolution and their succes-
sors in the immediate postindependence period. The term itself is an
emotive one in modern Indonesia, used not only in reference to the arts
but in all areas of national history to imply participation in the passion
and struggle which ultimately led to the birth of the Indonesian nation.
Those deemed to be a part of the Generation of 45 are seen as the
bearers of the spirit of the revolution, who through their experience and
their outlooks bequeathed to all subsequent generations the ideals of
struggle and commitment which freed Indonesia from colonial domina-
tion. Applied to literature, the term "Angkatan 45" conjures up an
expectation of the drama, excitement, and promise of the national
revolution captured in the writing of the times. Indeed, in standard
versions of Indonesian literary history, the Angkatan 45 is seen as the
work of young writers, almost exclusively male, who, fired by the times
in which they lived, rebelled against the literary conventions of their
prewar predecessors to produce literature in a new way, and in a new
language more in keeping with the demands of the time.[1]

A closer look at the historical context of those writers now called
the Angkatan 45 suggests that the expectations aroused by the term, and
the way in which their work usually is presented, may be misplaced.
The characteristics which came to define the literary Angkatan 45

emerged in the work of a small group of writers who were active in Dutch-occupied Jakarta between 1945 and 1949, and represented in purely literary terms an assimilation into Indonesian culture of certain modernist tendencies in European art and literature of the interwar years. This process of assimilation gave rise to a realist prose and a symbolist poetry that embodied, variously, fear and uncertainty, horror and compassion, or detachment and cynicism about the revolution and those actively engaged in it. All of these attitudes were formed from a necessarily limited view of the many and varied realities which made up the revolution outside occupied Jakarta itself. As such, what has come to be called the Angkatan 45 in Indonesian literature is a much more specific phenomenon than usually is recognized. Its origins and character, as well as its subsequent "construction" by observers and critics, all await more rigorous historical research than has hitherto been the case.

In what follows I suggest the type of reconsiderations which further research might bring to bear on our understanding of the Angkatan 45. The discussion proceeds initially from the proposition that the Angkatan 45 cannot be placed within its proper cultural-historical framework if we assume Indonesian literary history to be a continuous process of evolution from one Indonesian language text to another. Using this framework we proceed from the prewar generation of Indonesian writers and their tentative forays into a new literary culture, to the sudden and unexpected revolution brought about by the pioneers of the 45 Generation. Something new has come, seemingly ex nihilo. Yet setting the question of language to one side, it is possible to construct a different picture. For it is possible to see the 45 Generation as having evolved with a considerable degree of continuity out of an Indonesian cultural and intellectual tradition that first emerges in the late 1930s, with Dutch as its medium of expression. The all-important link, and the intellectual and cultural nexus within which all this takes place, is undeniably the Sjahrir stream of Indonesian nationalism.

Forerunners: Indonesian Intellectual Culture in the late 1930s

The story we have to tell is an interesting one, because it is full of moral and political ambiguities bearing upon the role of the modern Indonesian secular intellectual, standing between the people of Indonesia and the West; it also has something to say about the difficult position

222

of Western intellectuals and artists who are caught up in that complex play of relationships. Its beginnings lie with the Dutch Indies writer Edgar du Perron, who was born into a wealthy landowning family in the environs of Batavia (Jakarta) in 1899 and died impoverished in Holland in 1940 on the day of the German invasion. His major work, *Het Land van Herkomst* (Country of Origin), published in 1935, is in large part an evocation of what it meant to grow up in the confident security of identity afforded by a wealthy Indies environment in the first decades of the twentieth century.[2] Writing about his youth, Du Perron refers to those Netherlanders newly arrived in the Indies as "Dutchmen," quite distinct from himself as an "*indische jongen*," a Dutch-speaking Indies boy from an aristocratic French family long resident in the Indies and for whom the Indies was home. In his adult years, however, Du Perron experienced the full force of cultural dislocation, knowing himself to be split forever between the cultural environment of his birth and his intellectual identification with Europe. In this he anticipated the experience of a whole generation forced by the political upheavals that accompanied war and revolution to seek a point of equilibrium between their "country of origin" and their country of nationality.

The acute sense of his own individual identity may have contributed to Du Perron's passionate commitment to an ideology of individualism and the responsibilities of the individual, amid what he saw as the dangers of collectivism on both the right and the left in the Europe of the 1930s. Fleeing what he described as the madness of Europe, he returned to the Indies in 1936 after an absence of fifteen years in search of a milieu where he could live and work. What he found there, however, was a society where to be European was to exist in a condition of moral ambiguity. To him, the racialist and narrow-minded colonial society he discovered in the Indies was as abhorrent as the political collectivism of Europe. Knowing that the world of the indische jongen was now never to be recaptured, he tried to find a way of life which was consonant both with the movement towards a new Indonesia, and with his sense of commitment to the dignity of the individual human being.

All the accounts we have of Du Perron suggest that he was a striking and charismatic personality, warm and receptive of anyone who won his respect. In the late 1930s, moving between Bandung, Buitenzorg, and Batavia, he gathered about him a group of young Indonesian intellectuals who shared his passion for literature and valued his recognition of the moral inevitability of Indonesian nationalism. "When we sat for hours on the verandah of his house talking with him," wrote one, "we had the feeling as if Dutch was our own language. We discussed Dostojovsky [sic], Huxley, Thomas Mann, Malraux, Gide, Slauerhoff, Vestdijk, Van Schendel, forgetting that we were sitting opposite one of the giants of Dutch literature himself."[3]

The author of this remark, Soegondo Djojopuspito, was one of the original members of the Sjahrir-Hatta Pendidikan Nasional Indonesia (known as PNI-Baru), formed from the split which occurred in the original Sukarno-led PNI (Partai Nasional Indonesia) in 1931. It appears that most of Du Perron's Indonesian intellectual friends at the time were drawn from this circle, those European socialist-oriented nationalists who, especially under the influence of Sjahrir, evolved a nationalist outlook which stressed the need for study, education, and long-term planning as the most appropriate response to the political conditions faced by politically aware Indonesians in the 1930s.[4] Soejitno Mangoenkoesoemo, another member of this group, recalled the effect of Du Perron's complaint that these Indonesian intellectuals unknowingly had devalued their old cultures. They needed to be aware of the power exercised by these cultures, and more important, he said, the value they could still exert. "He touched a sore point in this," Soejitno remarked. "It happens very rarely that anyone manages to find the right balance, a 'fusion,' within themselves."[5]

In December 1938, Du Perron became associated with a Dutch-language journal, based in Bandung, called *Kritiek en Opbouw* (Criticism and Construction). It had been founded earlier in 1938, describing itself as a "general and independent Indies journal," and directed at a Dutch-Indonesian readership on a basis of equality. It dealt with social and political issues in Europe and Indonesia, and especially with their cultural ramifications, and was unequivocally anticolonialist in its outlook. An early contributor writing on women's issues was Soewarsih Djojopoespito, the wife of Soegondo, whose recollections of Du Perron have just been quoted. The contact between Soewarsih and Du Perron, which was made through their common involvement with *Kritiek en Opbouw*, is an   important point in our story, because from their friendship came the publication of perhaps the finest literary work by an Indonesian in the prewar period, Soewarsih's novel *Buiten het gareel* (Out of Harness).[6]

In 1937, living with her family in Yogyakarta while her husband sought work elsewhere, and suffering from a crisis in her marriage, Soewarsih had written a novel in her native Sundanese dealing with the problems faced by women in marriage.[7] She had sent it for publication to the government printer, Balai Pustaka, an institution much vaunted in the writing on Indonesian literature as a promoter of the efforts of young Indonesians to write in non traditional ways. Balai Pustaka, however, existed to promote a certain type of literary expression and exercised a strict censorship over works which did not meet its guidelines. Soewarsih's manuscript was returned, rejected for publication, because it contained too little "instruction" and was not written in simple enough style.[8] It was Du Perron, after their meeting in 1939, who encouraged Soewarsih to take up the pen again and write this time of herself and in Dutch, the language in which she thought and could better express herself than in Sundanese. The result was *Buiten het gareel*, an autobiographical novel about her life as a teacher in an independent *taman siswa* school run by her husband in Bandung between 1933 and 1937. Du Perron stood by her in the writing of the novel, discussing with her the problems of autobiography and of writing in general, and offering her instruction through examples of his own work.[9] Yet *Buiten het gareel* establishes Soewarsih's own literary voice, dealing in a remarkably open manner with her feelings, the tensions in her marriage and the frustrations of poverty and political repression. She allows her alter ego Soelastri to emerge as a woman possessed of her own self-worth, yet driven by devotion both to her husband and to the nationalist cause, and dealing with the unavoidable tensions that result.

Buiten het gareel was not published in Indonesia, and when Du Perron returned to Europe in late 1939, Soewarsih's manuscript was among his papers. It was first published in Holland in 1940, after the German invasion and after Du Perron's death, but prefaced by the introduction which he had written for it.[10] The bond he had established with Soewarsih had generated the first properly realist Indonesian novel, subsequently all but overlooked in Indonesia because it was written in Dutch, but the beginnings nevertheless of a new Indonesian cultural tradition. The influence which Du Perron had on her emerges in Soewarsih's fulsome and emotional memoir written to mark his death less than a year after their final meeting.[11] That his spirit remained with her until her own death in 1978 was obvious to all who met her in her later life.[12]

Du Perron never met Sjahrir, the intellectual and political center of his circle of Indonesian friends, because his three years in Indonesia between 1936 and 1939 coincided with Sjahrir's exile in Banda Neira.[13] Yet there are two well-known points of contact between the two men.

These are important for our story, because they assist in elaborating our view of the intellectual culture with which we are dealing, and its relationship to the development of Indonesian literature.

The first point of contact between Du Perron and Sjahrir came in Du Perron's response to the well-known article by Sjahrir, *Kesoesastraan dan Rakjat* (Literature and the People), written in Banda and originally published in the 1938 commemorative volume of *Poedjangga Baroe*, the independent Indonesian-language cultural and literary periodical founded by Takdir Alisjahbana and Armijn Pane in 1933. In its *Poedjangga Baroe* context Sjahrir's article had been quite striking, seeming to cut through the endless polemic and visionary theorizing which characterized most contributions to the journal with an attempt to define a concept of enlightened social-realist literature which could be developed and applied in Indonesia from the models offered by modern European literature.[14] The article was republished in Dutch in *Kritiek en Opbouw*, and drew a response from Du Perron in June 1939.[15] Gently chiding the naïveté with which Sjahrir had foreseen a popular, educative role for avant garde literature in Indonesia, and ironing out some of his misconceptions of European literature, Du Perron in his response entered into debate with Sjahrir on the type of problems implied by cultural renaissance in Indonesia, specifically in the construction of a modern Indonesian literature. Significantly, he concluded his remarks to Sjahrir with the observation that what was most needed for an Indonesian literature was an Indonesian language rich in expressive power. If Indonesia were to find within itself a great writer who was capable of giving form to a vital Indonesian language, so much the better. However, if vitality in language were to come through "storytellers" who seized the public imagination and were widely read, there was no cause for alarm. Vitality in literature could only follow from vitality in language.[16]

Du Perron's second communication addressed publicly to Sjahrir came in the form of a reply to a letter, which was published in *Kritiek en Opbouw* in August 1939 as part of a collection of works by Du Perron under the title *Indies Memorandum*.[17] It is his attempt to sum up the personal meaning of his three years in Indonesia and explain the reasons for his return to Europe, and it reads as a characteristic expression of the modernist sensibility of the interwar years. He begins by remarking that Sjahrir is right,

In any case it is true that in Holland I always remain a bit of the "awkward foreigner." It's to be expected; my parents were almost full blood French and "colonial patrician," something very different from Dutch bourgeoisie. Atavistically I am a Frenchman, by upbringing an indische jongen, and by language and some customs a Dutchman. At the moment I am again so Europeanized that some say there is not much of this Indies boy left—with which I don't agree. Put me with real Indies boys and in ten minutes they will recognize me as one of them.

Yet, he goes on, he cannot now stay in Indonesia. "In all kinds of ways it repels me morally and intellectually . . . not the land, but the pedestrian, hypocritical colonial society." Moreover, reaching the age of forty, he has the feeling of betrayal, desertion of Europe. "You see, I am not as 'individualist' and 'free' as you think!" (And in an aside with present-day relevance, "I have noticed that many young Indonesians use the word 'individualist' without any nuance as 'egoist.'")

Apparently responding to a remark made by Sjahrir, Du Perron agrees that he can be useful in Indonesia, but only in a very indirect way. "To be really 'on the good side' here, you must be Indonesian. If I were Indonesian, maybe I wouldn't be so . . . individualistic, but nationalistic to the fingertips. That makes sense here." Yet to stand wholly with the Indonesians, even if that were possible, means for him an unacceptable betrayal of his Europeanness. He tells the story of a young Indonesian who likened the role of Europeans in Indonesia to that of Drona, the teacher of the Pandawas in the Mahabharata. Drona was a member of the Korawa clan, and, much beloved as he was by the Pandawas, in the Bharata Yudha they still feel compelled to kill him and bury him with honor. "It's all too poetic for me. The role doesn't attract me," says Du Perron with perhaps unintended irony. He senses it is time to leave, not only to join the struggle to protect Holland from the threat of fascism, but also because his role in Indonesia cannot be prolonged indefinitely. Sjahrir had apparently written of what the West, through figures such as Du Perron, had to offer Indonesian intellectuals. He agrees there are tools to be gained from the West which are of use, but says in the end, the Indonesian must stand alone. "It is people like you who must develop the culture of this country (I say nothing of politics), not 'outside players' like me," he concludes.

In this document, Du Perron makes quite clear the political ambiguities of his cultural broker's role, and his response to them. The importance of the task, the assimilation of modern Europe to the Indonesian nationalist consciousness, is not foresworn, but its execution is, as it were, handed on to Sjahrir and his circle. It is they who write the next chapter in this story, and make the transition from an Indonesian culture in Dutch to one in Indonesian. In this way, the lines of cultural history flow from Soewarsih and Du Perron, through Sjahrir to Chairil Anwar and his circle and the idea of an Angkatan 45. We can be somewhat more specific about how this process takes place.[18]

The Sjahrir Circle and the Genesis of the Angkatan 45

In his study of the Sjahrir circle in occupied Jakarta, John Legge has given us a clear picture of the type of intellectual culture which developed around Sjahrir once the Japanese occupation put an end to his exile and returned him to nationalist politics in Jakarta. In addition to the presence of his prewar allies, men and women such as those we have met already, he drew about him a younger generation of followers who espoused his nationalism on democratic socialist principles and the type of social, political, and cultural thought which accompanied it. Their socialism rested on a loosely Marxist interpretation of the nature and logic of colonialism and imperialism; it was fiercely antifascist and anticommunist, and it saw political struggle as the struggle to perfect the condition of life for the individual human being.[19]

It was a framework of thought and action which had no difficulty reconciling the nationalist struggle for a free Indonesia with a respect for Western values and Western civilization. Sjahrir himself, long resident in Holland and married to a Dutch woman, had in the prewar period been acutely aware of the "divided consciousness" which beset Du Perron at the end of his life. Feeling his intellectual home to be in Europe, much of his prewar writing, as Legge notes of Du Perron's letters from exile, is "full of contemptuous references to the backwardness of Indonesian society."[20] Yet unlike Du Perron, Sjahrir had no direct line of retreat available to him, and his passionate intellectual striving was characterized by a restless search for cultural synthesis.[21]

Among Sjahrir's younger generation of followers, however, Legge suggests that there was not the same sense of marginality and the need for its resolution. For some there may have been a need to negotiate a path between hostility to the political role of the Dutch and respect for their culture,[22] but there were no perceived problems for them of cultural, or nationalist, identity in their sense of personal growth

228

through Western cultural values and the examples offered through Western art, literature, and philosophy. In other words, their nationalism was not a cultural nationalism; the concept barely seems to have entered their concerns, and in contrast to the generations that went both before and after them, they found no need to formulate what it meant to be an "Indonesian." It was as though one lived the commitment to Indonesia through one's very being; it was the rest of life that was the hard part, that involved the need for discussion, debate, and creative practice.

In attempting to gain a sense of the outlooks of this group, it is important to note the fundamental distinction which Legge draws between Hatta and Sjahrir, a distinction resting upon Sjahrir's secularism as against Hatta's personal commitment to Islam.[23] Sjahrir and his followers, of both generations, were secular intellectuals. While this should not be taken to mean, of course, that they were antireligious or even necessarily lacking in religious sensibility, the absence of Islam at the heart of their concerns and their identities probably helps to explain the ease with which they moved within Western culture and its products and the lack of any felt cultural basis to their nationalism. In their cultural makeup, there were no barriers to the free play of internationalism, in both its political and its cultural dimensions.

Thus there began to develop in Jakarta during the years of Japanese occupation an intellectual culture with links to the prewar *Kritiek en Opbouw* circle. There is no doubt that in the discussions that took place, centered in Sjahrir's home and the network of student *asrama*s (dormatories) with their varying degree of proximity to Japanese propaganda aims,[24] the question of modern literature was a part of the agenda. This was not an interest in *kesoesastraan baroe* (new literature), as it had been espoused by *Poedjangga Baroe* in the prewar period. As we have seen, the lines of continuity do not go in this direction.[25] Rather, it was an interest in primarily Dutch, and secondarily French, German, and English literature from the Romantics to the Moderns. Such interest was fed by the ready availability of books looted from Dutch houses or sold to buy food, which came onto the secondhand market all over Indonesia in the wake of the Japanese occupation. Literature in European languages was one of the sources of the complex of ideas which formed the outlooks of Sjahrir's followers; along with philosophy and politics, it was an access point to Western civilization.

229

Some time early in 1940, in the company of his mother who was fleeing an unhappy marriage in Medan, North Sumatra, a nephew of Sjahrir named Chairil Anwar arrived in Jakarta, and stepped into this scene. A precocious, unruly, and by all accounts unlikable twenty year old,[26] Chairil did not share the educational background characteristic of Sjahrir's younger followers. His formal education had not progressed beyond the MULO secondary school level, whereas most of the Sjahrir circle had received a tertiary education. Chairil, however, possessed a great talent for languages and a voracious appetite for reading. During the Japanese occupation he is said to have read his way through Sjahrir's personal library;[27] later, he appears to have developed a talent for pilfering books from bookstores.[28] At the same time, he began to write poetry, not in the languages he was reading, but in Indonesian. In so doing he created the next link in our story, because although he wrote within the cultural intellectual framework which went back to the *Kritiek en Opbouw* circle, it was he who took the decisive step of transferring that framework to Indonesian-language writing. Certainly, he himself was well aware of the *Poedjangga Baroe* phenomenon, and saw himself as a writer in rebellion against it. He is said to have destroyed all his early, *Poedjangga Baroe*-influenced work, which predated his discovery of his own poetic voice in 1942. But his discovery of that voice came about within a new framework, not as a result of individual inspiration or some vague spirit of the times in which he lived.

A well-known essay which Chairil published in 1945 perhaps contributes to the common tendency to see him as a literary maverick, taking on the *Poedjangga Baroe* generation single-handedly and overturning its concerns. This is the essay entitled "Hoppla!" where Chairil excludes only a handful of poems from the prewar period in his blanket dismissal of the poetry of *Poedjangga Baroe* as failing to reach a level of any significance.[29] As such, he does enter into participation in the world of *Poedjangga Baroe*, but he does not evolve out of it; rather he enters it by a different route. Moreover, the path he has taken is evident in "Hoppla!" itself. The essay betrays all the marks of the kind of cultural thought which developed around Sjahrir's political nationalism. Its starting point is an attack on *Poedjangga Baroe*'s failure to recognize the dangers of fascism in the world of its day; it castigates the "collaborationist" artists who worked with the Japanese propaganda apparatus in contrast to the hundreds of European artists who left homelands they loved rather than be subjected to political

230

directives; it concludes not with a shout of welcome for a new *literary* age, but with a call to light the fires of everlasting brotherhood among the world's nations—all marks of the Sjahrir style of democratic socialist thought. It is this context which carries by implication the need for a new literary culture. He rejects *Poedjangga Baroe* because it belongs to a cultural and intellectual framework which is different from the one with which he finds identification.

In his early poetry, written between 1942 and 1945, Chairil began to experiment with the new Indonesian language and his self-perception as a writer. In both these areas, he took the literature of Europe, particularly in the interwar years, as a model and became the first to reproduce the European idea of "the modern" in Indonesian-language literature. The somewhat self-pitying tone of the *poete maudit* suited the adult personality which had been built on the spoilt and indulged child of an unhappy marriage. Only later would poems of some genuine introspection begin to appear. But the vitality of his language and his ability to derive metaphor and ambiguity from the plasticity of everyday speech and communicate it with utter directness were the marks of a genuine pioneer. Here, perhaps, was someone who might be Du Perron's "great writer" at the same time that he was that more essential "former of the Indonesian language."

Chairil became known and admired as a writer in company which lay on the fringes of the Sjahrir circle. He established contact with people who by temper and cultural outlook could be considered to be within the Sjahrir stream of Indonesian nationalism, but who were not direct participants in Sjahrir's circle. As Indonesia moved into the excitement and promise of late 1945, Chairil was forming his own circle, men and marginally also women who would see themselves as the cultural voice of the new Indonesian nation. They were to be the writers and intellectuals who established a framework of thought and produced the works of literature which established the Angkatan 45 as a recognizable outgrowth of the Sjahrir tradition, even as it acquired a character of its own. As this occurred, and as part of the process, the Dutch connection was to be reestablished. In the Indonesia of the revolution, however, Dutch-Indonesian cultural interaction was not to be as uncomplicated as it had been from the Indonesian side less than ten years before.

Cultural Politics in Occupied Jakarta

The circle which grew up around Chairil in the first eighteen months of the revolution appears to have had its "core" in a group of self-consciously "modern" or "bohemian" artist-intellectuals who interacted to varying degrees with others expressing Indonesian cultural sentiment in and around Jakarta. Close friends of Chairil were the writers Asrul Sani, Rivai Apin, M. Balfas, and the painter and illustrator Baharudin; also a part of this group was the striking figure of the essayist Ida Nasution. They had connections in one direction with Balai Pustaka, now the publishing house of the nationalist government, where the key figures were the critic H. B. Jassin and the writer Idrus. In another direction they interacted with writer-journalists like Mochtar Lubis, Rosihan Anwar, and Gadis Rasjid. They had some connections with the revolutionary youth fighting outside Jakarta with the *lasykar* (army) militia groups, although this contact appears to have been in the form of intermittent adventure rather than a continuing relationship.[30] The lasykar connection was represented in the broad spectrum of literary activity by the early writing of Pramoedya Ananta Toer, the most politically radical point to which the literary scene of revolutionary Jakarta extended.

The Chairil group acquired its first formal channel of expression in 1948 with the establishment of the cultural periodical *Gema Suasana*. The editorial board consisted of Asrul Sani, Chairil, Mochtar Apin, Rivai Apin, and Baharudin, but the journal was published by the Dutch Opbouw (Pembangoenan) printing house and was from the start embroiled in the politics of cultural collaboration with the Dutch. It appeared at a time when the Indonesian republic was on the defensive against the Dutch, following the unilateral Dutch abrogation of the Linggadjati Agreement in July 1947, and it suffered from Dutch behind-the-scenes financial and editorial support.[31] Within six issues (June 1948) most of the original Indonesian editorial staff had resigned, and transferred to *Gelanggang*, a cultural supplement to the Sjahrir-oriented weekly news journal *Siasat*, which first appeared at the end of February 1948 under the editorship of Chairil and Ida Nasution. Indonesian control over financial and editorial matters was thereby assured (and, we might add, placed firmly within the Sjahrir stream of nationalist politics), but the question of cultural collaboration/cooperation with the Dutch remained a central issue. The Chairil group was by this time in close interaction with another center of cultural activity in occupied

232

Jakarta, which revolved around the Dutch-language biweekly cultural periodical, *Orientatie*.

Orientatie had begun publication in November 1947 with support from the Dutch administration's Information Office and Ministry of Social Affairs. It described its function as the provision of a cultural forum where both original literary work by Dutch and Indonesians might find publication, and where translations and cultural news from Western Europe and Indonesia might be made known.[32] Initially, it clearly was intended to advance Dutch political interests, encouraging cultural interchange and understanding in a climate characterized otherwise by mutual hostility and suspicion.[33] From its fourth issue, in January 1948, the journal came under the personal direction of the Indies writer Rob Nieuwenhuys, one of the original *Kritiek en Opbouw* circle. From this time until after the transfer of sovereignty, Nieuwenhuys attempted to give the journal a thoroughly literary character, to move it away from the propaganda interests of the Dutch administration and to make it a meeting place for individuals of whatever racial origin who saw a new Indonesia as their cultural homeland.[34] In its early years, prior to the death of Chairil in April 1949, the circle which established itself around *Orientatie* played a role comparable in some respects to that played by Du Perron in relation to the earlier generation of young Indonesian writer-intellectuals. The Dutch and Dutch-Indies writers associated with *Orientatie* provided a bridge by which Chairil Anwar and his immediate circle felt in touch with modern Europe, both in terms of the provision of books, and by debate and discussion. They also encouraged the Indonesians in their writing, and through the translations of a number of Indonesian literary works which appeared in *Orientatie*, they played a part in constructing a literary Angkatan 45 as the voice of the Indonesian revolution.

Nevertheless, political relations between the Indonesian Republic and the Dutch were tense at this time, and though they were not cultural nationalists, there was no doubt that Chairil and the full extent of the cultural circle around him were fully republican in their political sympathies. They tended to distinguish between the Indies element in the Dutch circles, those like Nieuwenhuys, Vuyk, and Resink, who were believed to have cast their lot with the Indonesian nation, and those *totok* Dutch, some of whom were seen as being linked to the political motives of van Mook and his cabinet. One of the latter was the Islamologist C. A. O. (Chris) van Nieuwenhuyze, who belonged to the Dutch-Indonesian cultural circle, but was also a member of the van Mook cabinet.

Van Nieuwenhuyze was a devotee of personalism, a school of philosophy which asserted that the basic features of the human personality represent a paradigm of all reality. He established a kind of study group in his home, where this and other schools of thought were subjects of discussion among the young Indonesians. Speaking many years later Jassin recalled that all kinds of things were discussed at these meetings, but that "we were very careful, because we knew he was a cabinet man."[35] (On the other hand, warm relations seem to have existed between the Indonesians and Dolf Verspoor, a Dutch writer-journalist and AFP corrrespondent, who was part of the *Orientatie* circle.[36] It was Verspoor who first translated Chairil, his elegant Dutch versions of five poems appearing with their originals in *Orientatie* as early as January 1948.)

So it was that cultural politics, the question of defining a basis for cultural cooperation with the Dutch, came to underlie much of the discussion which was carried on through the pages of, initially, *Gema Suasana* and then *Gelanggang*. Certainly, the journals do offer us as well a guide to broader questions which figured in the literary culture of the years of revolution in Jakarta. Issues of world political concern in the postwar environment figured prominently, as is reflected in the range of articles translated from American and European magazines. The international cultural and literary scene was also a focus of interest and activity. *Gema Suasana* included as a regular feature a column called *Puisi Dunia* where translations by Chairil and his group of both Asian and American/European poetry were included, following on the more prominent position given to an original Indonesian short story and poem published in each issue. (Some later well-known stories by Idrus and Balfas were first published in this column, as well as lesser-known works by writers such as Asrul Sani, Utuy T. Sontani, and Usmar Ismail.) The publication of literature, in both the original Indonesian and in translation, was not a feature of *Gelanggang*, which was more a forum for the discussion of ideas. The role of cultural digest was performed by *Orientatie*, which included as regular features sections devoted to film, book, and magazine reviews, mostly from Dutch-language sources, but also from English, French, and, of course, Indonesian publications.

In the discussion of ideas which took place in the Indonesian journals, however, the sense of the relationship among culture, the nationalist struggle, and relations with the Dutch is a constant theme. The first issue of *Gema Suasana* in January 1948 included an extract from Sjahrir's letters under the title "Barattimur," in which he argued in characteristic fashion against idealization of so-called Eastern and Western cultures, against the need to choose between "slave and master, capitalistic West and servile East." In Sjahrir's view both had to be rejected as belonging to the past, in the forging of a culture appropriate to the demands of the modern world. Yet the sense of debate is felt in the same issue of the journal, in the publication of a short article from the work of Walter Spies which expressed the awe of the Western musician confronted by the "other-worldly" skills of the musicians of Bali.[37] More extensively, in the same first issue is an interview with Pak Said, the widely respected head of the Jakarta *Taman Siswa*. Expressing the taman siswa ideal, Pak Said was quoted as arguing the need for Indonesian culture to be based firmly in regional cultural sources, so preserving the cultural roots of Indonesia's young intellectuals and their links with the Indonesian people in general. Pak Said said it was not a question of "choosing" and "taking" from Western culture, for those aspects of culture necessary for Indonesia's development would be assimilated passively, as they were required, and adapted to Indonesian cultural patterns.[38]

While it is clear, then, that something of a cultural debate was being pursued within Indonesian circles at the time, it did not develop in the highly idealized and theoretical prewar *Poedjangga Baroe* style. Rather, in the context of national revolution, it was constantly pulled back to issues of political concern. The question of world culture and Indonesian participation within it was not seen to be divorced from Dutch political goals in Indonesia. In his 1972 interview, Jassin provided an interesting example of how the two were perceived inevitably to be related. The second issue of *Gema Suasana* featured on its title page a statement by the Indian writer, political activist, and feminist Shrimati Sarojini Naidu which argued passionately in favor of the humanist calling of writers and against the use of literature for the expression of nationalist sentiment. In his interview Jassin referred to the inclusion of the quotation as an example of Dutch attempts to influence the direction of the thinking represented in *Gema Suasana*. He said he believed the source of the quotation to have been van Nieuwenhuyze, and that it represented in the broader sense the type of policies pursued by the Dutch to win over the hearts of Indonesian intellectuals in support of Dutch interests in Indonesia.[39]

Those at the center of the Chairil group attempted to define in their writing and thinking a way through their antipathy to Dutch

235

political motives and colonial Dutch culture and their equal suspicion of any form of cultural nationalism. One later writer recalled the contemptuous remarks made by Chairil in reply to the views expressed by St. Takdir Alisjahbana in a 1948 interview, in which Takdir had argued in favor of continuing cultural cooperation with the Dutch, expressing the view that it was through the Dutch language that Indonesians had access to the major scholarly work on their own cultures. In the writer's recollection, Chairil had asked whether it was culture or erudition which the Dutch had offered Indonesians, and whether Dutch scholarship was so much a part of Indonesians that they could not now do without it in the search for their own identity.[40] Similarly, in her articles of 1948, Ida Nasution had railed against the absence of any cultural sensibility in Dutch society in Indonesia.[41] At the same time, however, she welcomed what she saw as the passing of a time when Indonesians maintained a defensive attitude to foreign cultural influence. In her view, Indonesian youth had liberated itself from the thinking of a past generation which looked to foreigners for approval and could not countenance anything usual, in art as well as in political and social matters. In the climate of independence, the important thing was to maintain a freedom from dogma in pursuit of a level of understanding where a broader view of developments in international thinking could be obtained.[42]

This striving after the "international plane of understanding" becomes an important theme in the writing of the Chairil group. It is not the internationalism which offered Sjahrir and his circle a framework for understanding the struggle between fascism and capitalism during the Japanese occupation; rather, it derives from an identification with European modernist aesthetics.[43] In the sense in which it is used, the international framework places full responsibility on the integrity of the individual artist/intellectual as "culture builder." Cultural nationalism is eschewed because it obscures the responsibility of the individual. In Nasution's terms, the effort to be "different" produced only "eccentricity"; the real goal, "originality," required the assumption of personal responsibility.[44] Within this thinking, art had a role to play in the process of nation-building in Indonesia, but only as long as the artist remained faithful to ideals of self-examination and constant change; the price of anything less was rigidity, the death of art, and its irrelevance to the national struggle. In this way, republican allegiances and European modernism remained completely compatible, producing a new

236

literary ideology which represented a clear cultural counterpart to the political nationalism of Sjahrir.[45]

The implication of this stance, for the literature produced by Chairil and his group, was that the national struggle in the broadest sense was best served by the complete faithfulness of the artist to the inner exploration provoked by the social environment. The revolution itself figured in the literature only in as much as it provided the setting in which that inner exploration took place and the modernist calling of the artist was realized. In the poetry of Chairil, a restless inner energy, fed by the modernist conception of the artist as seeker after personal truth, was the persistent focus of expression. The sense of the revolution as collective struggle was largely absent from his work.[46] Only in a few poems, where the inner restlessness interacts with a sense of hesitation and uncertainty in the wider political and social environment was the presence of the revolution apparent. One such poem is the well-known "Catetan Th. 1946."[47] Another, lesser-known example is the following untitled poem, one of the very few works of literature to be published in *Gelanggang*. It appeared in the 12 December 1948 issue, and belongs to the later Chairil poems, which begin to be pervaded by a sense of impending death.

> Sudah dulu lagi terdjadi begini
> Djari tidak bakal terandjak dari petikan bedil
> Djangan tanja mengapa djari tjari tempat disini
> Aku tidak tahu tanggal serta alasan lagi
> Dan djangan tanja siapa akan menjiapkan liang penghabisan
> Jang akan terima pusaka: kedamaian antara runtuhan menara
> Sudah dulu lagi, sudah dulu lagi
> Djari tidak bakal terandjak dari petikan bedil.[48]

> (A long time now it's been like this
> Finger stuck fast to the trigger of the gun
> Don't ask me how it first got here
> I've forgotten when and why
> Nor ask who's to make the final resting place
> For what is to be bequeathed: peace amid the ruined towers
> A long time now, a long time now
> Finger stuck fast to the trigger of the gun)

The lines have the characteristic Chairil ring of living at the extremity of experience, under a vaguely defined threat. The central image of the finger resting on the trigger of a gun belongs to the revolution, but the poem is not about the revolution itself. Even the "peace amid the ruined towers," which seems to slide toward a melancholy statement about the outcome of the revolution, is to be seen as a vision of personal defeat, couched in terms that recall the wider social environment.

This type of expression, then, is the most characteristic treatment of the national revolution in the work of Chairil and his circle. As writers they were not chroniclers of the revolution; they were its observers, as they consciously pursued their individual destinies. Yet in their self-perception they were the Generation of 45. Chairil is said to have himself coined the term "Angkatan 45" in its cultural meaning;[49] by December 1948 the freedom to pursue individual destiny and the struggle against the Dutch were seen as inextricably interconnected.[50]

The Construction of the Angkatan 45

Chairil died on 28 April 1949, his body apparently destroyed by his "bohemian" excesses and was buried on a hot and sultry Jakarta Friday morning.[51] The funeral procession, swelled by young students who, like many among the generations who came after them, found a hero in the author of lines like *Aku ini binatang jalang*, went by way of Sjahrir's home. Sjahrir himself was already at Karet cemetery, however, waiting to deliver a funeral oration with Usmar (Ismail?) and (Moh.?) Natsir.[52] In a touching testimony to the secularism of the tradition which Chairil and Sjahrir both embodied, the *kiayi* charged with conducting the funeral was said to have been annoyed that not one among the assembled gathering could recite the "Surat Yassin," and cut the funeral short to return to his Friday mosque obligations.[53]

The testimonies to Chairil Anwar which marked his death indicate that his status as a culture hero was by then well assured in both Indonesian and Dutch circles. *Orientatie* marked his death with the inclusion of a suggestive obituary by Rob Nieuwenhuys, who described Chairil as the personification of the modern cultural form so urgently needed by Indonesians—"Western in character perhaps, but still its own." There is an undercurrent of debate in the obituary with radical nationalist assertions of Indonesian identity. Nieuwenhuys offers Chairil as the model in place of the tendency to seek one remedy for all of (Indonesia's) complaints, and defends him against the offense which his failure to express himself consistently in political terms caused political "dogmatists." Chairil's great contribution to Indonesia lay on quite another plane from politics as such. It was he who made the Indonesian language that of a modern literature. "Chairil's Indonesian is remarkably 'transparent,' even for Netherlanders. That is, we hear in Chairil's poetry a voice break right through the form, that touches at once, and wakes in us the feeling that 'this is it.'"[54]

One point in Nieuwenhuys's obituary provoked a response in *Gelanggang* which indicated the type of myth-making which would occur in the Indonesian response to Chairil after his death. Nieuwenhuys had written that at the end of his life Chairil had suffered something of a "crack-up" (using the English term), which had given many people the opportunity to say he had a weakness of character. Clearly, Nieuwenhuys intended to defend Chairil against such an accusation, but its very mention was a regrettable flaw in the obituary for the *Gelanggang* writer. Writing in the column on the emotive date of 17 August 1949, Zarah asserted that it was not a personality breakdown which Chairil suffered, but an awareness that he was to be defeated in the struggle to realize his ideals. "He had a great sense of responsibility in his efforts to give form to a language in tune with the national spirit of the present age," the article ran. "So he would not give in to a society which would not move with the linguistic changes he felt." There is an attempt to claim a secure political consciousness for Chairil in the writer's accusation that only a Dutchman could believe that Chairil took no interest in political developments in Indonesia.[55]

This article represents, in fact, the beginnings of the process foreseen by the editors of *Gelanggang* in their original note on Chairil's death. "In his life maybe not everyone could appreciate him. Since his death, he has been commemorated, honored, glorified—maybe this is a writer's fate." In an interesting indication that Chairil had his admirers in republican Jogjakarta as well as in occupied Jakarta, this same editorial note chose to reproduce, from among many tributes received, one from the "young artists of Yogyakarta," regretting that Chairil had failed to live, in the words of his famous line, "another thousand years."[56]

In the months following his death, it was not only the personality of Chairil and the significance of his poetry which began to acquire a particular interpretation. At the same time, the "international plane of understanding" which had guided Chairil and his group through their cultural and political explorations began to be formulated in terms of an aesthetic ideology with political overtones and implications. The impetus for this process appears to have come from the entry into the debate of certain radical nationalist intellectuals who had taken a different path through the national revolution from that represented by the Sjahrir political-cultural stream. As the revolution drew to its negotiated settlement in the later months of 1949, this group shared the radical nationalist sense of the failure of the revolution, and looked to identify the cultural counterpart of that failure. By August 1950, this line of activity was to culminate in the formation of LEKRA and an identification with the political analyses of the PKI. Along the way, however, and in reaction to it, came the construction of the Angkatan 45 as it was to be known to later generations.

Late in 1949, at the time of the negotiations which concluded the warfare, accusations began to appear in Jakarta that the Angkatan 45 as a whole, the pioneers of revolution in all fields, was dead, that it had failed in its attempts to realize the potential for genuine revolution that had existed in 1945.[57] Applied to the cultural arena, these accusations threatened to challenge the nationalist credentials and achievements of the art and literature of the revolution and its claims to any special status in the attempts to build a new Indonesian culture. In reaction, the claim that the Angkatan 45 was indeed the embodiment of the Indonesian revolution was thus immediately brought to the fore. Sitor Situmorang, making his first appearance as an essayist, wrote a series of articles for *Gelanggang* in November 1949 defining the Angkatan 45 and the special character of its art and literature. Chairil Anwar is described unequivocably as *pemuda revolusioner*[58] and his asocial restlessness declared to be not a fashion but a bitter necessity of the times.[59] For artists like Chairil, the idea of "East" and "West" had been superseded by the recognition of the "universal" within the human being and the "universality" of the problems confronting the human being. The art which the Angkatan 45 produced expressed an intuitive belief in humanism, a conviction that the problems of humanity start within universal human nature, and so there must their solution be found. Sitor expresses the idea that these ideas played a part in giving birth to the revolution, but not in determining its course. (Neither side of the debate, it seems, wished to be associated with the revolution's outcome.) The fire of revolution declined and was extinguished, to remain alive only in the hearts of a few special artists of the Angkatan 45.[60] Thus, there is an attempt to claim the emotive nationalist name, and the true revolutionary convictions, on behalf of the group which Chairil had led. The guiding ideals of the group are formulated as "universalist" and "humanist" at the same time as they are "nationalist."[61]

Not long after the publication of these articles by Sitor came the formulation of the famous Gelanggang Testimony of Beliefs, the "Surat Kepercayaan Gelanggang."[62] The document is dated 18 February 1950, suggesting that its context is an attempt to formulate the meaning of the experience of revolution, though it was not published in *Siasat* until 22 October 1950, possibly in reply to the LEKRA "Mukadimah," issued in August of that year. Importantly, it claims both a concept of ongoing revolution and a heritage in the mass of the Indonesian people for its formulators. As such, there is no question of denying the social and political context of its aesthetic and cultural concepts. In keeping with the thinking of the original Chairil group, however, the formulation specifically rejects the notion of cultural nationalism. The well-known opening words of the document are, "We are the true heirs of world culture and must perpetuate this culture in our own way." This is the stance already being thought of as universalism. It stands alongside the humanism which in Sitor's articles had been ascribed to Chairil: "In our findings we may not always be original; the important thing for us to find is the human being."

It is the combination of these two principles which leads within a year to the term "universal humanism" as the concept on which the Angkatan 45 was seen to have been based. In 1951 Jassin published a long essay under the title "Angkatan 45" which constructed an argument for the term as the appropriate designation for a literary generation that was definable both in relation to its break with the prewar generation of writers and as the voice of the Indonesian revolution. In attempting to describe its characteristics, Jassin used the term "universal humanism" quite without qualification: "*Angkatan 45 punya konsepsi humanisme universal*" (The Generation of 45 held the concept of universal humanism). The concept was reflected in the Surat Kepercayaan Gelanggang. In Jassin's construction it drew together all those writers who had been active in occupied Jakarta, as well as many lesser-known figures who had worked outside Jakarta. In his later work, his application of the concept of the Angkatan 45 and, by extension, the ideology of universal humanism was very wide-reaching. His anthology *Gema Tanah Air*, originally published in 1948 and incorporating literature written between 1942 and 1948, was extended in subsequent reprints. In 1966, he wrote a short preface to the fifth printing of the anthology which appeared in 1969. In this preface, Jassin explained that, acting on the instructions issued by the Minister of Education and Culture banning the work of writers associated with "LEKRA/PKI," he had removed some writers and replaced them with others who had been excluded from previous editions for reasons of space. "In this way, we can now offer a complete introduction to what is called the Angkatan 45 in the history of Indonesian literature," the preface ran.[63] Thus, by this time, the Angkatan 45 and universal humanism had reached the form in which they were to be known in New Order Indonesia.

At the time of the revolution itself, however, the process by which certain works of literature came to be deemed worthy of inclusion in the Angkatan 45 and others were excluded from it was a more subtle procedure. Jassin himself played a key role in the process, from his position of critic, editor, and publisher, finding "literary" grounds to exclude extremes of both radical and antiradical nationalist sentiment. This was important, for it was part of the process by which the works which defined universal humanism came into being.

Establishing the Canon

Despite his excision from the 1969 edition of *Gema Tanah Air*, Pramoedya Ananta Toer was the most prolific and most accomplished of the prose writers of the revolutionary period. As noted above, he was not a member of Chairil circle; differences in temperament and outlook seem to have resulted in a degree of distance and mutual dislike where there was any contact.[64] Pramoedya was active in the early part of the revolution in the lasykar militia forces, and, for most of the period discussed above, he was a prisoner of the Dutch in various internment sites in and around Jakarta.[65] His first appearance in *Gelanggang* appears to have been an article on religion and literature, not published until well into the independence period.[66] Yet during the revolution, both before and after his imprisonment, Pramoedya wrote prolifically, experimenting with various narrative forms in search of his own writer's voice. As he did so, he moved both inside and outside the type of literary ideology we have seen become associated with the Angkatan 45. The way in which the proponents of that ideology responded to his work provides us with an instructive example of how the Angkatan 45 "canon" was established.

Pramoedya's earliest writing dates from late 1946, when he acted for a time as commander of a unit of sixty soldiers fighting in the Kranji-Bekasi area outside Jakarta. He left the army in January 1947 once rationalizations began to take place, and went to work in Jakarta with the publishing section of the Republican Information Office, "the Voice of Free Indonesia." It was this body which published his first literary work, some time in 1947. This was the novelette *Krandji dan Bekasi Djatoeh* (The Fall of Kranji and Bekasi), the middle section of a longer work, which must have been written during or immediately after his time with the army. In the postindependence period, the first part of this work appeared under the title *Ditepi Kali Bekasi* (On the Banks of the Bekasi River),[67] but the third part of the work was lost after Pramoedya's arrest and subsequent imprisonment by Dutch marines in July 1947. Thus, it is *Ditepi Kali Bekasi* and its sequel, *Krandji dan Bekasi Djatoeh*, although published in reverse order, which represent Pramoedya's first sustained piece of writing.[68]

As has been made clear elsewhere in this volume, the novel is closely related to Pramoedya's own experience of this time, allowing an "insider" viewpoint on the *pemuda* world, as distinct from the cultural environment of occupied Jakarta which is represented by Chairil and his circle.[69] Through the description of events in the novel, interchanges between characters, and the reflections which circumstances provoke in the mind of its protagonist, there is a gradual elaboration of pemuda ideology and its view of the revolution.[70] In this view, the humanism which later was deemed to be a defining characteristic of the Angkatan 45 is specifically rejected, as for example when the narrator's voice, speaking through the main character after a vicious battle with Sikh and Dutch troops, asks whether it "was for this that God gave life to these men, to come from far away to shatter the happiness of the Indonesian people, only now to be destroyed by the bamboo spears of Indonesia's youth"?[71] There is no attempt in the novel to disguise the brutality and cruelty exercised by both sides in the struggle, but the justice and historical inevitability of the pemuda cause is never obscured. The moral dilemmas are acknowledged as an unavoidable part of the battle to realize the nationalist ideals.

Ditepi Kali Bekasi's link to the broader climate of revolutionary literature is recognizable in its stylistic experimentation based on foreign models; in particular the influence of Steinbeck, whom Pramoedya notes as one of his teachers, is clearly evident.[72] In his prison writing, the experiments with style underwent a shift, under the influence of William

Saroyan and the Flemish writer Lode Zielens,[73] to produce a more elaborate and sentimental style, before finding their way towards the irony and caricature which marks Pramoedya's best writing.[74] Works in the sentimental style exhibited as well a changed ideological outlook which moved much closer to Angkatan 45 conceptions. They are represented by the story "Blora" and the novels *Perburuan* (The Fugitive) and *Keluarga Gerilja* (A Guerilla Family), which—not coincidentally, I would suggest—are Pramoedya's best-known works from the revolutionary period.

The story "Blora," which relates a prisoner's dream of freedom and along with it a recognition of the horror of all the revolution has produced, was smuggled out of Bukitduri prison by Professor Resink and published simultaneously in the Balai Pustaka journal *Indonesia* and in Dutch translation in *Orientatie*.[75] The editors of *Orientatie* introduced the story in extravagant terms, describing it as a "protest against war as such." Both Jassin and Teeuw later noted that the story marked Pramoedya's recognition as a writer of substance.[76]

The short novel *Perburuan* underwent a similar process of reception, outside its author's own hands. From Resink the manuscript passed to Jassin, who entered it in a writing competition sponsored by Balai Pustaka, where it won first prize.[77] In contrast to the fast-moving narrative of *Ditepi Kali Bekasi*, *Perburuan* is a novel of ideas, and revolves around universal human attributes of fear and courage, betrayal and revenge, against the backdrop of the Japanese occupation and the outbreak of the revolution. The longer work, *Keluarga Gerilja*, similarly slows down the narrative pace to seek out the play of human values in conditions of extremity of experience. In the process the expression becomes highly sentimental and melodramatic. It is one of Pramoedya's least successful works, but it is also the one where he comes closest to the universal humanist ideal. His characters are committed to the revolution, but the narrative is so constructed as to focus on their attempts to come to terms with universal questions, and the cost to their humanity which the revolution exacts.

In mainstream Indonesian literary criticism, Pramoedya's writing, especially *Keluarga Gerilja*, has been much criticized for its sentimentality and immaturity, even as those works devoid of these stylistic characteristics remain largely ignored. Significantly, Jassin's later essay on Pramoedya was entitled "Pramoedya Ananta Toer, Pengarang Keluarga Gerilya" (Pramoedya Ananta Toer, the Writer of A Guerilla Family).[78] The reason for this, I believe, is that it is in works like

Keluarga Gerilja that the ideological outlook comes closest to the Angkatan 45 ideal, because the works are nationalistic as well as humanistic and universal. It seems highly significant that Jassin later recommended against the republication of *Ditepi Kali Bekasi*, when Pramoedya raised the possibility, because the story was "too localized" and lacking a "grand idea."[79]

It is worth noting, however, that nationalism, in the sense of a commitment to the republican political struggle, is also a component, though unspecified, requirement for the inclusion of works within the universal humanist canon. The one important exception to this rule must be, of course, the long story *Surabaya*, by Idrus. In the postindependence period, it would be left to the radical cultural nationalists to challenge the place of this story in the literature of the revolution because of its focus on the hypocrisy, immorality, and self-aggrandizement of the young freedom fighters. The story does not appear to have attracted much published discussion during the revolution itself, but it was certainly a part of the Angkatan 45 canon in the postindependence period. (Jassin's essay was entitled "Idrus Pengarang Surabaya."[80]) Something of a puzzle emerges when the history of *Surabaya* is placed alongside the fate of another long story by Idrus from the later part of the revolution, *Perempuan dan Kebangsaan* (Women and Nationalism).

Despite the expectations aroused by its title, *Perempuan dan Kebangsaan* is an autobiographical story in which Idrus creates a picture of his involvement with the Balai Pustaka circle and in particular his relationship with Jassin from the time of the Japanese occupation. Read with irony, it is an incisive look at the cult of the artist-as-writer in the circles in which Idrus moved, and is as unflattering to himself as it is to the other figures who appear thinly disguised within it. The superficial ease with which foreign literary models and psychological theories are adopted, and the artificiality of the profession of writer, are the lasting impressions of the story, intended or not. It was published as a special issue of the Balai Pustaka journal *Indonesia*, of which Idrus himself was editor at the time, in May 1949. Subsequently it was forgotten. (Teeuw later dismissed it as being of no literary value.[81])

The interesting point, however, is in the terms in which Jassin, at the center of the process of selection of the Angkatan 45 canon, rejected the work. In private correspondence he professed to be unconcerned, even amused, at recognizing himself as Idrus's adversary in the story.[82] In a lengthy letter to Idrus, and later in published form, he explained in detail his objections to the story's elevation of humanist, to the exclusion of nationalist, ideals. Idrus's persona in the story adopts a pacifist stance towards the revolution, arguing that warfare in the name of humanity is the greatest crime of all, "because it makes use of humanity to carry on something which will destroy humanity."[83] Jassin specifically rejects this position, arguing in terms which would later be used by the radical nationalist wing of the cultural-literary debates: "there is a humanity which can only be attained through warfare."[84] He accuses Idrus's character of a lack of pluralistic thought, by which he means an inability to recognize the complexities of the nationalist commitment.

The paradox of the inclusion of *Surabaya*, with an an applauding of its honesty,[85] and the dismissal of *Perempuan dan Kebangsaan* for its failure to equate humanity with Indonesian nationalism, may be simply the result of Jassin's personal discomfort at Idrus's portrait of him in the latter story, despite his claims to the contrary. *Surabaya* may have claimed its place in the canon because of its status as a model of the tight, sparse Indonesian prose which Idrus pioneered. As such its stylistic significance may have outweighed its antinationalist overtones. Yet the terms in which Jassin rejected *Perempuan dan Kebangsaan* are consistent with his suspicion of aspects of Dutch-Indonesian cultural contact mentioned above, and with the type of criteria which were used throughout the revolution and after to define a literary Angkatan 45. It appears that whatever the reason, *Surabaya* is the anomaly; the universal humanist position lies somewhere between the pemuda radicalism of *Ditepi Kali Bekasi* and the pacifism of *Perempuan dan Kebangsaan*. Once more, we find the historical and ideological context of the literary Angkatan 45 best defined as lying within the nationalism of Sjahrir and his followers.

Conclusion

In the bitterly fought cultural political debate of postindependence Indonesia, universal humanism over time came to acquire a meaning which differed from that of its original historical context. In the years leading up to 1965, the strength of the radical challenge meant that those writers and intellectuals who worked within the Angkatan 45 tradition increasingly found themselves denying the political-ideological context in which literature was produced. In its place, they asserted that the autonomy of the individual artist, free from political involvement, was the precondition for genuine aesthetic achievement. This was the sense in which the term "universal humanism" was inherited by New Order Indonesia, when it was seen as the forerunner of the Angkatan 66 catch-cry, "literature in the name of justice and truth." By the 1980s, when the term resurfaced in a new climate of cultural political debate, its meaning had narrowed further. It was then seen to be the heritage of a type of literary expression which regarded a historical and political consciousness as nothing to do with the business of the writer, and was more concerned with religious sensibility and aesthetic experimentation.[86] In just under forty years, the term had travelled a long way.

There is no doubt, of course, that the Angkatan 45, and the universal humanism ascribed to it, stood fundamentally in opposition to radical nationalist sentiment and its application to literature. As I have suggested, the early critical reception of Pramoedya's work is sufficient indication that this position was defined clearly during the revolution itself. What has been lost sight of, however, is the particular tradition of nationalist politics in which the Angkatan 45 rightly belongs. It is not the voice of a collection of anarchic individuals who happened to live during the revolution, as we are sometimes led to believe. The ideology of individualism which it embraced was an outgrowth of a particular tradition of nationalist thought, reaching back to the prewar period. It was a tradition which found its own synthesis between the political struggle for a free Indonesia and a focus on the integrity and personal responsibility of the individual artist. It was not the voice of what we think of as the fire and spirit of the revolution; this was to be found elsewhere. Neither did it point towards the cultural and political future of Indonesia in the postindependence period. The irony in the heroic claim embodied in the term "Angkatan 45" is that, like the Sjahrir tradition in Indonesian politics, its vision of the Indonesian revolution and the Indonesian future proved to be a vision which failed. The dynamics of Indonesian cultural and political life came to rest elsewhere. The Angkatan 45 was in cultural and intellectual terms a minority tradition, going by a name that evoked something other than what it was. It represents one voice among many which made up the Indonesian revolution; it embodies one particular synthesis between a recognition of one's self in secular, Western cultural traditions, and a commitment to the Indonesian nation and the Indonesian people.

247

NOTES

1. For a recent statement of this standard view of Indonesian literary history see H. B. Jassin, "The Literature of Revolution," in *Born in Fire, The Indonesian Struggle for Independence*, ed. Colin Wild and Peter Carey (Athens: Ohio University Press, 1988), 28-33.

2. The novel has been translated into English in the "Library of the Indies" series. See E. du Perron, *Country of Origin*, trans. Francis Bulhof and Elizabeth Daverman (Amherst: University of Massachusetts Press, 1984).

3. Soegondo Djojopoespito, "E. du Perron," *Kritiek en Opbouw* 3/13 (16 August 1940).

4. J. D. Legge, *Intellectuals and Nationalism in Indonesia, A Study of the Following Recruited by Sutan Sjahrir in Occupation Jakarta* (Ithaca: Cornell Modern Indonesia Project, 1988), pp. 13-41.

5. Soejitno Mangoenkoesoemo, "E. du Perron," *Kritiek en Opbouw* 3/13 (16 August 1940).

6. *Kritiek en Opbouw* and its relation to the Dutch "Ethical" tradition is discussed in Gerard Temorshuizen, "Protest als pleidooi voor de inlander: het 'ethische principe' in de Indisch Nederlandse literatuur," *Indische letteren* 3/1 (March 1988): 27-42.

7. Gerard Temorshuizen, afterword to *Buiten het gareel*, by Soewarsih Djojopoespito (The Hague: Nijgh and van Ditmar, 1986), 225-26.

8. Temorshuizen, afterword to *Buiten het gareel*, 225. See also the comments on the novel's rejection in A. Teeuw, "Een buitenbeentje in de literatuurgeschiedenis," *Indische Letteren* 1/4 (December 1986): 163-66.

9. Temorshuizen, afterword to *Buiten het gareel*, 226.

10. The novel reached Soewarsih, and an Indonesian audience, only in 1946, after its second printing. A third printing appeared in 1947 and a fourth in 1986 with the original introduction by Du Perron and the afterword by Temorshuizen referred to above. With financial support

from the Netherlands, Soewarsih translated the novel into Indonesian in 1975 under the title *Manusia Bebas*.

11. Soewarsih Djojopoespito, "In Memoriam E. du Perron," *Kritiek en Opbouw* 3/13 (16 August 1940). The testimonies written in memory of Du Perron at this time were especially emotional, in view of the assumption in Indonesia that he had been murdered by the invading Germans. In fact he died of a heart attack. His friend and colleague Menno Ter Braak, with whom Du Perron edited the influential journal *Forum*, committed suicide on the same day that Du Perron died, in fear of reprisals for the public stand against fascism which the two had taken before the German invasion. (See the introduction by F. Bulhof in Du Perron, *Country of Origin*.)

12. In a conversation I had with Soewarsih in July 1970, she described her contact with Du Perron as a turning point in her life, something which changed her personality from shy and withdrawn to confident and assertive, breaking down, for her, the screens which existed in colonial society.

13. See W. Schermerhorn, *Het dagboek van Schermerhorn; geheim verslag van prof. dr. ir. W. Schermerhorn als voorzitter der Commissie-Generaal voor Nederlands-Indie, 20 september 1946-7 oktober 1947* (Groningen: Wolters-Noordhoff, 1970), 203-4. The leader of the Dutch delegation which negotiated the Linggajati Agreement, Schermerhorn described in this diary entry of 15 January 1947 his reaction to Du Perron's work and his asking Sjahrir whether he had known Du Perron personally.

14. The essay is reproduced in E. du Perron, *Menentukan Sikap* (The Hague: W. van Hoeve, n.d.), a collection of Du Perron's works translated into Indonesian by Sitor Situmorang.

15. Du Perron, *Menentukan Sikap*, 22-44.

16. Du Perron, *Menentukan Sikap*, 41-44.

17. "Indies Memorandum XV P.P.C. (Brief aan een Indonesier)," *Kritiek en Opbouw* 2/12 (1 August 1939). An Indonesian translation is included in Du Perron, *Menentukan Sikap*, 42-50.

18. For further material on the questions dealt with here, see the important publication by Kees Snoek, *De Indische Jaren van E. du Perron* (Amsterdam: Nijgh & Van Ditmar, 1990). This work, appearing after the completion of the present essay, contains much which elaborates and deepens the picture of the intellectual tradition which evolved in prewar Indonesia around the figure of Du Perron.

19. A concise statement of the political philosophy of Sjahrir's follwers, as it was expressed in the postwar Partai Sosialis Indonesia (PSI), is given in Bernard Dahm, *History of Indonesia in the Twentieth Century* (London: Pall Mall Press, 1971), 156-57. See also the introduction to Sutan Sjahrir, *Our Struggle*, translated and introduced by Benedict Anderson (Ithaca: Cornell Modern Indonesia Project, 1968).

20. Legge, *Intellectuals and Nationalism*, 32-33. Legge quotes here the striking lines from the letter which ran, "We intellectuals here are much closer to Europe and America than we are to the Boroboedoer or Mahabharata or to the primitive Islamic culture of Java and Sumatra. Which is to be our basis: the West or the rudiments of feudal culture which are still to be found in our Eastern society?"

21. Legge, *Intellectuals and Nationalism*, 30.

22. Legge, *Intellectuals and Nationalism*, 127.

23. Legge, *Intellectuals and Nationalism*, 23.

24. Legge, *Intellectuals and Nationalism*, 45-47.

25. Legge, *Intellectuals and Nationalism*, 76. Legge comments that though his informants knew of *Poedjangga Baroe*, "it did not appear to have excited any of them." This ought not to be surprising, given the different thought world which *Poedjangga Baroe* represented.

26. Chairil Anwar seems to have spawned a remarkable amount of "My memories of the poet" type of writing, right up to the 1980s. (See the bibliography in the latest Indonesian edition of Chairil's collected poems, Chairil Anwar, *Aku Ini Binatang Jalang* [Jakarta: PT Gramedia, 1986]). Much of this writing gives an unflattering picture of the poet's personality, despite its general hagiographical intent. For a summary of two of the more useful accounts, see Arief Budiman, *Chairil Anwar, Sebuah Pertemuan* (Jakarta: Pustaka Jaya, 1976), 64-69. See also the

fictional portrait of Chairil in Achdiat K. Mihardja's novel *Atheis* (Djakarta: Balai Pustaka, 1949), 113-19 and 131-34.

27. Budiman, *Chairil Anwar*, 66-67.

28. See Mochtar Lubis, "Chairil Anwar, Sebuah Kenang-Kenangan," *Horison* 19/4 (April 1985): 113-14 and 117.

29. The essay was first published in *Pembangoenan* (10 December 1945). It is reproduced in H. B. Jassin, *Chairil Anwar Pelopor Angkatan 45* (Djakarta: Gunung Agung, 1968), 139-40, and in (poor) English translation in B. Raffel, ed., *The Complete Poetry and Prose of Chairil Anwar* (Albany: State University of New York Press, 1962), 174-75. Raffel published revised translations of Chairil's works in 1993 in *The Voice of the Night: Complete Poetry and Prose of Chairil Anwar*, revised edition, by Burton Raffel (Athens, Ohio: Center for International Studies, 1993).

30. See Budiman, *Chairil Anwar*, 67, which quotes a memoir recalling that Chairil acted as a "courier" for Sjahrir. The historian Robert Cribb recalled that in his research on the revolution in Jakarta he had gained the impression that Chairil had spent a short time "hanging around" the lasykar headquarters "doing useful jobs" (personal correspondence).

31. See H.B. Jassin, "Humanisme Universil," in his *Kesusastraan Indonesia Modern dalam Kritik dan Esei II* (Djakarta: Gunung Agung, 1962), 30-33. (This essay is missing from the revised 1985 edition of the collection.)

32. "In Plaats van een Inleiding," *Orientatie* 1/1 (8 November 1947).

33. See Liesbeth Dolk, "'Wat in de Gids zou kunnen staan, dat moeten wij niet opnemen.' Over Rob Nieuwenhuys, *Orientatie* (1947-1954) en Indo-Centrisme," *De Gids* 151/11 (November 1988), 840-58, esp. 842-43.

34. Dolk, "Wat in de Gids," 844-45.

35. See "Interview with H. B. Jassin" in Bruce Holcombe, "*Orientatie* and *Gema Suasana*, A Study in Cultural Cooperation and Western Influence on the Early Post-War Avant-Garde" (B.A. honors thesis, Department of Indonesian & Malayan Studies, University of Sydney,

1972). This thesis, completed under the supervision of M. Balfas, and including the interview made with Jassin during his visit to Australia in 1972, is a valuable documentary source, as it is shaped by the approach of Balfas, a member of Chairil Anwar's circle.

36. See H. B. Jassin, *Surat-Surat 1943-1983* (Jakarta: PT Gramedia, 1984), 43.

37. Walter Spies, "Bali Muda dan Eropah Modern," *Gema Suasana* 1 (January 48).

38. "Pak Said dan Taman Siswa-dan-Pak Said," *Gema Suasana* 1 (January 1948).

39. Holcombe, "*Orientatie,*" 130. See also Jassin, "Humanisme Universil."

40. "Kerdjasama Kebudajaan," *Gelanggang/Siasat*, 23 October 1949.

41. Ida Nasution, "Persatuan," *Gema Suasana* 3 (March 1948).

42. Ida Nasution, "Kesenian Angkatan Muda Indonesia," *Gema Suasana* 5 (May 1948).

43. For a discussion of European modernism see I. Howe, ed., *The Idea of the Modern in Literature and the Arts* (New York: Horizon Press, 1967), and F. Kermode, "Modernism," in his *Modern Essays* (London: Collins, 1971).

44. Nasution, "Persatuan."

45. Some observers have suggested that the thinking which was later seen as characteristic of the Angkatan 45 was already present in the prewar period, especially in the writing of St. Takdir Alisjahbana. See Subagio Sastrowardoyo, "Orientasi Budaya Chairil Anwar" in his *Sosok Pribadi dalam Sajak* (Jakarta: Pustaka Jaya, 1980), 11-55, esp. 36-37). Some continuity can be shown to exist, but in my view only in the same way that European Modernism is related to and an outgrowth from nineteenth-century Romanticism. Takdir's sources, and his own form of expression, were characteristic scholastic reformulations of Romantic thought. With Chairil Anwar the same ideals are expressed in the hard-

edged and more immediate framework of Modernism, which sought a more urgent interaction between "art" and "life."

46. Among Chairil Anwar's best-known poems are "Krawang-Bekasi" and "Persetudjuan dengan Bung Karno," both of which would seem to belie this statement. Yet despite their fame (brought about by the postwar need for poems of "revolutionary spirit"), they are not characteristic examples of his work. ("Persetudjuan" . . . is said to have been intended as a technical and linguistic experiment, while "Krawang-Bekasi" is an adaptation, not an original work.)

47. Originally published in the collection *Deru Tjampur Debu*, the poem's latest printing is in *Aku Ini Binatang Jalang*.

48. I am grateful to Peter Burns of the James Cook University of North Queensland, who suggested almost all of this translation of the poem to me. Burton Raffel's revised translation appears in *The Voice of the Night: Complete Poetry and Prose of Chairil Anwar*, trans. Burton Raffel (Athens, Ohio: Center for International Studies, 1993), 129.

49. There is some uncertainty about this. Writing in *Gelanggang* on 6 November 1949, Sitor Situmorang attributed the term to Chairil Anwar. The articles by Rosihan Anwar, appearing in *Gelanggang* in December 1948/January 1949, are apparently the first written use of the term, however. See H. B. Jassin, *Kesusastraan Indonesia Modern dalam Kritik dan Esei II* (Jakarta: PT Gramedia, 1985), 2.

50. Rosihan Anwar, "Angkatan 1945 buat Martabat Kemanusiaan," *Gelanggang/Siasat*, 26 December 1948.

51. The extreme point of celebration of Chairil Anwar's "bohemianism" occurs in the writing of Burton Raffel, an image loosely constructed on inaccurate translations of his work. See Raffel, *Complete Poetry and Prose*, xiii-xxii.

52. "Kismet, Tjerita buat Chairil Anwar," *Gelanggang/Siasat*, 15 May 1949.

53. "Kismet, Tjerita buat Chairil Anwar."

54. R. N., "In Memoriam Chairil Anwar," *Orientatie* 20 (May 1949), 63.

55. Zarah, "Rob Nieuwenhuys Keliru tentang Chairil Anwar," *Gelanggang/Siasat*, 17 August 1949.

56. Zarah, "Tawa Chairil," *Gelanggang/Siasat*, 8 May 1949.

57. See the response by Mochtar Lubis, "Hidup, Mati?" *Gelanggang/Siasat*, 4 December 1949.

58. Sitor Situmorang, "Angkatan 45," *Gelanggang/Siasat*, 6 November 1949.

59. Sitor Situmorang, "Konsepsi Seni Angkatan 45," *Gelanggang/-Siasat*, 27 November 1949.

60. Situmorang, "Konsepsi Seni."

61. The Indonesian-Dutch connection, in which Chairil Anwar had played a central role, appears to have declined at this time. In a letter dated 14 August 1949, Jassin described the attempt of the "progressive Dutch" (the *Orientatie* group) to establish regular meetings and to exchange ideas with the centers of Indonesian nationalist publications in Jakarta. Jassin notes that the initial meeting was a failure and the idea was not pursued. The arrangement had a formal air about it, in contrast to the spontaneous personal interaction which characterized the earlier period (Jassin, *Surat-Surat*, 55).

62. An English translation of the text of the declaration appears in A. Teeuw, *Modern Indonesian Literature*, vol. 1 (The Hague: Martinus Nijhoff, 1979), 127.

63. H. B. Jassin, *Gema Tanah Air* (Djakarta: Balai Pustaka, 1969), 16.

64. I have gained this impression from a variety of remarks and references noted in random contexts, without being able to nominate a specific source.

65. For details, see Teeuw, *Modern Indonesian Literature*, vol. 1, 164-66.

66. Pramoedya Ananta Toer, "Masalah Tuhan Dalam Kesusastraan," *Gelanggang/Siasat*, 27 June 1952.

67. Pramoedya Ananta Toer, *Ditepi Kali Bekasi I* (Djakarta: Gapura, 1951).

68. A short story, "Kemana??," later published in *Pertjikan Revolusi* (Djakarta: Gapura, 1950), and possibly other stories in the collection predate the novel.

69. What follows here is a summary of the argument elaborated in my chapter 7 "The Early Fiction of Pramoedya Ananta Toer, 1946-1949" of the present volume.

70. The standard work on the pemuda role in the revolution is Benedict R. O'G. Anderson, *Java in a Time of Revolution, Occupation and Resistance 1944-1946* (Ithaca: Cornell University Press, 1972).

71. Pramoedya, *Ditepi*, 96.

72. See Pramoedya Ananta Toer, "*Perburuan* 1950 and *Keluarga Gerilya* 1950" (trans. Benedict Anderson), *Indonesia* 36 (October 1983), 41.

73. Pramoedya, "*Perburuan*," 41.

74. In his writing during the revolution, this style is marked by some of the stories in *Pertjikan Revolusi*, especially the story "Djongos + Babu." See my "Early Fiction."

75. See *Indonesia* 2 (1950) and *Orientatie* 26 (November 1949).

76. Jassin, *Kesusastraan*, 1985 ed., 76; and Teeuw, *Modern Indonesian Literature*, vol. 1, 169.

77. Pramoedya, "*Perburuan* 1950," 42.

78. Jassin, *Kesusastraan*, 1985 ed., 69-147.

79. Jassin, *Kesusastraan*, 1985 ed., 75.

80. Jassin, *Kesusastraan*, 1985 ed., 46-68.

81. Teeuw, *Modern Indonesian Literature*, vol. 1, 163.

82. Jassin, *Surat-Surat*, 34-42.

83. Jassin, *Surat-Surat*, 40.

84. Jassin, *Surat-Surat*, 40.

85. Jassin, *Kesusastraan*, 1985 ed., 57.

86. Such an interpretation of the term lay behind many expressions of opinion in the "Sastra Kontekstual" debates of 1984-85. See, for example, Hendrik Berybe, "Tentang Sebuah Sastra Kiri," *Kompas*, 30 January 1985.

9

WRITING THE PAST: THE LIMITS OF REALISM IN CONTEMPORARY INDONESIAN LITERATURE

Paul Tickell

In Western literary criticism both from the left and the right of the political spectrum, an implicit and often an explicit assertion exists of the superiority of realism as a mode of literary representation. Whether justified in terms of its factual accuracy or its capacity to depict class conflict and ideological contradictions,[1] realism and the realist novel in particular hold a special position in the pantheon of Western literary genres. This system of values dismisses realism's "others"—whether labelled as fantasy or romance—as essentially inferior, trivial, and escapist, even as downright dangerous.[2] More recently, critics have valued nonrealistic fiction-fantasy, science fiction, melodrama for their subversive political and expressive potentials. Guided by structuralist (and poststructuralist) linguistic theory and by Althusserian understandings of ideology, many contemporary critics have come to reject realism as a privileged form of literary discourse, seeing it as part of a wider ideological construct. As Catherine Belsey has noted, the reader of

> the form of the classic realist text . . . is invited to perceive and judge the "truth" of the text, the coherent, non-contradictory interpretation of the world as it is perceived by the author whose autonomy is the source and evidence of the truth of the interpretation. . . . In this way classic realism constitutes an ideological practice in addressing itself to readers as subjects, interpellating them in order that they freely accept their subjectivity and their subjection.[3]

For critics like Belsey, nonrealist literary models are seen as formally appropriate to contemporary experience. This essay will avoid assertions of a qualitative metaphysical difference between the past and present. Nor will it see the latter as less fragmented, more integrated, more coherent, and, where collective anxiety and fears are concerned, as less intense than at the present. Some of realism's more articulate defenders have pointed out that such assertions remain essentially untested.[4]

Instead, the following discussion will argue the superiority of such writing over realistic alternatives in the contemporary Indonesian context, not in the sense that Indonesian nonrealist writing is innately better than its alternative, but more that such value is essentially contextual, dependent on the circumstances governing its production. In contemporary Indonesia, fantasy is able to evoke certain aspects of contemporary experience about which realism, for reasons to be noted, is unable satisfactorily to speak.

Realism's high status reflects the influence of nineteenth-century romantic literary models on the colonially sponsored Indonesian literature of the 1920s and 1930s. For it is precisely these classics which have become institutionalized through school curricula and through literary criticism as the beginnings of modern Indonesian literature.[5] This realism also reflects an ideology of the modern as the appropriate vehicle for a new, consciously modern and increasingly Westernized literary culture wishing to shed a moribund, feudalistic tradition.

Behind this veneer lies the indelible individuality of the author, with his or her inhibitions, traumas, prejudices, and predilections. In the Indonesian context one has also to contend with the real coercive power of a repressive state, with the power and often the will to censor and ban literary works deemed to be unacceptable—morally, politically, religiously, or any other way—and to imprison those who produce and disseminate such material. Thus, even if claims for realism's accuracy are accepted and the boundaries between representation and actuality elided, in certain circumstances and as regards certain topics realist modes are incapable of accurately depicting the world "as it really is." Indeed, in many cases they are deficient and more: a public and private liability. The operative constraints force author and work alike to mouth the orthodoxy of the powers-that-be.[6] In such cases representation becomes little more than vertically imposed, agitational propaganda.[7]

In contemporary Indonesian literature the problem of devising an "appropriate mode, radical both formally and politically, revolutionary both as fiction as well as transmitted . . . consciousness"[8] is nowhere more apparent than in the representation of the coup of the 1 October 1965 and the subsequent massacre of alleged communists or communist sympathizers.[9]

More than twenty years after the event, the coup possesses an immediate presence for most Indonesians, either in personal memories of the actual period and its consequences or as the contrived memories of the New Order state, projected through film, novels, written documentary material, and the education system.[10]   The coup's continuing centrality to the New Order is also manifested in administrative ways, with Indonesian citizens requiring a Surat Bebas G-30-S (Certificate of Non-involvement in the 30th September Movement) for access to such things as state-sponsored employment, credit, and passports.

For both the victors (the Right) and the losers (the Left, their families, and ex-detainees) these events and the subsequent upheaval remain a continuing source of pain and trauma. The sensitive nature of the topic and the personal pain involved mean that the events are neither open topics of conversation nor a frequent subject of creative literature. As the winner, the Right has a greater, indeed an almost exclusive, opportunity to broadcast its view of events. Frequently, however, what is produced amounts merely to ex post facto rationalization rather than personal experience. For the Left, trauma and the real danger of (re)imprisonment do little to loosen tongues and release memory. Their voice is muted, or dumb.[11] Obviously there is still much about the coup and its aftermath which remains a prohibited area in the collective memory of the Indonesian nation. Prohibited, in the sense that the forms of its representation are limited to the officially peddled line and are rarely—perhaps never—able to transgress these prohibitions, even partially.

In the years immediately following the coup a number of short stories appeared in literary journals (*Horison* and *Sastera*) associated with non-leftist, liberal intellectuals.[12] Their thematic concerns provide an immediate and direct link to the postcoup social upheaval and individual trauma of late 1965 and 1966. For our purposes, three short stories will be discussed: Satyagraha Hoerip's "Pada Titik Kulminasi" (1966) (At the Culmination), Zulidahlan's "Maka Sempurnalah Penderitaan Saya di Muka Bumi" (1966) (And My Suffering on the Face of the

Earth was Complete), and Usamah's "Perang dan Kemanusiaan" (1966) (War and Humaneness).[13] As texts, these short stories are unambiguously partisan. Their considerable value derives therefrom—and in some cases, I suspect, from the involvement of the authors in events similar to those depicted in the stories. This quality suggests that measured critical distance could hardly have been a feature of these fictions.

Such lack of detachment may be read both as a conscious expression of a deep conviction of being justified in beliefs and actions and as an explicit indictment of the "other side." These stories reveal certain immanent contradictions which are denied, suppressed, or glossed over and which can be detected in the asymmetry between ideals (and their underlying ideological bases) and certain actions. They reveal the "unsaid" and the "unsayable" both of the text and of the contemporary Indonesian imagination. They can be found in the narrative in three areas. In all cases, the general "humanist" ideology of the authors (and their narrator personae) conflicts with the depiction of and a wider social reality at odds with it.[14] There are, as well, divergences from the Indonesian aesthetic/literary ideology known as Universal Humanism with its denial of engagement and its eschewal of politically charged narrative.[15] Finally, there is a conflict with a overarching concept of truth and veracity, free from "sloganeering" and a literary practice involving the selection and suppression of events, a practice in turn producing a loaded text.[16]

The *Humanisme Universil* just alluded to, emphasizing a respect for the dignity of human life, represents itself as the basis of civilized and civilizing behavior. The clash is essentially between this ideology and the imagination of circumstances which threaten the humanity of people through torture and murder. This in turn generates fundamental crises of conscience for the narrators. It is important to ask what literary strategies are available to the writers of these realist short stories in dealing with these crises and with their resolution. Several such strategies are on offer. Within the boundaries of what can be said, both in the specific context of Indonesian literature and in the wider context of New Order Indonesia as a whole, each must suppress much that is uncomfortable and/or politically dangerous or delegitimizing. Credible resolution of conflict, therefore, becomes difficult.

In an attempt to work within the constraints of this framework, our authors focus on the emotional reaction of individuals in hard times. But the effect is to neutralize and sublimate the political understanding crucial to a grasp of these stories or else to consign it to their background. The postcoup violence becomes a rather grisly backdrop against which are played out the narrators' *pertarungan batin* (inner conflicts). Underlying this apparently apolitical stance lies the intense conviction that the violence meted out to the Left was entirely deserved. While latent in creative representations of the coup and its aftermath, this conviction surfaces in the critical writings of the contemporary Indonesian literary establishment on this matter. The coup and its aftermath are depicted effusively as "*awal sejarah baru yang pantas kita syukurkan*" (the beginning of a new age, for which we should be appropriately thankful), or, less exuberantly, as just retribution.[17]

> Boleh jadi, memang benar . . . bahwa khususnya di antara tahun 1965-1970, tak sedikit orang LEKRA yang "diamankan" haknya. Boleh jadi memang benar. Akan tetapi, apa yang mereka alami itu tidak akan mampu menghapuskan apa yang telah mereka lakukan selama 1959-1965.[18]

> (Maybe it is true that between 1965 and 1970 many LEKRA supporters were imprisoned and denied their rights. Maybe it is true. However, what they experienced will never be capable of wiping out what they did between 1959 and 1965.)

The refusal of both creative literature and critical commentary to come directly to terms with the attendant political and ethical dilemmas is hardly neutral. Silence on these matters becomes as tendentious and as potent as any slogan and represents, in effect, an acceptance of, even support for, things as they are.

Numerous means are used to turn the stories into subtle (and not so subtle) apologies. Each of the stories is related from the perspective of an involved first-person narrator—an "I" figure. This gives them an inwardness which concentrates on the narrators' emotions and reaction. Other human beings are little more than names, without the problematic inner life of the speaker. This becomes especially convenient for the depiction of the leftist victims of the violence, who are shown to be effective nonentities, making the ethical and moral problems of their (permanent) disposal somewhat less invidious. "*Persoalan eksistensi*" (problems of existence) are cast in terms of the narrator's own inner turmoil—the problems of living with one's conscience after the event. It is the narrator's "existential crisis" rather than the victims' that is central. This can be seen clearly in the following quote for "Pada Titik Kulminasi":

> Hal itu sama sekali lain daripada dua yang jika ditambah tiga lalu dikurangi empat, pastilah menjadi satu. Tak lain sebab ini adalah persoalan eksistensi, dan sekali-kali bukan aritmetika sederhana. Bukan pula penulisan fiksi yang plotnya sewaktu-waktu bisa kita rubah, namun suatu momen yang harus benar-benar terjadi dalam pentas kehidupan yang riil. Dan itulah sebabnya aku sampai bisa dibuatnya tegang kegelisahan.[19]

> (It is not merely a matter of $2 + 3 - 4 = 1$. It is a problem of existence and in no way simple arithmetic. Nor is it fiction, whose plot we may change according to whim, but a particular moment that must take place on the stage of real life. And it is for this reason that I have come to be in a state of nervous anxiety.)

Bearing in mind that death or torture is the fate awaiting victims in at least two of these short stories, it would seem that the victims' existential problems were somewhat more pressing than those of the narrators. The alleged communist victims are significant only in terms of their impingement upon the narrator's own life or security. Thus, in "Pada Titik Kulminasi," the "disposal" of Kuslan, who is both the narrator's brother-in-law and a member of the Indonesian Communist party (PKI), is not in itself an issue. The issue is how his death will affect the narrator's sister, and ultimately the narrator himself:

> Bisa dimengerti bahwa juga di jalan pikiranku balau-kacau. Seluruh syarafku mencongak bagai tiang-tiang tilpon. Kuobral-kan macam-macam makian kepada molekul-molekul di jalan, bisa jadi kepada diriku sendiri, mulai dari kata-kata kerja yang haram, binatang-binatang yang najis, sampai-sampai ke benda-benda yang kotor. Kenapa aku dulu sampai-sampai mendesak ibuku supaya mau meluluskan lamaran Kuslan kepada adikku, Yayuk? Sedang aku tahu betul Yayuk sebenarnya membalas cintanya semata-mata sebab ditinggal kawin pilot kekasihnya dengan gadis Rusia di kota dia dikirim belajar. Bukankah itu waktu Yayuk baru berumur duapuluhsatu, dan itu artinya belum mendesak benar untuk menerima lamaran pertama yang tiba? Siapa tahu

262

tak lama kemudian akan ditemunya jodohnya yang benar-benar dia cintai juga? Dan kini? Setelah lahir anak-anaknya dan harus ditinggal mati ayah mereka, tidakkah aku orang yang tersiksa nanti? Siksaan yang takkan boleh kubuka-dan-bagi-bagikan meski ke isteripun. Adapula bila ibuku (yang sejak kepergian Kuslan ke luar negeri lalu tinggal bersama Yayuk menjaga cucunya di sana) kelak sampai tahu: Bahwa akulah sebetulnya yang bisa menyelamatkan jiwa Kuslan padahal tak ada kulakukan; tidakkah siksaan itu makin memburu-burukan saya.[20]

(Understandably as I walked along my thoughts were in a state of complete chaos. My nerves were standing on end like telephone poles. I muttered various curses to the molecules in the road, even swore at myself—ranging from everyday expletives, through various types of filthy animal, to vile and dirty objects. Why had I come to the point where I pressured my mother into accepting Kuslan's proposal to marry Yayuk, my little sister? In fact I really knew that she was in love with Kuslan only because she had been ditched by her pilot boyfriend, who had married a Russian girl from the town where he had been sent to study. Wasn't Yayuk only twenty-one at the time and surely this meant that there was really no pressure to marry her to the first man that came along? Who knows, maybe later on she would have met a husband whom she really would have loved? And now? After her children have been born then left fatherless by Kuslan's death, won't it be me who will suffer? A torment that I cannot expose and share, even with my own wife. And what will happen when my mother (who since Kuslan had gone overseas had gone to stay with Yayuk and look after her grandchildren) finds out that I could have in fact saved Kuslan's life, but that I didn't. Won't the torment then pursue me even further?)

The concern is pragmatic, selfish even, rather than with the rights and wrongs of taking the victim's life; or else it is with more abstract ethical considerations, coloring the surface elsewhere in the narrative.

A similar pragmatism can be seen in Usamah's "Perang dan Kemanusiaan" where the narrator is haunted by the fear of disclosure, having had a close acquaintance with the alleged communists with whose interrogation and torture he is charged. The fear is that he will become a suspect, suffering the same fate as the victims. It is reflected in the following passages from the short story:

> Ada segi yang tidak mengenakkan bagi orang-orang yang banyak tahu akan ikhwal komunis di sana. Umumnya mereka-mereka ini dalam Team akan diperintah untuk menginterogasi tawanan. Dan saya sudah sejauh itu, tanpa saya sadari bahwa kedudukan saya membahayakan hidup saya sendiri. Sungguh tidak enak. Tentu tidak enak untuk bicara dengan orang-orang yang dalam matanya membayang dendam. Lebih-lebih lagi kalau di antara mereka terdapat kenalan-kenalan. Dua kali saya terpaksa menginterogasi kenalan saya sendiri. Begini.

> (There was an unpleasant side to all of this for those who knew all about the communists there. In general they were part of teams ordered to interrogate the prisoners. It had gone so far that unbeknown to me my position was endangering my life. It was really unpleasant. Certainly it was disturbing to talk with people whose eyes were full of revenge. Especially if you knew them personally. Twice I was compelled to interrogate people I knew. This is what it was like.)

and

> "Di mana," tanya saya.

> "Sungguh mati, dik Us, saya di rumah saya," jawabnya.

> Panggilan dik Us yang saya yakin didengar pula oleh petugas-petugas lain, membahayakan sekali kedudukan saya. Setiap orang di Solo ketika itu penuh curiga. Setiap orang harus dicurigai, termasuk orang-orang dalam Team Pemeriksa. Beberapa hari sebelum saya memeriksa Bu Y, ada seorang yang terpaksa 'diamankan' sendiri karena ternyata punya terlalu banyak kenalan tawanan, dan ternyata telah memanfaatkan kedudukannya untuk membantu kenalan-kenalannya itu.

> Saya jengkel sekali mendengar Bu Yu memanggil saya dengan 'dik Us', walaupun panggilan itu panggilan biasa. Sudah saya

264

peringatkan sebelumnya bahwa 'saya' yang duduk di belakang meja pemeriksa, bukan 'Usamah' kenalan Bu Y, tapi tidak diperhatikannya peringatan-peringatan itu. Beberapa petugas pasti curiga. Oleh karena kekuatiran barangkali, saya terpaksa memerintahkan seorang petugas khusus:

"Siksa perempuan ini"![21]

("Where?" I asked.

"I swear to God, dik Us, I was at home—nowhere else!" she answered.

I was convinced that often officials had heard her call me by the familiar form of address "dik Us" (little brother Us) and that this was very dangerous in my position. Everyone in Solo was then very suspicious. Everyone was a suspect, even those in the Investigation Teams. Several days before I interrogated Mrs. Y. one of the team was arrested because clearly he knew too many of the prisoners and was using his position to help his acquaintances.

I was very annoyed to hear Mrs. Yu call me "dik Us," even though this is what people normally called me. I had previously warned her that the person who sat behind the investigator's table was not the "Usamah" that she knew, but she did not take any notice of these warnings. Several officials were obviously suspicious. Perhaps out of fear, I had to give this order to one of the men from the special section.

"Torture this woman!")

The narrator's fear may in fact have been well founded at the time given the wide net cast for alleged communists and fellow-travellers. But such a fear equally expresses pragmatic and self-interested concerns that sort ill with humanism and with the values it places on life. When viewed in concert with other assumptions, the stories themselves become something far more than an exposition of authorial angst. They become a powerful if unconscious series of justifications for the internecine violence that followed the coup.

265

The short story "Maka Sempurnalah Penderitaan Saya di Muka Bumi" appears at first glance to work against the loaded narrative methods adopted in the other short stories. "Maka Sempurnalah" appears different in that the narrator is a leftist. Yet instead of a narrative allowing unconditional sympathy and understanding to be expressed for the narrator as an individual in horrific circumstances, what we get is subtly loaded and presented in a way which precludes any sympathy for the speaker's seeing the error of his ways. He must recognize that forgiveness, redemption, and reintegration into the community are possible only through embracing Islam and rejecting communism.

The story opens in early morning, with the narrator confronting his mother's death and facing the ritual obligations which this entails. These rites of passage are impossible without community support, a support which he believes will not be forthcoming because of his family's associations with the Indonesian Communist party. He gives vent to his anxiety thus:

> Akan kukatakan bahwa aku seorang diri tanpa pamili dengan para tetangga yang sedang membenci kami, tapi tidak jadi. Dan aku berlalu dengan lesu setelah menyampaikan rasa syukurku.

> Bayangkan ketakutan menyergap aku di perjalanan. Bayangan cerita-cerita yang kudengar, bahwa tak seorangpun mau mengurusi jenazah-jenazah kami orang-orang yang diasingkan ini. Bahkan tanah kuburpun haram kami tempati.

> Lalu apakah yang harus kubuat? Mengubur mayit ibu di halaman rumah sendiri? Betapa akan marah tetangga-tetangga nanti.

> Bertumpang-tindih pikiran-pikiran ini, seperti martil yang memalu botak kepalaku. Tuhan kalau memang benar Kau ada, beri aku jalan. Kemana aku mesti melangkah? Aku tidak bisa berpikir.

> (Would I tell the neighbors who still detested us that I was alone and had no family? I didn't. I walked on, exhausted after expressing my feelings of relief.

266

Just imagine the fear that came over me on the road. Haunted by stories that no one would lay out the bodies of people like us after death—pariahs in our own community. They would not even let us rest in a cemetery.

Then what could I do? Bury my mother's body in the backyard. The neighbors would be really angry then.

My brain throbbed like a mallet pounding down on the top of my head. God, if You really do exist, show me the way. Where must I go? I cannot think.)

His mother's death does not, however, lead to his greater estrangement from the community. The community extends its support and, by implication, its forgiveness. At the same time he recognizes the power of God and his own guilt. Reintegration is presaged first by his turning his back to atheism and embracing the "truth" of religion, and second by his seeing the folly of his and his colleagues' ways. In the remembered words of his mother,

Jangan lanjutkan dendam keluarga ini, Mintalah maaf karena keluarga kita yang bersalah. Berbuatlah baik bagi sesamamu. Dan celakalah manusia yang selalu membawa prasangka dan kebencian serta dengki terhadap sesamanya.

(End this family's vendetta, my son. Ask them for forgiveness, for it is our family who is guilty. Do good to your fellow man. Disaster comes to he who constantly bears prejudice, hate, and malice to his fellow man.)

Just as the previous short stories assume the guilt of the communists, "Maka Sempurnalah" puts such assumptions into the mouth of its narrator. Implicit assumptions become explicit confessions; popular belief is reinforced.

The narrator's journey from alienation towards reintegration, from deceit to truth, from the darkness of communism to the light of Islam, is reinforced by a metaphor which develops through the story. The story opens in predawn gloom in an atmosphere of death, fear, loathing, suspicion, and heathen alienation. As it progresses, the light grows in intensity:

Satu dua mulai datang berkunjung ke rumah. Bertanya ini itu tentang penyakit ibu dan aku sendiri. Dan hari semakin siang dan tetangga-tetangga semakin banyak datang.

Tak ada yang aku kerjakan kecuali hanya melihat ibu dalam rawatan tanpa prasangka dan dendam mendendam. Duduk aku di antara mereka dan mengenang semuanya itu. Dan berpikir, bahwa di antara mereka, yang mati maupun yang masih hidup itu, ada sesuatu. Yang selama ini di luar jangkauan kami sekeluarga, jangkauan orang-orang yang semacam keluarga kami. Begitu agungnya Dia, sampai airmata ini menitik tidak terasa.[22]

(First of all one or two of them came to visit the house. They asked about this and that, about my mother's illness, and about me. As the day wore on, more and more neighbors came.

I did nothing other than look at my mother in the care of people free of prejudice and revenge. I sat among them and thought about it all. And I realized that among them—those who had died and those who were still alive—there was something. Something that had up to now been beyond the reach of us as a family, beyond the reach of people like our family. Such was His power, that I was unaware that I was crying.)

In the full light of day the narrator faces not loathing and suspicion, but the prospect of reintegration into the local community and true belief in God. Both superficially and symbolically the narrative emphasizes the essentially delinquent character of communists and communism. In such a worldview, communism can be seen only as an alien deceit and truth be obtained in only one way.

What is left unsaid, indeed what is unsayable in "Maka Sempurnalah" and the other short stories, is as important as what was inscribed on the surface of these narratives. How does a forgiving, God-fearing community come to grips with the massacre of tens of thousands of its members? Explicitly it can, and indeed does, do so only by denial or by rationalization. Denial may take the form of simply desisting from writing of the slaughter. This is perhaps the least pernicious course. It is the rationalizations, the touting of accepted "truths," that are the most pernicious. All three short stories share a deep commitment to the belief in the inexpungable guilt of the communists, and in the outland-

268

ishness of their ideology in a local context. Their guilt is not just for the alleged involvement in the 30th September Movement, for 500,000 people could hardly have been involved directly in events at Lubang Buaya. It is, rather, for a wider, more generalized treachery. Where forgiveness is extended, it is dependent on one thing only: the denial of previous conviction and the taking on board of the religious convictions of the other side. This, precisely, was one of the methods of used by the Indonesian government to "rehabilitate" political prisoners.

The stories themselves are a way of dealing with a disturbing and horrific experience which cannot be coped with except through sublimation. This is not to suggest that they are based on pure expediency or are merely New Order propaganda. They possess an emotional power stemming from deep conviction as well as from profound anxiety. So, rather than seeing them as a not-too-subtle form of self-delusion, we must understand them in terms both of their historical context and of their formal literary genre. Realist fiction is, I believe, incapable of accounting for events of such absolute awfulness. The very pain of the memory, the nature of the New Order government, its symbolic legitimacy deriving as it does in large part from its "saving" the Indonesian nation from the perils of communism; the alliance between parts of Indonesian Islam, the Western-oriented intelligentsia and the Indonesian army; all combine to make anything else unlikely. Alternative representations may imply less-than-absolute guilt on the part of Indonesian leftists and (therefore) that the Indonesian Right may, in however small a part, share some of the blame. And admissions even of partial guilt or responsibility are not permissible insofar as the guilt of the PKI remains an unquestioned and unquestionable article of official faith.

With some justification it might be suggested that our authors were forbidden critical distance and balanced views by their situations. The stories were produced at a time when the New Order and its supporters were establishing their legitimacy and their credentials for ruling Indonesia. Part of this process involved the discrediting of previous rivals and of the only potential challenge. After the extreme polarization of Indonesian politics in the early 1960s and the explosive postcoup violence of 1965-66, the Indonesian Right was in no mood to forgive or forget. The views expressed in the previous short stories in so charged a context were as inevitable as they were unremarkable. Just as temporal immediacy is seen as an impediment to forgiveness, so time is seen as a balm, soothing painful memories. The logic of this is that

269

Indonesian literature eventually will be able to depict the coup, the polarization before it, and the violence subsequent to it, in ways which do not content themselves with echoing officially acceptable versions of the truth.

In some ways, precisely this appears to be happening in Indonesian literature. In it, there can be seen a certain ambivalence about the absolute and unmitigated guilt of the Left. Changes in the way this theme is handled can be seen in two quite remarkable and very different recent Indonesian novels: Ajip Rosidi's *Anak Tanahair* (A Son of this Land) and Putu Wijaya's *Nyali* (Guts). Ajip's is written within a mainstream realist tradition and does not bear directly on the events in question but takes as its backdrop the Indonesian cultural scene of the 1950s and early 1960s.

The novel is unique in its depiction of the main character, Ardi. Rather than shying away from politics and asserting the autonomy of art from wider considerations, as does much post-1966 writing, Ajip Rosidi confronts these issues and most importantly the issue of commitment in a way that does not depend on the recourse to conventional wisdom and cliche which characterizes the earlier short stories. Because of Ajip's ambiguous relations with the Indonesian literary and cultural center in the 1950s and 1960s, and also possibly because the novel was written in Japan, it does not fall into the characteristic mold. While Ajip's own views are echoed forcefully through the character Hasan, other characters and, importantly, the Left-leaning Ardi are allowed to develop and to do so without being paralyzed by the stigma of indelible guilt. As Keith Foulcher notes,

> Importantly, Ajip allows Ardi a well-drawn moral and intellectual basis to his development, as well as making room for the more familiar personal frustrations and disappointment at his failure to gain recognition and satisfaction as an individual and an artist. We see, moreover, how the circumstances which Ardi faced were at a certain point beyond his control as an individual. Acting initially on the basis of personal conviction, the need to express a social conscience without wishing to become aligned with any particular group, he is propelled into a situation where his personal and artistic survival is only guaranteed by coming to terms with the broader social and political conditions in which he finds himself. All of this represents a way of viewing recent Indonesian history which as a published statement inside

Indonesia is perhaps unique. It is not a story of "innocent victims" of a national tragedy, but a detailed attempt to illustrate the circumstances that might have led an individual artist to make a left-wing political commitment in 1950s Indonesia.[23]

Ardi's social conscience is credibly depicted as developing from his own experience of life; his background, class, and childhood all contribute to its growth. For instance, Ardi experiences in the flesh the feudalism and class distinctions of Indonesian society, which lead in the first instance to a sense of being *malu* (ashamed, but with overtones of inferiority), but then form the basis of his appreciation of what is just and right, and his sense of a division between "them" and "us." Ardi has no inferiority complex. In fact, a strong sense of self and self-respect pervade the novel. He is, however, aware of his inferior status within society and gradually grows conscious of how this is produced by a mutable social order, one sustained by language, religion, wealth, and power. Note how social differentiation, class distinctions and, above all, Ardi's reactions to these things, are manifested.

> Tiba-tiba terdengar derai Asep. Muka Ardi "menjadi" merah padam. Ia salah memakai perkataan "tuang" untuk dirinya sendiri, padahal perkataan itu hanya boleh dipergunakan buat orang lain yang dihormati saja. Ya, ia salah. Tetapi mengapa dia ditertawakan? Ia sadar bahwa perkataan yang harus dipakainya adalah "neda"—seperti pernah dihapalkannya untuk pelajaran bahasa. Ia memang hanya memakai kata-kata begitu dalam kelas saja. Itupun dalam bahasa Sunda. Di rumahnya dia mempergunakan bahasa kanak-kanak "emam," yang terus dipergunakannya walaupun sekarang dia sudah bukan anak kecil lagi. Bahkan ibunya pun mempergunakan kata tersebut. Dan tak seorangpun merasa itu sebagai kesalahan!
>
> Tak hanya itu, Asep bahkan berteriak-teriak kepada ibunya, memberitahukan betapa lucunya bahasa yang dipakai Jang Ardi, karena mengacaukan undak-usuk basa.
>
> Ia hampir tak dapat bernafas. Ia merasa dipermalukan secara tak sepertinya. Berapa usianya ketika itu? Delapan? Sembilan? Betapa hatinya merasa tersinggung. Harga dirinya terbakar. Dan tanpa mempedulikan lagi Asep dengan kata-kata yang harus

terpelihara rapi, ia berlari menemui ibunya dan mengatakan bahwa is akan pulang lebih dulu. Ia tak mau mempedulikan kata-kata Asep Suwangsa yang membujuknya agar terus bermain dengannya. Juga bujukan ibunya yang menahannya agar pulang bersama, tak dihiraukan.[24]

(Suddenly Asep roared laughing. Ardi blushed deeply. He had used the word *tuang* [to eat] and applied it to himself, whereas that word could only be applied to other, respected persons. Yes, he was wrong. But why was he mocked? He knew that he should have said *neda*—just like he had learned in his language classes. Of course, he only ever used words like that in class—that was in his Sundanese language classes. At home he used the children's word *emam*, even though he was no longer a child. Even his mother used this word. Nobody thought that was wrong.

Not only that, Asep even yelled out to his mother, telling her how funny Ardi's language was, because he had mixed up his speech levels.

Ardi almost couldn't breathe. He was unbelievably embarrassed. How old was he? Eight? Nine? He felt so hurt. His self-esteem was destroyed. And without taking any more notice of Asep with his neatly cultivated vocabulary, he ran off in search of his mother and told her that he was going home early. He couldn't give a damn for Asep Suwangsa who was trying to persuade him to stay and play with him. He also took no notice of his mother's entreaties to stay so that they could go home together.)

and

Ia tahu Menteng. Itulah daerah rumah gedongan. Yang aspal jalannya licin berkilat. Yang rumahnya seluruhnya batu. Banyak yang bertingkat. Halamannya luas-luas. Tamannya indah-indah. Ada garasi selalu. Listriknya benderang. Rumput hijau terpelihara. Jendela dengan terali besi. Daun pintu kayu jati yang tinggi dan berat. Di pagar depan tergantung peng-

272

umuman dengan huruf balok pada sekeping logam berwarna
hitam: Awas Anjing Galak.

Itu sebuah dunia lain. Dunia yang tidak pernah dikenalnya.
dunia Asep dan Askin yang selalu berbahasa halus, berpakaian
rapi diseterika. Dunia untuk setiap orang telah disediakan kata-
kata yang khas yang tak boleh dipercampurkan, karena orang
yang mempercampurkannya akan dianggap tak layak masuk ke
dunia itu.[25]

(He knew Menteng. That's where the flashy houses were.
Where the roads were smooth and shiny. Where all the houses
were made of brick. Lots of them multi-storied. With big
grounds. Beautiful gardens. All of them had garages. The
windows were covered with wrought iron guards. Their heavy
tall door panels were made out of teak. On their front fences
were metal signs with bold black lettering: Beware of the Dog!

It was another world. A world unfamiliar to him. It was the
world of the Aseps and Asikins with their refined language and
their neatly ironed clothes. A world in which they all had their
own special languages which couldn't be intermixed, because
people who mixed them up were regarded as unfit to enter that
world.)

and

Mengapa ia menangis? Karena berpisah dengan ibunya? Waktu
ia berangkat meninggalkan kampung halamannya dengan Paman
Manan, ia tidak menangis. Malah gembira. Padahal itulah
pertama kalinya ia akan meninggalkan ibunya ke tempat yang
jauh. Ketika ia pergi ke ibukota kabupaten taklah dianggapnya
jauh, karena hanya beberapa belas kilometer dari kampungnya,
dan kalau mau ia menangis: Karena sedihkah ia dengan ibunya
dari dunianya. Yang merenggut dan melemparkan ibunya itu
kemudian ke dunia lain yang tak dia kenal.

Juga dunia yang dia kira tidak dikenal ibunya. Ia merasa bahwa
ibunya dalam bahaya, tetapi ibunya kelihatan seakan-akan tidak
menyadari hal itu. Ha, memang bukan bahaya, melainkan

273

penistaan yang hina, yang merendahkan martabat dirinya. Ya, itulah yang menyedihkan. Ibunya tidak menginsafi hal itu![26]

(Why was he crying? Because he was leaving his mother? When he left his village with his uncle Manan, he didn't cry. In fact he was happy, even though it was the first time he had left his mother to go away. When he went to the regional capital, he didn't think that was far, because it was only maybe a dozen kilometers from village, and if he had wanted to he could have gone home every day. He didn't know. He felt that he was being separated from his mother, separated by a thick, but invisible wall. All that was snatching his mother from his world. It was snatching her and then throwing her into a world of which he knew nothing.

It was also a world of which his mother knew nothing. He felt that she was in danger, but it seemed as if she was unaware of this. Oh, of course, it wasn't danger, but a low form of humiliation, which lowered their self-esteem. Yes, that was what was sad. She just didn't know what was happening.)

Ardi's rejection of religious belief arises from hard-won personal experience, of corrupt religious leaders, the terror carried out by the Darul Islam movement in the name of Islam, and the general dissonance of religious theory with practice. The depiction of class division (and of potential class conflict) and the rejection of religious belief are unique in contemporary Indonesian literature, for both are outlawed areas of public discussion and debate.

Ardi's political commitment and his orientation towards the left of the political spectrum proceed naturally from his experiences, the development of his social conscience, and his artistic principles. To some degree the novel, as Foulcher observes, represents Ardi's politicization as being beyond his own personal control. He is the victim of circumstances and is seen as being imperfectly aware of the consequences of his own actions and alliances. Yet the vision of the novel is sufficiently broad and liberal to make any alternative alliances, or indeed any alternative mode of behavior on Ardi's part, quite unthinkable. The strength of his character(ization) means that he is unlikely to see the light and convert to Islam. Although Hasan—a strong Muslim voice in the novel—and other characters who voice the

Indonesian Socialist party (PSI) position make their objections known to Ardi's leftist tendencies, their own commitment is shown in parts one and two of the novel to have no greater claim to truth. The pluralism of the time meant that Islamic, communist, and Western-oriented socialist voices were just some of the many being heard in Indonesia. Because Ardi's characterization is more complete and more sympathetically handled than other characters', his views appear to possess equal (or greater) credibility. Given that Ajip Rosidi was not, nor is he still, seen as a leftist, this sympathy and the novel's balance and neutrality are the more remarkable.

For all the power of this form of literary representation, there is an irresolvable tension that ultimately limits what can be written and in what form. The novel goes beyond, and in many ways may be in conflict with, the conscious views of the author. If the mode of literary representation were to have continued in the same vein, the result would have verged, politically speaking, on the subversive. The formal frame of the novel gives clues as to how Ajip chose to resolve these tensions. The first two parts of the novel are written straightforwardly and respectively tell the story in the omniscient third person and in the first person. It is significant that these first two sections of the novel relate events up to circa 1962-63. Although the Indonesian political climate was increasingly polarized and tensions were on the increase, these tensions were relatively mild in comparison with what was to follow from 1963 to 1965. Ajip discards dramatized narrative in part three of *Anak Tanahair*, so that the novel then becomes a series of epistolary entries, written in diary form by Hasan, who is Ajip's persona; the sentiments expressed by Hasan are those of Ajip himself.[27] Standing as it does in structural contrast to the previous narrative, it is as if Ajip has "put the brakes" on a narrative that has run out of authorial control. The diary entries regain control of the novel and foreclose upon its interpretative possibilities. The Islamic interpretations of Indonesian history, culture, and politics emerging from these diary entries are Ajip's. With this strong authorial guidance the possibility of further understanding Ardi on his own terms also disappears. His actions, motives, and emotions, which in the second part of the novel in particular become understandable in terms of his own experiences and interaction with others, in the third part are interpreted through Hasan's eyes and worldview. The final part of the novel jars in a stylistic and structural sense and makes for less compelling fiction. It also renders the narrative politically and emotionally safer, and subject to greater control.

The first two narrative parts of the novel, however, cannot be erased and *Anak Tanahair* remains a powerful and unique piece of contemporary Indonesian fiction. It takes Indonesian realist writing to its very limits. Political and personal pain are such that if Indonesian literature is to transcend limits on the representation of the past, it will, for the time being, do so only through alternative modes. For these modes offer authors (and readers too) a degree of protection. In a world where many people's consciousness is structured in ways not unlike a realist novel,[28] the power to expose and subvert associated with fantastic literature is easily denied. The exposure, and the subversion, either are not seen by those in power or else can be easily dismissed as harmless by those who write, distribute, or read such material.

Without suggesting that Putu Wijaya's novel *Nyali* should be read as outright political allegory, corresponding more or less exactly to contemporary Indonesian political reality, I will suggest that the novel can be read in the light of the experience of the last twenty-five to thirty years. The novel is undoubtedly a political fiction, revolving around issues of ideology and power and involving insurgency, counter-insurgency, propaganda, and a coup. While many elements intimate at lived experience, and may indeed be read as directly allusive to the world, the novel as a whole keeps its distance from such direct parallels. It would be wrong, therefore, to see *Nyali*'s General Leonel as an allegorical Suharto, Zabaza as the PKI, or His Majesty as Sukarno.

The novel does, nevertheless, constitute a commentary on political behavior and discourse. Inevitably it must be read against the only other political rhetoric familiar to most Indonesians—that of the New Order State. The action of *Nyali* constantly must be read and assessed in terms of the known and familiar. The result is a kind of resonance bordering on *déjà vu*.

The interrogation of seldom-questioned articles of faith in which *Nyali* specializes is achieved through exposure of their immanent contradictions. These include patriotism, leadership, the need for tight social control, and leaderly rhetoric. Patriotism becomes entwined with its apparent opposites—treachery, sedition, insurgency. The ideal of dedicated and selfless leadership is scrutinized and shown to be permeated with duplicity, personal ambition and self-interest. Social control in the novel's fictional world is achieved and maintained by the threat of violence—apparently from without—and by a powerful martial

276

ideology deemed necessary for the survival of the state. Finally, the novel shows political speech to be manipulated, subject to abuse, and absorbed into an apparatus of social control.

The novel initially reads as a simple conflict between a *kerajaan* (kingdom, state) and a mysterious insurgent group called Zabaza. It appears as an uncluttered fight between good and evil, legitimate and illegitimate power, and civilization and barbarism. This is reinforced by initial descriptions of Zabaza, baleful to say the least. The following is an example:

> Gerombolan yang digerayanginya itu buas dan berdarah. Mereka terdiri dari berbagai kelompok yang putus asa. Gerang. Dendam menyala-nyala. Bulat tekad. Bersedia mati untuk kepentingan bersama. Apa saja yang mereka genjot dengan hati beku dan tertutup. Karena mereka sangat yakin kepada kemulyaan tujannya.[29]

> (This group that he had infiltrated was vicious and bloodthirsty. It consisted of various desperate sections. Wild. Flaming with hatred. Totally dedicated. Ready to die for the collective good. The members did everything cold heartedly and without mercy. For they were utterly convinced of the grandness of their aims.)

Zabaza is characterized by gratuitous violence, steely determination, and mercilessness. Kropos, an agent of the kerajaan, is charged with infiltrating this organization. At this early stage the kerajaan and Zabaza appear as poles in irreconcilable conflict. What either side actually believes is never stated. The Zabaza group appears to prize loyalty, discipline, and group solidarity and is motivated by its unseen but charismatic leader. The kerajaan, and especially its high-profile military clique, esteems similar things though its values appear to be attenuated superficially by a quality of mercy or else are applied with less rigor than those of Zabaza.

Zabaza is at this early stage depicted as a threat to the kingdom, which devotes its all to countering it. Opposition to Zabaza is therefore a patriotic act and Kropos, in risking his life to infiltrate this organization, is performing a duty of the highest order. As the novel progresses the narrative makes a number of unexpected and disconcerting turns. The external threat is revealed as having a peculiar relationship to the kingdom in that Zabaza is gradually revealed to be a de facto instrument of the state, performing a vital function for those who rule it. If the state faces a real threat from real enemies, it is not from Zabaza, who is a fabrication, an agent provocateur, diverting other potentially dangerous tendencies. No matter how apparently random and illogical they may seem, all events directed both by and at Zabaza are part of a *rencana* (plan). This is subject to fitful control by powerful individuals and, in the final analysis, is greater than any one of them.

In a moment of private candor, but also of deep mutual suspicion, the king, the legitimate head of state, and General Leonel, the commoner upstart who ultimately usurps power and is clearly identified as Zabaza, both talk of Zabaza, the rencana, and the positive role played by this supposed enemy:

> Baginda tahu sendiri bagaimana brengsek mental mereka waktu Ayahanda Baginda almarhum masih bertakhta. Ada alasan kenapa tiba-tiba moral tentara kerajaan sedang berada di puncaknya sekarang. Karena ada Zabaza. Zabaza yang telah berjasa mengembalikan semangat kepada mereka dengan cara paksa. Dalam hal ini Baginda harus berterima kasih pada Zabaza. Dia penjahat tapi sekaligus pahlawan, barangkali lebih besar dari semua pahlawan-pahlawan yang kini dipajang di Makam Pahlawan Kerajaan. Tapi Baginda tahu semua itu.[30]

> (Your majesty knows for himself just how demoralized they were when your late father was on the throne. There is a reason why the morale of the royal army is suddenly at its peak now. Because we have Zabaza. Zabaza has done us a service in forcefully revitalizing them. Your majesty should be grateful to Zabaza for this. He is a criminal, yet at the same time he is a hero. Perhaps he is even a greater hero than all of those heroes who have been laid to rest in the Royal War Cemetery. But your majesty knows all of this.)

When the real threat to the state arrives, it is not from Zabaza but from Leonel himself and his own personal ambition. It is Leonel who usurps power. The rencana and the mysterious Zabaza which were supposed to strengthen the state by disarming potential rivals and diverting popular attention to life-and-death struggles apparently runs out of control to the point where the order it was designed to strengthen is subverted—ostensibly by Leonel. The king and his family are killed, and the kerajaan declared a republic. This transition from the old order to the new is described in terms which ring bells for contemporary observers of Indonesia, and in a manner not untinged with irony:

> Usaha untuk menjadikan negeri itu untuk tidak tergantung lagi pada tanah sudah mulai dilakukan. Rencana-rencana pembangunan beberapa buah industri disebarkan. Sawah dirubah menjadi rimba beton yang setiap hari akan gemuruh menggerakkan asap ke udara—sambil menghisap ribuan tenaga kerja.[31]

> (Efforts to reduce this country's dependency on agriculture had already begun. Development plans for several industries were made public. Rice fields became concrete jungles that every day roared and pushed smoke into the atmosphere, while exploiting the labor of thousands of workers.)

By making the subversive Zabaza a creation of the state, the novel starkly questions the notion of patriotism. Who is really the enemy? For whom the sacrifice? Does the state oppress or protect its citizens? Patriotism, Zabaza, and the pretext for violence that they create, are depicted finally as a form of planful control and as gross deception.

The deception is most clearly stated by the wife of General Leonel. Although she is described as "*seorang wanita yang putus asa, frustrasi, cacat mental. Seorang yang pintar akan tetapi sakit*" (a desperate, frustrated, and mentally ill woman. A clever person, but a sick person), what this mad woman says is as valid and as consistent as anything else in the eccentric world of the novel: "*kata-katanya mengalir dengan manis dan menyerakkan kebenaran yang mengerikan*" (her words flowed sweetly and spread a horrible truth). She describes the situation and the connections between Zabaza, the kingdom, Leonel, the king, and the state and its people in the following speech:

> Seperti sudah saya ceritakan dari tadi. Saya memang mata-mata Baginda. Tetapi kemudian saya jatuh cinta pada suami saya. Kemudian saya betul-betul kecewa karena merasa dipermainkan. Kedua orang itu sebenarnya tidak bermusuhan. Mereka hanya melakukan permainan. Keduanya menipu saya. Jalan satu-satunya adalah membunuh anak-anaknya. Tetapi ternyata itu belum cukup menjadikan saya seorang Zabaza. Tetapi ini malah

mendekatkan saya pada gerakan itu. Gerombolan ini tidak memiliki target merebut pemerintahan. Dia adalah usaha untuk menegakkan moral baru. Semacam revolusi kepribadian yang membuat setiap orang menjadi hamba kerajaan yang baik. Ini terjadi karena sekarang setiap orang sudah terlalu banyak bicara tentang kepentingan-kepentingannya. Dalam kelompok Zabaza, tidak ada lagi kepentingan pribadi. Setipa orang merasa dirinya alat. Dan ini menimbulkan kerukunan.

(As I was telling you before, I was really a spy for the king, but then I fell in love with my husband. I then became really disappointed because I felt as if they were deceiving me. In fact they were not really enemies. It was a game for them. They were both deceiving me. The only thing for me to do was to kill the children. But clearly that was not enough to make me into a Zabaza. It did however make me closer to the movement. This movement had no intention of taking control of the government. It was an attempt strengthen a new moral order. A kind of personal revolution to turn everyone into a faithful subject of the kingdom. This happened because they all now only talked of their own interests. In Zabaza there are no private interests. Everyone sees himself or herself as an instrument. And this creates harmony.)

She continues:

Dan tiba-tiba sekarang beberapa hal berbalik. Leonel dan Baginda sudah merasa kini waktunya untuk benar-benar menghancurkan Zabaza sebelum terlalu besar. Mereka tidak menginginkan robotnya melakukan serangan total, lalu menghabisinya. Sementara itu sudah pasti mereka akan memberikan peluang baru untuk robot yang lain. Karena rupanya itu satu-satunya cara untuk membangun persatuan di kerajaan ini.[32]

(Suddenly now several things have changed. Leonel and His Majesty now feel that it is time to completely destroy Zabaza before it becomes too big. They do not want their robot to carry out a total attack; then they will finish it off. Then they will give an opportunity to another robot. Because it seems that this is the only way to develop unity in this kingdom.)

280

Much of the rhetoric of this speech rings familiar to contemporary Indonesian ears: *menegakkan moral baru* (give rise to a new moral order); *membangun persatuan* (develop unity); the corporatism implied in the rejection of *kepentingan pribadi* (vested interests). These items are not far removed from current Indonesian New Order jargon.

The use of patriotism and of Zabaza, the manufactured enemy, to deceive ordinary people is linked to one of Leonel's previous admissions to the king. This stands notions of both popular sovereignty (*kedaulatan rakyat*) and enlightened leadership (*yang dipimpin oleh hikmah yang bijaksana* . . .) on their head. It is not the people who select the leader, nor their will that determines legitimacy, but the contrary. After outlining his conception of military honor, his code of chivalry, Leonel proceeds to given his vision of the future:

> Saya tak ingin jalan yang damai, tapi jalan yang berdarah. Bukan karena haus darah, tapi karena segala kekerasan ini akan mengatur suasana tertentu. Dia merupakan satu proses yang akan berguna untuk menyeleksi rakyat kita menuju hari depan yang gemilang. Di masa depan, bayangan saya kerajaan ini akan menjadi satu republik dengan rakyat pilihan. Yang tak berhak untuk hidup harus cepat dibuang.[33]

> I don't want the peaceful way, but rather the bloody way. Not because of blood lust, but because all of this violence will give rise to a certain situation. It constitutes a useful process in selecting the population for our glorious future. In the future, I see this kingdom becoming a republic with a chosen and choice population. Those without the right to live must be quickly disposed of.

This martial elitism seriously questions and undermines the ethos of strong leadership as necessary for the public good. It brings the inherent dangers of military *dwifungsi* (dual function—the Indonesian military doctrine espousing both a civil and military role for the armed forces) to the surface. The message for Indonesia, a country ruled by a "retired" general and by a military clique, would seem clear.

Not only are the immanent contradictions between roles of soldier and statesman exposed in *Nyali*, but the myth that leaders are selfless individuals working for the common good is scrutinized and finally destroyed. Leonel's usurpation of leadership from the king and their previous collusion in creating Zabaza are revealed as an elaborate plan to perpetuate their own power. Far from struggling for the common good, it is self-interest, cloaked in cliche, that motivates these men.

With personal ambition as the motive for action, the key to staying in power is violence. Ostensibly this originates outside of the state with Zabaza, but is in fact revealed as an instrument of the state itself. The instrument is one which *berjasa mengembalikan semangat* (has served to return spirit/enthusiasm); *mempersatukan seluruh kekuatan kerajaan* (has united all of the kingdom's strength); *mempersatukan seluruh potensi angkatan bersenjata kerajaan* (has united the whole potential of the kingdom's armed forces); *menegakkan moral baru* (has strengthened a new moral order); and *membuat setiap orang menjadi hamba kerajaan yang baik* (made everyone into faithful subjects of the kingdom).[34] While this violence appears initially as a means to an end (though an end not recognized as such at the time), ultimately it becomes an end in itself, with an impetus of its own, consuming those who created it. It is gratuitous, with no particular purpose—a model, in fact, of absolute terror.

As a novel, *Nyali* is constructed from language and its primary reality is the words on the page. While it is not a novel that speaks of its own writing—and therefore not one that dismantles its own verisimilitude by pointing to its own literariness—it emphasizes the arbitrary nature of language. The novel is in a continuous state of taking language apart, refusing to fix concepts and situations with any certainty. The nature and identity of Zabaza are good examples of this. Who or what Zabaza is changes over time. At different points in the novel, the title/identity of Zabaza is assumed, though never incontrovertibly, by different people—by Leonel, by Kropos, perhaps, finally, by Leonel's wife. What Zabaza is and does depends on who you are and where you stand. For his/her/its victims, Zabaza is mortal danger. For the kingdom, the king, and, at times, Leonel, Zabaza is a tool and a "robot" to unify the state. At other times, Zabaza becomes for Leonel a vehicle for his own ambition. At the end of the novel a neo-Zabaza is the cause of his downfall.

In *Nyali* hardly anything has a fixed meaning. Everything is susceptible to manipulation and ultimately disintegrates. This is also apparent in the all-pervasive rencana—a word with strong governmental overtones in Indonesian. In *Nyali* the rencana includes elements of both the rational and irrational which make it the antithesis of a normal

282

"plan" with all that word suggests of rationality and order. *Nyali* is a novel in which belief must constantly be suspended and where credibility can never been assured.

One may ask what this sustained attack on fixity of meaning achieves. On the one hand *Nyali* and writing like it can be dismissed as "fantastical and bizarre literary styles to obscure . . . lack of social commitment."[35] I would suggest that such an interpretation represents a misreading and an overly narrow vision of the means whereby a social and political vision can be expressed in literature. It is an inadequate reading, in the sense that it ignores literature's subversive potential and may ultimately lead to the style of narrative that Carlos Fuentes describes this way:

> The revolutionary hero, too often, has simply illustrated the fairy-tale-truth of boy meets rifle before settling down to the eternal domestic triangle between two Stakhanovites[36] and the tractor.[37]

This kind of idealism, more important, its insistence on realism as the only effective mode of literary expression, especially of radical expression, goes some way towards explaining the failure of much Indonesian leftist literature of the 1950s and 1960s.

The power of *Nyali*'s dystopian vision lies in its capacity to question what is real. The mistrust and, indeed, skepicism with which it surrounds notions of truth and free will may carry well beyond the novel. It creates a vision which may undermine the politics of the contemporary Indonesian experience. Literary representation does not necessarily need to be "realistic" to be socially and politically potent. Symbols may be powerful, and fantasies dangerous. This has been the burden of this paper, which has attempted to show that, for all its vaunted "objectivity," verisimilitude does not necessarily represent the world as it really is but, often, as people wish it to be. In many cases realistic modes of it tells us only part of the story. The other part, blocked out by pressures of anticipated or externally-imposed censorship, can be revealed only by exposing the immanent contradictions to be found in the narrative surface. What results from this sort of reading is both contrary and insubordinate. Contrary, in that this reading refuses to accept that the surface of the narrative is all there is. Insubordinate, in that it reads against this surface in an attempt to expose the pressures that organize a narrative.

NOTES

1. For example Georg Lukacs, *The Historical Novel* (London: Merlin Press, 1974), and *Studies in European Realism* (London: Merlin Press, 1975); and L. Goldmann, *The Hidden God* (London: Routledge and Kegan Paul, 1964).

2. Note, for example, Lukacs' rejection of Kafka in the following quotation: "In Kafka, the descriptive detail is of an extraordinary immediacy and authenticity. But Kafka's artistic ingenuity is really directed towards substituting his angst-ridden vision of the world of objective reality" (*The Meaning of Contemporary Realism* [London: Merlin Press, 1963], 25-26). Lukacs also notes "the obsession with psychopathology in modernist literature as a desire to escape from the reality of capitalism. But this implies the absolute primacy of the *terminus a quo*, the condition from which it is desired to escape. Any movement towards a *terminus ad quem* is condemned to impotence. As the ideology of modernist writers asserts the unalterability of outward reality (even if this is reduced to a mere state of consciousness), human activity is, *a priori*, rendered impotent and robbed of meaning. . . . The apprehension of reality to which this leads is most consistently and convincingly realised in the work of Kafka" (36). For the context of contemporary Indonesian literature, see David Hill's rejection of certain contemporary Indonesian writers in the following quotation: "New order artistic champions, like Sutarji Calzoum Bachri, Danarto and Putu Wujaya, concentrated on *fantastical and bizzare literary styles to obscure their lack of social commitment*" [my emphasis]. David Hill, *Who's Left? Indonesian Writers of the 1980s* (Melbourne: Monash University Centre of Southeast Asian Studies, Working Paper No. 33, 1984), 2.

3. Catherine Belsey, *Critical Practice* (London: Methuen, 1980) 68-69.

4. Noted for example in R. Tallis, *In Defence of Realism* (London: Edward Arnold, 1988), especially 9-20.

5. On the "institutionalization" of Indonesian literature and the writing of its history, see P. Tickell, "The Writing of Indonesian Literary History," *Review of Indonesian and Malaysian Affairs* 21/1 (1987).

6. See Arswendo Atmowiloto, *Pengkhianatan G-30-S/PKI* (Jakarta: Sinar Harapan, 1986). This novel and the film on which it was based are essentially propaganda commissioned by the Indonesian "New Order" government to reinforce its vision and version of the events surrounding the abortive coup of 1 October 1965.

7. "Vertical" propaganda is defined by Jacques Ellul as "made by a leader, a technician, a political or religious head who acts from the superior position of authority and seeks to influence the crowd below. Such propaganda comes from above. It is conceived in the secret recesses of political enclaves; it uses all technical methods of mass communication; it envelops a mass of individuals; but those who practice it are on the outside." Jacques Ellul, *Propaganda: The Formation of Men's Attitudes* (New York: Knopf, 1973), 79-80.

8. Michael Wilding, *Political Fictions* (London: Routledge and Kegan Paul, 1980), 20.

9. For further details of the events surrounding the coup d'état and interpretations as to the significance of these events see H. Crouch, "Another Look at the Indonesian Coup," *Indonesia* 15 (April 1973).

10. For instance, films like *Pengkhianatan G-30-S*, noted above in note 6. Documentary material outlining the role of the PKI in antistate activities and rebellions can be found in the following pseudohistorical volume: *Lukisan Pemberontakan PKI di Indonesia dan Penumpasannya* (Illustrations from Rebellions by the Communist Party of Indonesia in Indonesia and their Suppression) (Jakarta: Dinas Sejarah, Tentara Nasional Indonesia, Angkatan Darat, 1979).

11. Some leftist recollections of the events of this period and their subsequent experiences have been published. See, for example, Teguh, *Catatan di Sela-Sela Intaian* (Limburg: Yayasan Langer, 1981). It is important to note that these have been published by exiles outside of Indonesia. Naturally they are not readily available in Indonesia itself.

12. For a list of literary material dealing with the events of the coup see Satyagraha Hoerip, "Pemberontakan GESTAPU/PKI dalam Cerpen-cerpen Indonesia," in Pamusuk Eneste, *Cerpen Indonesia Mutakhir* (Jakarta: Gramedia, 1983).

13. Satyagraha Hoerip, "Pada Titik Kulminasi," *Horison* 1/1 (1966) (translated as "The Climax," in *Gestapu: Indonesian Short Stories on the Abortive Communist Coup of 30th September 1965*, ed. H. Aveling [Honolulu: University of Hawaii, 1975], 36-50). Zulidahlan, "Maka Sempurnalah Penderitaan Saya di Muka Bumi," *Horison* 2/3 (March 1967) (translated as "The Valley of the Shadow of Death," in Aveling, *Gestapu*, 77-82). Usamah, "Perang dan Kemanusiaan," *Horison* 4/8 (August 1969) (translated as "War and Humanity" in Aveling, *Gestapu*, 12-22). Subsequent page references in the following notes are references to the *Horison* publications.

14. See T. Eagleton, *Criticism and Ideology* (London: Version, 1975), especially 54-63. The term "literary ideology" is also taken from this source, especially 44-63.

15. For an outline of the main tenets of Universal Humanism, see H. B. Jassin, "Humanisme Universil," in his *Kesusastraan Indonesia Modern dalam Kritik dan Esei* (Jakarta: Gunung Agung, 1954), and A. Teeuw, *Modern Indonesian Literature*, vol. 1 (The Hague: Martinus Nijhoff, 1967) 126-29.

16. The concept of literature as a vehicle of truth versus literature as political sloganeering is raised by Indonesian critic and commentator Goenawan Mohamad. In this case the accusation of "sloganeering" is levelled at the Indonesian Left—in particular writers associated with LEKRA, an Indonesian Communist party affiliated organisation. Goenewan takes it for granted that Indonesian liberal writers (in whose ranks he himself would usually be counted) are the purveyors of truth and genuine literature. See Goenawan Mohamad, *"Seribu Slogan dan Sebuah Puisi": Potret Seorang Penyair Sebagai Si Malin Kundang* (Jakarta: Pustaka Jaya, 1972), 31-32.

17. Satyagraha, "Pada Titik Kulminasi," 56.

18. Wiratmo Sukito, "Satyagraha Hoerip atau Apologia Pro Vita Lekra," in *Kesusasteraan dan Kekuasaan* (Jakarta, 1984), 40.

19. Sukito, "Satyagraha," 73.

20. Sukito, "Satyagraha," 75.

21. Usamah, "Perang dan Kemanusiaan," 231.

22. Zuliahahlan, "Maka Sempurnalah," 73-74.

23. Keith Foulcher, "Historical Past and Political Present in Recent Indonesian Novels," *Asian Studies Association of Australia Review* 11/1 (July 1987): 95.

24. Ajip Rosidi, *Anak Tahahair* (Jakarta: Gramedia, 1985), 19.

25. Rosidi, *Anak Tanahair*, 37-38.

26. Rosidi, *Anak Tanahair*, 45.

27. Foulcher, "Historical Past," 96.

28. Note, for example, the following comment from Marcel Proust: "In this conclusion I was confirmed by the thought of the falseness of so-called realist art, which would not be so untruthful if we had not in life acquired that habit of giving to what we feel a form of expression which differs so much from, and which we nevertheless after a little time take to be, reality itself." Proust, quoted in M. Bradbury, *The Modern World: Ten Great Writers* (London: Secker and Warburg, 1988), 150-51.

29. Putu Wijaya, *Nyali* (Jakarta, 1983).

30. Wijaya, *Nyali*, 41-42.

31. Wijaya, *Nyali*, 82.

32. Wijaya, *Nyali*, 64.

33. Wijaya, *Nyali*, 40.

34. Wijaya, *Nyali*, 41-42, 51, 62, 64.

35. Hill, *Who's Left*, 87.

36. Stakhanovites—n. (esp. Russian) worker who increases his output to an exceptional extent, and so gains special awards (*OED*).

37. Quoted in Barbara Harlow, *Resistance Literature* (London: Methuen, 1987), 37.

10

INTERPRETING THE INDONESIAN NATIONAL CHARACTER: MOCHTAR LUBIS AND *MANUSIA INDONESIA**

David T. Hill

There can be few Indonesian journalists, authors, or cultural figures who have achieved and sustained the kind of international prominence enjoyed by Mochtar Lubis.[1] For more than three decades now he has been invited to major international forums as a representative of, and spokesperson for, his society, a role enhanced by his reputation as Indonesia's primary liberal advocacy journalist and one of her best-known political prisoners, detained for nearly ten years prior to 1966. Until surpassed only recently by his ideological rival, the left-wing author Pramoedya Ananta Toer, Mochtar Lubis was Indonesia's most translated novelist and short story writer. His *Senja di Jakarta* (Twilight in Jakarta), published in 1963, was the first Indonesian novel to appear in English translation.[2] Mochtar[3] has cultivated his transnational role assiduously, having recognized early in his career the benefits of a foreign constituency.[4]

After outlining the turbulent course of Mochtar's career and drawing attention to his importance as an international spokesperson for his country, this essay will examine his most important and controversial analysis of his society. A succinct presentation of the main features

---

* I would like to thank Dr. Krishna Sen for her unfailing willingness to read and discuss previous versions of this paper, which benefited incalculably from her suggestions. The many remaining weaknesses display my own limitations, for which I take full responsibility.

which Mochtar identifies in the Indonesian "national character" will be followed by a critique of his position, in the light of varying responses from his Indonesian audiences.

Credentials

Although never a member of a political party and unfailingly assertive of his political "independence" of party politics, Mochtar has been sympathetic to the liberal policies of Sutan Sjahrir, founder of the Indonesian Socialist party (PSI) and one of Indonesia's most respected intellectual and political figures.[5] The secular "democratic socialist" stream of Indonesian political thinking, identified by Feith and Castles[6] and associated primarily with the PSI though always numerically small, was both highly vocal and privileged by the mainstream tradition of English-language scholarship on Indonesian politics.[7] Mochtar circulated on the fringes of Sjahrir's inner circle, being, at times, both a sharp critic of the Indonesian Socialist party and an articulate sympathizer of Sjahrir's democratic socialism.

Since Mochtar's early years as the combative editor of *Indonesia Raya* daily newspaper, established with military support in December 1949, he was viewed by foreign observers as a sharp-tongued editorializer for anticommunist and anti-Sukarnoist forces sympathetic to Sjahrir and the PSI. In the Cold War chill he was a vocal Indonesian representative on the US-aligned, Zurich-based International Press Institute (IPI) from 1951 and an enthusiastic member of the American-funded intellectuals' lobby, the Congress for Cultural Freedom (CCF), since 1954.[8] His house arrest in December 1956, after *Indonesia Raya*'s support for a simmering anti-Jakarta regionalist movement among army officers in Sumatra, brought down a storm of international protest upon the Indonesian government. Released in April 1961, Mochtar flew to the IPI General Assembly in Tel Aviv to deliver a strongly worded speech interpreted back home as a veiled attack on the Sukarno government. Dismissing the assumed perils, he returned in July and was promptly rearrested. Despite continued international protests, including his adoption by the newly formed Amnesty International as their first Indonesian prisoner-of-conscience, he remained in jail until the fall of Sukarno and the change of government in 1966 which expedited his eventual release in May of that year.

In October 1968 Mochtar relaunched *Indonesia Raya*, ten years after its demise in the wake of his earlier detention. Like many of the inheritors of the Sjahririan tradition, dubbed the "secular modernizing intellectuals," he was initially a staunch supporter of the Suharto regime which had freed him.[9] Yet he soon became a vocal critic of government once again. In November 1969, catching the scent of the financial mismanagement within the national Pertamina oil company (which ultimately needed government intervention in 1975 to avoid bankruptcy), *Indonesia Raya* signalled its return to advocacy journalism with a broadside aimed at the presidentially protected head of Pertamina, Ibnu Sutowo, for budgetary and administrative "irregularities" which were turning the company into a virtual fiefdom.[10] Mochtar's growing reservations about official economic policy, and in particular his suspicion of Suharto officer-protegees who facilitated Japanese investment in Indonesia, dovetailed with burgeoning anti-Suharto student protests in late 1973. These erupted in January 1974 into three days of demonstrations and civil disorder known as the January Fifteenth Incident and usually referred to as *Malari*, acronymic of *Malapetaka Limabelas Januari*.[11] The closure of *Indonesia Raya* brought to an end Mochtar's career as a daily editor and accelerated his shift into other pursuits.

Domestic Constraints on Expression

By the mid-1950s Mochtar's early fiction, particularly *Jalan Tak Ada Ujung* (Road With No End), published in 1952, had established him as a writer of some distinction.[12] With the translations of *Senja di Jakarta* and *Jalan Tak Ada Ujung* in 1963 and 1968 respectively, he had direct access to readers of English (and the numerous other languages into which these works have been translated), a rare opportunity for an Indonesian writer of the period. Within weeks of his release in May 1966 he had drawn around him young students and artists to publish the influential cultural monthly, *Horison*. In apparent recognition of his numerous contributions to literary and cultural life, he was elevated in 1970 to the prestigious twelve-member Jakarta Academy (modelled on the *Academie Francaise*), apex of the cultural establishment of President Suharto's New Order Indonesia.

During the 1970s Mochtar reworked several incomplete fictional works begun in jail prior to 1966. But always he regarded himself primarily as a journalist, and his inability to report publicly on day-to-day political developments after the 1974 ban on *Indonesia Raya* frustrated him greatly. He wrote occasional columns in various papers

290

and journals but tended to relinquish his role as regular political commentator, instead increasing his involvement in several businesses which he had established previously, and pursuing his professional activities overseas. A recipient of the Philippines's Magsaysay Award for Journalism and Literature in 1958, he was active in a number of regional professional, cultural, and publishing ventures in Southeast Asia, including the Manila-based Press Foundation of Asia in which he held several senior posts. He was one of four Indonesians to have been on "blue ribbon" United Nation bodies, serving on UNESCO's International Commission for the Study of Communications Problems (known as the MacBride Commission) from 1977 to 1979. He remained a frequent participant in international, regional, and local conferences and seminars. Foreign fellowships, grants, and publishing contracts enabled him to complete two Dutch-language glossy "coffee-table" books on Indonesia for a foreign readership (one has since been published in English, but neither as yet in Indonesian).[13]

Much as he appreciated the opportunity of appearing before an overseas public, in the decade after the Malari ban, Mochtar sought new avenues to present his opinions to Indonesians. While fiction provided one outlet,[14] his most comprehensive domestic statements and social critiques took the form of public lectures, three of which have been published as monographs: *Manusia Indonesia* (Indonesian Humanity), *Bangsa Indonesia* (The Indonesian Nation), and *Transformasi Budaya untuk Masa Depan* (Cultural Transformation for the Future).[15] His major fictional works have been the focus of frequent attention by foreign academics.[16] His lectures, however, have eluded any such analysis. Yet an examination of them as distinct from his more voluminous journalistic and fictional writings provides an insight into the perspective of one of Indonesia's best-known and most vocal intellectuals a decade into the New Order. The most controversial was his attempt in one lecture at a critical examination of the nature of the Indonesian national character. From his criticisms, and from their reception, it is possible to develop a critique of the lecture as an ideological statement and illustration of Mochtar's political and social attitudes.

The Lecture

When Mochtar addressed a packed Arena Theatre at the prestigious Jakarta Cultural Centre, Taman Ismail Marzuki (TIM) on 6

April 1977, the audience, which spilled out of the seating onto the theatre floor, was in an expectant, almost festive, mood. The tenth anniversary of the endorsement of General Suharto as acting president by the Indonesian Parliament in March 1967 had only just passed and the second general elections under Suharto's New Order were less than a month away, on 2 May 1977.[17] The election atmosphere permeated the theatre's crowd, with students, aware of his support for the 1973-1974 protest movement, looking for a rousing campaigning diatribe from the political maverick. The two hour and twenty minute lecture, and the battery of questions that followed, were punctuated by ebullient applause, underscoring his key criticisms and dry-humored asides.[18]

One of the most popular and controversial held at TIM, the talk, entitled "The State of Present-day Indonesians, Viewed from the Perspective of Culture and Human Values," represents his most explicit and comprehensive statement about contemporary Indonesian society in the late 1970s.[19] The lecture has since become a rubric—the term *manusia Indonesia* itself entering popular parlance—in public discussion of Indonesian society.[20] In part this is due to the spirited reaction and polemic it generated in the national press, taken up by newspapers such as *Kompas* (Compass), *Sinar Harapan* (Ray of Hope), *Pelita* (Lamp), *Suara Karya* (Work Voice), and *Angkatan Bersenjata* (Armed Forces).[21] Showing glimpses of the provocative style that had become Mochtar's trademark, it was not intended as an academic study but succeeded in its goal of triggering public debate. An eighty-page monograph based on the lecture, in its sixth edition by 1985, was a best-seller for the publisher, the Idayu Foundation (Yayasan Idayu) and a major commercial success for a nonfiction work.[22] So successful was the publication that Idayu commenced a series of "character study" analyses of particular Indonesian ethnic groups.[23] *Manusia Indonesia* is also the only one of his lectures to reach an international audience through an English translation.[24] Asked some days after the lecture about the implicit political constraints to open debate, he admitted to being on the horns of a dilemma that "if one is too subtle, no attention is paid to the criticism. If one is too outspoken, action is taken against you."[25]

It was, therefore, a restrained Mochtar who identified six major and many minor traits of the Indonesian character (manusia Indonesia). Insofar as it is possible to reproduce them here, briefly and without interpolation, what were these traits and in what terms did Mochtar present them?

The first was hypocrisy. Mochtar attributes this to Indonesians' need to hide their true feelings when confronted by outside force, for fear of retaliation. Feudalism and forced proselytization inclined people to feign acceptance while masking their true beliefs. In addition, he wrote that

> we have been ravished by the Portuguese, the Spanish, the Dutch, the Japanese, the Chinese,[26] and other peoples, and for the last thirty years by international consumerism, and greed-oriented giant multinational enterprises, not to mention our own selfish people.[27]

An ingrained hypocrisy manifests itself in attitudes toward sex, Mochtar continues. Nowadays, while perfectly respectable at home, when this manusia Indonesia goes overseas he heads straight for the nightclubs in search of women. Damning corruption, he is himself a corruptor.[28] National hypocrisy allows major criminals to go free or to serve brief sentences, while petty criminals languish in prison. It allows large-scale corruption within government institutions like Pertamina to go unchecked for decades. In that particular instance, although "the facts are crystal clear, to this day no legal action has been taken against the senior participants" (24). Mochtar blames this corruption upon an "ABS mentality" which justifies all behavior, *Asal Bapak Senang* (as long as the boss is happy), thereby encouraging underlings to avoid reporting unpleasantness to their superiors. He believes this tendency to have been implanted well before the coming of the colonialists, when "Indonesian feudal lords ruled over the land, oppressed the people, and violated the values held by Indonesians" (24). Subservience continues in the use of terms such as *bapak* (father) for seniors or superiors, which negate the democratic spirit of the Indonesian struggle for independence.

Yet another feature of the national character is an unwillingness to accept responsibility for one's actions. Again Mochtar points to the behavior of such senior executives of Pertamina as former chief Ibnu Sutowo. Yet many other Indonesians also accept official awards and approval without having earned them. It is always the figureheads and not the real workers who get the praise, unwarranted though this may be.

A feudalistic mentality is the third attribute of manusia Indonesia. This is evident in such things as the nomination of the wives of very senior government officials for candidature in general elections. In women's associations it is the status of her husband which determines a wife's position, not her own qualities of leadership or experience. While those in "high" positions expect to be treated according to their station, those beneath "have no less a spirit of feudal mentality in their service to their bapak" (29). In traditional Indonesian societies, the king was believed to have a divine right, a *wahyu cakraningrat*, which fitted him to rule. Though the title "king" may have changed, nowadays "[those] in power do not like to be criticized, and their subordinates are very reluctant to criticize them . . . . Communication between the powerholder and the people goes only from the top downwards. It is a one-way street."[29]

The fourth characteristic is superstition, the investment of natural objects with supernatural powers. Indonesians place faith in symbols, talismans, and *mantera* (magic formulae) for protection; this Mochtar sees as a pollution of rationality by mysticism. Even the most rational and highly skilled of them often surrender to the pull of *kebatinan* in times of crises.[30] So far as he is concerned, "this mystical ideology has control of the largest segment of Indonesia's population, especially those on the island of Java."[31] Mochtar is skeptical of animistic beliefs and mystical practices. He cannot accept as valid any reason for modern, educated people to turn to mysticism: "Try to imagine," he urges his audience sarcastically, "what would happen if all our government policies were based on *wahyu* (messages from God) and other entirely irrational guidance. How dangerous it would be for the life of our nation" (15).

Traditional mystical belief embodied in divine messages has its modern equivalent in political rhetoric, which encourages people to place faith in oft-repeated words rather than tangible achievements. He is critical of "new magic formulae and slogans" promoted by the Suharto government. Though bandied about as a concept, the idealized society based on the five-point state ideology of *Pancasila* is not given form in statutes governing taxes, social welfare, and equal access to education.[32] While he hopes that Indonesia will one day create a *"manusia Pancasila"* (the Pancasila-guided person) who personifies the highest ideals of human society, Mochtar doubts this will be achieved before 2000.

"Modernization" and "economic development," he observes, are new superstitions. Instead of bringing about a just and equitable distribution of wealth, "modernization" encourages consumerism. The warning is about the damage to human values, the environment, and natural resources posed by technological and economic "advances" in industrialized societies. Language is manipulated to obscure contradictions between what people say and what they do, making it difficult to evaluate politicians' statements about "the rule of law"[33] or the freedom and responsibility of the press since "the meaning of words or other symbols is not in the words themselves, but in our semantic reaction to those words" (37).

The fifth characteristic, and the only one to offer hope for the future, is artistic ability, developed through closeness to nature, an intimacy exemplified by ascribing spiritual powers to inanimate objects. As for the sixth, this, according to Mochtar, is weakness of will, or indecision. He criticizes intellectuals who have trimmed their philosophies to suit prevailing politics, a practice he calls "intellectual prostitution" *(pelacuran intelektuil)*.[34] The Javanese attitude of *tepa slira* (knowing one's place),[35] he regards as a weakness of character and a manifestation of "ABS" behavior.

The discussion of "Other Characteristics" describes the Indonesian as wasteful, extravagant, and not an "economic animal."[36] Typically, he or she seeks instant wealth, success, and status as a public servant, only to exploit it for personal gain. Jealousy and covetousness are widespread. The "average Indonesian" is pretentious *(manusia-sok)*, power-hungry, and avaricious, preferring foreign products to local ones. A favorable physical environment has made him lazy and impecunious. On the positive side, he is gentle, peace-loving, quick to learn, dexterous, endowed with a sense of humor, and patient to a fault.

Mochtar is critical of the *penguasa* (powerholder) who wants to be seen as a servant of the people, a defender of justice and the rule of law, but who in practice is malicious, power-hungry, greedy, and egotistical. He criticizes the hierarchical and neofeudalist language used by and about powerholders and particularly the ambiguous, platitudinous headlines used by newspapers. He mocks the flamboyant lifestyle of the Indonesian "elite," a superwealthy clique of powerholders increasingly distanced from the population they claim to lead. "As the years go by we allow this elite of ours to enrich itself by corruption and theft of the rights and property of the people, in ever-increasing amounts" (53). He quotes Gandhi's famous dictum, "Earth provides enough for everyone's need, but not for everyman's greed."[37] To benefit from natural resources "we must control science and technology. But we must be careful. Science is power, and power is never neutral."[38]

As the lecture's focus gradually shifts from national character to Indonesia's place in the world economic order, so too does the criticism come to center on the predominance of foreign investment in Indonesia in capital—not labor—intensive areas. In redress, Mochtar recommends that a popular voice must counterbalance government control: "Social supervision of our natural resources, our capital, our use of labor, our science and technology, our country's ecological balance, and the prevention of environmental disaster needs to be institutionalised."[39] He stresses that, since the transfer of sovereignty in 1949, there is a growing gap between national pretensions (such as Pancasila, justice, human rights, and the rule of law) and the actual behavior of Indonesians, individual or collective.

The lecture's substantive penultimate section, "Today's World," discusses global economic developments and speaks of an increasing gap between developed and underdeveloped or developing countries, a distinction measured according to criteria determined by Western economists.[40] Such economic indicators misleadingly suggest that wealthier countries are more advanced in all areas of human civilization and culture. Mochtar calls for a reconceptualization of such loaded terminology. He questions the direction of Western economic development with its stress on materialistic gains and relegation of human considerations.[41] "How primitive and backward," he insists (59), is a theory which stresses Gross National and Domestic Product, the pursuit of goods and profits: "'modernization' should not mean computers or giant factories, but 'a certain mental attitude and rationality of thought, which always strives to find solutions to the problems of human life in a rational and all-encompassing manner'" (61).

While attacking piecemeal approaches to the problems created by economic development, he lambasts the West (America particularly) for seeking ever-increasing opulence without thought for the developing world. The goal should be the alleviation of hunger, provision of adequate clothing, housing, equality of educational opportunity, with guarantees that neither life nor death will be too expensive. This is achievable through a simpler lifestyle for the wealthy countries, with an emphasis in Indonesia on small-scale agricultural industries producing food, the most vital commodity for the future. Appropriate or intermediate technology *(teknologi madya)* must take priority, especially in developing renewable energy resources. Mochtar sets little store by North-South debates or dialogues on the proposed New International Economic Order. Unfair trade flows will continue to mean low returns

296

for primary producers and high prices for industrial goods, which developing countries must buy because "we have been deceived and impressed by their advertising and consumerist propaganda" (68). The industrialized countries will have to either "defend their extravagant, luxurious standard of living at all costs (including forcing their will upon those countries which possess the reserves of raw materials they need), or change their lifestyles, adjusting and learning to live simply once more" (70).

Mochtar recognizes that

> the more we are drawn along in the currents of consumerism of the rich countries, the more we make ourselves dependent upon their aid, whether in the form of their capital or technology, the more we make our safety dependent upon their weaponry, the more we weaken our ability to protect our individuality as a nation and as people, and the more we fall further and further into dependence upon them. (71)

Indonesia must become self-sufficient in food, reduce dependence upon the wealthy countries by efficiently utilizing financial, human, and natural resources, end corruption, and improve the life of the people. Otherwise, he greatly feared "that, in our own homeland, we will become just unskilled laborers for multinational companies from Japan, America, Germany, the Netherlands, France, England, and the rest" (75).

The conclusion to the lecture reiterates the need for Indonesians to free themselves from the constraints of a semifeudal or neofeudal society. They should return traditional art forms to their deserved place as an inspiration for developing the Indonesians' inherent creativity and artistry, since "through artistic expression we will be able directly to attain truth" (77).

He proposes "a closer relationship among powerholders, the private sector, and the artistic community," in the hope of tempering power with humanistic principles and artistic sensitivity;[42] "we have to make culture and art tools for liberating our people from the grip and fetters of a value system which has long inhibited us and dwarfed and constrained the Indonesian capacity for inspiration and creativity" (78). He urges a regeneration of a national self-confidence, and a redevelopment of those strengths of character which enabled his people in precolonial times to explore and trade as far afield as Madagascar and

Africa. Ethics are to reach beyond personal relations in public life, embracing ecological responsibility and environmental preservation. The educational system must meet modern challenges and satisfy demands for rapid flow of information to allow for keeping abreast of current scientific developments.

After nearly two and one-half hours, Mochtar closed his talk with two proverbs: one, Minangkabau,

> I have told you all I know;
> The rest, that I know not,
> I must leave to others . . .
> To those who know more than I.

the other, Javanese,

> What you are after is not available,
> What you are not after is everywhere.[43]

The lecture reveals Mochtar's attitudes as a social critic, deliberately setting out to provoke public reaction.[44] How successful he was in issuing his challenge, and the degree to which his comments represent wider-held views in Indonesia, may be gauged by the public response to his lecture, which suggested his ideas both enjoy a wide currency and have been themselves subjected to criticism.

The Context and Responses

Public lectures at TIM seldom generate extensive press coverage. They are usually reported in the literary or cultural columns of the inner pages. Few make the front page or the feature columns. *Manusia Indonesia* did both, with front page reports, a detailed summary of the lecture's contents, a number of substantial articles devoted to the subsequent polemic being given prominence on the prestigious "features" page together with various "letters to the editor" suggesting a spirited debate within the newspaper-reading public.[45] Significantly, most respondents praised Mochtar for his outspokenness. They regarded the lecture as evidence of his sincere concern for his community but wanted to provide other perspectives or to correct some of Mochtar's assumptions.[46] Critical responses ranged from chidings of aristocrats offended by Mochtar's accusations to more fundamental challenges to the "national character" approach.

Margono Djojohadikusumo (1894-1978), head of an influential aristocratic Javanese family closely linked with the Indonesian Socialist party, was, for example, "a little hurt" by Mochtar's criticisms of feudalism and his representation of Javanese culture.[47] Mochtar, he thought, gave the impression of being anti-Javanese, an impression which he, Margono (saying he had know Mochtar well for thirty years) knew to be erroneous. Mochtar, it seems, had misunderstood Javanese culture and the noblesse oblige of the Javanese aristocracy. Margono defended the latter, arguing that what distinguished them from commoners was not wealth, but behavior and a view of life.

This distinction between the benevolent aristocracy and a plutocracy which wields power because of its wealth was echoed by Abu Hanifah who claimed that the traditional aristocracy had generally dispensed with the trappings of privilege during the upsurge of democratic ideals after 1928.[48] It was unfair for Mochtar to blame the nation for the shameful behavior of the "new Aristocrats," Abu Hanifah's term for those who recently had become wealthy through their powerful bureaucratic and military positions. Mochtar's lecture had inspired Abu Hanifah to reread and to reflect upon previous studies of the Indonesians and their character. He recalled that the writings about Indonesians by various foreign "Orientalists" were often motivated by political considerations. Their depreciatory assessments were often used to justify the extension or maintenance of colonial power. As a nationalist he "suspected the authors of such books intended to find the weaknesses in the Indonesian nation" (119). He claimed there was no reason to think that "the attributes of the Indonesian character are different from the attributes of people anywhere else in the world" (124). Subtly linking the *Manusia Indonesia* lecture with traditions of Orientalist scholarship, Abu Hanifah's response foreshadowed more radical critiques, to which I shall later return.

A frequent objection was that the lecture was based upon its author's own necessarily limited experience and was devoid of supporting data. Social psychologist Sarlito Wirawan Sarwono wrote that Mochtar tended to mislead by presenting an attribute as if it were exclusively Indonesian, when, for example, superstition and corruption "are not an Indonesian monopoly" (84). Instances of subservient behavior in the community, Sarlito observed, do not mean that Indonesians are characteristically feudalistic, for such behavior arises from within the pattern of power-relations into which people are pressed and was linked inextricably to structural causes. Equally fundamental was his criticism that Mochtar had limited his observations to

> those who, in their daily lives, had the opportunity to come directly face to face with influences coming in from outside, in relation to development and modernisation. They live in the large cities and consist of government officials, wealthy business people, intellectuals and others of the elite, as well as their families.[49]

Mochtar's description is not true for Indonesian working people, since the

> vast majority of Indonesians are farmers and workers who are industrious, persevering, resolute in the face of the challenges of nature, appreciating moral values, upholding religious values, and respecting honesty and courage. (89)

Some observers argued that from the outset Mochtar had intended his disparagement to apply only to those with political and bureaucratic power. They assumed that, under pressure of prevailing political constraints on expression, he had chosen to gloss criticisms of specific leaders and influential groups in more general terms. However, in answering those who attacked his broad-brush caricature (and in effect countering the charge that he had in mind specific targets) Mochtar denied that such vices were those of a minority only. He maintained that the lecture described practices which "have spread to a great number of Indonesians."[50] He attempted to counter Sarlito's claim that his observations were applicable only to the urban elite, arguing that the "idealist and romantic image of the Indonesian peasant" as "industrious, persevering, determined, respecting honesty and courage" was mistaken, for "many of the bad things we see in our large cities are even reflected in villages nowadays" (95).

Such assertions failed to convince author Wildan Yatim, who stressed that "the common people could not possibly be corrupt, laze about, not take any responsibility, and the like."[51] Such behavior finds a breeding ground within the government apparatus. In an article published twenty-two days after the 1977 general election, he argued that the attitudes under attack are generated by an unrepresentative political structure which does not serve the needs of the ordinary people. The current political system was at the root of the characteristics Mochtar described. For example, he pointed to the electoral system, arguing that it encourages politicians to tolerate corruption because they are dependent not on an electorate but on those in the political hierarchy. Crucially, it is this hierarchy, not the electorate in any real sense, which determines the ranking of candidates on electoral lists and thus their political future. In varying degrees, then, the criticism of Yatim, Sarlito, and Hanifah were of biases inherent in Mochtar's perception of his society, biases which may be revealed by looking closely at the text of the lecture.

The Author's "Strategic Location"

The year Mochtar delivered this lecture on the Indonesian character saw the publication by the Indonesia-born Malaysian Syed Hussein Alatas of an analysis of the image of the Malays, Filipinos, and Javanese from the sixteenth to the twentieth century and its function in the ideology of colonial capitalism.[52] In embarking on his task of deconstructing the European myth of the indolence and inferiority of Southeast Asians, Alatas cited Karl Mannheim's view that it is only by being conscious of the social roots of one's ideas and attitudes that one could hope to escape the distorting influence of ideology upon scholarship.[53] In opening his pathbreaking work on the production of images of "the Oriental," the Palestinian-American Edward Said declared similarly that "no production of knowledge in the human sciences can ever ignore or disclaim its author's involvement as a human subject in his own circumstances."[54] Both these contemporaneous texts, whose authors are critically aware of their own disposition, provide instructive contrasts with Mochtar's *Manusia Indonesia*.

Mochtar seems to lack in such an awareness. There is no acknowledgement of his own class, religious, ethnic, or gender position. In examining writings of non-"Orientals" about the "Orient," Said tests them for their "strategic location," "the author's position in a text with regard to the Oriental material he writes about."[55] Mochtar opens his lecture with an anecdote in which he nearly comes to blows with a "loud-mouthed whitey" *("si mulut lancang bule")* who had insulted Indonesians by claiming "you can buy everybody in Jakarta" (8). From the outset he presents himself as a defender of Indonesians against outside critics, identifying himself as author firmly with the manusia

Indonesia which forms his subject. This attempted insertion of himself into his subject is reinforced by his use of the inclusive first-person plural, *kita*, in the discussion of the characteristics of Indonesians.

His posture throughout the lecture, however, negates this insertion and identification. He is at pains to establish the national character as a reality separate from himself, something tangible and objective, there to be analyzed. This has two effects. First, highly personal views are presented as knowledge of an objective reality. As the closing Minangkabau proverb illustrates, he has told the audience all he *knows*; opinions have become knowledge. Occasionally he poses rhetorical questions to this audience, bidding them judge the accuracy of his picture of manusia Indonesia; this device encourages their agreement and takes it for granted. Secondly, his distancing from his subject and this attribution of mainly negative characteristics to his manusia Indonesia establish a pattern of images which reinforces the stereotype which had incensed Mochtar when articulated by the "whitey" in his opening anecdote. All his primary characterizations, with the single important exception of artistic ability, are consonant with the stereotypical images of the colonial ideology.

The lecture opened with questions, "Who is this Indonesian person? Does he really exist?" (7). It answered them in detail, testifying to the reality of such a creature. In this description negatives predominate, reinforcing the exclusion of author from subject. By implication he does not share the traits he observes in the national character but stands apart, a signpost to danger. Responding to Sarlito's hopes that the next generation would approximate the ideal Indonesian, Mochtar hints at his self-assigned role in asking rhetorically, "How can this happen if there is no example *(tauladan)* to motivate them?" (97). His own practice is taken to have deviated from the norm he establishes for this manusia Indonesia.

Identifying a "National Character"

Sarlito Wirawan Sarwono criticized Mochtar for basing his lecture on observations of the Indonesian urban elite and for conflating limited practices with general features. "Excessive generalizations," he concluded, "will be dangerous because they can give rise to misleading impressions about national character" (90). Unaware of his own strategic location, Mochtar presents an image of a national character largely devoid of such things as class, religion, ethnicity, and gender.

302

A feudal mentality can be observed equally in both status superiors and status inferiors, and while criticizing superstition *(takhyul, kebatinan)*, Mochtar revealingly excuses himself from a discussion of religion, saying that "[we] cannot talk too' much about religion tonight, because it will lead to many sensitive matters, and will never bring us to an agreement. Each religion says that it is the absolute truth, because it is a belief" (57). Implied criticisms of the Javanese prompted Margono Djojohadikusumo's spirited defense. Yet in general Mochtar's approach was not consciously to differentiate amongst various ethnic groups in his remarks, but instead to extend traits he observed in one such group to a national character. As for gender, there is no integrated consideration of women. Throughout the lecture *manusia Indonesia* appears to be male, and gender is seen to have no bearing of all on national character. The result of this reductionist perspective, in Said's words, is "to eradicate the plurality of differences" in the interest of establishing one essential difference, that between "good" and "bad" characteristics.[56]

If one premise crucial to the lecture is that analysis of national character is indeed possible, another is that the perspective of an urban intellectual is its appropriate point of departure. Other social scientists working on Orientalism are doubtful of this. As Alatas has noted,

> There are serious problems connected with national character study which have baffled the best brains in social sciences; one of these is the definition of national character. The difficulty of defining the national character is due to the fact that there are many classes in society with their sub-cultures; there are also the differentiations into age groups, into male and female, and into responses which arise from the situation only, without the dominant influence of the national character.[57]

Mochtar is caught between attempting to define the national character and being forced to acknowledge specificities of classes or groups. At one point he suggests that "Indonesian feudal lords . . . violated the values held by Indonesians" (24). The behavior of the rulers was in contrast with Indonesian values *("nilai-nilai manusia Indonesia")*, although later the vices of the Indonesian personality are seen to be precisely those of the elite. As Alatas asserts, just as ideology influences an observer's perspectives, so it influences one's identification and selection of as well as one's approach to problems.[58] The national character approach is premised on the existence of a

303

(relatively) homogeneous, undifferentiated character within political/geographical boundaries. It excludes or subsumes other variables which contradict the existence of such intrinsic features or else it misrepresents them as national.

Contradictions

Early in his lecture, Mochtar referred humorously to colonial scholars' views of various Indonesian ethnic groups. Given Hanifah's deft association of his lecture with Orientalist perceptions, can *Manusia Indonesia* be interpreted justifiably as an extension of the Orientalist tradition?

Said's exploration of that tradition identified key elements in the view of "the Orient" and "the Oriental" held by non-Orientals, from early contacts to the 1970s. While local manifestations changed, what he called Modern Orientalism, after World War II, perpetuated the fundamental dogmas: that there is an absolute and axiomatic difference between the (positive) West and the (negative) Orient; that abstractions about the Orient are preferable to direct evidence; that it is eternal, uniform, incapable of defining itself, and therefore is to be defined by a "scientifically objective" West; and that it is to be feared and controlled.[59] Said warns those who assume such attitudes to be the preserve of non-Orientals that to some degree, the intelligentsia in "the modern Orient . . . participates in its own Orientalizing" by accommodating itself to a "new imperialism."[60] Using a different terminology, Alatas documents this process in Malaysia in two influential studies of the Malay national character written by Malays in the early 1970s. *Manusia Indonesia*'s English title, *The Indonesian Dilemma*, is an obvious allusion to the better-known of these studies, *The Malay Dilemma*, whose author, Mahathir bin Mohamad, was by the time this translation appeared prime minister of Malaysia![61]

There are parallels among the Orientalist tradition as summarized above, the two works Alatas examines, and *Manusia Indonesia*. In the last, the systematic difference is not between West and Orient/Asia, though such categories are assumed. Nevertheless, a polar opposition is set up between categories such as tradition and modernity, superstition and rationality. The approach is essentially ahistorical and abstract, sustained by little evidence. This entity, dubbed "manusia Indonesia," does not speak *through* the text: the lecture is not *his* perspective; he is spoken for by an external mouthpiece, who offers a definition in negative, would-be objective terms, the tone betraying apprehension about long-term social consequences.

One recurrent feature of this kind of thinking which stands out is the reproduction of arguments against mysticism and superstition which parallel colonial scholars' low opinion of indigenous faiths. Djojohadikusumo claimed that Mochtar did not adequately understand the attitude of the Javanese toward such mystical practices as the keeping of a *keris* (dagger), to take one example selected by Mochtar. All peoples have myths which are fundamental to their "security need," wrote the psychologist Sarlito. There is a distinction in the lecture between "mystical spirituality" *(kebatinan)*, regarded as negative, and the religions of the Great Tradition, such as Islam and Christianity, which are approved. Indigenous mystical beliefs are excluded from its use of the term "religion" *(agama)*.[62] While kebatinan is depicted as contrary to "rational" thought, belief in an approved religion is not. Mochtar thus throws his weight behind one side of an argument between conventional institutionalized religion and other forms associated with mysticism and animism.[63] Yet he does so without conveying any sense of meaningful Islamic conviction.

In apparent contradiction to the preceding comments, Mochtar also borrows concepts from dependency theory in commenting on the way aid and capital investment link with the First World to reinforce Indonesia's dependency upon the wealthy countries. He questions the goal of modernization (he calls it a new "superstition") set by Western economists. While his perspective had led him to define and speak for manusia Indonesia, he asserts the right of Indonesians to seize the definition of their own economic goals from foreign hands. At one point he argues that *"we* still have to be able to define for *ourselves* what is meant by 'developed country,' 'rich country,' 'poor country'" (58) (my emphasis), stressing that what people regard as modern varies historically. In ten or twenty years it might be thought very modern to reject environmentally damaging technologies. Modernization should amount to "a certain mental attitude and rationality" (61), in implicit contrast with traditional superstitions.

But the terminology of dependency is tangential to the basic thrust of Mochtar's argument, which draws on modernization theory of the 1960s. This theory, heir to the intellectual tradition of Orientalism, held that traditional societies had to undergo a cultural metamorphosis in order to develop into modern states (modelled on a Western paradigm) capable of achieving First World levels of economic success.

Dependency theory challenged this by showing how Third World countries reinforce rather than reduce their dependence upon Western economies in taking an imitative path to modernity. While adopting aspects of radical dependency theory to criticize the directions of Indonesia's growth, the *Manusia Indonesia* lecture retains elements of modernization theory, proposing a transformation of negative traditional values—superstition, evasion of responsibility, a feudalistic mentality—leading to a more desirable rational modern culture.[64]

This perspective locates culture and national character outside the political system and the power relations governing the community. In so doing, it contributes to crucial silences in the text. The military's role in social and political control is ignored or seen to have no bearing upon the formation of manusia Indonesia. Nor does the lecture make any reference to the national electoral system, its inadequacies in relation to political representation, or its implications for democratic life, though it was delivered only weeks before the 1977 general elections.

It should be noted that while adopting dependency theory's criticisms of international consumerism and of the advertising industry for promoting acquisitive values detrimental to manusia Indonesia (and thereby increasing dependency), Mochtar is not advocating economic isolationism. At the time of the *Manusia Indonesia* lecture, he was, in fact, president-director of one of Indonesia's major national advertising companies, PT Fortune Indonesia Advertising, whose clients included several major transnational companies, among them Cathay Pacific Airways, Nestlé, Bristol-Myers, and Peugeot.[65] In *Manusia Indonesia*, he criticized the entry of foreign capital-intensive investment and stressed the need for labor-intensive technology. The question of foreign investment and imported technologies could hardly have been a theoretical one, for he had been a founder, along with Professor Sumitro Djojohadikusumo, of Indoconsult Associates business consultancy firm, which from its inception in mid-1967 had a clientele of transnational companies anxious to invest in Indonesia.[66] This involvement may have sharpened his awareness of the nature of dependency, making him conscious of the financial benefits and costs.

Conclusion

Consistent with Mochtar's practice since his release from the post-Malari detention in 1975, practical politics found little place in defining the parameters of his lecture. The approach has elements of the

Sjahririan heritage in that it allows for praise of some of the achievements of Indonesia's precolonial past and of her traditional art but also for a general disparagement of traditional beliefs and practices, particularly those identified as Javanese.[67] There is little explanation of how positive values from this past have decayed, but plenty of exasperation at the resilience of mysticism and superstitions, despite the influence of (Western-style) education designed to inculcate rationality. Social justice, equal education opportunities, a just prosperity, personal human freedoms, and humanistic ethics are the ideals to be achieved by a cultural transformation, seen as an aggregate cultural shift generated by individuals changing. The hope is of a closer relationship among powerholders, the private sector, and the artistic community, tempering power with humanistic and artistic sensitivity. This implies a tremendous faith in gradual reform through collaboration.

The lecture retains the moralistic tone and the fervor appropriate to a man long considered a public conscience. But Mochtar takes up this role of conscience not for the regime but for society at large, at which are levelled most of his criticisms.[68] The lecture's subtitle, "A Statement of Responsibility" *(Sebuah Pertanggungjawaban)*, may refer to society's obligation to take note and change, or else to the intellectual's duty to reveal its failings. It reinforces the assumption that the intellectual is spokesperson *for* society. It is through education and through reflection upon information presented by educated, rational individuals that people within the broader community will become civic-minded and reformist, and begin to agitate for legally sanctioned change within the society. The clear implication is that only a handful are currently thus disposed since "[perhaps] only a few Indonesians have succeeded in freeing themselves from the various kinds of shackles and pressures to which they have been subjected for these past centuries" (22). Although Mochtar shared few of the deprivations of his poorer compatriots, in a subsequent public lecture he closed by venturing "to speak for the orphans of our nation, the 50 percent who are still below the poverty line, who still suffer calorie and protein deficiencies, . . . and also for the future, and for the generations to come in this, our homeland."[69]

The lecture conjures up the image of a conciliator, seeking the middle road to avoid conflict. Taking into account the industrialized countries' immense demand for the world's scarce resources, he outlines two possible scenarios: either these countries will defend their lifestyle at any cost, or else they will voluntarily embrace a simpler, less consumption-oriented lifestyle. His is a call for global conciliation, voluntary temperance, and self-restraint, a request for concessions to the developing countries lest their resentment lead to sharp confrontation. Cultural change unrelated to political action lies at the heart of the lecture. In effect, Mochtar keeps options for change in the hands of the powerful. If the powerful, internationally, are the rich nations, domestically they are a greedy self-serving Indonesian elite "essentially becoming increasingly distanced from the community because of its behavior, and communication between it and the people is becoming increasingly more awkward and difficult day by day" (54). Yet, on the other hand, the lecture is an appeal to those who have attained a degree of economic and political control over their own lives to work for general change.

These are the tactics of a nonparliamentary opposition to the Suharto New Order, made up of individuals convinced of their right to exercise authority yet with a shared revulsion for mass political action and for the chaos and disorder that might ensue. In such a category along with Mochtar are his colleagues in the Institute for Constitutional Awareness (LKB) and signatories of the Petition of Fifty (Petisi Limapuluh).[70] In earlier years, many key members of such major informal Opposition groups like the LKB and the Petition of Fifty, particularly retired military officers, had been in power or at least in positions of substantial influence. Their tactics in opposition involve lobbying and appealing to particular factional groups within the government, groups believed to be concerned with ruling in a respon- sible, restrained manner: dubbed by Southwood and Flanagan the "critical collaborators."[71]

Mochtar's criticisms, then, far from being threats to the essential principles of the current regime, are recommendations to consider the changing nature of his country within the context of world development. His dilemma is common to those occupying a privileged social position and needing to maintain a working relationship with government and bureaucracy for practical or other reasons. There is no indication that *Manusia Indonesia* angered the Indonesian authorities.[72] Its approach to sociological study is one which sidelines domestic political factors, focussing, on the one hand, on domestic "cultural" characteristics and, on the other, under the influence of dependency theory, on the economic and political relationship *between* states.

It is interesting to note that the lecture remains contentious in private discussion among the Jakarta intelligentsia, a leading young member of whom (and a strong supporter of Mochtar during the 1960s) adduced it as an example of ignorance of one's own biases, assuming one's perspective to be objective. Mochtar failed to analyze himself or the political structures of the state, this observer noted, assuming that the state and the military were fundamentally neutral.[73] Some commentators interpreted the lecture as an indication of the weakening political grip of senior secular intellectuals whose mantle was passing to a younger and theoretically more rigorous generation both from secular and Islamic constituencies. Articulately putting this view was a prominent spokesperson for progressive, less orthodox Muslims.[74] He noted a disillusionment, which he attributed to a growing political desperation among secular intellectuals. What he called a derogatory style exemplified Mochtar's loss of authority *(wibawa)* as an oppositional figure. Increasingly erratic criticisms, bland statements, and intellectually dubious cliches were seen by him as displaying a lack of zest or intellectual agility, an incapacity to read the mood in the broader, nonintellectual community beyond the urban centers. Such weaknesses, he argued, were symptomatic of a broader lack of political direction. Despite such evaluations in the national press, which took exception to various assumptions of the lecture, the sentiments expressed by Mochtar on this occasion seem nevertheless to have struck a chord within the middle-class urban secular modernizing community. *Manusia Indonesia* was much praised by those impressed by the views of this articulate New Order opposition figure about society, and, by implication, about his own role within it.

Still, it was a role increasingly criticized by younger political and cultural activists and intellectuals as too placatory. Two years earlier, the poet and dramatist Rendra had contrasted such a position with that of artists who reject institutionalized links with government and choose to "live in the wind." For Rendra, the Jakarta Academy's eminent membership (which included Mochtar) were like the *empu* of old Java, the religious scholars whose task it was to guard society's spiritual values. By compromising with the center of state power and moving into the palace, the empu lost the political freedom which came from "residing in the wind."[75] The *Manusia Indonesia* lecture, with its exhortations for a closer relationship among powerholders, the private sector, and artists, led critics to conclude that Mochtar was moving out of the draft.

309

NOTES

1. More detailed studies of Mochtar Lubis include Henri Chambert-Loir, *Mochtar Lubis: Une Vision de l'Indonésie Contemporaine* (Mochtar Lubis: A Vision of Contemporary Indonesia) (Paris: Publications de l'École Française D'Extrême-Orient, 1974); F.X. Mudji Sutrisno, "Man and the State in the Works of Mochtar Lubis and Mangunwijaya: An Inquiry into the Relations Between the "Ideal" and the "Real" in Mochtar Lubis' and Mangunwijaya's Political Philosophies," (PhD thesis, Pontifical Gregorian University, Rome, 1986); and David T. Hill, "Mochtar Lubis: Author, Editor, Political Actor," (Ph.D. thesis, Australian National University, Canberra), 1988.

2. *Twilight in Jakarta*, trans. Claire Holt (London: Hutchinson & Co., 1963; 2d edition, Kuala Lumpur: Oxford University Press, 1983). The Indonesian "original" appeared in 1970 as *Senja di Jakarta* (Twilight in Jakarta) (Jakarta: Penerbit Indonesia Raya; 2d Indonesian ed., Jakarta: Pustaka Jaya, 1982). For clarity, citations of works by Mochtar Lubis are referred to by *title* (abbreviated where appropriate) and date, rather than by author and date.

3. In using Mochtar Lubis's "first" name, I follow common practice in Indonesian, where he most frequently is referred to either as *"Pak Mochtar"* (Father/Mr. Mochtar), *"Bung Mochtar"* (Brother Mochtar), or simply *"Mochtar."* This usage implies neither disrespect or excessive familiarity.

4. Mochtar's detention diary for 1956-1966, published as *Catatan Subversif* (Subversive Notes) (Jakarta: Sinar Harapan, 1980), reveals his elation at having been able to "speak to the world" through his writings (302, dated 13 June 1964).

5. On the Sjahrir circle in the 1940s and 1950s, see J. D. Legge, *Intellectuals and Nationalism in Indonesia: A Study of the Following Recruited by Sutan Sjahrir in Occupation Jakarta* (Ithaca: Cornell Modern Indonesia, 1988). On Sjahrir's influence on the intellectual politics of the 1970s, see R. William Liddle, "Modernizing Indonesian Politics," in *Political Participation in Modern Indonesia*, ed. R. William Liddle (New Haven: Yale University Southeast Asia Series, 1973), 177-206.

6. See Feith's Introduction to Herbert Feith and Lance Castles, eds., *Indonesian Political Thinking 1945-1965* (Ithaca: Cornell University Press, 1970), particularly 13. The five "streams of political thinking" were Radical Nationalism, Javanese Traditionalism, Islam, Democratic Socialism, and Communism.

7. Hill, "Author, Editor," 11-17, elaborates this point with particular attention to the American George McTurnan Kahin and the Australian John D. Legge.

8. On Mochtar Lubis's involvement in the IPI and CCF, see Hill, "Mochtar Lubis: The Artist as Cultural Broker in New Order Indonesia," *Review of Indonesian and Malaysian Affairs* (RIMA) 21/1 (Winter 1987): 54-88.

9. The term "secular modernizing intellectuals" was coined by Liddle, "Modernizing Indonesian Politics."

10. On the Pertamina collapse see Bruce Glassburner, "In the Wake of General Ibnu: Crisis in the Indonesian Oil Industry," *Asian Survey* 16/12 (December 1976): 1099-1112.

11. *Indonesia Raya* was among the twelve banned newspapers and periodicals, and Mochtar Lubis was the last of the 470 arrested, being jailed without trial in February 1975 for two and one-half months on suspicion of inciting student leaders. On *Indonesia Raya* and Malari, see David T. Hill, "Press Challenges, Government Responses: Two Campaigns in *Indonesia Raya*," in Paul Tickell, ed., *The Indonesian Press: Its Past, Its People, Its Problems* (Clayton: Monash University Center for Southeast Asian Studies, 1987), 21-38. On Malari, see Harold Crouch, "The 15th January Affair in Indonesia," *Dyason House Papers* 1/1 (August 1974): 1-5. Mochtar's prison diary was published as *Kampdagboek* (Camp Diary), translated into Dutch by Cees van Dijk and Rob Nieuwenhuys (Alphen aan den Rijn: A. W. Sijthoff, 1979).

12. See *Jalan Tak Ada Ujung* (Jakarta: Balai Pustaka, 1952); *A Road With No End*, trans. and ed. Anthony H. Johns (Singapore: Graham Brash, 1968; 2d ed. 1982).

13. The two Dutch books, which were written directly in English then translated by the publishers, were *Het Land Onder de Regenboog: de geschiedenis van Indonesië* (Land under the Rainbow: The History of

311

Indonesia) (Alphen aan den Rijn: A.W. Sijthoff, 1979), which has appeared in English as *Indonesia: Land under the Rainbow* (Manila: Solidaridad Publishing House, 1987, and Kuala Lumpur: Oxford University Press, 1990); and *Het Land Onder de Zon: Het Indonesië van nu* (The Land Under the Sun: Indonesia Now), (Alphen aan den Rijn: A.W. Sijthoff, 1981).

14. Post-Malari, this includes *Harimau! Harimau!* (Tiger! Tiger!) (Jakarta: Pustaka Jaya, 1975); *Maut dan Cinta* (Death and Love) (Jakarta: Pustaka Jaya, 1977); *Kuli Kontrak* (Contract Coolies) (Jakarta: Sinar Harapan, 1982), a collection of older, previously published short stories; and *Bromocorah: Dua Belas Cerita Pendek* (Jakarta: Sinar Harapan, 1983), translated into English by Jeanette Lingard as *The Outlaw and Other Stories* (Singapore: Oxford University Press, 1987).

15. Mochtar Lubis, *Manusia Indonesia (Sebuah Pertanggung-jawawaban)* (Indonesian Humanity: A Statement of Responsibility) (Jakarta: Idayu, 1980, 4th edition, to which all subsequent page references refer; 1st ed., 1977), based on a lecture at the Jakarta Cultural Centre, Taman Ismail Marzuki (TIM); *Bangsa Indonesia: masa lampau, masa kini, masa depan* (The Indonesian Nation: Its Past, Its Present, Its Future) (Jakarta: Yayasan Idayu, 1987), based on a lecture at the Building of National Awakening (Gedung Kebangkitan Nasional) on 30 January 1987; and *Transformasi Budaya untuk Masa Depan* (Cultural Transformation for the Future) (Jakarta: Idayu, 1985), based on another TIM lecture on 18 October 1983.

16. Recent examples included D. M. E. Roskies, "Politics and the Novel in Contemporary Indonesia: The Fiction of Mochtar Lubis," in *Discharging the Canon: Cross-cultural Readings in Literature*, ed. Peter Hyland (Singapore University Press, 1986), 73-100; and Peter Wicks, "Independence Corroded: Twilight in Djakarta. Revisited," *Asian Profile* 14/1 (February 1986): 41-48.

17. In the light of Mochtar's acceptance, prior to his release in May 1966, that military dominance in government was inevitable for at least ten years (see his *Catatan Subversif*, 489), it is significant that this lecture evaluating his society occurred at the close of the first decade of New Order rule.

18. A description of the presentation of the lecture and the audience response is given in "Mochtar Lubis: Manusia Indonesia Cenderung Boros" (Mochtar Lubis: Indonesians Tend to be Wasteful), *Kompas*, 9 April 1977, 1 and 12. See also "Ceramah Budaya Mochtar Lubis: Manusia Indonesia Yang Sebenarnya Makin Jauh Dari Manusia Ideal Kita" (Mochtar Lubis: Indonesians Are Actually Moving Further Away from Our Ideal National Character), *Sinar Harapan*, 7 April 1977, 1. I am grateful to Eka Budianta, who attended, for his description of the audience's reactions (London, March 1989).

19. Originally *"Situasi Manusia Indonesia Kini, Dilihat dari Segi Kebudayaan dan Nilai Manusia."*

20. The appropriate English translation of *Manusia Indonesia* depends on the context. Literally, *manusia* means *human, human being, humankind (Man)*. Thus, *Manusia Indonesia* could be translated as *Indonesian humanity*, but in the lecture it is used to refer to the "national character," or the typical "Indonesian person." In lower-case, it refers to these definitions; when capitalized, it refers to the lecture's title.

21. *Kompas* and *Sinar Harapan* were the largest, most prestigious dailies, broadly associated with Catholic and Protestant publishing groups. *Pelita* was aligned with Islamic interests. *Suara Karya* was the voice of the government political organization, Golkar, and *Angkatan Bersenjata* was a military paper.

22. "Sebisa Mungkin Menyimpan Semua Hal Tentang Indonesia" (Insofar As Is Possible, To Collect All Things To Do with Indonesia), *Kompas*, 31 November 1981; 6.

23. The series includes Marbangun Hardjowirogo, *Manusia Jawa* (The Javanese) (Jakarta: Idayu, 1983); Ajip Rosidi, *Manusia Sunda* (The Sundanese) (Jakarta: Idayu, 1984); and Hamid Abdullah, *Manusia Bugis Makassar* (The Bugis-Makassarese) (Jakarta: Idayu, 1985). That the stimulus to start the series was the public response to Mochtar's *Manusia Indonesia* lecture is acknowleged in the preface to *Manusia Bugis*.

24. It appeared initially as *We Indonesisans*, trans. Florence Lamoureux, ed. Soenjono Dardjowidjojo (Honolulu: Asian Studies Program,

University of Hawaii, 1979). Lamoureux's revised translation was published as *The Indonesian Dilemma* (Singapore: Graham Brash, 1983), and reprinted 1986. These translations will be identified as Lamoureux (1979) and (1983).

25. "Dalam Setiap Masyarakat Kritik Mempunyai Tempat" (In Every Society Criticism Has Its Place), *Kompas*, 19 April 1977, 4 and 9.

26. Mochtar uses the once-derogatory term for the Chinese, *Cina*, which he himself opposed during a polemic in the early postcoup years in favor of the older, more neutral *Tionghoa*. See "Surat dari Bangkok" (Letter from Bangkok), *Kompas*, 28 April 1967, cited in Charles A. Coppel and Leo Suryadinata, "The Use of the Terms 'Tjina' and 'Tionghoa' in Indonesia: An Historical Survey," in *The Chinese Minority in Indonesia: Seven Papers*, ed. Leo Suryadinata (Singapore: Chopmen Enterprises, 1978), 123.

27. Since page references to the *Manusia Indonesia* monograph (4th edition, 1980) are frequent and *passim*, they will be omitted unless identifying direct quotations. Translation adapted from Lamoureux (1983), 7. All translations are mine unless otherwise acknowledged.

28. The Indonesian word for third-person singular, *dia,* is not gender-specific; however, Mochtar's use of the term assumes *manusia Indonesia* to be male. Lamoureux (1983) uses the masculine pronoun, e.g., 18.

29. Translation adapted from Lamoureux, (1983), 23. Lubis (1980), 30.

30. Lamoureux (1983), 5, translates *kebatinan* as "one's inner-self," but it is generally used to refer to spiritual movements in Indonesia outside the Great Tradition religions. It also often relates to the role of the *dukun* (mystic, shaman healer). See Niels Mulder, *Mysticism and Everyday Life in Contemporaty Java: Cultural Persistence and Change* (Singapore University Press, 1980), 21-22. On the place of kebatinan in Indonesian political life, see Paul Stange, "'Legitimate' Mysticism in Indonesia," RIMA 20/2 (summer 1986): 76-117.

31. Translation by Lamoureux, (1983), 6. Lubis (1980), 12.

32. Sukarno formulated the *Pancasila* (Five Principles) in 1945 to symbolize, in broad terms, the ideological basis for the Indonesian state and these were then incorporated into the preamble to the 1945 Constitution as "One Deity, just and civilized Humanity, Indonesian Unity, and People's rule guided wisely through consultation and representation, in order to achieve Social Justice for the whole Indonesian people" (translated in Feith and Castles, *Indonesian Political Thinking*, 50). Since 1978 the New Order has implemented compulsory two-week Pancasila indoctrination programs (P4) for all civil servants, to assert a monopoly over interpretation of the principles. This interpretation reinforces the government's "ideology of containment rather than [Sukarno's intended ideology] of mobilization" (according to Michael Morfit, "Pancasila: The Indonesian State Ideology according to the New Order Government," *Asian Survey* 21/8 (August 1981): 846.

33. In English in the original.

34. In 1969 *Indonesian Raya* published a series entitled "Examples of 'Intellectual Prostitution' during the period of the Sukarno Regime" (14-18 April 1969), attacking people like Prof. Mohammad Sadli, Prof. Ismail Suny, Prof. R. M. Sutjipto Wirjosuparto, Barli Halim, and Emil Salim, who had cooperated with the Sukarno government yet switched loyalties once the Suharto regime established itself (see Hill, "Author, Editor," 143-45). In this lecture Mochtar Lubis is extending similar arguments to those in the *Indonesia Raya* series.

35. According to Lamoureux, (1983), 33.

36. The English term is used in the original.

37. Original in English. Lubis (1980), 54.

38. Translation adapted from Lamoureux, (1983), 48. Lubis (1980), 55.

39. Translation adapted from Lamoureux, (1983), 30. The original Indonesian (Lubis 1980, 56) is, *"Kita memerlukan pengawasan sosial dilembagakan terhadap sumber-sumber alam kita, terhadap modal, pemakaian tenaga manusia, terhadap ilmu dan teknologi, terhadap ancaman-ancaman yang mungkin terjadi terhadap keseimbangan ekologi, terhadap pencemaran alam kita. "* This was toned down in Lamoureux, (1983), 49, to, "We must learn to be farsighted and carefully control the

exploitation of our natural resources, our capital, our manpower, science, and technology, so as not to upset our country's ecological balance and thereby cause an environmental disaster." This translation removes the element of social supervision or control of resources.

40. Both English and Indonesian terms are given. Lubis (1980), 58.

41. In English in the original. Lubis (1980), 59.

42. The Lamoureux (1983) translation (68) is, "I propose a closer involvement of those in private business with the arts. An exchange of ideas would be beneficial to all, tempering strong views with humility." This rendering does not express fully the original (Lubis, 1980: 77-78): *"Saya mengusulkan pergaulan yang lebih erat antara penguasa, swasta dan dunia seniman, agar pandangan kekuasaan mereka diimbangi oleh pandangan-pandangan dan pengalaman artistik dan kemanusiaan."* Notably, this translation omits mention of the powerholders (penguasa). The argument that the "exchange of ideas would be beneficial to all" is not apparent in the original, which emphasizes that it is those who hold "views on power" *(pandangan kekuasaan)* who need to balance these with artistic and humanitarian concerns.

43. Translations from Lamoureux, (1983), 71.

44. See his "Kondisi dan Situasi Manusia Indonesia Masa Kini" (The Current Condition and Situation of the Indonesia Character), *Kompas*, 14 May 1977, 4 and 9, reprinted in his *Manusia Indonesia* 1980, 91-92.

45. Most of the written responses were based upon the summary in the prestigious Jakarta daily newspaper *Kompas* (12 April 1977). There was widespread informal discussion of the lecture (according to "Gebrakan Mochtar Lubis—borok-borok Manusia Indonesia" [Mochtar Lubis's Attack—The Ugly Face of Indonesians], *Horison* 8 [August 1977]; 240-42); but my comments in this section are based on published material.

46. See, e.g., the responses by Sarlito Wirawan Sarwono, "Kondisi dan Situasi Manusia Indonesia Masa Kini, Dilihat Dari Sudut Psikologi" (The Current Condition and Situation of Indonesian Character, from a Psychological Perspective), *Kompas*, 5 May 1977, iv and ix (included in *Manusia Indonesia* 1980, 82-91); and also Margono Djojohadiku-sumo, "Feodalisme, New-Feodalisme [Sic], Aristokrasi" (Feudalism,

65. Michael H. Anderson, "Transnational Advertising in Indonesia," unpublished paper read at Eighth Annual Conference on Indonesia Studies, University of California, Berkeley, 1979, 16.

66. Mochtar Lubis stepped down as director in 1972, saying later that the multinational clients were ignoring his warnings about the negative side effects of their projects. He remained a major shareholder in the company. (Interview with Mochtar Lubis, 24 April 1981.) On Mochtar's business activities, see Hill, "Author, Editor," 133-35.

67. Syahririan heritage is identified by Liddle, "Modernizing Indonesian Politics," 179.

68. Chambert-Loir, *Mochtar Lubis*, 101, noted this trend in *Indonesia Raya*'s position in the early 1970s.

69. Mochtar Lubis, *Bangsa Indonesia*, 50.

70. The LKB (Yayasan Lembaga Pengembangan Pengertian dan Kesadaran Berkonstitusi Menurut Undang-Undang Dasar 1945) was founded on 1 June 1978 by a group of opposition figures, including former vice president Mohammad Hatta, former defense minister General A. H. Nasution, former Jakarta governor Lieutenant General Ali Sadikin, former chief of the national police, General Hugeng Imam Santoso, and Mochtar. In May 1980 a Statement of Concern signed by fifty citizens from different ideological and generational groups (including at least fourteen members of the LKB) was presented to Parliament, objecting to certain unscripted speeches by the president. The criticisms made by the signatories, who became known as the Petition of Fifty group, were strongly supported by Mochtar, who was abroad when the original signatures were collected. David Bourchier's "The 'Petition of 50': Who and What Are They," *Inside Indonesia* 10 (April 1987), 7-10, gives a good summary of the issues.

71. Julie Southwood and Patrick Flanagan, *Indonesia: Law, Propaganda and Terror* (London: Zed Press, 1983), 4, 52.

72. This lack of interest in Mochtar's lecture contrasts sharply with the reaction to the lecture "The Role of Intellectuals in Indonesia Life" given at the University of Indonesia in September 1981 by his rival Pramoedya Ananta Toer. Four student organizers of the lecture were detained for several months before being expelled from the university.

Pramoedya, while not formally arrested, was harassed, interrogated frequently over several months, and forbidden to speak in public.

73. Confidential interview, Jakarta, 1981.

74. Confidential interview, Jakarta, 1982.

75. When accepting an award from the Jakarta Academy at TIM on 22 August 1975, Rendra's speech argued that artists and intellectuals have to choose between being tied down to the state institutional "body" or remaining free as "spirit." He regarded the Academy as "half-body" because of its institutional function. See Rendra, *The Struggle of the Naga Tribe*, translated and introduced by Max Lane (St. Lucia: University of Queensland Press, 1979). The speech is translated as Appendix A, 75-85.

SELECTED PUBLICATIONS BY MOCHTAR LUBIS LISTED BY DATE OF PUBLICATION

Jalan Tak Ada Ujung (Road With No End). Jakarta: Balai Pustaka, 1952. Translated from the Indonesian and edited by Anthony H. Johns. Singapore: Graham Brash, 1968. Reprinted 1982.
Senja di Jakarta (Twilight in Jakarta). Jakarta: Penerbit Indonesia Raya, 1970; 2d Indonesian ed., Pustaka Jaya, 1982.
Harimau! Harimau! (Tiger! Tiger!). Jakarta: Pustaka Jaya, 1975.
Maut dan Cinta (Death and Love). Jakarta: Pustaka Jaya, 1977.
"Kondisi dan Situasi Manusia Indonesia Masa Kini" (The Current Condition and Situation of the Indonesian Character). *Kompas*, 14 May 1977, 4 and 9 (reprinted in *Manusia Indonesia* 1980, 91-92.
"Tanggapan atas Tanggapan" (Response to a Response). *Kompas,* 1 June 1977, 4 (included in *Manusia Indonesia* 1980, 105-107).
Bangsa Indonesia (masa lampau, masa kini, masa depan) (The Indonesian Nation: Past, Present and Future). Jakarta: Idaya, 1978.
Kampdagboek (Camp Diary). Translated by Cees van Dijk and Rob Nieuwenhuys. Alphen aan den Rijn: A. W. Sijthoff, 1979. Translation of 1975 prison diary, not published in Indonesian.
Het Land Onder de Regenboog: de geschiedenis van Indonesie (Land Under the Rainbow: The History of Indonesia). Alphen aan den Rijn: A. W. Sijthoff, 1979. Published in English as *Indonesia:*

Land Under the Rainbow. Manila: Solidaridad Publishing House, 1987, and Kuala Lumpur, Oxford University Press, 1990.

Manusia Indonesia (Sebuah Pertanggungjawaban) (Indonesian Humanity: A Statement of Responsibility). Jakarta: Yayasan Idayu, 1977. Fourth printing in 1980. Translated by Florence Lamoureux and edited by Soenjono Dardjowidjojo as *We Indonesians.* Honolulu: University of Hawaii, 1979; revised as *The Indonesian Dilemma.* Singapore: Graham Brash, 1983.

Catatan Subversif (Subversive Notes). Jakarta: Sinar Harapan, 1980.

Het Land Onder de Zon: Het Indonesië van nu (The Land Under the Sun: Indonesia Now). Alphen aan den Rijn: A. W. Sijthoff, 1981.

Kuli Kontrak (Contract Coolies). Jakarta: Sinar Harapan, 1982.

Bromocorah: Dua Belas Cerita Pendek. Jakarta: Sinar Harapan, 1983. Translated into English by Jeanette Lingard as *The Outlaw and Other Stories.* Singapore: Oxford University Press, 1987.

Transformasi Budaya untuk Masa Depan (Cultural Transformation for the Future). Jakarta: Idaya, 1987.

MONOGRAPHS IN INTERNATIONAL STUDIES

ISBN Prefix 0-89680-

Africa Series

38. Wright, Donald R. *Oral Traditions From the Gambia: Volume II, Family Elders.* 1980. 200pp.
084-9 $15.00

43. Harik, Elsa M. and Donald G. Schilling. *The Politics of Education in Colonial Algeria and Kenya.* 1984. 102pp.
117-9 $12.50

45. Keto, C. Tsehloane. *American-South African Relations 1784-1980: Review and Select Bibliography.* 1985. 159pp.
128-4 $11.00

46. Burness, Don, and Mary-Lou Burness, eds. *Wanasema: Conversations with African Writers.* 1985. 95pp.
129-2 $11.00

47. Switzer, Les. *Media and Dependency in South Africa: A Case Study of the Press and the Ciskei "Homeland."* 1985. 80pp.
130-6 $10.00

48. Heggoy, Alf Andrew. *The French Conquest of Algiers, 1830: An Algerian Oral Tradition.* 1986. 101pp.
131-4 $11.00

49. Hart, Ursula Kingsmill. *Two Ladies of Colonial Algeria: The Lives and Times of Aurelie Picard and Isabelle Eberhardt.* 1987. 156pp.
143-8 $11.00

51. Clayton, Anthony, and David Killingray. *Khaki and Blue: Military and Police in British Colonial Africa.* 1989. 235pp.
147-0 $18.00

52. Northrup, David. *Beyond the Bend in the River: African Labor in Eastern Zaire, 1864-1940.* 1988. 195pp.
151-9 $15.00

53. Makinde, M. Akin. *African Philosophy, Culture, and Traditional Medicine.* 1988. 175pp.
152-7 $13.00

54. Parson, Jack ed. *Succession to High Office in Botswana. Three Case Studies.* 1990. 443pp.
157-8 $20.00

55. Burness, Don. *A Horse of White Clouds.* 1989. 193pp.
158-6 $12.00

56. Staudinger, Paul. *In the Heart of the Hausa States.* Tr. by Johanna Moody. 1990. 2 vols. 653pp.
160-8 $35.00

57. Sikainga, Ahmad Alawad. *The Western Bahr Al-Ghazal Under British Rule: 1898-1956.* 1991. 183pp.
161-6 $15.00

58. Wilson, Louis E. *The Krobo People of Ghana to 1892: A Political and Social History.* 1991. 254pp.
164-0 $20.00

59. du Toit, Brian M. *Cannabis, Alcohol, and the South African Student: Adolescent Drug Use 1974-1985.* 1991. 166pp.
166-7 $17.00

60. Falola, Toyin, ed. *The Political Economy of Health in Africa.* 1992. 254pp.
168-3 $17.00

61. Kiros, Tedros. *Moral Philosophy and Development: The Human Condition in Africa.* 1992. 178pp.
171-3 $18.00

62. Burness, Don. *Echoes of the Sunbird: An Anthology of Contemporary African Poetry.* 1993. 198pp.
173-X $17.00

63. Glew, Robert S., and Chaibou Babalé. *Hausa Folktales from Niger.* 1993. 136pp.
176-4 $15.00

19. Sung Ho Kim and Thomas W. Walker, eds., *Perspectives on War and Peace in Central America.* 1992. 150pp.
172-1 $14.00

Southeast Asia Series

47. Wessing, Robert. *Cosmology and Social Behavior in a West Javanese Settlement.* 1978. 200pp.
072-5 $12.00

56A. Duiker, William J. *Vietnam Since the Fall of Saigon.* Updated edition. 1989. 383pp.
162-4 $17.00

64. Dardjowidjojo, Soenjono. *Vocabulary Building in Indonesian: An Advanced Reader.* 1984. xviii, 256pp.
118-7 $26.00

65. Errington, J. Joseph. *Language and Social Change in Java: Linguistic Reflexes of Modernization in a Traditional Royal Polity.* 1985. xiv, 211pp.
120-9 $20.00

66. Binh, Tran Tu. *The Red Earth: A Vietnamese Memoir of Life on a Colonial Rubber Plantation.* Tr. by John Spragens. Ed. by David Marr. 1985. xii, 98pp.
119-5 $11.00

68. Syukri, Ibrahim. *History of the Malay Kingdom of Patani.* Tr. by Connor Bailey and John N. Miksic. 1985. xix, 113pp.
123-3 $12.00

69. Keeler, Ward. *Javanese: A Cultural Approach.* 1984. xxxvi, 522pp., Third printing 1992.
121-7 $25.00

70. Wilson, Constance M., and Lucien M. Hanks. *Burma-Thailand Frontier Over Sixteen Decades: Three Descriptive Documents.* 1985. x, 128pp.
124-1 $11.00

71. Thomas, Lynn L., and Franz von Benda-Beckmann, eds. *Change and Continuity in Minangkabau: Local, Regional, and Historical Perspectives on West Sumatra.* 1986. 363pp.
127-6 $16.00

72. Reid, Anthony, and Oki Akira, eds. *The Japanese Experience in Indonesia: Selected Memoirs of 1942-1945.* 1986. 411pp., 20 illus.
132-2 $20.00

73. Smirenskaia, Zhanna D. *Peasants in Asia: Social Consciousness and Social Struggle.* Tr. by Michael J. Buckley. 1987. 248pp.
134-9 $14.00

74. McArthur, M.S.H. *Report on Brunei in 1904.* Ed. by A.V.M. Horton. 1987. 304pp.
135-7 $15.00

75. Lockard, Craig Alan. *From Kampung to City. A Social History of Kuching Malaysia 1820-1970.* 1987. 311pp.
136-5 $16.00

76. McGinn, Richard. *Studies in Austronesian Linguistics.* 1988. 492pp.
137-3 $20.00

77. Muego, Benjamin N. *Spectator Society: The Philippines Under Martial Rule.* 1988. 232pp.
138-1 $15.00

79. Walton, Susan Pratt. *Mode in Javanese Music.* 1987. 279pp.
144-6 $15.00

80. Nguyen Anh Tuan. *South Vietnam Trial and Experience: A Challenge for Development.* 1987. 482pp.
141-1 $18.00

81. Van der Veur, Paul W., ed. *Toward a Glorious Indonesia: Reminiscences and Observations of Dr. Soetomo.* 1987. 367pp.
142-X $16.00

82. Spores, John C. *Running Amok: An Historical Inquiry.* 1988. 190pp.
140-3 $13.00

83. Malaka. *From Jail to Jail.* Tr. and ed. by Helen Jarvis. 1990. 3 vols. 1,226pp.
150-0 $55.00

84. Devas, Nick. *Financing Local Government in Indonesia.* 1989. 344pp.
153-5 $16.00

85. Suryadinata, Leo. *Military Ascendancy and Political Culture: A Study of Indonesia's Golkar.* 1989. 250pp.
154-3 $18.00

86. Williams, Michael. *Communism, Religion, and Revolt in Banten.* 1990. 356pp.
155-1 $14.00

87. Hudak, Thomas John. *The Indigenization of Pali Meters in Thai Poetry.* 1990. 237pp.
159-4 $15.00

88. Lay, Ma Ma. *Not Out of Hate: A Novel of Burma.* Tr. by Margaret Aung-Thwin. Ed. by William Frederick. 1991. 222pp.
167-5 $20.00

89. Anwar, Chairil. *The Voice of the Night: Complete Poetry and Prose of Anwar Chairil.* 1993. Revised Edition. Tr. by Burton Raffel. 180pp.
                                                                         $17.00

90. Hudak, Thomas John, tr. *The Tale of Prince Samuttakote: A Buddhist Epic from Thailand.* 1993. 275pp.
174-8 $20.00

91. Roskies, D. M., ed. *Text/Politics in Island Southeast Asia: Essays in Interpretation.* 1993. 321pp.
175-6 $25.00

ORDERING INFORMATION

Orders for titles in the Monographs in International Studies series may be placed through the Ohio University Press, Scott Quadrangle, Athens, Ohio 45701-2979 or through any local bookstore. Individuals should remit payment by check, VISA, or MasterCard.* People ordering from the United Kingdom, Continental Europe, the Middle East, and Africa should order through Academic and University Publishers Group, 1 Gower Street, London WC1E, England. Orders from the Pacific Region, Asia, Australia, and New Zealand should be sent to East-West Export Books, c/o the University of Hawaii Press, 2840 Kolowalu Street, Honolulu, Hawaii 96822, USA.

Other individuals ordering from outside of the U.S. should remit in U.S. funds to Ohio University Press either by International Money Order or by a check drawn on a U.S. bank.** Most out-of-print titles may be ordered from University Microfilms, Inc., 300 North Zeeb Road, Ann Arbor, Michigan 48106, USA.

Prices are subject to change without notice.

*   Please include $3.00 for the first book and 75¢ for each additional book for shipping and handling.

**   Please include $4.00 for the first book and 75¢ for each additional book for foreign shipping and handling.